AF540654

UNDERSTANDING PLANT HORMONES

UNDERSTANDING PLANT HORMONES

By

Dr. Shubhrata R. Mishra
Deptt. of Botany
Vikram University
Ujjain (M.P.)
(India)

Published by:
Tilak Wasan
DISCOVERY PUBLISHING HOUSE PVT. LTD.
4831/24, Ansari Road, Prahlad Street
Darya Ganj, New Delhi-110002 (India)
Phone: +91-11-23279245, 43764432
Fax: +91-11-23253475
E-mail: parul.wasan@gmail.com
info@discoverypublishinggroup.com
discoverypublishinghouse@gmail.com
web: www.discoverypublishinggroup.com

First Edition: 2011
ISBN: 978-81-8356-865-4

Understanding Plant Hormones

Printed at:
Shree Balaji Art Press
Delhi

PREFACE

The present title "*Understanding Plant Hormones*" provides a structured approach to learning by covering all the important topics in a uniform, systematic format. The book has been comprehensively designed incorporating recent advances in this fast moving field. It is written to provide accessible information on plant hormones in compact form for undergraduate students in biology and related life sciences. It will be useful for both beginning students and those who are more advanced. In addition, busy lecturers who require a quick reference compendium will find it useful, particularly for tutional planning. Simple, yet hopefully clear figures and tables are provided throughout the book.

The over-riding goal of this book, and indeed of the whole *Understanding series,* is to present the essential information concering microbiology in a compact, readily accessible form which leads itself to student learning and revision. The convergence of various approaches has generated a rich panorama of detail, the significance of which we are still attempting to unraval. The present text has been written as an introduction to this rapidly growing field.

To make the work more comprehensive and informative, the author has consulted many authoritative books, research journals, abstracts, monographs etc., so there can be no claim to originality except in the manner of treatment.

The author expresses his thanks to his friends and colleagues whose continue inspirations have initiated him to bring out this book.

The author expresses his gratitude to Mr. Wasan and staff of M/s Discovery Publishing House Pvt. Ltd. for their whole hearted co-operation in the publication of this book.

In the mean time, the author will remain sincerely responsible for any shortcomings of the book and be grateful to the readers for their suggestions and constructive criticism for the continuous betterment of the book. He takes this opportunity to appeal to the readers to send their suggestions straightaway to his Publisher.

Author

CONTENTS

Introduction

A number of bioactive substances found in plants exhibit some similarities to hormones in the endocrine system of animals. However, plants have developed an amazing variety of mechanisms regulating phytohormone distribution and activity.

Distribution of phytohormones can depend on a concentration gradient established in the plant body, or it can be mediated by free diffusion, as is the case for the gaseous compound ethylene.

On the other hand, polar transport of the phytohormont auxin, which occurs in a strictly unidirectional fashion, depends on a complex machinery of carrier proteins, mediating cellular uptake and efflux steps that ensure establishment and maintenance of hormone gradients in the developing plant body.

In this chapter we address and compare phytohormone distribution of three examples, representing the quite distinct mechanisms in the control of phytohormone activities: auxin, which is actively transported throughout the entire plant body; gibberellin (GA), which appears to be transported in some circumstances and brassinosteroid (BR), for which no clear-cut evidence for transport is so far available.

Moreover, we address points concerning regulatory cross-these growth regulators, integrating distinct mechanisms of hormone distribution in the control of plant growth and development.

AUXINS: DISTRIBUTION AND TRANSPORT

Auxin Distribution

Auxin has a prominent position among the classical plant hormones since it mediates multiple aspects of plant growth and development. Besides its involvement in division, enlargement and differentiation of individual plant cells, auxins also function as signals between cells, tissues and organs.

A key role in these responses has been attributed to temporal and spatial control of auxin levels (homoeostasis), which would be required to initiate and perpetuate developmental events or growth responses that occur because of variation in intrinsic or environmental cues.

The conceptual framework regarding the biological function of auxin in higher plants is essentially based on the view that auxin is primarily synthesised in the apical parts of the shoot and subsequently delivered to other parts of the plant body where it exerts its activity in the regulation of a variety of growth responses.

This view remained more or less unquestioned for many years, as reflected in an often oversimplified presentation of sites and mechanisms of auxin biosynthesis and distribution. This somewhat unsatisfactory scenario was mainly based on the fact that quantitative analysis of free auxin or inactive auxin conjugates in a given cell file represented a major challenge for analytical phytochemistry.

That situation has changed dramatically in the last few years, providing us with a contemporary picture of sites of auxin biosynthesis and auxin distribution during plant development, specifically in the model organism *Arabidopsis thaliana*.

Auxin Biosynthesis

Control of auxin steady-state levels is thought to involve changes in biosynthesis, in metabolism, or in transport into and out of the tissue concerned. The most abundant naturally occurring auxin is indole-3-acetic acid (IAA); but other auxins including indole-3-butyric acid (IBA) and 4-chloroindole-3-acetic acid (4-Cl-IAA) have also been identified in plants.

Besides these physiologically active auxin forms, inactive auxin conjugates linked to sugars, amino acids or to small peptides have been isolated. Importantly, regulation of the ratio between conjugated and de-conjugated forms of auxin could represent an effective means to control steady-state levels of active auxin in a given tissue.

The oxidative degradation of auxin also has been implicated in the control of auxin concentrations. All these findings are suggestive of a scenario in which a complex interplay between metabolic events mediating auxin biosynthesis, conjugation and degradation would play an important role in cell- and tissue-specific control of auxin homoeostasis.

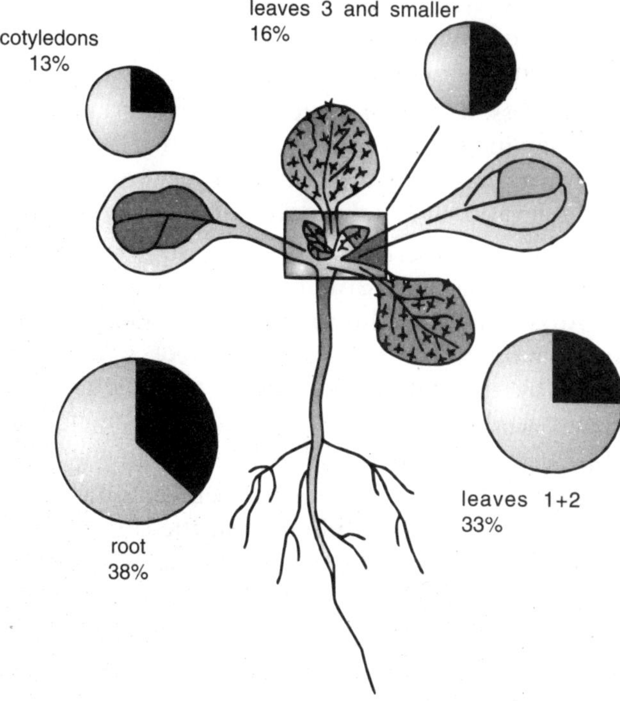

Figure 1.1: Auxin pool sizes in 10-day-old Arabidopsis plants, grown under long-day conditions.

With the availability of novel techniques such as micro-scale gas chrocoupled mass spectrometry, together with skilled hands capable of dissecting plant tissue nearly to the cellular level, it has become possible to study distribution and biosynthesis of auxin at a very high resolution.

Analyses performed in *Arabidopsis* confirmed some of the older views, as auxin concentrations were found to be highest in the youngest leaves formed by the shoot apical meristem (SAM). While it turned out that essentially all vegetative organs are capable of synthesising IAA *de novo*, in general, rates of auxin biosynthesis were found to be highest in meriste, also correlating with the important role of auxin in the control of cell proliferation.

For example, a comparison of IAA pool sizes in different organs demonstrated that *de novo* auxin synthesis in 10-day-old roots contributes a significant amount to the entire auxin pool synthesised in *Arabidopsis*. Thus, roots apparently do represent a major auxin source.

Nevertheless, as demonstrated by labelling and inhibitor studies, a significant amount of auxin found in root tissue derives from shoot sources raising questions about the biological relevance of two distinct auxin pools found in roots.

An answer to these questions came from the analysis of auxin biosynthesis and distribution in a spatiotemporal context. Auxin found in the roots of very young *Arabidopsis* plantlets is most likely derived from shoot sources, a view supported by the analysis of lateral root emergence on decapitated seedlings.

Removal of shoot-derived organs, such as the first true leaves, inhibited lateral root emergence, indicative of a requirement for shoot-derived auxin in the control of lateral root growth at early developmental stages.

By contrast, upon removal of aerial tissues at later developmental stages, lateral root emergence was significantly less affected, indicative of a correlation between root development and an increasing competence of the root to synthesise auxin.

Further support for this idea came from the analysis of auxin biosynthesis in roots. In particular, primary root meristems as well as emerged lateral roots appear to represent important sources for root-synthesised auxin.

From that it auxin, derived from the root as well as from the shoot, exerts a combinatorial effect on the regulation of auxin-mediated responses in the control of root growth.

AUXIN TRANSPORT

Another means of controlling auxin homoeostasis at specific locations involves the controlled, coordinated transport of auxin throughout the plant body. The first indication for a biological relevance of auxin transport dates back to Darwin's experiments on phototropism, which indicated the existence of transported signals.

Several decades later, Went and Cholodny performed growth experiments suggestive of a scenario in which transport of an externally applied regulator would regulate plant tropisms and the responsible substance was subsequently termed auxin by Kogl and Haagen-Smit (1931).

Two physiologically distinct and spatially separated mechanisms appear to be involved in auxin transport over long distances in plants. One mechanism appears to translocate auxin rapidly by mass flow in the mature phloem, wher mechanism controls auxin transport in a strictly polar fashion.

The major route of such polar auxin transport (PAT) involves relocation of the growth regulator from immature tissues close to the shoot apex downwards towards the root tips.

In addition, auxin reaching the root tip appears to be redistributed back towards the base of the root, presumably via the outer most cell layers of the root. Polar transport of auxin is much slower *(ca.* 7–15 mm/h) than mass-flow-dependent auxin distribution, and involves, carrier-dependent, cell-to-cell polar transport.

In that respect, auxin is unique among plant hormones,

as it is actively transported from source organs in young, apical regions to target cells where it might exert its biological activity.

Mass-flow-dependent Distribution of Auxin

There is considerable evidence that IAA is a constituent of phloem sap. After entering the phloem in the leaves, IAA would then be passively translocated to and unloaded at auxin sinks. The direction and velocity of auxin translocation in phloem cells thus primarily depends on spatial variations in auxin concentrations.

However, while substantial quantities of auxin can be found in the phloem sap the role of this auxin pool in auxin-mediated growth responses is still poorly understood.

Polar Auxin Transport

Physiological Aspects

Unlike mass-flow-dependent distribution, PAT has been shown to exhibit characteristics of a carrier-mediated process that is energy dependent, saturable, and which involves cellular uptake as well as efflux of the growth regulator.

Long before the first molecular players involved in PAT were characterised, a number of elegant physiological experiments already predicted the involvement of specific carrier proteins in this process. Specifically, saturable auxin uptake and efflux activities have been demonstrated in single plant cells as well as in tissue segments. Remarkably, these carrier activities exhibit quite distinct substrate specificities.

Auxin uptake could be demonstrated for IAA and 2,4 dichlorophenoxyacetic acid (2,4-D), whereas carrier-dependent auxin efflux is efficient for IAA and naphthalene-1-acetic acid (NAA). Besides differences in substrate specificity, auxin uptake and efflux activities can be distinguished using a set of synthetic auxin transport inhibitors.

Auxin efflux inhibitors were characterised in the 1970s and were subsequently shown to inhibit auxin efflux in single cells as well as in entire plants. Well-known inhibitors of auxin efflux are 2,3,5-triiodobenzoic acid (TIBA) and N-1-naphthyl-

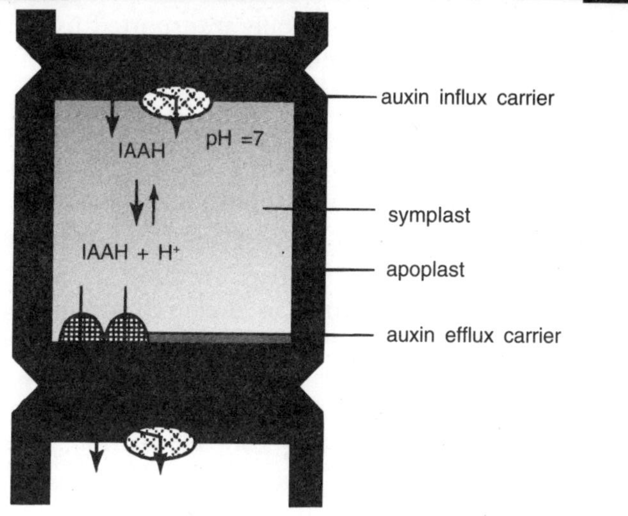

Figure 1.2: Chemiosmotic model for PAT.

phthalamic acid (NPA), which are both commonly used to study physiological and developmental consequences of inhibition of PAT.

Recently, however, treatment with high concentrations of synthetic auxin efflux inhibitors has been shown to exhibit a quite general effect on the control of membrane protein cycling, raising questions about the specificity of these compounds.

Interestingly, a group of plant metabolites, namely aglyconic flavonoids, appear to inhibit auxin efflux, leading to the suggestion that these compounds might act as natural regulators of PAT. However, these compounds also appear to interfere with a large variety of biological processes.

Thus, a specific role of flavonoids in the regulation of PAT remains to be determined. In addition, substances interfering with carrier-mediated cellular uptake of auxin have been identified. Specifycally, 1-naphthoxy-acetic acid (1-NOA) and 3-chloro-4-hydroxyphenylacetic acid (CHPAA) were shown to inhibit auxin uptake in tobacco culture cells.

In addition to the pharmacological characterisation of PAT, the site that mediate such transport have been well characterised. Auxin is basipetally transported from the apex to the base of the shoot. PAT in the stem has been localised to the vascular cambium.

In addition to basipetal auxin transport, evidence for lateral auxin transport has been found in the shoot as well. Once auxin has passed the shoot-to-root-junction, further polar transport of auxin proceeds in the root vasculature towards the root tip.

From the root tip, auxin is then redistributed upwards into the root elongation zone . Thus, roots exhibit both acropetally and basipetally oriented auxin streams, both of which have been implicated in a variety of auxin-mediated growth responses, including root elongation, lateral root formation and root tropisms.

A conceptual framework for the mechanisms underlying the coordinated polar distribution of auxin was proposed in the mid-1970s. The chemiosmotic hypothesis for PAT was proposed by Rubery & Sheldrake (1974) and Raven (1975), and is based on the observation that only the protonated form of auxin efficiently move across the plasma membrane, whereas the auxin anion (IAA^-) is unable to cross the membrane.

In the relatively acidic environment of the cell wall, a fraction of IAA is in its protonated form (IAAH), which could therefore efficiently enter the cell via concentration gradient-dependent diffusion.

Moreover, activity of auxin uptake carriers could further reinforce cellular uptake of auxin. The higher pH found in the cytoplasm then forces the majority of IAAH to dissociate. As a result, the highly polar IAA^- anion is "trapped" in the cell because of its poor membrane permeability.

Further transport of IAA^- thus requires specific carriers that mediate the efflux of auxin into the surrounding apoplast. The polarity of auxin transport would be the result of an asymmetric distribution of efflux carriers in cell membranes that allows auxin transport to proceed in only one direction.

Polar auxin export from a single cell would then multiply

in a file of neighbouring cells that all exhibit the same asymmetric distribution of auxin efflux carrier proteins.

This classical hypothesis has remained essentially unchallenged for the last 30 years, and was recently supported by the identification of candidate proteins, seemingly involved in facilitating uptake and efflux of auxin in a concerted mechanism that controls the polar distribution of auxin.

Auxin Transporters

In contrast to mass-flow-dependent auxin transport, PAT can be strictly regulated by the plant via control of influx and efflux carriers. Most of the research to date has been on *Arabidopsis thaliana,* in which the following set of putative auxin carriers have so far been identified:

(1) The AUX1/LAX influx carriers comprising four members of amino acid permease-type proteins.

(2) The PIN efflux carriers comprising eight members resembling putative bacterial transporters.

(3) The MDR/PGP efflux carriers comprising many members homologous to multidrug resistance/P-glycoproteins transporters.

A role for these proteins in PAT is primarily demonstrated by the phenotypes of the corresponding mutants, such as altered PAT and associated growth defects.

Their role as actual carriers has been implied from two features: firstly, their highly polar localisation in cells which supports the chemiosmotic hypothesis, and secondly, their homology to other permeases/transporters.

To date, the PINs have featured most prominently in research on PAT. Their role in PAT is further supported by the strong phenotypes of the pin1 (pin-formed inflorescences) and *pin2* mutants (agravitropic), which clearly demonstrate PAT deficiencies.

However, whether or not the PINs are true auxin *carriers* is less certain—although PINs are known to be homologous to bacterial proteins with mostly predicted functions in transport across membranes. This similarity, however, is restricted to the transmembrane region, whereas the large hydrophilic loop can only be found in plant PIN proteins.

The MDR/PGPs are implicated in PAT as they can bind the auxin efflux inhibitor NPA, and due to the PAT-related defects exhibited by pgp1 and pgp19/m*dr*] mutants. Moreover, although MDR/PGPs are less polarly localised, their homology to known ABC transporters is highly suggestive for a function as auxin efflux transporters.

As the chemiosmotic model predicts that auxin influx can be passive, the requirement for a specific influx carrier such as AUX1 seems at first redundant.

However, the agravitropic phenotype of aux1, the polar localisation of AUX1 and its homology to known permease-type proteins supports its role as an influx carrier. In addition, aux1 is more resistant (in root elongation assays) than wild-type (WT) plants to auxins-like 2,4-D and IAA, suggesting that active auxin uptake is crucial for at least some PAT-related processes, particularly in the root tip.

To be considered true auxin carriers, it is essential to prove actual auxin transport activity for these putative carriers. This has been a difficult task for several reasons. Firstly, any measurement of "activity" refers to the amount of auxin transported or retained in whole cells or tissues.

Thus, what is being measured is not the activity of a specific carrier but the combined effect of all influx and efflux activities, including passive diffusion. Unfortunately, comparisons between WT and mutants of the various carriers do not overcome this problem due to the redundancy of the carriers, for example the absence of one PIN can be compensated by an increase in the other PINs.

Secondly, evidence of auxin transport activity can also mean that the "carriers" are required as part of a complex that transports auxin. This might be particularly true for the PINs, as they are not homologous to established transporters/permeases and their function in PAT is thus less certain.

Thirdly, one has to show specificity for auxin. This is probably most relevant for the MDR/PGPs, as MDRs can have a broad range of substrates. Measurements of auxin transport performed in heterologous systems (i.e. expressing the plant carriers in non-plant hosts) are also subject to these limitations.

With the above limitations in mind, there is evidence to support auxin transport activity for AUX1 and PIN2 in root, and some weak evidence when PIN2 is expressed in yeast . PGP1 appears to facilitate auxin transport when expressed in yeast and HeLa cells, but Noh *et al.* (2001) failed to find auxin transport activity in the same yeast system for PGP19.

Regulation of the Carriers

As with any cellular process, regulation of PAT can be directed at changing either the amount of protein (e.g. by increasing transcription or reducing degradation of protein) or the actual *activity* of the protein (e.g. by covalent modification or allosteric activation).

However, it is often not possible to distinguish between these two specific changes. In most cases, PAT is simply measured in tissue segments, or more often, a secondary effect of PAT is observed (e.g. root length or gravitropic response).

PIN mRNA expression is tissue and developmental-stage-specific and in some cases circadian-regulated. Specific changes in mRNA (or expression of transcriptional reporter genes) have been reported for the PINs and MDR/PGPs following a variety of treatments that can be linked to PAT.

These include treatment with IAA and auxin transport inhibitors NPA and TIBA, mechanical or gravitational stimulation or dark/light transition Geisler. However, changes in mRNA are indicative of transcriptional control, but may not be matched by corresponding increases in protein (e.g. 200-fold increases in PIN mRNA levels were matched by little or no increase in PIN protein.

This illustrates the importance of following up any RNA analysis with protein analysis. Levels of mRNA are affected in certain mutant backgrounds and such data may be useful in identifying possible components in the control of PAT.

For example, PIN3 and *PIN4* are downregulated in i*fl*1.

As *ifl1-2* mutants have reduced PAT and exhibit the distinct pin1 phenotype, that is pin-formed inflorescence stems, this indicates that IFL (a homoeodo-main-leucine zipper protein) could be required for PIN control.

There is a scarcity of data showing actual quantitative changes (e.g. Western blot analysis) in total carrier protein levels as part of a regulatory process. To an extent this certainly reflects the difficulties of dealing with plant membrane proteins, but it is also due to a unique aspect of the carriers, that is their function is dependent on their membrane localisation.

Thus, adjusting the amount of carrier protein at the membrane compared to the amount that is in internal compartments could affect their activity. Changes in the rate of cycling or the polarity of distribution also could affect the rate or direction of PAT.

It has also been suggested that the cycling of PINs may be part of their transport activity, such that auxin is transported in cargo vesicles which are then exocytosed in the manner of mammalian neurotransmitter release.

Studying the distribution of carrier proteins between the membrane and internal compartments (or changes in polarity) requires *in situ* analysis (e.g. immunolocalisations or fluorescent reporter proteins). The majority of reported results comprise such visual analysis and have revealed fascinating insights as to how carrier proteins are regulated.

However, the disadvantage is that such analysis is more subjective, particularly for quantitative comparisons. Membrane localisation of the carriers can be affected by the following:

(1) Gravitropic and phototropic stimulation, which leads to relocation of PIN proteins. Moreover, control of PIN2 endocytosis (via a putative auxin-dependent mechanism) has also been implicated in the root gravitropic response.

These processes may mediate asymmetric auxin redistribution and cell elongation during tropic responses.

(2) Auxin treatment, which can increase the internalisation

of PIN1 in hypocotyl and root tip cells. This is also supported by analysis of the *tt4* mutant, roots of which have higher auxin levels than WT and a diffuse PIN1 pattern. In contrast to these data, auxins may also enhance PIN1 or PIN2 membrane localisation.

(3) The vesicular cycling inhibitor brefeldin A (BFA), which has been widely used to demonstrate the cellular internalisation and cycling of PINY in roots Geldner. PIN3 can also be internalised by BFA, while the data on PIN2 are more equivocal. The BFA-sensitive cycling of PIN1 requires GNOM, a GDP/GTP exchange factor for small G-proteins and in the gnommutant embryo, PIN1 polar distribution is disorganised. BFA has also been shown to internalise AUXY, although this required much higher BFA concentrations (100μM) than that required to see an effect on AUXY-dependent phenotypes and is in contrast to studies that show a lack of effect of BFA on auxin influx.

(4) The auxin transport inhibitors TIBA and NPA, which can prevent the reversibility of the BFA-induced internalisation of PINs. Also, in big/tir3/doc1 mutants, NPA by itself can cause internalisation of PINY. However, doubts have been raised about the high amounts of NPA required to see these effects (up to 200 μM NPA, whereas auxin efflux is already inhibited by Y-Y0 μM NPA). Notwithstanding such doubts, the observation in big/tir*3/docl* is interesting, as BIG has been implicated in mediating the effect of auxin on PIN cycling.

(5) Various mutations; for example in the PINOID kinase mutant *pid* or in PID over-expression plants, the normal apical or basal locations of PIN Y, PIN2 and PIN4 are shifted. A diffuse rather than polar patterning of PINY is seen in flavonoid-deficient mutants *tt4* and in *mdr/pgp* hypocotyls[1]; the latter raises interesting possibilities of links between the two carrier families. PINY polarity and PIN3 distribution

are altered in the sterol methyltransferase mutant *smtl /orc.* In all of these mutants, PAT and PAT-processes are also affected, thus illustrating the correlation between PAT and correct PIN positioning. However, whether or not PAT is dependent on PIN localisation, or *vice versa,* is still an open question.

As mentioned above, the activity of the carriers is closely tied to their membrane localisation. Conditions that perturb localisation of the PINs have generally been shown to affect PAT rates. For example, BFA treatment causes intracellular accumulation of PINs, correlating with an inhibition of auxin efflux or PAT in tobacco suspension culture cells, zuchinni hypocotyls and Arabidopsis.

In agreement with its effects on auxin transport, BFA also affects processes dependent on PAT, for example it inhibits lateral root growth, decreases root and hypocotyl length, and inhibits gravitropism.

BFA also affects the polarity of root hair initiation, a process that is auxin gradient dependent and has been linked to AUX1 activity. In addition to the effects of cellular mislocalisation of the carriers, the following have also been shown to affect PAT, although the mechanisms or the connection to the auxin carriers are uncertain:

(1) Various protein kinase and phosphatase inhibitors in general inhibit auxin efflux or basipetal PAT; but may also enhance basipetal PAT. The latter is in agreement with the increased PAT seen in the r*cn* mutant, which has reduced phosphatase 2A activity (RCN codes for a regulatory subunit of protein phosphatase 2A. Moreover, PINOID kinase also affects auxin distribution, that is a decrease in IAA accumulation in root tips.

(2) Acidification of the intracellular pH of cells reduces active auxin influx and efflux, while alkalinisation of the extracellular pH reduces influx. The transient alkalinisation observed in root columella cells following gravistimulation has been suggested to be involved in the control of PIN activity or localisation.

(3) NPA is widely used as an inhibitor of general auxin efflux and PAT. The mechanism of action is not entirely clear but there is accumulating data to make some reasonable hypotheses been shown to bind directly to distinct proteins including the MDR/PGP carriers. Moreover, MDR/PGP interacts with the cyclophilin-like protein TWISTED DWARF1 (TWD1); this interaction is disrupted by NPA, and the twd1 mutant has decreased PAT. These data suggest that the inhibitive effect of NPA on auxin efflux could be due to the direct binding of NPA to MDR/PGP carriers. Alternatively, as PIN1 is mislocalised in *mdr/pgp* mutants, a scenario where the PINs and the MDR/PGPs operate in a complex has been postulated. Apart from MDR/PGP proteins, NPA also binds to aminopeptidases and a gluthathione-S-transferase. Intriguingly, GSTF2 also binds auxin and has been suggested as a cytoplasmic escort for auxin.

(4) Flavonoids have a negative effect on PAT and can inhibit auxin efflux/leakage from roots and hypocotyls. In agreement, defects in flavonoid biosynthesis in the *tt4* mutant correlate with elevated PAT and with phenotypes associated with elevated PAT.

The structural resemblance of flavonoids to NPA, and their ability to compete for NPA-binding sites on the various NPA-binding proteins, indicates that NPA may inhibit PAT by mimicking the natural flavonoids. In addition, NPA can compensate for flavonoid deficiencies in *tt4* mutants.

An intriguing possible mechanism of flavonoid/NPA action arises from the fact that flavonoids are known to compete for ATP-binding sites in ATP-binding proteins and in this way act as physiological negative regulators. In particular, flavonoids can displace ATP in mouse MDR/PGP homologues.

Thus, by analogy with the situation in mammals, NPA/flavonoid-type molecules might bind to the nucleotide-binding region of plant MDR/PGPs and in this way inhibit MDR/PGP activity in catalysing auxin transport.

Conclusion

We mentioned earlier that measurements of PAT reflect the sum of all influx and efflux paths of auxin in cells or tissues, and that it was thus not possible to measure activities of the individual carriers.

However, the fact that PIN localisation can change has given researchers a good tool to observe direct effects on these carriers in response to a certain treatment.

Following up this with PAT measurements (or observing secondary effects of PAT) allows further postulations on the putative role of the PINs in mediating PAT. The technical inability to assign any observed changes in PAT to specific carriers is a disadvantage when analysing the role of each carrier, but it also simply reflects the true situation, that is the carriers act together.

For example, an emerging model of PAT is that the PINs and the MDR/PGPs form a complex to facilitate auxin transport against an electrochemical gradient. The AUX1 influx carrier would enhance the direction of PAT in tissues where tight regulation of this absolutely crucial for a response (e.g. gravitropic response in the root tip). And no doubt future research will also discover other proteins involved in the carrier machinery.

GAS: DISTRIBUTION AND TRANSPORT

The second major hormone group to be discussed here are the GAs. The GAs are potent promoters of elongation growth, in both shoots and roots.

Their physiological characterisation has long been associated with dwarf mutants, many of which are grossly deficient in bioactive GAs.

When applied to such mutants, GAs dramatically promote growth, even in parts of the plant distant from the application site. However, this does not mean that *endogenous* GAs are normally transported long distances within the WT plant, as the ensuing discussion will demonstrate.

Seeds and Fruits

The developing seeds of many plant species typically contain higher levels of GAs, and a greater diversity of these compounds, than do vegetative tissues.

Young seeds, in particular, often contain some unusual GAs and compounds; for example, young pea seeds contain substantial amounts of GAS dihydrodiol, whereas this compound is much less abundant in other parts of the plant.

On the other hand, older pea seeds (at the "table-ready" stage) tend to contain very high levels of a more limited number of GAs.

This aspect, coupled with their large size, made older pea seeds ideal for early studies on GA biosynthesis, and the sequence of steps in the early 13-hydroxylation pathway of GA biosynthesis was established using this system.

Ironically, however, GAs do not appear to be important for seed development at these later stages, since the is-1 mutant, which blocks GA production early in the biosynthetic pathway, dramatically reduces GA content in maturing seeds without affecting seed set or seed size.

GAs are critical at the early stages of seed development, however, since the *lh-2* mutation (which, like ls-1 imposes a block early in GA biosynthesis reduces bioactive GA levels in young seeds and results in substantial seed abortion, while the *lh-2* seeds that do develop are smaller than WT seeds.

In earlier work it was suggested that seeds might act as sources of GAs for developing fruits. However, in pea, the ls-1 mutant contains normal levels of the main bioactive GA, GA1, in young seeds, but is deficient in GA_1 in the pods. The same appears to be true for early blocking mutation, *na-1*.

The *na-1* mutation does not affect the GA content of maturing seeds, but dramatically reduces that of the pods. This indicates that in normal circumstances, the seeds do not export bioactive GAs (such as GA1 and GA_3) or their precursors into the elongating pods.

Vegetative Tissues Grafting Studies

GA levels are generally much lower in vegetative tissues

than in developing seeds. However, the phenotypic effects of GA synthesis mutations are often more dramatic in the vegetative plant, and much early GA research addressed the related questions of GA distribution and transport at that developmental stage.

It is well established that young, rapidly growing shoot tissue contains higher levels of bioactive GA than does fully mature tissue. However, where is that GA synthesised?

With the isolation of dwarf, GA-deficient mutants, this question could be revisited, because in certain species, mutant and WT plants could be grafted together to determine whether or not GAs move from one genotype into the other. In pea, the first such grafting studies were performed with the *le-1* mutant that blocks the final step in GA_1 biosynthesis.

The dwarfing effect of this mutation was not graft-transmissible; that is, it could not be reversed by grafting to WT stocks. This result was confirmed by Reid *et al.* (1983), and by this time, the *na-1* mutant was also available *(na-1* blocks GA biosynthesis early in the pathway).

Grafting *na-1* shoots (scions) to WT stocks (consisting of mature leaves and internodes) resulted in a dramatic promotion of elongation in the mutant. This provided evidence for the "long-distance" transport of a compound or compounds from one portion of the shoot (mature tissue) to another (immature tissue), where growth is stimulated.

The *le-1/WT* and *na/WT* grafting results, taken together, indicate that a GA_1 precursor, but not GA_1 itself, is the mobile factor. It would appear that this precursor is a GA after GA_{12} in the pathway, since *na-1* blocks before GA_{12}.

Other graft combinations showed that a major source of this mobile GA is mature shoot tissue, although a contribution from the roots cannot be ruled out. Interestingly, although the le-1/*WT* grafts indicated that *endogenous* GA_1 is not subject to long-distance transport in pea, it is well known that applied GA_1 is at least partially transported from leaves to other parts of the plant.

Further evidence that the endogenous mobile factor is a

GA was provided by Proebsting *et al.* (1992), who showed that grafting *na scions* to WT rootstocks increased the actual GA content of the mutant scions. Proebsting *et al. also* presented evidence that the mobile GA is GA_{20}, and not GA_{19} (the precursor of GA_{20}).

The idea of GA_{20} as the mobile GA is consistent with the finding that in phloem diffusate from pea leaves, GA_{20} was approximately 7-fold more abundant than GA_{19} or GA_{1}.

Grafting studies showed that GA1 precursors can be exported from mature WT tissue to immature mutant tissue across a graft union, but does this mean that such transport normally plays a significant role in providing GAs to the young growing tissues?

Grafting also showed that WT scions elongated to approximately the same extent whether grafted to *na* or WT mature stocks, indicating that a supply of GA1 precursors from the mature tissue is *not* necessary for the normal elongation of young internodes.

However, it must be realised that as the WT scion develops, its own leaves expand and mature, and could be acting as sources of GA_{20} for the elongating internodes.

Thus, the extent to which elongating internodes rely on other tissues for GA_{20} or other GA precursors is not yet known. It is relevant, however, that young internodes typically contain more $GA1_{9}$ than GA20, and this GA_{19} might well have been synthesised in situ, since GA19 might not be transported to a great extent.

Furthermore, the internodes themselves are capable of converting GA_{19} to GA_{20} and GA_{20} to GA1. Therefore, there is considerable evidence that young internodes might be autonomous for GAs, and that they might not depend on imported GA precursors to maintain normal GA1 levels.

Can mature shoot tissue synthesise GAs?

During the 1990s, the sites of GA biosynthesis were also being studied using a different method. This approach relied on the logic that ent-kaurene, as the first committed intermediate in GA biosynthesis, represents a "gateway" into the GA biosynthesis pathway. On the basis of studying ent-kaurene biosynthesis, it was suggested that ent-kaurene synthesis, and therefore GA synthesis, is largely restricted to the rapidly expanding, immature shoot tissue. By implication, this research suggested that GA synthesis does not occur in mature tissue to any significant extent.

The Aach *et al.* (1995, 1997) articles were widely quoted, but the idea that GAs are not synthesised in mature tissue did not seem to fit with the grafting results, which indicated that mature shoot tissue can synthesise and export a GA_1 precursor, probably GA_{20}, into other parts of the shoot.

Therefore, Ross *et al.* (2003) reexamined the issue, by monitoring GAs in mature shoot tissue after excision of the immature material (decapitation). It was found that after decapitation, GA_{19} and GA_{20} levels were maintained in the mature tissue; in other words, it appeared that the GA_{19} and GA_{20} found in mature tissue was not coming from the immature region.

Furthermore, evidence was obtained that these GAs were not coming from the roots. The maintenance of normal GA_{19} and GA_{20} levels in decapitated plants did not seem to be due to slow metabolism of these GAs.

Indeed, metabolism experiments with radiolabelled GAs indicated that mature tissue from both intact and decapitated plants rapidly converted GA_{19} to GA_{20}, GA_{20} to GA1, GA_1 to GA_8, GA_{20} to GA_{29} and GA_{29} to GA_{29}-catabolite. Ross *et al.* (2003) concluded that in pea, mature tissues are able to synthesise GAs such as GA_{19}, contrary to the suggestions of Aach *et al.* (1995, 1997).

Nevertheless, there is little doubt that mature tissues contain much lower levels of the bioactive GA_1 than do immature tissues; in other words, there is co-localisation of GA1 accumulation and rapid elongation in pea shoots.

Ross *et al.* (2003) reported that the main reason for the steep gradient of GA1 down the shoot is that mature tissues contain very strong GA1 deactivation (2-oxidation) activity. GA_{20} is also a substrate for 2-oxidation, and consequently GA_{20}

levels also decrease dramatically in older parts of the plant. GA19, on the other hand, is not 2-oxidised in pea, and mature tissue still contains substantial amounts of this GA. The end product of GA_{20} 2-oxidation, GA29-catabolite, actually accumulates in the mature portion of the shoot. In immature tissues, GA 2-oxidation activity is weaker, and GA1 and GA_{20} accumulate.

The conclusion that mature shoot tissue produces but rapidly deactivates GA_I is supported by the expression pattern of a range of GA synthesis and deactivation genes. The synthesis genes *LS, LH, NA, PsGA20ox1* and *LE* (PsGA3ox1) are all strongly expressed in mature tissues, when the mRNA level is quantified in terms of the amount of mRNA per unit total RNA.

The GA deactivation (2-oxidation) gene PsGA2ox*] (SLN)* is also strongly expressed in mature shoot tissue. In potato, the theory that endogenous GA_{20} is mobile, whereas endogenous GA_I is not, would provide an explanation for the apparently anomalous tuberisation behaviour of certain transgenic potato plants.

In this specie GAs in the stolons inhibit tuber formation. It would be expected, therefore, that over-expression of GA synthesis genes would lead to an inhibition of tuber formation. In short days, this proved to be the case with a GA 20-oxidase gene, but not with a GA 3-oxidase.

These genes encode enzymes for the steps GA_{19} to GA_{20} and GA_{20} to GA1, respectively. Prat (2004) has suggested that endogenous GA_{20}, but not endogenous GA1, is a mobile GA in potato (as in pea), an GA 3-oxidation occurs rapidly in the shoot (as in plants over-expressing a 3-oxidase gene), this consumes GA_{20}, reducing the supply of GA_{20} available for export from the shoot to the stolons.

When a GA 20-oxidase gene is over-expressed, in contrast, GA_{20} becomes abundant in the shoot, from where it can be transported to the stolons and converted to GA1, which inhibits tuber formation. There is also evidence for the movement of endogenous GAs in germinating *Arabidopsis* seedlings.

In this case, the suggestion is again that the precursors of bioactive GAs, rather than bioactive GAs themselves, are transported. In *Arabidopsis* an early GA precursor, possibly ent-kaurene, is thought to move from the provasculature to the cortex and endodermis of the germinating seedling.

The gene encoding the enzyme for ent-kaurene synthesis was expressed exclusively in the provasculature, while genes for later steps, including the step immediately after ent-kaurene, were expressed in the cortex/endodermis of embryo axes.

Interestingly, the mobility of ent-kaurene may not be limited to the plant body itself. It appears that ent-kaurene can be emitted from *Arabidopsis* plants over-expressingent-kaurene synthase (from a GA-producing fungus).

Furthermore, the airborne ent-kaurene then appeared to be taken up and converted to bioactive GAs by other *Arabidopsis* plants sharing the same container as the overproducers.

Otsuka *et al.* (2004) also reported evidence that ent-kaurene is released by WT *Chamaecyparis obtusa* and *Cryptomeria japonica* plants, suggesting that emission of this GA intermediate may be a natural phenomenon. However, ent-kaurene was not released by seedlings of tomato, lettuce, pea or pumpkin.

Monocotyledonous Species

While the grafting studies in pea indicated that GA1 is not transported, similar experiments in maize yielded a different result. Katsumi *et al.* performed approach grafts, in which two seedlings were joined, but with each retaining its own root system.

Two mutants were used: d_5 and d1, which impose early and late blocks on the GA biosynthesis pathway, respectively. Similar to the le-*1* mutation from pea, the d1 mutation is defective in the step from GA20 to GA1.

The key results were that grafting d1 plants to the WT promoted elongation in the mutant, and that grafting d_5 to d1 promoted elongation in the d_5 partner. These findings indicate than both GA1 and its precursors are transported in maize, in contrast to pea where there is only evidence for transport of the precursors.

Using a different approach, Winkler and Freeling (1994) also obtained evidence that endogenous GA1 is transported in maize. These workers created a mosaic plant consisting of WT leaves with sectors of genotype d1.

The d1 sectors, which comprised up to 45% of the distance from mid-vein to leaf margin, were immediately recognisable because they also carried *cl,* which conferred whiteness (lack of chlorophyll) to the tissue.

The reasoning was that if GA1 did not move from the WT section of the leaf, where it was produced, the mosaic leaves would become distorted as they grew, because d1 sections, lacking GA1, would elongate to a lesser extent (by approximately 50%).

However, no such distortion was observed, and the elongation of the mutant sectors appeared to be normal. These observations indicate that a mobile factor, probably GA1 itself, moved from WT tissues into the d1 sections, promoting elongation.

It is possible, therefore, that there is a difference between monocotyledonous and dicotyledonous plants with respect to the potential of endogenous GA_1 to be transported.

However, even though endogenous GA1 appears capable of being transported in monocotyledonous species, we need to again ask: in these species, does the transport of GA1 and/ or its precursors normally make a substantial contribution to the GA1 pool at sites where GA acts?

In other words, is there, or is there not, co-localisation of the sites of GA synthesis and GA action? This question was addressed for rice by Kaneko et al. (2003), who monitored the expression of GA biosynthesis and signaling genes in various plant parts at several stages of development.

On this basis Kaneko et al. (2003) suggested that at most developmental stages, bioactive GA is synthesised (from its immediate precursors) in the same zone in which it acts. For example, in 2-week-old seedlings, the synthesis and signaling genes were all expressed in young leaves surrounding the SAM, whereas little or no activity was detected in the developed leaves.

However, since the genes monitored were from late in the GA pathway, the gene-expression data on their own do not preclude the *possibility that early* GA intermediates move from another part of the seedling to the young leaves enclosing the SAM.

In grasses, the major exception to the co-localisation pattern reported by Kaneko *et al.* (2003) involves the germinating grains, where there is clear spatial separation between GA synthesis and GA action. In germinating cereal grains GA1 is transported from the embryo (specifically, the epithe-embryo) to the aleurone layer, where it stimulates the production and s-amylases and other hydrolases.

In support of this classical model, Kaneko *et al.* (2003) found evidence for the expression of GA signaling genes, but not GA synthesis genes, in the aleurone layer. Earlier experiments indicated also that GAs were synthesised in the embryo rather than in the aleurone.

Another situation in which a GA is thought to be a critical mobile signal in grasses relates to flowering in *Lolium temulentum.* In this species one long day, perceived by the leaves, is sufficient to promote flowering at the shoot apex, and it is suggested that the communicating signal is GA_5, which possesses strong florigenic activity in this species.

Conclusion

In summary, for dicots there is evidence that in certain circumstan grafts), GA precursors can move from mature tissues into the elongating zone, where they are converted to bioactive GAs that in turn promote elongation growth.

In the grasses, there is evidence for the potential mobility not only of GA precursors, but of the bioactive species as well. However, the contribution that transport normally makes to the GA pool of rapidly growing tissues is still not what is clear is that the highest levels of bioactive GA are usually found in zones of rapid growth. Nevertheless, the co-localisation of bioactive GA and rapid growth should not be confused with the co-localisation of GA *biosynthesis* and growth. There is little doubt that mature pea shoot tissue, well past the growth stage, can still synthesise GAs.

That bioactive GA does not accumulate in mature pea tissue is attributable to rapid GA deactivation.

BRS: DISTRIBUTION AND TRANSPORT

The third hormone group to be discussed are the BRs. The BRs are steroidal compounds now known to be essential for normal plant growth and development.

Extensive research over the past two decades has revealed the importance of BRs in a wide variety of processes, including cell elongation, cell division, vascular differentiation, reproductive development, and pathogen and abiotic tolerance.

As a consequence, this group is now widely recognised as an important class of plant hormones, alongside the "classical" hormones such as auxin and GA.

BR Distribution

BRs were originally isolated from pollen which other reproductive organs such as seeds, generally contains the highest concentration of these substances.

With the development of techniques for the analysis of endogenous BR levels and the expression of BR biosynthesis genes, researchers have recently been able to address specific questions regarding the distribution of BRs in other plant tissues.

Such studies have revealed clear spatial patterns of distribution of BRs in a wide range of plant species. For instance, Bancos *et al.* (2002) showed that BRs were present in both the shoot and root tissues of pea, *Arabidopsis* and tomato plants.

However, the levels of the early interme BR biosynthesis pathway were generally higher in the roots, while the late-pathway BRs, castasterone (CS) and 6-DeoxoCS, were more abundant in the shoots.

In 2003, Shimada *et al.* published a comprehensive report on both endogenous BR levels and BR biosynthesis gene expression, in a wide range of different tissues from *Arabidopsis* seedlings.

This study demonstrated a widespread distribution of endogenous BRs throughout the plant, with the greatest accumulation of late-pathway BRs occurring in the young actively growing tissues.

Significantly, there was a close association between the tissues that show the highest BR concentrations and those that showed the highest expression levels of BR biosynthesis genes.

Symons and Reid (2004) have demonstrated a similar distribution pattern of BR levels in pea. The occurrence of the highest BR levels in the young, actively growing tissues is consistent with a key role for these hormones in plant development.

Given the importance of BR we would expect the existence of mechanisms that strictly control endogenous BR levels and their distribution in the target cells or tissues.

As is the case for other hormones, such mechanisms could include the relative rates of BR synthesis, destruction, inactivation and transport within the plant.

The close association between BR levels and the expression of BR biosynthesis genes suggests that *in situ* BR biosynthesis may be one such mechanism that plays a significant role in regulating the endogenous BR levels.

However, the widespread distribution of endogenous BRs also raises the possibility that long-distance transport of these compounds may occur between different plant tissues, and that this may also play a role in regulating localised BR levels.

BR Transport

Exogenous BRs

Early attempts to understand BR transport involved

monitoring the movement of radiolabelled BRs after application to the plant. Such studies provided some evidence that BRs may be transported acropetally from the roots to the shoots.

For instance, a small percentage of [^{3}H]brassinolide (BL) or [^{3}H]castasterone (CS) applied to the roots of rice plants was reported to be translocated to the shoots.

Similarly, when [^{14}C]epiBL was applied to the roots of cucumber and wheat seedlings ^{14}C was soon detected throughout both plant species. In contrast to BRs applied to plant roots, exogenous BRs applied to shoot tissues of different species have proven to be relatively immobile.

For instance, Symons and Reid (2004) showed that [^{3}H]BL and [^{3}H]CS applied to the shoot tissues of pea entered the plant, but did not move beyond the site of application.

These results are consistent with previous studies, which show that the majority of radiolabelled BL and CS incorporated into leaves of rice remained in the treated leaves 24 h after it was applied. In this study a small amount of radioactivity was shown to accumulate in the roots after 72 h, but this was largely in the form of water-soluble BR metabolites.

Similarly, in wheat, exogenously applied [^{14}C]epiBL was not transported from the treated leaf even after 7 days. Despite these relatively clear outcomes, we must be cautious in our interpretation, because the observed movement of exogenous radiolabelled substances may not accurately reflect transport of endogenous hormones.

Therefore, while some of these studies demonstrate that *exogenous* BRs *can* move acropetally from the roots, they do not necessarily prove that *endogenous* BRs are normally transported in a similar manner. It is inherently difficult to make definitive conclusions about hormone transport on the basis of hormone application studies alone.

Endogenous BRs: grafting studies

As was the case for the GAs, grafting studies have provided invaluable insights into the transport of *endogenous* BRs in plants. Initial grafting studies using the pea *lkb* mutant were conducted prior to the discovery that the *lkb* mutation causes BR deficiency, by blocking BR biosynthesis.

In this initial study, young *lkb* scions were grafted onto mature leafy WT stocks, but the presence of this WT root and shoot tissue did not restore internode elongation in the *lkb* scion.

With the benefit of hind sight we now know that this result indicates that *endogenous* bioactive BRs are not transported acropetally (upwards) in pea shoots.

However, these initial studies revealed little about the possibility of basipetal tran the shoot (e.g. from the apical bud to the internodes), or from the shoot to the root. Armed with techniques for the quantification of endogenous BR levels, Symons and Reid (2004) revisited grafting studies using WT and *lkb* mutant plants.

Significantly, this study revealed further compelling evidence that endogenous, bioactive BRs do not undergo long-distance transport. For example, it was confirmed that a WT rootstock does not restore the growth of a BR-deficient *lkb* shoot, and the reason was shown to be that bioactive BR levels in the *lkb* shoot are not increased by the presence of the WT rootstock.

Assuming that grafting does not disrupt normal BR transport pathways, these results provide further evidence that the maintenance of normal bioactive BR levels in the pea shoot is not dependent on acropetal BR transport from the roots.

In the reciprocal graft combination (a WT shoot grafted onto an *lkb* rootstock), the presence of the WT shoot did not increase BR levels in the BR-deficient *lkb* root.

Once again, if we assume that grafting does not disrupt normal BR transport pathways, this result suggests that the maintenance of normal bioactive BR levels in pea roots is not dependent on basipetal BR transport from the shoots.

Comparable grafting studies in tomato, using WT and the BR-deficie dwarf *dx* mutant plants, have also yielded similar results, with no phenotypic recovery of the *dx* phenotype in either reciprocal graft combination.

These results reinforce the conclusion that *endogenous* BRs do not undergo long-distance transport between shoots and roots, and show that this phenomenon is consistent in different plant species.

Therefore, it is likely that the acropetal movement of *exogenously* applied BRs from the roots may not accurately reflect the transport of *endog*enous BRs in plants.

BR Transport within the Shoot?

While the grafting studies clearly show a lack of BR transport (acropetal or basipetal) between shoot and root, they provide only limited information regarding the possible transport of BRs within these tissues.

This issue was also addressed by Symons and Reid (2004), who examined the effects of decapitation (removal of the apical bud) and defoliation (removal of leaves) on endogenous BR levels in the shoot.

In this case, neither decapitation nor defoliation resulted in a decrease in endogenous BR levels in the remaining shoot tissues. This suggests that the maintenance of normal BR levels in the stem is not dependent on BR transport from either the apical bud or the mature leaves.

Furthermore, the maintenance of normal BR levels in the mature leaves does not depend on BR transport from the apical bud and *vice versa*. Other evidence that BRs do not move over long distances (from one organ to another) within plant shoots has come from characterisation of the BR-deficient *dx* mutant of tomato.

In this study several transposon-induced *dx* mutant lines were shown to exhibit a variegated phenotype, consisting of revertant WT sectors within shoots that otherwise exhibited *a dx* mutant phenotype. The fact that these WT sectors (presumably with normal BR levels) exist within *a dx* background, without restoring the *dx* phenotype, indicates that BRs are not freely diffusible around the shoot.

Such results are also consistent with the apparent immobility of *exogenous* BRs when applied to the shoot.

"Short-distance" BR transport?

While many of the studies discussed above rule out long-distance transport of bioactive BRs between the shoot and roots, and between different organs within the shoot, they do not exclude the possibility that BRs may move short distances within or between plant cells.

Indeed, a closer examination of the phenotype of the transposon-induced d^x mutant lines provides some evidence that such short-distance BR transport may occur in plants.

For instance, the boundaries between the *dx* mutant tissue and revertant (WT) sectors were reported to be diffuse, and were found mainly at physical boundaries such as the veins.

Based on this observation it could be suggested that BRs might move over a short distance (i.e. cell to cell, within the leaflet), a scenario in which a small number of genotypically revertant cells would be sufficient to generate comparably large phenotypically revertant sectors.

A potential mechanism for BR transport in plants has been proposed by *Markovic Housley et al.* (2003). This involves binding of BRs to a specific pathogenesis-related protein (PR-10) to form a complex that would allow the relatively apolar BRs to be transported from the cytosol to their receptors.

It has been suggested that this mechanism may be of crucial importance in the plant defence response to pathological situations as well as in plant growth and development.

Clearly the possible existence of short-distance or micro-scale BR transport, the mechanism by which this occurs, and its potential role in the regulation of BR levels and plant development are all worthy of further investigation.

Conclusion

The weight of evidence clearly suggests that endogenous BRs do not undergo long distance transport between the shoot and root or between different organs within the shoot.

While short-distance or micro-scale BR transport remains a possibility, it appears that endogenous BR levels are regulated primarily through site-specific control of BR biosynthesis, catabolism and conjugation.

GENERAL DISCUSSION

This chapter has highlighted some significant similarities and differences regarding the distribution and transport of three of the main growth-promoting hormones that have been discovered and characterised so far.

All three (IAA, GAs and BRs) occur at higher levels in young, rapidly expanding tissues than in more mature shoot, although in pea, the steepness of this gradient down the stem is greatest for GA1 and the least for the BRs, with IAA intermediate.

All three hormones can be detected in mature shoot tissue, and although GA1 levels are very low in that case there seems little doubt that mature shoot tissue can synthesise GA precursors.

It is when we turn to hormone transport that major differences between the hormones emerge. Plants appear to have evolved a specialised transport system for only one of the three: auxin.

Certain GAs may well be transported, but there is no evidence that this occurs in any system other than the plant's normal vasculature (probably the phloem). There is good evidence that in some circumstances precursors of bioactive GAs (in dicotyledonous species) or possibly the bioactive GAs (in grasses) are transported, although it is not clear at present what contribution this makes to the GA pool in young, rapidly growing tissues.

It may well be the case that elongating internodes can both synthesise GA precursors and convert these to the bioactive form, given the right conditions.

As far as the BRs are concered, there is no definitive evidence at present for transport from one plant part to another. The auxin transport system allows the plant to develop auxin gradien turn convey positional information. The discovery that auxin dramatically affects GA biosynthesis helps us to understand how this can then affect development and why apparently only one of the hormones requires a specialised transport system. Auxin may well promote elongation, at least in stems, by upregulating the level of active GA.

According to this model, auxin is the mobile factor that communicates between the apical bud and the elongating internodes, and bioactive GA is the ultimate hormonal effector of stem elongation growth, synthesised in the internodes themselves under the influen imported from above.

In this way a single specialised transport system influences the level not only of the hormone actually transported, but of a second hormone as well. The classification of plant-growth-regulatory substances as "hormon occasions, created conceptual problems by implying a similarity to animal endocrine systems.

This has led to the assumption that a plant hormone must be synthesised by one organ before being transported and perceived by other tissues. Although this may be true for auxin, this scenario does not seem to apply to the BRs: it seems likely that BRs are synthesised and act in the same tissues, or perhaps even in the same cells.

Therefore, not all growth-promoting hormones meet the "transport" criterion regarding their status as plant "hormones". Nevertheless, the recent characterisation of mechanisms controlling perception and signal transduction of auxin, GAs and BRs leaves no doubt about the vital importance of these signaling compounds in the control of plant growth and development.

Auxin Analysis

Plant hormones are present and active in minor concentrations in plant tissue. To allow quantification in a restricted amount of material, i.e., protoplasts, chloroplasts, seedlings, seeds, buds, or apical root- and stem regions, a sensitive analytical technique is a prerequisite.

During the last two decades, procedures for phytohormone analysis as well as the available hardware have improved substantially. Fluorimetry is widely used for the analysis of indole-3-acetic acid (IAA) because it is more specific and therefore more sensitive than ultraviolet detection.

Good detection limits for derivatized IAA are obtained in Electron Impact (EI^+) or negative ion chemical ionization (NICI) GC-MS. IAA can be analyzed by GC-MS after methylation, heptafluorobutyryl acylation, N-trifluoroacetyl or N-heptafluorobutyryl derivatives, trichloroethyl esterification, pentafluorobenzyl esterification, or trimethylsilylation.

During these derivatization procedures, special attention should be paid to avoid degradation of the derivatized IAA in contact with trace amounts of water. Special storage under desiccated conditions are in most cases advised.

The stability of these derivatives was analyzed and compared by Schneider et al.. The method described by Epstein and Cohen provides quantitative yields of pentafluor-obenzyl (PFB)-esters without anhydrous conditions and uses reagents that are stable under normal storage conditions.

Moreover, because of the presence of the pentafluorobenzyl group, the molecule yields additional electron capture characteristics. This allows the analysis of the negative ion [M$^-$] after electron capture in a chemical ionization mode. This ionization mode is far more specific, and therefore results in a lower background noise. Many undetected impurities will not interfere with the analysis.

Netting and Millborrow adapted the derivatization procedure to produce PFB-IAA to allow simultaneous derivatization and analysis of IAA and ABA. We adapted the derivatization procedure as described by Epstein and Cohen for the following reasons:

1. It has an easy derivatization protocol.
2. This derivative is stable for several months.
3. Anhydrous conditions are not required.
4. ABA and GAs are derivatized in a similar manner, which allows the simultaneous analysis of the latter phytohormones during one GC-MS run.

The first reports on the analysis of IAA-conjugates and catabolites used LC-frit fast atomic bombardment (FAB)-MS, but usually IAA-conjugates are analyzed after alkaline hydrolysis. We described the use of LC(ESI)-MS/MS for the analysis of indole compounds.

The electrospray ionization process by itself is extremely soft, optimizing the probability of obtaining molecular mass information, and is therefore very suitable for the analysis of phytohormones, such as auxins and cytokinins.

In combination with conventional LC, a detection limit of 0.1 pmol IAA injected on-column was achieved under single reaction monitoring conditions.

Despite the structural analogy between the different compounds analyzed simultaneously, the unique diagnostic transitions for each individual compound used for single reaction monitoring (SRM) channel enabled fast analysis under less chromatographic resolution.

Mass sensitivity can be improved 230 times by miniaturization in LC instrumentalization as well as in sample size as compared to conventional HPLC.

In combination with GC analysis, microscale analysis of IAA from a few milligrams to <1 mg starting material should be obtained by optimizing the extraction volumes.

Although Ribnicky et al. showed the analysis of IAA in <1 mg starting material by El GC-MS after methylation, an ideal sensitivity is obtained in combination with a more selective detection, such as NICI, or double-focusing high resolution mass spectrometry.

MATERIALS

Preparation of the Diethylaminoethyl (DEAE)

1. Dissolve 100 g dry DEAE Sephadex A_{25} in 500 mL distilled water for swelling following the manufacturer's guidelines. Never use a magnetic stirrer because this might damage column particles.
2. Rinse the swollen DEAE with 3 L 1 M NH_4-formate. A sep-aration funnel is very useful for this purpose.
3. Rinse the column material with distilled water until pH 6.0 is reached.
4. Check if the pH of the column material is between 5.0 and 7.0 before use. If not, then rinse with additional water or 50% methanol.
5. Always use freshly prepared column material.
6. Pour 2 mL of column material in a 5-mL syringe containing a polypropylene frit.

C_{18} Column Cartridges

The reversed phase (RP)- C_{18} cartridges used are single-use prepacked 1 or 0.5 mL cartridges. Prerinse the cartridges with 10 mL technical grade ethanol for conditioning the column matrix followed by 20 mL distilled water and 10 mL of the solvent to be used.

Although these columns are single use, they can easily be reconditioned by rinsing with 10 mL acetone. We could recycle these cartridges over 50 times without reducing the capacity.

Extraction and Purification of Free IAA

1. Liquid nitrogen.
2. -70 or -20°C freezer.
3. 80% Methanol (HPLC grade).
4. Phenyl-$^{13}C_6$-IAA
5. Mortar and pestle.
6. MeOH-resistant centrifuge tube or, for small sample volumes, an Eppendorf microtube.
7. High-speed centrifuge (Centrikon T-124, Kontron, Milan, Italy) or scintered glass filter. For small amounts an Eppendorf centrifuge is appropriate.
8. C_{18} cartridge.
9. Distilled water.
10. 0.0-14.0 pH indicator strips.
11. 50% MeOH (HPLC grade).
12. DEAE-Sephadex A_{25} cartridge.
13. 6% formic acid.
14. $NaSO_4$ cartridge (isolute sodium sulfate drying cartridge, IST Ltd 2.5 g, or MN Chromafix 1200-Dry, 1.2 g) (optional).
15. Diethylether.
16. 1 or 3 mL reaction vial.
17. Evaporator using a nitrogen stream, i.e., a Pierce Reacti-Vap Evaporator.

Purification of IAA-Amino Acid Conjugates

1. 10 mL Snap cap reaction vial.
2. 7 N NaOH.
3. Water-saturated nitrogen circuit (obtained by applying a water trap in a nitrogen flow).
4. Incubator at 100°C.

5. Ice.
6. Distilled water.
7. 2 *N* HCl.
8. 0.0–14.0 pH indicator strips.
9. 0.05 *N* HCl.
10. 80% MeOH (HPLC grade).

Purification of IAA-Sugar Conjugates

1. 10 mL Snap cap reaction vial.
2. 1 *N* NaOH.
3. Water-saturated nitrogen circuit.
4. Distilled water.
5. 2 *N* HCl.
6. 0.0–14.0 pH indicator strips.
7. 0.05 *N* HCl.
8. 80% MeOH (HPLC grade).

Synthesis of the Pentafluorobenzyl Derivative of IAA (PFB-IAA)

1. A 1- or 3-mL gas-tight reaction vial.
2. Evaporator using a nitrogen stream, i.e., a Pierce Reacti-Vap Evaporator.
3. Acetone p.a.
4. 1-Ethylpiperidine.
5. α-Bromopentafluorotoluene (= pentafluorobenzyl bromide).
6. Incubator at 60°C, i.e., a Pierce Reacti-Therm Heating module.
7. Ethylacetate p.a.
8. H_2O (milliQ or HPLC grade).
9. Methanol 100% (HPLC grade).

Synthesis of the IAA Methyl Ester (Me-IAA)

The methylation of IAA is appropriate when analysis will

be performed by LC-MS/MS. Electron impact (EI) GC-MS of the IAA methyl ester is possible and on a routine basis applied in several laboratories.

However, the larger the diagnostic ion, the higher the specificity will be. Therefore, we prefer the PFB-IAA derivative for GC-MS analysis.

1. A 1- or 3-mL gas-tight reaction vial.
2. Acidified methanol (2 drops of fuming HCl added to 100 mL 100% methanol).
3. Ethereal diazomethane.
4. Nitrogen stream for drying samples, i.e., a Pierce Reacti-Vap Evaporator. Vacuum evaporation (i.e., using a Speed-Vac) is not appropriate as the IAA methyl ester is volatile.
5. 100% Methanol (HPLC grade).
6. 20% Methanol (HPLC grade methanol, MilliQ water).
7. MilliQ water.
8. Eppendorf centrifuge.

GC-MS Analysis

1. Chemical ionization energy moderator: methane or ammonium gas (Air Liquide).
2. Column: J&W (Folsom, CA) DB-XLB 15 m, id 0.25 mm, film thickness 0.25 μm (J&W).
3. Labbase or Masslynx GC-MS software.
4. GC-coupled mass spectrometer with chemical ionization or electron impact source (VG Micromass Trio 2000).
5. Hewlett Packard 5890 Series II gas chromatograph (Hewlett Packard, Avondale, PA) and HP 6890 injector with a Gerstel Sys3 cooled large volume injection system.

LC (+)ESI SRM MS/MS Analysis of IAA

1. Kontron 465 injector equipped with a 10-, 25-, or 100-μL sample loupe, depending on the sample volume injected.

2. Injector-driven 10-port multifunctional valve with microelectric two position valve actuator.
3. Through-hole 0.5-mm SS precolumn filter unit.
4. Prodigy 5 μm OD83 100 *A* 30 × 1 mm (Phenomenex, Torrane, CA) precolumn.
5. HPLC pump (Kontron 325).
6. 0.01 M NH_4OAc pH 7.
7. MeOH (HPLC grade).
8. Hypersil 5 μm C8 BDS 100 × 1 mm id (Alltech) analytical column, Prodigy 5 μm OD83 100 A 50 × 1 mm, or a 30 × 1 mm (Phenomenex). The Alltech columns have as an extra advantage that column filter frits can easily be replaced.
9. Two HPLC pumps (Kontron 422) equipped with 0.01–2 mL/min pump heads in master-slave configuration. This is a cheaper alternative for an HPLC gradient pump with a maximal 0.01–2 mL/min pump head volume.
10. Biocompatible PEEK Mixing Tee (JOUR Research) as a low-volume solvent mixing device to couple two Kontron 422 in gradient mode.
11. Quattro II mass spectrometer equipped with an electrospray interface and a megaflow probe.

METHODS

Extraction

1. After harvest, immediately freeze the excised plant material in liquid nitrogen. Keep samples at –70°C until analysis.
2. Homogenize the plant material in liquid nitrogen using a mortar and pestle. For calli or soft, nonlignified tissue.
3. Extraction can easily be obtained immediately in a centrifuge tube.
4. Add 80% methanol to 5 mg–2 g plant tissue (9 mL/gram fresh weight).

5. Add the $^{13}C_6$-IAA internal tracer. The amount used (10–1000 pmol) depends on the amount of starting material. The exact amount added should be registrated.
6. IAA is extracted overnight from the tissue at –20°C in darkness.

Purification of Free IAA

1. Remove cell debris by centrifugation: 24,000g, 4°C, 15 min. For alternatives.
2. Pass the supernatant at 80% MeOH over a C18 cartridge to remove chlorophylls.
3. Rinse the column after application of the sample with an additional 10 mL of 80% MeOH.
4. Collect the effluent, containing IAA and pool with the cartridge's 10 mL wash volume.
5. Dilute the sample with water until 50% MeOH is obtained.
6. Purify the sample using a DEAE-sephadex A_{25} cartridge (prerinsed with 50% MeOH; control the column's pH [5.0–6.0]).
7. Rinse the DEAE cartridge after application of the sample with an additional 75 mL of 50% MeOH.
8. Prerinse a C18 cartridge sequentially with 5 mL ethanol, 10 mL water, and finally 5 mL 6% formic acid.
9. Couple the C18 cartridge underneath the DEAE-sephadex cartridge.
10. Elute IAA from the DEAE-sephadex with 20 mL 6% formic acid. IAA is retained on the C18 matrix. The effluent of the C18 can be discarded.
11. Pass one syringe of air through the C18 cartridge.
12. Couple a $NaSO_4$ cartridge underneath the C18 for on-line drying of the ethereal sample (optional).
13. Elute IAA from the C18 cartridge with 1 mL diethylether. Collect the diethylether immediately in a reaction vial.

14. Discard the water phase, if any, underneath the ether phase.
15. Evaporate the ether phase under a nitrogen stream. Cap the vial upon storage.

Purification of IAA-Conjugates

Although IAA-conjugates can be analyzed in their native form by LC-MS, we prefer to analyze IAA-conjugates after alkaline hydrolysis. This is merely because heavy labeled internal tracers for the different IAA-conjugates are not easily available.

When alkaline hydrolysis is performed, Note 9 should be taken into account. The amount of IAA analyzed after alkaline hydrolysis corresponds to the total amount of IAA (free + conjugated).

Therefore, the amount of free IAA as analyzed following should be subtracted.

IAA-Amino Acid Conjugates

1. Take one-half to one-tenth of the original extract after stage and transfer to a 10-mL snap cap reaction vial.
2. Add NaOH until a final concentration of 7 *N* NaOH is obtained.
3. Apply a water-saturated nitrogen circuit by applying a water trap in a nitrogen flow.
4. Flush the vial to obtain a water-saturated nitrogen atmosphere.
5. Incubate the vial at 100°C for 3 h.
6. Cool down the sample on ice.
7. Dilute one-half with distilled water and titrate the sample with 2 *N* HCl until pH 2.5 is obtained.
8. Desalt the acidified sample on a C18 cartridge that is equilibrated with 0.05 *N* HCl.
9. Rinse the cartridge with an additional 10 mL 0.05 *N* HCl.
10. Elute the cartridge with 80% MeOH.

11. Dilute with distilled water to obtain a final MeOH concentr-ation of 50%.

IAA-Sugar Conjugates

1. Take one-half to one-tenth of the original extract after and transfer to a reaction vial.
2. Add NaOH until a final concentration of *1 N* NaOH is obtained.
3. Apply a water-saturated nitrogen circuit by applying a water trap in a nitrogen flow.
4. Flush the vial to obtain a water-saturated nitrogen atmosphere.
5. Incubate the vial at ambient temperature for 1 h.
6. Dilute one-half with distilled water and titrate the sample with 2 *N* HCl until pH 2.5 is obtained.
7. Desalt the acidified sample on a C_{18} cartridge that is equilibrated with 0.05 *N* HCl.
8. Rinse the cartridge with an additional 10 mL 0.05 *N* HCl.
9. Elute the cartridge with 80% MeOH.
10. Dilute with distilled water to obtain a final MeOH concentration of 50%.

Derivatization of IAA

Pentafluorobenzyl Ester of IAA (PFB-IAA)

This derivatization procedure is essential for the NICI GC-MS analysis of IAA. Different derivatization methods are described for the analysis of IAA. We have chosen the most stable and easiest derivatization, which in addition allows chemical ionization analysis (because of the electron capture characteristics of the pentafluorobenzyl group).

Warning: Most of the derivatization mixtures are toxic; work in a fume-hood during the entire derivatization procedure.

1. Transfer the sample in a reaction vial and dry entirely.
2. Dissolve in 50 gL acetone p.a.

3. Add 1 gL 1-ethylpiperidine and 5 gL a-bromopentafluorotoluene (= pentafluorobenzyl bromide) and mix vigorously. 4. Incubate at 60°C for 45 min.
5. Add 300 gL ethylacetate and mix vigorously.
6. Add 300 gL H_2O (milliQ or HPLC grade) and mix vigorously.
7. Remove and discard the lower water phase.
8. Repeat from *step 6* on.
9. Dry the ethylacetate fraction under a nitrogen stream.
10. Dissolve the sample in 20 gL methanol 100% (HPLC grade).

IAA Methyl Ester (Me-IAA)

This derivatization procedure is performed prior to LC (+)ESI SRM MS/MS analysis of IAA. Although methylation is not essential, this manipulation improves the detection limit by a factor of 100. Methylation is performed following Schlenk and Gellerman.

Warning: The diazomethane is toxic. Work in a fumehood during these steps. Take care that the vial containing the sample is resistant to ether, i.e., glass.

1. Transfer the sample in a glass reaction vial and dry entirely. Avoid water condensation inside the reaction vial at any circumstance throughout all further steps.
2. Dissolve in 100 μL acidified methanol.
3. Add ethereal diazomethane until a slight yellow colour remains for 10 min at room temperature.
4. Dry the sample under a nitrogen stream. Avoid vacuum evaporation (i.e., Speed-Vac) because the IAA methyl ester is volatile.
5. Dissolve in 50 μL 100% methanol (HPLC grade).
6. Transfer the sample to an LC-MS insert.
7. Dry the methanol fraction under a nitrogen stream.
8. Dissolve in 10 μL 20/80, v/v, methanol/H_2O.
9. Add 30 μL MilliQ water until a final MeOH concentration of 5% is reached.

10. Mix vigorously.
11. Spin down the sample in the insert.

Analysis

Two different analysis methods are outlined here. GC is on a routine base used for the analysis of IAA. ESI LC-MS/MS have, however, several advantages in terms of selectivity, especially when several indole compounds are analyzed in parallel.

NICI GC-MS Analysis of IAA

GC-MS SETTINGS

1. Injection volume: 1–10 μL.
2. GC oven gradient: 2 min 175 °C followed by a linear gradient at a temperature rate of 15°C min to 300°C and finally 2 min at 300°C.
3. Solvent delay (2 min).
4. Injector temperature: temperature gradient from 150 to 325°C in 2 min.
5. Source temperature: 140°C by constant filament emission.
6. Source vacuum pressure: 7–8 10^{-5} mbar.
7. GC carrier gas: helium (Air Liquide), He flow: 1.5 mL/min.
8. Ionization potential: 35 eV.
9. Ionization current: 100 μA.
10. Negative chemical ionization mode.
11. Analysis by selective ion monitoring (SIM).
12. Diagnostic ion IAA-PFB: m/z at 174.
13. Diagnostic ion $^{13}C_6$-IAA-PFB: m/z at 180.
14. Dwell time: 0.01 s.
15. Inter channel delay: 0.01 s.

Integration and Calculation

All data were processed by Labbase or Masslynx (VG Micromass) software.

The endogenous concentration of IAA is calculated from the spectra obtained using the following equation:

$$(area_x/area_y) = (x/y) \quad (1)$$

where : $area_x$ = peak integration value for the specific diagnostic ion for the nonlabeled IAA, $area_y$ = peak integration value for the specific diagnostic ion for the $^{13}C_6$-labeled IAA, x = endogenous IAA content initially present in the tissue analyzed, and y = amount of $^{13}C_6$-labeled IAA added to the extract before purification.

Correct for the 180/174 ratio of the $^{13}C_6$-IAA tracer. The detection limit of this method is 0.5 fmol injected.

LC/LC (+)ESI SRM MS/MS Analysis of IAA

On-line sample concentration can be obtained by on-column focusing or a column switching setup, the latter having an additional on-line purification.

Chromatographic Conditions

1. Precolumn: Prodigy 5 gm OD83 30 × 1 mm (Phenomenex).
2. Analytical column: Hypersil 5 gm C8 BDS 150 × 1 mm id column (Alltech, Deerfield, IL), or a Prodigy 5 gm OD83 100 or 50 × 1 mm (Phenomenex).
3. Injection volume: 25 μL.
4. Solvent A: 0.01 M NH_4OAc pH 6.6.
5. Solvent B: Methanol 100%.
6. Solvent delivery for loading precolumn: 100% solvent A.
7. Solvent delivery for backflushing: 4 min sample loading at 5/95, B/A; from 1 to 3 min: linear gradient from 5/95 to 90/10 B/A.
8. Flow rate: 100 μL/min.
9. Pump systems: two Kontron 422 pumps equipped with 0.01–2 mL/min pump heads in master-slave configuration using a Biocompatible PEEK Mixing Tee (JOUR Research) as a low-volume solvent mixing device.

10. The effluent was directly introduced into the MS source at a flow rate of 100 μL/min.

Mass Spectrometry Conditions

A crossflow counter electrode (Micromass) was used to avoid excessive contamination of the source for routine analysis of biological samples. The mass spectrometer was tuned using a 10^{-5} M Me-IAA solution dissolved in 100% methanol.

1. Source temperature: 80°C.
2. Nebulizing gas flow: 20 L/h.
3. Drying gas flow: 400 L/h.
4. Capillary voltage: +3.5 kV.
5. Cone voltage: 28 V.
6. Collision gas: Argon, P_{AR} of 4 10^{-3} mbar
7. Collision energy 20 eV.
8. Quantification: single reactant monitoring (SRM) of the [MH]+ ion and the appropriated product ion (190-130 for IAA-Me, 196-136 for the $^{13}C_6$-IAA-Me).
9. Dwell time: 0.05 s.
10. Inter channel delay: 0.01 s.
11. Span: 0 amu.
12. The effluent of the analytical column is directly introduced into the MS source at a flow rate of 100 μL/min.
13. Sample loading by a Kontron 325 pump for 6.5 min.
14. After 6.5 min sample loading, the precolumn is backflushed.
15. While sample 1 is introduced to the analytical column, a second sample was loaded on a parallel precolumn.

Integration and Calculations

All mass spectra is background subtracted and smoothed once. All data is processed by Masslynx software. Endogenous IAA concentrations are calculated using Eq. 1. The detection limit of this method is 1 fmol injected.

NOTES

1. Different heavy-labeled tracers for IAA are available. A tracer should always be chosen in terms of a high enrichment and a large amount of labeled sites (at least two or more). Deuterated tracers are shown to be less stable and exchange in alkaline or acidic conditions may occur.
2. –70°C is preferred for the storage of samples before analysis. However, for storage <3 mo, –20°C is also acceptable.
3. For calli or soft, nonlignified tissue, the extraction is performed by diffusion without prior homogenization.
4. Plant or bacterial cells are lysed by sonication using a Vibra Cell VCX400 High Intensity Untrasonic Processor (Sonics and Materials Inc., Danbury, CT) with a stepped microtip to allow small volume (200 μL–10 mL) processing. Sonicate under a pulsed regimen of 5 s (5 s sonication–5 s rest) for a 4 min total time span. Use a power of 400 W at 40% gain. Continuously cool the samples on ice during processing.
5. Extract protoplasts in 500 μL 80% methanol in an Eppendorf tube.
6. Small amounts of sample are easily extracted in an Eppendorf microtube after homogenization using an Eppendorf size conical pestle.
7. Cell debris can also be removed by filtration using a scintered glass filter under vacuum.
8. Small amounts of plant material that are extracted in an Eppendorf microtube are centrifuged at full speed using an Eppendorf centrifuge.
9. If IAA-conjugates are hydrolyzed under alkaline hydrolysis, data obtained for the total IAA fraction are contaminated because of degradation of IAN into IAA. The use of an $^{13}N_1$-IAN tracer (gift from Dr. N. Ilic, University of Maryland) is essential to calculate

the sample-specific correction factor measuring the IAA+1 diagnostic ion.

10. Concentration of the sample prior to alkalization is advised in case the original extract volume is too large.
11. Avoid traces of water during methylation.
12. For additional purification after derivatization, a C_{18} cartridge or, if large amounts of samples are processed, C_{18} 96-well extraction plates are useful. The small eluting volume of the latter makes immediate elution (100 μL 100% MeOH) in LC or GC inserts possible. Sample processing can either be achieved manually using a 96-well vacuum manifold or it can be automated using a number of commercially available sample processors. The apolar characteristics of the IAA-derivative allows loading of a sample in neutral watery conditions and subsequent elution in 100% MeOH.
13. In case the chemical ionization mode (CI, NICI) is not available, IAA can easily be analyzed by electron impact (EI) GC-MS after pentafluorobenzylation or methylation: diagnostic ion IAA-PFB or IAA-Me: m/z at 130; diagnostic ion 13C6-IAA-PFB or 13C6-IAA-Me: m/z at 136. Source temperature: 270°C by constant filament emission. Source vacuum pressure: 7–8 10–5 mbar. Ionization potential: 70 eV. Ionization current: 250 μA.We prefer to analyze the PFBIAA using a chemical ionization interface although electron impact is also perfectly acceptable. Because of the specificity of CI (correlated to the rare ion-capture characteristics), the background noise is much more reduced, resulting in improved sensitivity.
14. Sometimes we experienced contaminating compounds, although with a retention time slightly different from PFB-IAA, which could result in altered peak shape for IAA. We experienced these interfering compounds as less stable. In this case, storage of derivatized samples at –20°C for at least 1 wk before

GC-MS analysis always resulted in a improvement of the chromatography for PFB-IAA without significant recovery losses. The PFB-IAA derivative is stable for several months without any significant degradation.

3

Chapter

Metabolism of Auxin

Auxin responses in plants were first observed and described in the 19th century. Elegant but simple experiments by early investigators indicated that a system for mobile signaling existed that allowed plants to respond to environmental signals such as light and gravity distant from their site of perception.

While the 20th century saw great progress in studies of auxin chemistry and physiology, we nevertheless approached the 21st century with many unanswered questions about how plants perceive and respond to auxin, how auxin is made within the plant, and how such processes are themselves regulated.

In this review, we will focus on these central questions and the impressive progress that has been made to illuminate those areas that have remained perplexing issues for a very long time.

AUXIN METABOLISM

Indole-3-Acetic Acid Biosynthesis

For the past 60 years, research on indole-3-acetic acid (IAA) biosynthesis in plants has focused on the degradation of the amino acid tryptophan by sequential oxidative deamination and decarboxylation.

Although there were questions raised, the basic concept remained relatively unchallenged until the early 1990s when

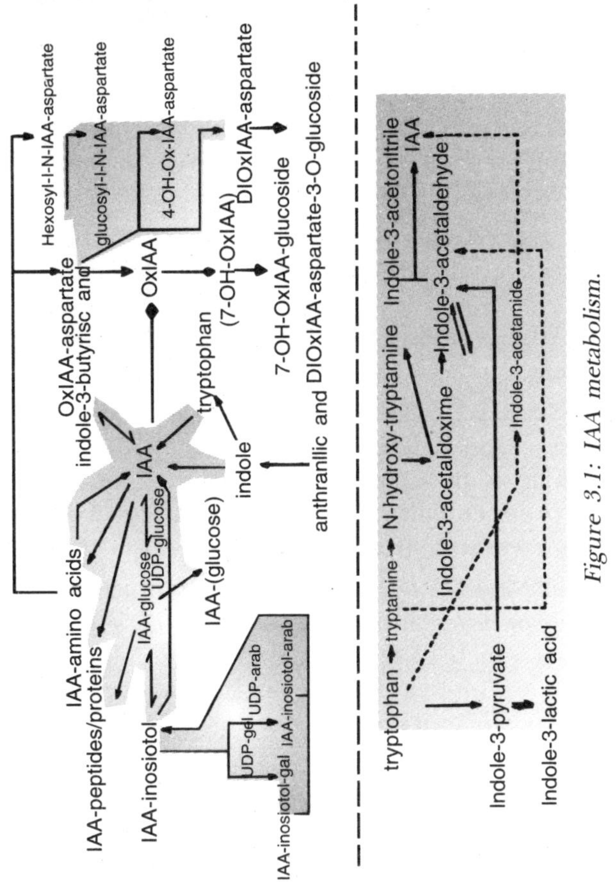

Figure 3.1: IAA metabolism.

work on several systems showed that IAA biosynthesis occurs via two separate pathways.

The metabolism of IAA plays an important part in the growth and development of plants, from embryogenesis through fruit ripening and senescence. Fundamental reassessments have occurred regarding the metabolic processes involved in making indolic auxins and consequently our ideas concerning the complexity of the metabolic control of these regulatory hormones have changed.

The Tryptophan-Independent Pathway

One of the first uses of stable isotope methods to track

IAA biosynthesis by mass spectrometry (MS) illustrated the advantages of such methods.

Baldi *et al.* (1991) compared normal plants to an IAA-overproducing mutant, jsR1, of *Lemna gibba* in an effort to examine the theory that D-, not L-tryptophan was the closer precursor to IAA.

These experiments indicated that while [^{15}N]D-tryptophan was ineffective, [^{15}N]L-tryptophan was also converted at relatively slow rates, suggesting that the widely held views about IAA biosynthesis from tryptophan needed a critical reevaluation.

Rapid kinetic studies have shown that, even in *Lemna gibba,* L-tryptophan labeling overestimates the contribution of tryptophan as an auxin precursor since exogenous tryptophan was preferentially used to label IAA as compared to tryptophan synthesized *in vivo.*

The only known non-conditional tryptophan auxotroph, *orp (orange pericarp),* proved to be a uniquely suitable genetic system with which to reevaluate the tryptophan precursor hypothesis. *orp* mutants completely lack tryptophan synthase β-activity due to mutations in two unlinked loci, *orpl* and *orp2.*

When grown on media containing 30% [$^{2}H_{2}$]O or [^{15}N]anthranilate, only the wild-type seedlings showed significant incorporation of label into tryptophan, while both wild-type and mutant seedlings showed substantial incorporation into IAA.

Thus, in *orp* seedlings, *de novo* IAA biosynthesis occurs without tryptophan as a precursor. A similar series of studies using *Arabidopsis* conditional tryptophan auxotrophs extended the results from maize. These studies focused on three mutants, *trpl -100, trp2,* and *trp3,* which are deficient in anthranilatephosphoribosyl transferase, tryptophan synthase β, and tryptophan synthase β activities, respectively. The tryptopha-mutant showed elevated levels of IAA.

The other two mutants had normal levels of IAA. Based on [$^{2}H_{2}$]O labeling, all three mutants were synthesizing IAA *de novo.* These results suggest that the branch point for IAA biosynthesis from the pathway to tryptophan is between tryptophan synt.

Ouyang *et al.* (2000), using an antisense approach to lower the levels of indole-3 glycerolphosphate (IGP) synthase activity in plants, showed a decrease in IAA levels and a low auxin phenotype.

The authors concluded that IGP was the likely precursor to IAA, however the results are subject to some interpretation since the conversion of IGP to indole is reversible.

An unassociated tryptopha-like gene appears to be present in *Arabidopsis* based on sequence analysis, and the encoded protein could account for the production of free indole, as has been shown for the maize tryptophan synthase 0-like genes, *IGL* and BX1. Another model system used for studies of IAA biosynthesis is carrot cell cultures, which can be induced to form somatic embryos by removal of auxin (i.e. 2,4-D) from the medium.

In suspension cultures, L-tryptophan can be converted to IAA. However, when these same cells are induced to undergo embryogenesis, the tryptophan-independent pathway predominates.

Carrot suspension cell cultures grown in the presence or absence of the synthetic auxin 2,4-D incorporated label from $[^2H]2O$ into IAA, indicating that *de novo* biosynthesis was occurring. Cells grown on media-containing $[^{15}N]$indole, both with and without 2,4-D, gave the same result.

However, when cells were labeled with $[^2H_5]$L-tryptophan, only the cultures grown in the presence of 2,4-D incorporated the ring deuterium into IAA. In all cases, with or without 2,4-D, tryptophan pools were equally labeled.

Thus make IAA by two different pathways at different developmental stages, because label incorporation into IAA from tryptophan changed without a change occurrng for label incorporation from the earlier precursors, indole or $[^2H]2O$.

Subsequent studies have confirmed both developmental and environmental regulation of IAA biosynthetic path ways, as determined by changes in labeling patterns, in several plant species and in an evolutionary context.

IAA biosynthesis was studied by several laboratories using *in vitro* enzymes prepared from maize tissues. Rekoslavskaya and Bandurski (1994) showed that extracts from liquid endosperm tissue converted indole to IAA, suggesting that the tryptophan independent pathway might contribute to the newly synthesized IAA.

However, extensive tryptophan to IAA conversion was also detected (Rekoslavskaya, [199]stin *et al.* (1999) described an *in vitro* enzymatic system from maize seedlings in which [^{14}C]indole was converted into [^{14}C]IAA. Biosynthesis was shown to be independent of tryptophan in this system because:

(1) [^{14}C]tryptophan was not converted to [^{14}C]IAA

(2) The addition of cold tryptophan did not inhibit conversion of [^{14}C] indole to [^{14}C]IAA

(3) Serine did not enhance the same conversion

(4) Addition of non-labeled indole decreased the formation of [^{14}C]IAA.

IAA biosynthesis was also shown to occur in an *in vitro* system derived from extracts of *orp* maize seedlings, which lack a functional tryptophan synthase.

IAA Biosynthesis from Tryptophan

The combined techniques of stable isotope labeling and gas chromatog-raphy-mass spectrometric (GC-MS) analysis of isotopic enrichment of suspected intermediates provide more data and allow evaluation of labeling patterns in detail not previously possible.

Thus, it is now feasible to obtain a more accurate assessme-nt of precursor-product relationships. Stable isotope techniq-ues, however, are also subject to error if multiple pools of compounds exist within the cell and if only specific pools are involved in the biochemical process being studied.

Some direct experimental analysis of the impact of these problems has shown that although multiple pools of tryptophan exist in carrot cell cultures, both pools can be labeled following isotopic tryptophan application. Time, as well as pool localization, can be an issue.

Bialek *et al.* (1992) showed that tryptophan conversion to IAA accounted for essentially all of the IAA production in germinating axes of bean when label incorporation was analyzed after several days of labeling following the surgical removal of the cotyledons.

However, a decade later, using methods allowing shorter labeling times, this experimental system was revisited in a series of studies where it was shown that tryptophan conversion was only operative in the first hours after cotyledon removal, followed by several days when the tryptophan-independent pathway predominated, suggesting wound activation of tryptophan to IAA conversion.

Compelling evidence from precursor and deuterium oxide labeling experiments indicate that intact etiolated maize seedlings do not produce significant IAA from *de novo* biosynthesis, which is likely a result of exceptional biosynthetic activity of the endosperm during seed development.

Maize liquid endosperm *in vitro* extracts are capable of converting radioactive indole to both IAA and tryptophan. Most remarkably, IAA accounted for up to 60% of the product and, although initial results suggested that tryptophan might not be directly involved, subsequent experiments showed that most of the labeled indole actually was converted to tryptophan before going onto IAA.

IAA biosynthesis in this system has since been shown to be sensitive to oxidation potential, which is unexpected because the previously described routes from tryptophan are oxidative or simple transferase reactions.

In addition, tryptamine, indole-3-acetamide, indole-3-acetonitrile, and indoleacetaldoxime (IAOx) were shown to be not directly involved in the reaction, while a peptide-bound tryptophan intermediate was isolated.

This experimental system, where relatively large rates of IAA biosynthesis occur, clearly shows promise for understanding at least one route for IAA biosynthesis.

The relative contribution of the tryptophan-dependent biosynthesis pathway in *Arabidopsis thaliana* has been examined critically, however experimental levels of tryptophan and indole (IAN) used were 15–25X of their endogenous levels yielding results difficult to interpret.

Similarly, Park *et al.* (2003) took a high substrate approach with maize activities converting IAN (a possible intermediate in the tryptophan-dependent pathway) where they reported assays in the millimolar range, although the reported IAN endogenous concentrations were lower orders of magnitude. Redundant pathways have been defined within the tryptophan-dependent pathway by using gain-of-function methods in *Arabidopsis.*

Activation tagging identified the *YUCCA* gene that encodes a novel flavin monooxygenase catalyzing the rate-limiting N-hydroxylation of tryptophan to create N-hydroxyl tryptamine.

This defined a new pathway not formerly predicted for IAA biosynthesis from tryptophan. Although at least two paralogs are present in *Arabidopsis*, the YUCCA-like flavin monooxygenase from petunia is apparently a single-copy gene.

Recent advances concerning the genetics of secondary product metabolism have resulted in increased focus on the role of cytochrome P450s in the reactions leading to indolic glucosinolates and has resulted in important advances in our knowledge of IAA biosynthesis as well.

For example, overexpression of an *Arabidopsis* gene encoding the cytochrome P450, CYP83B1/SUPERROOT 2, or overexpression of a related cytochrome P450, CYP83A1, both resulted in increased indolic glucosino late levels and a morphologic phenotype consistent with underproduction of IAA.

Conversely, *sur2* mutants exhibit increased adventitious rooting and epinasty, consistent with IAA overproduction. It has been suggested that CYP83B1 serves as a gatekeeper between IAA and indolic glucosinolate biosynthesis, but downstream from the most likely branch point from IAA production where IAOx is an intermediate.

The conversion of tryptophan to IAOx is catalyzed by two other cytochrome P450s, CYP79B2 and CYP79B3 in *Arabidopsis,* but whether IAA or only glucosinolates were produced from IAOx was not clear.

The CYP83B 1/CYP83B2 results pointed to the most likely role for these cytochrome P450s being to supply IAOx for conversion to 1-aci-nitro-2-indolyl-ethane, the committed step of indolic glucosinolate biosynthesis.

Analysis of CYP79B2 and CYP79B3 function as it relates to YUCCA function, however, puts these two proteins squarely in the middle of another pathway utilizing IAOx in *Arabidopsis* for the production of IAA from tryptophan.

The complexity of understanding IAA biosynthesis appears to be well illustrated in *Arabidopsis,* where several potential pathways compete for attention of the research community.

It appears likely that several pathways are present, perhaps in different cells, developmental stages, or as regulated by environmental inputs.

In addition to the pathways involving monooxygenases and/or cytochrome P450s, reports of the presence of indole-3-pyruvic acid and indole- as well as the amidase, a multienzyme complex, and nitrilases suggest that the potential for many unique routes to IAA remains a very real possibility.

IAA Conjugates in Plants

All plants and plant parts so far examined contain most of their IAA in conjugated form and only minute amounts of the phytohormone as the free acid.

Some of the IAA conjugates that have been identified are esters or acyl anhydrides with simple sugars or cyclitols, larger-molecular-weight polysaccharides, or the carbohydrate component of glycoproteins. IAA can also be conjugated by amide linkage to amino acids, such as aspartate, or to peptides or proteins.

IAA-Peptide Conjugates

The known higher-molecular-weight amide conjugates consist of a hydrophobic 3.6 kDa peptide a 35 kDa protein from bean and several immunologically related proteins of higher-molecular-weight from *Arabidopsis* and several other species, and a class of maize zein protein.

Bialek and Cohen (1986) isolated a compound with very low mobility on thin layer chromatography (TLC), stained positive for indole compounds, and was subsequently isolated from bean seeds and found to yield IAA upon hydrolysis in 7 N NaOH at 100°C.

The properties of this compound were quite different from those of simple IAA–amino acid conjugates and it proved to be a conjugate consisting of two moieties of IAA attached to a 3.6 kDa peptide.

Several early studies had indicated that protein-like compounds were formed by plants from supplied radioactive IAA. More recently, such methods have shown that IAA–proteins are formed based on [^{14}C]-IAA feeding experiments with melon tissue.

Antibodies against the 3.6 kDa IAA–peptide from bean localized immunoreactive materials in immature melon fruit to the vascular tissue and epidermal layers, consistent with mass spectral measurements of amide IAA localization.

In bean, amide conjugated IAA does not begin to accumulate in significant amounts until late in seed development. By the time the seed is mature, however, most of the total IAA is present as protein conjugates.

During seed germination the protein conjugates, after an initial rapid decline, began to increase in amount again early in seedling growth. The content of free IAA as well as the content of amide IAA in the embryonic axes began to increase the growth of the axes started, and the level of IAA conjugates in the whole seed remained relatively high even after a week of growth.

The gene for the major bean IAA protein (iap1) was isolated and cloned from bush bean *(Phaseolus vulgaris)* seeds.

Walz *et al.* (2002) showed that the 957bp sequence encoded a 35 kDa protein and their immunologic and analytical data suggested that auxin modification of a small class of proteins may be a feature common to many plants.

Quantitative GC-MS analysis of the purified IAP1 showed a protein to IAA ratio of 2:1. Previous studies showed that *Arabidopsis* has both ester and amide conjugated IAA; however, in total the low-molecular-weight conjugates identified did not account for the bulk of the conjugate pool.

Immunostaining of different Arabidopsis tissues showed that putative IAA–proteins were localized to the root meristem and outer cell regions of the cotyledons and radical of Arabid*opsis* seeds. *Arabidopsis* seed IAA–proteins were partially purified and subjected to alkaline hydrolysis. GC-MS analysis confirmed the presence of IAA covalently bound to protein.

These results established the presence of IAA-proteins in dicots other than bean and confirmed that the major IAA conjugates in *Arabidopsis* are peptides and proteins. Leverone *et al.* (1991) showed that IAA–peptide formation might be more wide spread among plants by finding that the maize storage protein zein contained amide bound IAA.

In this case, however, IAA was present in only a very minor fraction of the total seed zein (1 molecule IAA to 175 molecules of zein), thus it is possible that a discrete class of zein peptides is conjugated.

Amino Acid Conjugates

In most higher and many lower plants, applied IAA is rapidly conjugated to form IAA–aspartate. The formation of IAA conjugates is widely believed to be a means of removal of excess IAA produced during certain times of plant development, and in mutant plants where indolic precursors accumulate.

The ability of plant tissues to make IAA-aspartate, as well as aspartate conjugates of a variety of synthetic auxins, is induced by pretreatment with active auxins, and this induction is blocked by inhibitors of RNA and protein synthesis.

After almost 50 years of study, recently an *in vitro* system from plants has been described that accounts for the formation of IAA-amide conjugates via a mechanism where the acid auxin is adenylated followed by acyl transfer to the amino acid.

The actual gene for this reaction had been discovered almost 20 years previously, when *GH3* from soybean was shown to be rapidly induced following auxin treatment, however the biochemical activity of the gene product remained undefined.

A number of different IAA–amino acid conjugates (e.g. IAA–aspartate, –gutamate, –alanine) have been identified in plants and plant cell cultures, and it appears that several of these could be formed by similar mechanisms.

Amide Conjugate Hydrolysis

Auxin conjugates can be used as "slow release" forms of IAA in plant tissue cultures, probably because of their slow hydrolysis in plant cells.

In vitro hydrolysis was shown by Bialek *et al.* (1983) for specific applied conjugates, and Ludwig-Muller *et al.* (1996) showed that a specific conjugate hydrolase was induced in Chinese cabbage upon infection with *Plasmodiophora brassicae.*

A genetic approach to the analysis of IAA conjugate hydrolysis in plants resulted in the first identification of a gene (ILR1) coding for a hydrolase of IAA conjugates. This enzyme preferentially hydrolyzes IAA–leucine and IAA–phenylalanine.

ILR1 is representative of a gene family whose members exhibit varying substrate specificities. IAR3, for example, shows a high level of specificity for IAA–L-alanine while ILL2 shows the highest *in vitro* activity and is also the most promiscuous in its substrate requirements. ILR1 and IAR3 are found predominately in roots, while ILL2 is predominately found in shoots.

Triple mutant (*ilr1*, *iar3*, and *ill2*) analysis has shown that lateral shoot number, hypocotyl elongation, auxin sensitivity and IAA levels are altered, suggesting that conjugate hydrolysis is involved in regulation of such processes *in planta.*

Enzymes from bacterial sources that are capable of highly selective hydrolysis of IAA–amino acids have been reported. For example, an IAA–L-aspartate hydrolase was purified and subsequently cloned.

Additional characterization at the level of the gene and analysis of the enzyme protein revealed that it is related to other bacterial amido-hydrolases, shows homology to the ILR1 gene of *Arabidopsis,* and transformation into *Arabidopsis* shows a mild high auxin phenotype.

Subsequent analysis revealed that two zinc-binding histidine residues conserved in bacterial and plant enzymes, His-404 and His-405, were critical for determination of substrate specificity and activity, respectively. A bacterial enzyme with specificity for IAA–L-alanine was recently reported from *Arthrobacter ilicis* and related bacterial strains.

Ester Conjugates

The ester conjugates of maize endosperm have been extensively reviewed. The higher-molecular-weight ester compound is a cellulosic glucan and the lower-molecular-weight compounds include IAA–glucose, IAA–myo-inositol and IAA–inositol glycosides.

IAA–myo-inositol esters have also been found in rice and horse chestnut. Horse chestnut was also shown to contain the esters IAA–rutinose (IAA–glucosyl-rhamnose) and an IAA desoxyaminohexose.

The *in vitro* synthesis of 1-O-(-D-IAA–glucose from IAA and uridine diphosphate (UDP)–glucose has since been described and the full array of conjugate-synthesizing reactions of *Zea mays* have also now been studied *in vitro.*

In maize, IAA–glucose is transacylated to *myo-inositol to* form IAA–myo-inositol. IAA–inositol may then be *glycosylated* to form IAA-*myoinositol-galactoside* or IAA–myo-inositol-arabinoside by reaction with the uridine diphosphosugar.

The enzyme *catalyzing* the synthesis of 1-O-IAA–glucose,

IAA–glucose synthetase, was purified to *homogeneity*, characterized and cloned. Kowalczyk *et al.* (2002) showed that the enzymatic activity and protein levels of IAA–glucose synthase are increased following auxin treatment of maize coleoptiles.

The reaction catalyzed by IAA–glucose synthase

IAA + UDP–glucose ⇔ IAA–glucose + UDP,

yields a product in which the acyl alkyl acetal bond between IAA and the aldehydic oxygen of glucose is approximately 1.4 kcal above that of the bon glucose and UDP. This energetically unfavourable reaction is "pulled" in the direction of conjugate formation by the energetically favoured transacylation of the IAA moiety.

Isolation of the *Arabidopsis* gene encoding an IAA–glucose forming enzyme as well as the availability of the maize gene has resulted in several groups generating transgenic plants with elevated and/or reduced capacity for IAA–glucose formation.

As the reaction leading to the formation of IAA–glucose is dependent on factors in addition to the level of active enzyme, the biochemical basis for the phenotypes obtained with the transgenic plants is not easy to inte effect of the transgene likely depends on the availability of both excess UDP-glucose and a suitable transacylation receptor in the transformed plant.

While dicotsmonocots form IAA–glucose and some dicots contain IAA–myo-inositol, the potential IAA–acyl acceptor in most dicots remains unknown.

The potential does exist for amino acids or other amines to serve as an alternative substrate for such transacylations from IAA–glucose or, as recently proposed, IAA–peptides or IAA–proteins could result from such a acyl transfer mechanism.

Although proposed, such reactions have never been demonstrated *in vivo* and are proposed based on the concept that the constitutive route to IAA–amides would differ from the induced mechanism via the GH3 adenylation reaction.

Antisense tomato seedlings showed reduced levels of IAA–glucose and in ester IAA pools, but no corresponding alteration in the levels of amide conjugates, suggesting that ester and amide conjugation are not linked via a common acyl transfer intermediate of IAA–glucose, and that amino acids may not, in this instance, serve as suitable indole-acyl acceptors.

Surprisingly, levels of free IAA either are unaffected by the level of expression of enzymes for IAA–glucose formation or increase or decrease in parallel with IAA–glucose changes. Kowalczyk and Bandurski (1990, 1991) and Jakubowska and Kowalczyk (2005) reported on the co-fractionation of IAA–glucose synthetase and two enzymes for IAA–glucose hydrolysis, a 1-O-IAA–glucose hydrolase and a 6-O-IAA-glucose hydrolase, and suggested that these enzymes exist as a hormone-metabolizing complex.

Kowalczyk *et al.* (2003) described a bifunctional indole-3-acetyl transferase that catalyzes synthesis and hydrolysis of indole-3-acetyl–myo-inositol in immature endosperm of *Zea mays.* These studies may indicate that at least some aspects of IAA ester metabolism occurs via enzyme complexes.

IAA Degradation

Ideas concerning IAA catabolism have also undergone substantial revision. IAA catabolism was thought to occur primarily through the action of IAA oxidase, a companion activity to most peroxidases of plant origin. It is likely that the contribution of the decarboxylation pathway has been overestimated when studying IAA oxidation in homogenates or with cut tissue pieces.

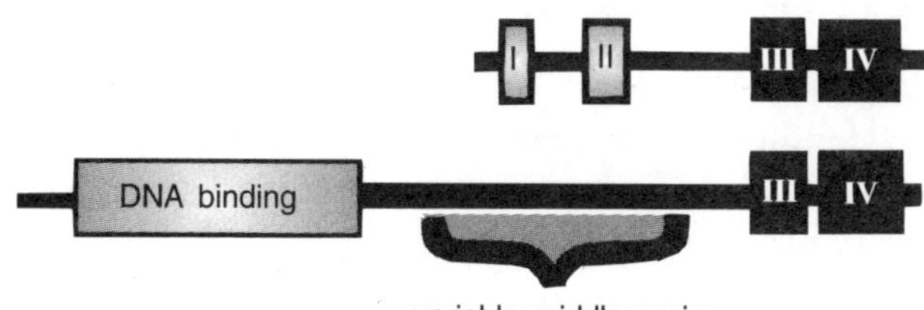

Figure 3.2: Conserved domains of Aux/IAA and ARF Proteins.

The concept of an "IAA oxidase" has received several serious challenges and this has been extensively reviewed. In maize, oxidation of IAA *in vivo* yields oxindole-3-acetic acid (oxIAA).

The general process of ring oxidation followed by glycosylation appears to a general theme, although variable in its specific details in different species. The discovery that the IAA conjugate, IAA–aspartate, can be either hydrolyzed to yield free IAA or serve as an entry point into IAA catabolism placed new emphasis on understanding the biochemistry of this branch point compound.

Pluss *et al.* (1989) found IAA–aspartate and oxIAA–aspartate were the major metabolites present after feeding IAA to *Populus tremula.* At least three different pathways for the direct oxidation of this IAA conjugate in different plant species are known.

Thus, IAA–aspartate has a significant role in IAA degradation, and these findings demonstrate that links exist between the processes of conjugation and degradation.

AUXIN SIGNALING

The application of auxin to plant tissues elicits a multitude of effects including electrophysiologic and transcriptional responses, and changes in cell division, cell expansion, and cell differentiation.

A central question in plant biology has long been how this simple molecule controls this staggeringly diverse array of responses. While this question is far from being answered, recent years have witnessed dramatic advances in our understanding of the molecular events underlying auxin action.

Auxin-Responsive Genes

Early molecular approaches to elucidate auxin action revealed that the hormone induces rapid and specific changes in gene expression and identified several auxin responsive genes. Among the most thoroughly characterized are three gene families *(SAURs, GH3s,* and Aux/IAAs), which are rapidly induced in response to an auxin stimulus.

Table 3.1: Dominant gain-of-function *Aux/IAA* mutants.		
Mutant	**Domain II lesion**	**Phenotypes**
axr2/iaa7	VVGWPPVR	Auxin, ABA, and ethylene resistant, Wilson *et al.* (1990) dwarf, gravitropism defects
axr3/iaa17	VVGWPPVR	Auxin resistant, increased apical Leyser *et al.* (1996) dominance & adventitious rooting, reduced root hairs and gravitropism
axr5/iaa1	IVGWPPVR	Auxin resistant, reduced photo- and Yang *et al.* *(2004)* gravitro-pism, no apical hook
bdl/iaa12	VVGWPPIG	Seedling lethal, fails to establish Hamann *et al.* *(2002)* embryonic root meristem
iaa28	VVGWPPVR	Dwarf, auxin resistant, reduced Rogg *et al.* *(2001)* lateral root development, bushy
msg2/iaa19	VVGWPPVC	Reduced hypocotyl photo- and Tatematsu *et al.* *(2004)* gravitro-pism and lateral root development
shy2/iaa3	IVGWPPVR	Short hypocotyl, auxin resistant, Tian and Reed (1999) long root hairs, reduced lateral roots
slr/iaa14	VVGWPPVR	No lateral roots, auxin resistant, Fukaki *et al.* (2002) gravitropism defects, few root hairs

The -SMALL AUXIN-UP RNAs *(SAURs)* were initially identified in soybean as rapidly accumulating transcripts following a short auxin treatment. *SAUR* genes have subsequently been identified in many other plants, including 77 predicted *SAURs* in the *Arabidopsis* genome.

Several *SAUR* transcripts are highly unstable due to a conserved downstream element (DST) found in the 3' untranslated region. These transcripts encode small proteins of 9–15kDa, however sequence analysis provides few clues as to their function.

Maize ZmSAUR2 has been shown to be a short-lived nuclear protein, and both ZmSAUR2 and ZmSAUR1 have been found to bind calmodulin *in vitro* in a calcium-dependent fashion. What role, if any, the SAURs play in auxin signaling however remains to be established.

Arabidopsis contains 19 *GH3* genes, several of which are auxin inducible. Recent findings demonstrate that at least some *GH3* family members encode a novel class of acyl-adenylate-forming enzymes capable of acting as IAA–amino synthases in the conjugation of IAA to amino acids.

This suggests that the auxin induction of *GH3* genes acts as a feedback mechanism that attenuates the auxin signal by inactivating IAA via conjugation. Consistent with this possibility, *Arabidopsis* seedlings overexpressing *GH3.6* exhibit resistance to applied IAA, while seedlings containing mutations in *GH3.5* or *GH3.17* exhibit increased sensitivit.

It should be noted that not all *GH3* genes are auxin inducibl GH3 proteins exhibit IAA–amino synthase activity. For example, *GH3.11/JARI* is not transcriptionally regulated by auxin and has instead been shown to function as a jasmonic acid–amino synthase.

The AUXIN/INDOLE-3-ACETIC ACID *(Aux/IAA)* genes comprise the third large class of auxin-inducible transcripts. Originally identified from soybean and pea, *Aux/IAA* genes have subsequently been identified in many plants, including *Arabidopsis,* which contains a 29-member gene family.

As is the case for auxin induction of the *SAUR* genes,

Aux/IAA induction occurs within minutes of auxin treatment and does not require new protein synthesis. The extent of induction, as well as the kinetics of expression varies considerably between different *Aux/IAA* family members.

The *Aux/IAA* genes encode 20–35kDa proteins that localize to the nucleus in all cases examined to date. Several lines of genetic and molecular evidence indicate that these proteins function as negatively acting transcription factors that repress auxin response.

Albeit a few exceptions, Aux/IAA–proteins share four highly conserved motifs termed domains I, II, III, and IV. The C-terminal domains III and IV mediate dimerization with other Aux/IAA–proteins and with AUXIN RESPONSE FACTORS (ARFs), which also share these two motifs.

Domain I functions as a putative transcriptional repression motif, and domain II constitutes a degron that targets the Aux/IAA–proteins for degradation by the ubiquitin–26S proteasome proteolytic pathway. The function of these highly conserved motifs and the role of Aux/IAA-proteins in auxin response are discussed in more detail below.

Auxin Response Factors

The upstream regulatory regions of several auxin-responsive genes contain one or more copies of the consensus sequence TGTCTC. This sequence, known as the Auxin-Responsive Element, or *AuxRE,* has been found capable of conferring auxin-regulated gene expression to reporter constructs.

The identification of the AuxRE sequence led to the isolation of the Arabido*psis ARFI* gene in a yeast one-hybrid screen. Subsequent genetic, genomic, and molecular studies have led to the identification of 23 *ARF* genes in *Arabidopsis.*

ARF-mediated transcriptional regulation has been extensively studied in protoplast co-transfection assays employing reporter constructs. ARF proteins share a conserved N-terminal DNA-binding domain that mediates binding to the *AuxRE* sequence.

When fused to the VP16 transcriptional activation domain,

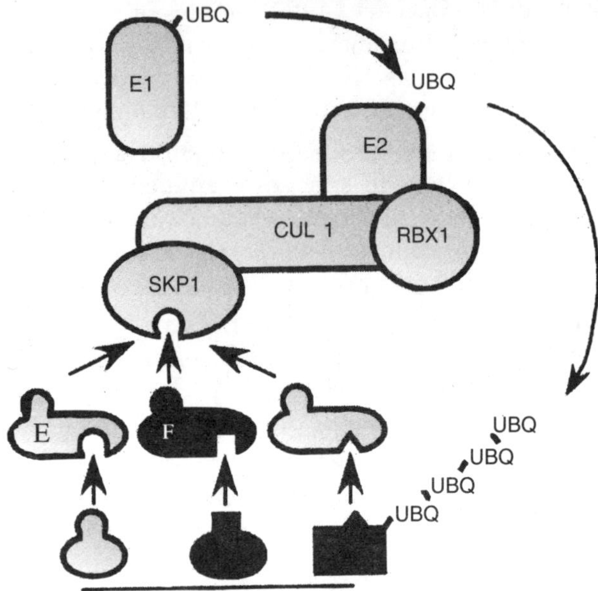

Figure 3.3: The SCF ubiquitin–ligase model. F-box proteins (F) bind to the core SCF subunits (SKP1, CUL1, and RBX1) and recruit specific substrates to the complex, facilitating ubiquitinylation by the associated E2 enzyme. Ubiquitin conjugation targets the substrates for proteolysis by the 26S proteasome. E1 = ubiquitin-activating enzyme; E2 = ubiquitin-conjugating enzyme.

this N-terminal domain is sufficient to target the ARF fusion protein to an AuxRE-containing promoter. Auxin does not appear to influence DNA binding.

The middle regions (MR) of ARF proteins are highly divergent, with some ARFs possessing serine-rich (S-rich) and others glutamine-rich (Q-rich) MRs. In all cases examined to date, the S-rich ARFs repress auxin-responsive gene expression in protoplast transfection assays, whereas the Q-rich ARFs act as transcriptional activators.

This functional divergence of the ARF transcription be attributed to the disparate MRs since these domains are sufficient to either activate or repress transcription when targeted to a heterologous promoter as a GAL4 DNA binding domain fusion protein.

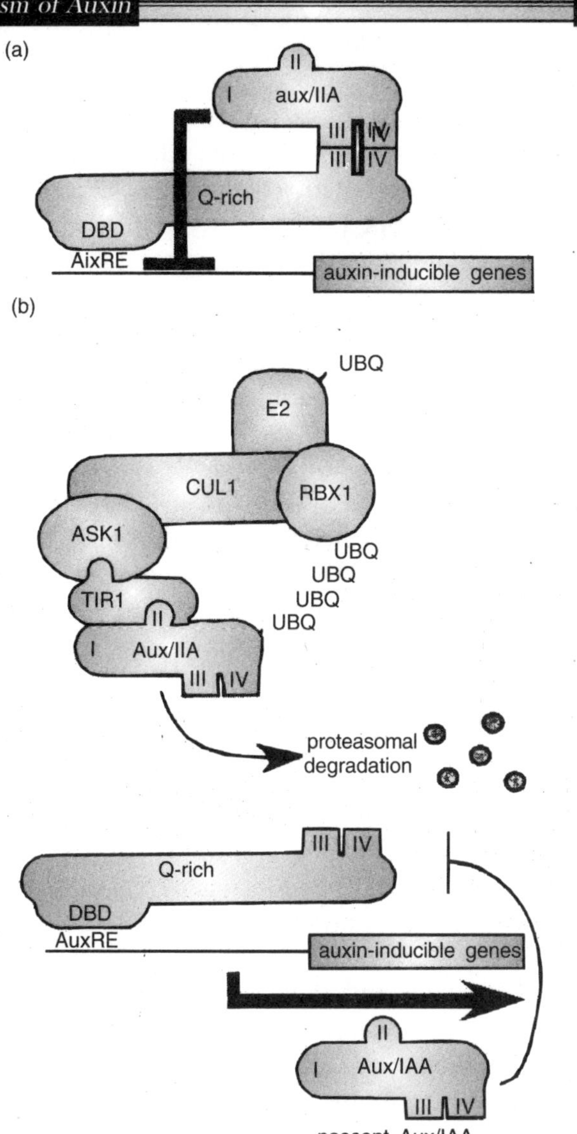

Figure 3.4 Regulation of auxin response by the SCF^{TIR1} ubiquitin–ligase. (a) Under sub threshold auxin concentrations, Aux/IAA–proteins are stable and dimerize with ARF transcriptional activators, repressing the activation of auxin-inducible genes. (b) Upon an auxin stimulus, the TIRI F-box protein recruits the Aux/IAA repressors to the SCF^{TIR1} complex, which ubiquitinylates the Aux/IAA proteins, thus targeting them for degradation by the 26S proteasome.

The majority of ARF proteins also contain a C-terminal dimerization domain highly related to motifs III and IV of Aux/IAA–proteins. These C-terminal domains mediate homo- and heterodimer formation between ARF proteins as well as heterodimerization with Aux/IAA–proteins.

While *in vitro* DNA-binding assays with a palindromic *AuxRE* repeat suggested that ARF–ARF dimerization might facilitate the binding of these transcriptio their target site, more recent protoplast transfection assays employing ARF derivatives lacking the C-terminal dimerization elements clearly indicate that ARF dimerization is not essential for *AuxRE* binding.

In the case of the activating ARFs, dimerization with Aux/IAA–proteins provides hormonal control of ARF transcriptional activity. Several members of the Aux/IAA family can interact with Q-rich ARFs and repress transcriptional activation in protoplast assays.

Aux/IAA domain I, recently shown to be capable of acting as a transcriptional repressor, may be responsible for this negative regulation although the mechanism remains to be elucidated. In response to an auxin stimulus, Aux/IAA–proteins are degraded by the 26S proteasome.

This reduction in Aux/IAA–protein levels relieves the repression on the Q-rich ARFs, resulting in increased transcription of auxin-responsive genes. Consistent with such a model, dominant gain-of-function mutations have been isolated in several Aux/IAA genes that confer dramatic auxin-related phenotypes and reduced auxin response.

Molecular studies have found that all of these mutations map to the domain II degron sequence and result in a dramatic increase in the stability of the mutant Aux/IAA repressor.

In contrast, the loss of-function mutations in *Aux/IAA* genes that have been described to date confer only subtle or no apparent phenotypes, suggesting that there is considerable functional redundancy among the *Aux/IAA* family members.

Analysis of several ARF mutants of *Arabidopsis* has

provided insight into the various auxin-dependent processes these transcription factors regulate. Mutations in *ETTIN/ ARF3,* an atypical S-rich ARF that lacks the C-terminal dimerization motifs, confer gynoecium patterning defects similar to those observed in flowers treated with the auxin transport inhibitor NPA.

A screen for mutations restoring ethylene-mediated apical hook formation to the *hookless* 1 *(hls1)* mutant identified HOOKLESS SUPPRESSOR 1 (HSS1/ARF2). Ethylene and light act though HLS1 to regulate protein levels of this S-rich ARF to mediate differential cell elongation in the hypocotyl.

While *arf2* mutants exhibit several phenotypes including increased size of several organs, agravitropic stems, and delayed senescence and abscission, microarray analysis using RNA prepared from 7-day-old *arf2* seedlings did not detect any difference from wild-type in auxin-regulated gene expression.

T-DNA insertion mutants in most of the remaining S-rich ARFs have recently been characterized and do not confer any obvious phenotypes suggesting functional redundancy. The recent demonstration that *arf10* arf16 double mutants, but neither single mutant, exhibit agravitropic root growth due to aberrant root cap cell differentiation supports this possibility.

In the case of the Q-rich activating ARFs, mutations in MONOPT-EROUS *(MP/ ARF5)* confer defects in embryo patterning with severe alleles lacking all basal structures.

In contrast, mutations in NON-PHOTOTROPIC HYPO-COTYL 4 *(NPH4/ARF7)* result in diminished tropic responses in the shoot due to reduced auxin-mediated cell expansion.

While the *mp* and *nph4* mutant phenotypes indicate that these two ARFs regulate distinct auxin responses, the recent finding that *nph4* mutations enhance the rootless phenotype of weak *mp* alleles suggests some functional overlap between these two transcriptional activators. ARF19 also appears to act redundantly with ARF7.

While arf19 mutants exhibit no apparent phenotype, arf19 enhances np*h4* tropism defects, and the double mutants exhibit additional auxin-related phenotypes including auxin-resistant root elongation and reductions in leaf expansion and lateral root development. The *arf8* mutants exhibit increased apical dominance, lateral root proliferation, and longer hypocotyls in the light.

Such hyper-auxin phenotypes are characteristic of IAA overproduction mutants such as *yucca* and sur2, and at first glance appear to contradict the notion that ARF8 is a transcriptional auxin-responsive genes.

However, further analysis revealed that the expression of several *GH3* genes encoding IAA conjugating enzymes is reduced in a*rf8* mutants, while elevated in plants overexpressing ARF8. These data suggest that ARF8 may specifically be involved in a negative-feedback pathway controlling

IAA levels via activation of GH3 expression and suggest a close connection between auxin signaling and auxin homeostasis. Although the analysis of *ARF* and *Aux/IAA* mutants suggests considerable functional redundancy among the individual members of the respective gene families, the fact that several *arf* mutants exhibit specific auxin-related defects clearly indicates some functional specialization.

Likewise, the phenotypes of the different dominant gain-of-function *Aux/IAA* mutants that have been characterized vary considerably. All of the ARF proteins thus far tested bind to a common regulatory sequence, the *AuxRE.* Additionally, at least among the activating ARFs, Aux/IAA–proteins do not appear to exhibit a high degree of interaction specificity.

For example, several different Aux/IAA–proteins were found to equivalently repress ARF5- and ARF7-mediated transcriptional activation of a reporter construct when co-expressed in carrot protoplasts. This begs the question of how specific auxin responses are generated.

Recent work suggests that this specificity may be achieved in large expression patterns of pairs of Aux/IAA and ARF proteins. Dominant gain mutations in the *BODENLOS (BDL/IAA12) Aux/IAA* gene result in embryo development defects virtually identical to loss-of-function mutations in MP/ARF5, suggesting that BDL regulates MP activity. In contrast, equivalent domain II mutations in *SHY2/IAA3* confer a short hypocotyl phenotype, but embryogenesis is unaffected suggesting it regulates a distinct ARF.

Weijers *et al.* (2005) employed a promoter-swap strategy to determine whether differential transcriptional regulation of these two *Aux/IAA* genes contributed to the distinct mutant phenotypes. Remarkably, transgenic seedlings expressing the dominant *shy2-2* allele from the BD*L* promoter exhibited an embryo phenotype qualitatively identical to *bdl* mutants.

Reciprocally, hypocotyl elongation and shoot development in pSHY2::bdl plants were strikingly similar to *shy2-2* mutants. These findings suggest that the SHY2 and BDL proteins are functionally equivalent for these specific auxin responses, and that transcriptional control of *Aux/IAA* gene expression is a major determinant for directing which auxin responses are regulated by a specific Aux/IAA family member.

However, it should also be noted that the same study found strong evidence for functional specialization of Aux/IAA–proteins. Whereas the *pSHY2::bdl* transgene was able to phenocopy the shoot phenotypes of *shy2-2* plants, the auxin-resistant and agravitropic root growth phenotypes characteristic of *shy2-2* seedlings were not observed in the transgenics.

Although additional study is needed, the regulated expression of specific Aux/IAA and ARF family members undoubtedly plays a large role in determining developmental specificity. Several recent studies suggest that post-transcriptional control of ARF expression is also involved in defining expression patterns.

Both micro RNAs (miRNAs) and trans-acting short-interfering RNAs (tasi-RNAs) have recently been identified that direct the cleavage of several ARF transcripts. For example, the miR160 miRNA targets ARF10, *ARF16,* and *ARF17* transcripts.

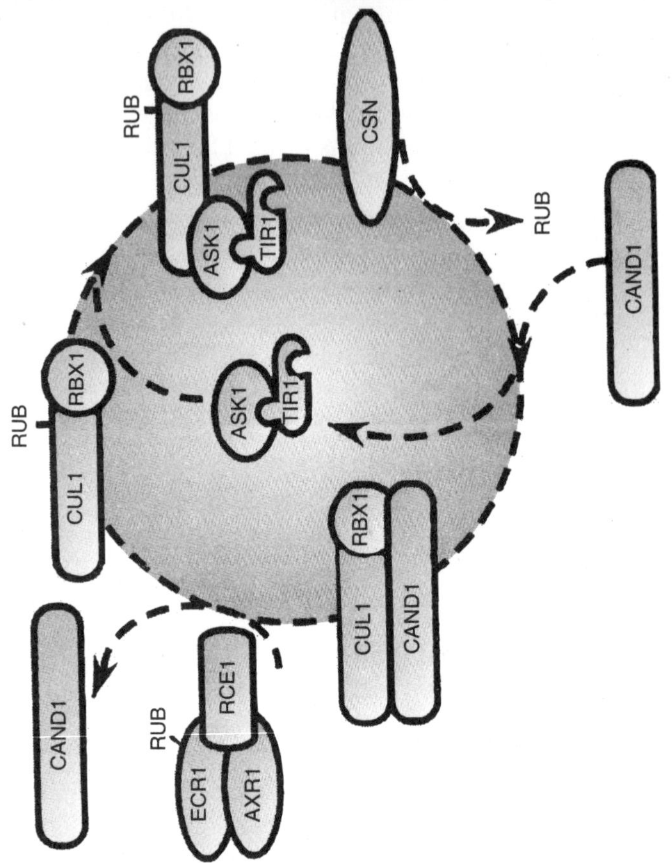

Figure 3.5: A model for SCF^{TIR1} regulation by the cyclic RUB modification of CUL1.

Constitutive overexpression of miR160 results in root cap defects similar to those observed in arf10 arf16 double mutants, while expression of cleavage-resistant forms of ARF16 or ARF17 confers numerous auxin-related defects, demonstrating that miRNAs likely play a crucial role in restricting ARF expression domains.

Regulation of auxin response by the SCF^{TIR1} ubiquitin–ligase

The genetic identification and analysis of auxin-resistant mutants in *Arabidopsis* has proven invaluable in elucidating the molecular mechan-isms underlying auxin action. Molecular and biochemical studies of the gene products affected by thes have positioned the SCF^{TIR1} ubiquitin–ligase complex as a central regulator of auxin signaling. Ubiquitin–ligases, or E3 enzymes, catalyze the conjugation to substrate proteins.

Once ubiquitinylated, these substrates are targeted for proteolysis by the 26S proteasome.

SCF-type ubiquitin–ligases comprise the largest family of E3 enzymes in *Arabidopsis.* These multi-subunit enzymes contain Skpl, Cullinl, an F-box protein, and the small RING domain protein Rbx1/Roc1/Hrtl. CUL1 acts as a scaffold protein, binding RBX1 through its C-terminal domain and SKP1 via its N-terminal domain.

F-box proteins bind to this hetero-trimeric core via an interaction between their F-box domain and the SKP1 protein, and function as interchangeable adaptor subunits that recruit specific substrates to the SCF complex for ubiquitinylation.

TIR1 is one of approximately 700 F-box proteins encoded in the *Arabidopsis* genome. Mutations in TIR1 confer modest auxin-response defects including auxin-resistant root growth and reduced lateral root development, and molecular studies confirmed TIR1 as *a bona fide* F-box protein by demonstrating that it assembles into a complex with *Arabidopsis* orthologs of the core SCF subunits.

Mutations in the *AXR6* (AUXIN RESISTANT 6) gene encoding the CUL1 subunit have also been isolated in auxin-resistance screens, and reverse genetic approaches have been used to demonstrate that *the* ASK1 *(Arabidopsis* SKP1-like 1) and RBX1 genes are also required for auxin response.

Unlike mutations in *TIRI,* mutations or transgenes perturbing core SCF subunits do not specifically affect auxin signaling but instead confer pleiotropic phenotypes, consistent with their participation in additional SCF complexes.

These findings established the SCF^{TIR1} ubiquitin-ligase complex as a positive regulator of auxin response and suggested a model involving the SCF^{TIR1}-mediated ubiquitinylation of a repressor of auxin signaling. The genetic isolation of several dominant gain-of-function alleles of *Aux/IAA* genes in auxin-resistance screens first implicated the Aux/IAA–proteins as repressors of auxin response. As detailed in Table elsewhere in this chapter, molecular analysis revealed that all of these dominant lesions affected amino acids in the highly conserved core of domain II.

Early studies on Aux/IAA–proteins indicated that these proteins were highly unstable. This instability is due to domain II, which acts as a degron, targeting Aux/IAA–proteins for ubiquitinylation by the SCF^{TIR1} complex in response to an auxin stimulus.

This was elegantly demonstrated using a combination of molecular, genetic, and biochemical approaches. First, domain II confers auxinstability to luciferase and (-glucuronidase fusion proteins *in vivo.* Second, TIR1 binds to Aux/IAA–proteins in cell-free extracts in an auxin-regulated fashion.

This binding requires domain II and is disrupted by the gain-of-function Aux/IAA mutations. And third, mutations affecting the SCF^{TIR1} complex stabilize endogenous Aux/IAA–proteins, as well as the domain II-fusion reporter proteins *in vivo.*

These and other findings suggest that in response to an auxin stimulus, Aux/IAA–proteins are recruited to the SCF^{TIR1} complex and ubiquitinylated. Subsequent Aux/IAA degradation by the 26S proteasome derepresses the ARF transcription factors, thus enabling auxin-dependent transcriptional changes.

Since domain II mutant derivatives are not recognized by TIR1, these stabilized repressors are immune to this auxin-regulated proteolysis and constitutively repress of ARF activity.

While it may seem counterintuitive that auxin promotes both the proteolysis of Ateins and increased Aux/IAA gene transcription, this latter response is likely a form of negative feedback that attenuates the auxin signal, ensuring a transient auxin response.

Regulation of SCF^{TIR1} Activity

The analysis of additional auxin-resistant mutants has identified several regulatory components modulating SCF^{TIR1} function. axr1 mutants exhibit severe auxin response defects. *AXR1* encodes a protein related to the amino-terminal half of the ubiquitin-activating enzyme, and biochemical studies have revealed AXR1 interacts with the E1-LIKE CONJUGATING ENZYME RELATED 1 (ECR1) protein.

Together, AXR1 and ECR1 form a RELATED TO UBIQUITIN (RUB) activating enzyme. *Arabidopsis* encodes three RUB proteins (known as NEDD8 in mammals) sharing approximately 60% sequence identity with ubiquitin. Once activated, RUB is transferred to the RUB1 CONJUGATING ENZYME 1 (RCE1), which using RBX1 as a RUB E3 ligase, catalyzes the addition of RUB to a lysine residue near the C-terminus of the CUL1 subunit of the SCF^{TIRI} complex.

Unlike ubiquitin, RUB conjugation does not result in substrate proteolysis, but rather is a regulatory modification required for SCF ubiquitin–ligase activity as demonstrated by the finding Aux/IAA stability is increased in RUB pathway mutants.

The RUB modification of CUL1 is a dynamic process. The SCF in the COP9 signalosome (CSN), an 8-subunit complex resembling the 26S protea some lid. The CSN possesses an isopeptidase activity that cleaves the RUB modifier off of CUL1.

Surprisingly, plants with impaired CSN function exhibit diminished auxin response and increased Aux/IAA stability indicating that like RUB conjugation, RUB cleavage off of CUL1 is also required for optimal SCF^{TIR1} activity.

Also consistent with the notion that RUB cleavage plays an important role in SCF function, plants overexpressing RBX1 exhibit hyper-modification of CUL1, yet display several auxin response defects and reduced SCF^{TIR1} activity.

The molecular function of RUB modification is unclear. Biochemical assays suggest RUB modification of CUL1 may enhance SCF activity in *vitro* by facilitating interactions with ubiquitin-charged E2 enzymes. An additional posemerged with the identification of CULLIN ASSOCIATED AND NEDD8 DISSOCIATED 1 (CAND1). Biochemical studies with human CUL1 identified CAND1 as a CUL1-binding protein. CAND1 specifically interacts with unmodified can be dissociated by the RUB modification of CUL1 *in vitro.*

Furthermore, CAND1 and SKP1 binding to CUL1 are mutually exclusive, suggesting a model whereby CAND1 sequesters a fraction of the CUL1 pool, thus negatively regulating ubiquitin ligase activity by preventing SCF complex assembly.

Genetic studies of *Arabidopsis cand*1 mutants, however suggest a more complicated scenario. Rather than exhibiting increased SCF^{TIR1} activity as might be expected, cand1 mutants are defective in Aux/IAA proteolysis and display diminished auxin response phenotypes similar to SCF mutants.

To reconcile these observations, it has been suggested that the RUB pathway, CAND1, and the CSN sustain SCF activity in *vivo* by promoting cycles of SCF assembly and disassembly. Although such a cycle is not required for SCF activity in *in vitro* ubiquitinylation assays, it may be essential in a cellular context where many F-box proteins are competing for access to the common core SCF subunits.

While additional studies are required to test this model, it is clear that CAND1, the CSN, and the RUB pathway are intimately linked and required for normal SCF^{TIR1} function. SGT1b, which also interacts with SCF complexes and is required for SCF^{TIR1} activity in *vivo* has also been suggested to potentially regulate SCF assembly.

Identification of an Auxin Receptor

Central to understanding the molecular basis of auxin action is the elucidation of how auxin is perceived. Classical studies provide support for both plasma membrane and intracellular sites of auxin perception. Biochemical efforts to isolate the auxin receptor identified AUXIN BINDING PROTEIN 1 (ABP1) as a protein that binds biologically active auxins with high affinity.

Originally purified from maize coleoptiles, this 22kDa protein has subsequently been found in many species and is apparently unique to the plant kingdom. The protein seque-nce of ABP1 reveals little functional information.

Consistent with the presence of a C-terminal KDEL endoplasmic retention motif, the majority of ABP1 is ER localized. However, a small fraction escapes to the cell surface, and several lines of evidence implicate plasma membrane associated ABP1 in early auxin-mediated electrophysiologic responses.

Genetic approaches to elucidate ABP1 function have found that its overexpression promotes auxin-mediated cell expansion. Furthermore, *Arabidopsis abp1* null mutants display an early embryo-lethal phenotype, indicating that ABP1 is an essential gene.

However, the molecular activity of ABP1 remains undete-rmined, and it does not appear to be involved in the SCF^{TIR1}-mediated signaling pathway.

The demonstration that auxin, when added to a crude protein lysate, could promote the binding of Aux/IAA–proteins to the SCF^{TIR1} complex indicated that an auxin receptor was functional in these extracts and provided a new approach for receptor identification.

Studies of several F-box protein–substrate interactions in yeast and animal systems have revealed that in virtually every case, the substrate must be post translationally modified before it can be recognized by its cognate F-box protein.

Generally, this involves substrate phosphorylation by a stimulus-activated kinase, although other types of modifica-tions have also been reported. Since domain II is not only necessary, but is sufficient for auxin-induced binding to TIR1, it was hypothesized that an auxin-activated kinase or other enzyme modified domain II, thus targeting the Aux/IAA–protein for SCF-mediated ubiquitinylation and ultimately degradation.

However, the domain II degron does not contain any essential phosphorylatable residues, and no detectable modifications were detected by MS analysis following incubation of the domain II peptide with auxin-treated extracts. This led to the alternative possibility that auxin acted through TIR1.

Two recent reports have implicated the TIR1 F-box protein as an auxin receptor when it was found that radiolabeled IAA added to crude Arabidops co-purifies with the SCF^{TIR1}–Aux/IAA complex. This binding is both saturable and specific for active auxins, with an estimated K_d in the 20–80 nM range.

While this alone only suggests that an auxin receptor is associated with SCF^{TIR1}, the finding that TIR1 expressed in animal cells also interacts with a recombinant Aux/IAA–protein in an auxin-dependent manner is more telling.

As TIR1 and the Aux/IAA–protein are the only plant-derived components in these assays, it seemed that one of these proteins must be responsible for auxin binding. Furthermore, since a 17-amino-acid domain II peptide can substitute for the intact Aux/IAA–protein, and an auxin pretreatment of TIR1, but not of the Aux/IAA–protein, also promotes the TIR1–Aux/IAA interaction *in vitro*, the TIR1 F-box protein appears to be the long sought auxin receptor.

It should be noted however, that direct IAA binding to purified TIR1 in the absence of an Aux/IAA–protein remains to be demonstrated. The fact that tir1 null mutants exhibit a relatively weak auxin response defect compared to axr1 or dominant *Aux/IAA* mutants suggested that TIR1 might not be the only auxin receptor. Indeed, three additional AUXIN SIGNALING F-BOX proteins,

AFB1, AFB2, and AFB3, displaying 60–70% sequence identity to TIR1 were recently shown to exhibit auxin-dependent binding to Aux/IAA–proteins *in vitro*.

Correspondingly, the introduction of *afb* mutations into *tirl* plants results in a progressive reduction in auxin response, culminating with tir*l afbl afb2 afb3* quadruple mutants exhibiting a seedling-lethal phenotype similar to *mp* and *bdl* mutants.

Aux/IAA pull-down assays with quadruple mutant extracts detected no saturable IAA-binding activity, indicating that auxin binding is dependent on these F-box proteins. The molecular details of auxin binding to the TIR1/AFB receptors remain to be elucidated, including the identification of the binding site and how hormone binding facilitates interactions with the Aux/IAA-proteins.

CONCLUSIONS

The identification of the TIR1/AFB family of receptors fills in a crucial piece of the auxin puzzle. Though many details remain to be worked out, we now have a frame work for a potentially complete signaling pathway leading from hormone perception to transcriptional response.

Can such a simple pathway with the TIR1/AFB receptors sensing IAA to trigger the ubiquitinylation of Aux/IAA–proteins and thus derepressing the ARF transcription factors account for the multitude of responses elicited by the hormone?

Differential expression of the many *ARF* and *Aux/IAA* genes coupled with the large number of potential combinatorial interactions between these proteins could potentially provide both developmental specificity and the complexity needed for a large array of auxin responses.

However, it is also likely that additional auxin signaling pathways await discovery, as some responses appear too quickly to result from transcriptional changes. Analysis of auxin response in plants lacking the TIR1 and *AFB* genes may be a useful approach for identifying such pathways.

Furthermore, the SAUR proteins, ABP1, a MAP kinase, the IBR5 dual specificity phosphatase, Rac GTPases, and a host of other potential signaling factors have been implicated in auxin signaling but are presently without a home in current models for auxin response, clearly indicating that there is much yet to learn about the mechanics of auxin signaling.

Likewise, Aux/IAA and ARF function are only beginning to be unde number of potential Aux/IAA–Aux/IAA, Aux/IAA–ARF, and ARF–ARF dimer combinations is massive, yet so far the only interaction ascribed any biologic significance is the negative regulation of the activating ARFs by Aux/IAA–proteins.

Are all Aux/IAAs negative regulators? Do Aux/IAA–proteins regulate the S-rch ARFs? If not, are these repressing ARFs subject to hormonal regulation, and if so, how?

The answers to these questions, as well as the identification of the downstream effector genes that are the targets of ARF regulation will greatly improve our understanding of auxin-regulated growth and development.

Molecular and biochemical processes involved in auxin biology have in common an impressive complexity and, in the case of auxin metabolism, functional redundancy.

Key areas of future research will be the understanding of the network–IAA biosynthesis and degradation, conjugation, transport, signaling, and response together.

Many links between these individual pathways have already been established, such as auxin induction of *GH3* expression and its resultant predicted effects on conjugation and oxidation, however it is likely that many more connections await identification.

An even greater challenge is elucidating the coordination of auxin with other signaling pathways. IAA does not act in isolation, but in concert with other phytohormones and developmental and environmental signals to control plant growth and development.

Understanding the integration of auxin with these other pathways is a daunting task, but is necessary to truly understand the role of this amazing hormone in plant biology.

Chapter 4 Analysis of Gibberellins

Gibberellins (GAs) are involved in a wide range of plant *developmental* processes. The biosynthetic pathway is discussed in othe chapter of this book but it should be noted here that of all the plant hormones the GAs represent perhaps the most diverse group, with currently 125 different *structures* known.

This diversity compounds the analysis of GAs in that not only must extraction ensure quantitative recovery of all the types, but these need to be resolved following partial purification.

Moritz and Olsen (1) have described the analysis of GAs from *milligram* amounts of *plant tissues.*

MATERIALS

Qualitative Analysis

Extraction

1. Methanol:water (4:1 v/v).
2. 833 Bq Each of the following tritiated GA standards, GA_{19}, GA_{20}, GA1, GA_4, and GA_9.
3. Methanol.
4. 2 M HCl.
5. Ethyl acetate.
6. 5% (w/v) sodium bicarbonate.
7. 1 M KOH.

8. PVP (Polyclar AT, sieved to remove fine (<100 mesh) particles) column (3 mL bed vol) pre-equilibrated with 0.1 M KH_2PO_4 (pH 3).
9. QAE Sephadex A25 (Pharmacia [Uppsala, Sweden]) anion exchange column (5 mL bed vol) pre-equilibrated with sodium formate (0.5 M).
10. 0.2 M formic acid.
11. C_{18} SepPak cartridge (Waters Associates [Watford, Hertfordshire, UK]).

Derivatization and Resolution of GAs.

1. Methanol.
2. 2 *mM* Acetic acid.
3. Hypersil 5 μm octadecylsiloxane (ODS) high-performance liquid chromatography (HPLC) column (4.9 mm id × 250 mm).
4. Ethereal diazomethane.
5. N-Methyl-N-trimethylsilyltrifluoroacetamide (MSTFA).
6. Ethyl acetate.
7. Aminopropyl cartridge (100 mg).

Quantitative Analysis

As above plus:

1. [17-$^2H_2$]GAs, the appropriate standard for each GA to be quantified.
2. A gas chromatography-mass spectrometry (GC-MS) system capable of selected ion monitoring (SIM) or selected reaction monitoring (SRM).

   An example of this is a Hewlett-Packard 5890 gas chromatograph coupled to an HP5970 mass selective detector.
3. A fused silica WCOT capillary column (25 m × 0.22 mm × 0.25 μm film thickness) coated with either BP1 or SE52/54 or equivalent.

Analysis by GC-MS with Selected Reaction Monitoring Using a Simplified Purification Procedure

1. QAE Sephadex A25 (Pharmacia) anion-exchange column (5 mL bed vol) pre-equilibrated with sodium formate (0.5 M).
2. 0.2 *M* formic acid.
3. C_{18} SepPak cartridge (Waters Associates).
4. Methanol.
5. 2 mM acetic acid.
6. Hypersil 5 μm ODS HPLC column (4.9 mm id × 250 mm).
7. Ethereal diazomethane.
8. MSTFA.
9. Ethyl acetate.
10. Aminopropyl cartridge (100 mg).
11. An external source ion trap mass spectrometer (Finnigan GCQ [Hemel Hempstead, UK]) or equivalent.
12. CH_2Cl_2. (10–20 μL).
13. A fused silica WCOT BPX5 capillary column (25 m × 0.22 mm × 0.25 mm film thickness) (Scientific Glass Engineering) or equivalent.

METHODS

Qualitative Analysis

Extraction

1. Plant tissues are frozen immediately in liquid N_2 and stored at –80°C or freeze-dried and stored at –20°C.
2. Samples (10–50 g fresh weight) are homogenized in cold (4°C) methanol:water (4:1 v/v) (>10 mL solvent/ g fresh weight of tissue). Small amounts (833 Bq each) of the following tritiated GA standards, GA_{19}, GA_{20}, GA1, GA_4, and GA_9, are added to the homogenate

and the extract stirred overnight in the cold (4°C).

3. After filtration, the residue is re-extracted with methanol (>10 mL solvent/g fresh weight of tissue) for 4 h and refiltered. Methanol is removed from the combined filtrates under reduced pressure at 35°C, and the aqueous residue is adjusted to pH 2.5 (2 M HCl), and partitioned against ethyl acetate (4× equal vols).
4. The combined organic phases are partitioned against 5% (w/v) sodium bicarbonate (3 × 1/5 vol). The aqueous phases are acidified to pH 3.0 (2 M HCl) and partitioned against ethyl acetate (4 × equal vol), which is then reduced to dryness *in vacuo* at 35°C.
5. The extract is dissolved in 5 mL water, adjusted to pH 8.0 (1 M KOH), and loaded onto a PVP (Polyclar AT, sieved to remove fine [<100 mesh] particles) column (3 mL bed vol) pre-equilibrated with 0.1 M KH_2PO_4 (pH 3.0). After loading, the column is washed with water (2 × 5 mL) at pH 8.
6. The eluate is combined and loaded onto a QAE Sephadex A25 (Pharmacia) anion-exchange column (5 mL bed vol) pre-equilibrated with sodium formate (0.5 M) then washed with formic acid (0.2 M) and water (pH 8.0). After loading, the column is washed with water (pH 8.0) (15 mL) and GAs are eluted with 0.2 M formic acid (20 mL).
7. The eluate is then applied directly to a pre-equilibrated C18 SepPak cartridge (Waters Associates). After washing with water (pH 3.0) (5 mL), GAs are eluted with methanol:water (4:1 v/v) (5 mL), and are then evaporated to dryness *in vacuo*.

Derivatization and Resolution of GAs

1. Samples are dissolved in 80 μL methanol, made up to 400 μL with 2 mM acetic acid.
2. GAs are resolved by reverse-phase HPLC using a 4.9 mm id × 250 mm column containing Hypersil 5 μm ODS. Samples are injected onto the column using a

Rheodyne 7125 valve fitted with a 500 μL loop and eluted using a linear gradient of increasing methanol in 2 mM acetic acid (20 to 100% methanol over 40 min) at a flow rate of 1 mL/min. Forty 1-mL fractions are collected.

3. Aliquots (50 μL) are removed for scintillation counting to locate the tritiated standards. Fractions, based on the location of these GAs, are combined and taken to dryness *in vacuo*.
4. The dried fractions are methylated with excess ethereal diazomethane, transferred to glass ampules, and trimethylsilylated with MSTFA (5 mL) at 90°C for 30 min.
5. If necessary, further purification can be achieved by dissolving the methylated fraction in ethyl acetate (1 mL), partitioning against water (1 mL), and then passing the ethyl acetate phase through a small (100 mg) aminopropyl cartridge that has been pre-equilibrated with ethyl acetate.
6. The aqueous phase is partitioned once more against ethyl acetate (1 mL), and the organic phase passed though the aminopropyl cartridge.
7. The combined ethyl acetate phases are taken to dryness and then transferred to ampules and trimethylsilylated.
8. Derivatized samples are analyzed by combined GC-MS in full-scan mode. Samples (1 μL) are coinjected with Parafilm in hexane to determine KRI values and the mass spectra and KRIs are compared with those of standards or with published data.

Quantitative Analysis

1. Samples (5–20 g fresh weight) are extracted. and in addition to the tritiated standards, $[17\text{-}^2H2]$GAs are added as internal standards.

   The appropriate standard is added for each GA to be quantified; the amounts of standards added should approximate the anticipa-ted amount of endogenous

Table 4.1: Characteristic Parent and Product Ions for Representative GAs and Internal Standards.

Gibberellin	*Excitation voltage*	*Parent ion m/z*	*Production mass range m/z*	*Production m/z*
GA_1	0.8	506	350–506	448
[17-$^2H_2$]GA_1	0.8	508	350–508	450
GA_4	0.7	284	150–284	224
[17-^{2}H2]GA_4	0.7	286	150–286	226
GA_8	0.9	594	430–594	448
[17-^{2}H2]GA_8	0.9	596	430–596	450
GA_{15}	0.8	284	180–284	239
[17-^{2}H2]GA_{15}	0.8	286	180–286	241
GA_{19}	0.8	434	250–434	374
[17-^{2}H2]GA_{19}	0.8	436	250–436	376
GA_{20}	0.8	418	300–418	375
[17-^{2}H2]GA_{20}	0.8	420	300–420	377
GA_{24}	0.7	314	200–314	286
[17-^{2}H2]GA_{24}	0.7	316	200–316	288
GA_{29}	0.9	506	350–506	477
[17-$^2H_2$]GA_{29}	0.9	508	350–508	479
GA_{34}	0.8	506	350–506	416
[17-$^2H_2$]GA_{34}	0.8	508	350–508	418
GA_{44}	0.8	432	200–432	207
[17-^{2}H2]GA_{44}	0.8	434	200–434	209
GA_{53}	0.8	448	350–448	388
[17-^{2}H2]GA_{53}	0.8	450	350–450	390

analyte determined from preliminary experiments.

2. After purification but omitting the PVP step, samples are analyzed by GC-MS with SIM using, for example, a Hewlett-Packard 5890 gas chromatograph coupled to an HP5970 mass selective detector.
3. Typically, samples (1–3 mL) are injected into a fused silica WCOT capillary column (25 mm × 0.22 mm ×

0.25 μm film thickness) coated with either BP-1 or SE52/54 at an oven temperature of 60°C. After 0.5 min, the splitter (50:1) is opened and 1 min later the temperature is increased at 20°C/min to 240°C and then at 4°C/min to 300°C. The He inlet pressure is 0.09 MPa and the injector, interface and MS source temperatures are 220, 270, and 200°C, respectively.

4. Characteristic ions are monitored with dwell times of 50 ms (for example, GA8, m/z 594,448; [17^2H2]GA8, m/z 596, 450; GA_1, m/z 506, 448; [17^2H2]GA1 *m/z* 508, 450; GA_3, *m/z* 504; [17^2H2]GA3, m/z 506; GA_{20}, m/z 418, 375; [17^2H_2]GA_{20}, m/z *420,* 377; GA19, m/z 434, 402; [17^2H_2]GA_{19}, m/z 436, 404). The concentration of GAs in the original extracts are determined from previously established calibration curves of the peak area ratios for unlabeled and deuterated GAs plotted against varying molar ratios of the two compounds (3).

Analysis by GC-MS with SRM Using a Simplified Purification Procedure

This method is used in conjunction with SRM for quantitative analysis using 0.5–5 g fresh weight of tissue. The method is the same as that described in other section of this chapter except that the solvent partitioning and PVP steps are omitted.

1. The extract is taken to dryness, then dissolved in water (5 mL), adjusted to pH 8.0 (1 M KOH), and loaded directly onto the QAE Sephadex A-25 (Pharmacia) anion-exchange column. Thereafter, the procedure is the same as above.
2. For GC-MS analysis using SRM, an external source ion trap mass spectrometer (Finnigan GCQ) is used.
3. Derivatized samples are diluted with CH2Cl2 (10–20 μL) and injected (1 μL) into a fused silica WCOT BPX5 capillary column (25 m × 0.22 mm × 0.25 mm film thickness) (Scientific Glass Engineering) at an oven temperature of 60°C. After 1 min the splitter

50:1 is opened and the temperature is increased at 20°C/min to 220°C and then at 4°C/min to 300°C. The He flow is controlled at a constant linear velocity of 40 cm/s. The injector, interface, and MS source temper-atures are 220, 270, and 200°C, respectively. The mass spectrometer is operated in dual SRM mode.

4. Characteristic parent ions are selected and monitored with an isolation wave-form notch of 1 amu. Full product ion scans at 0.5 s/scan are obtained for all GAs analyzed. The concentration of GAs in the extracts is determined from previously establi-shed calibration curves of peak area ratios of the product ion for unlabeled and deuterated GAs plotted against varying molar ratios of the two compounds. Parent and product ions for representative GAs and internal standards are listed in Table elsewhere in this chapter.

NOTES

1. During extraction, for many plant species the PVP purification step can be omitted.
2. If the samples are evidently very dirty, further purification can be achieved prior to trimethylation by dissolving the methylated samples in ethyl acetate (1 mL), partitioning against an equal volume of water and passing through an aminopropyl column as described anywhere else in this chapter.

Metabolism of Gibberellins

The term gibberellin was introduced by Teijiro Yabuta in 1935 for a growth active substance produced by the phytopathogenic fungus *Gibberella fujikuroi.* Two crystalline substances were obtained from fungal extracts and named gibberellin A and B, the former being subsequently shown to be a mixture of three compounds, gibberellin A_1, A_2 and A_3.

This system of nomenclature was later adopted for newly characterised gibberellins from all sources, and to date 136 different structures have been identified from higher plants, fungi or bacteria. It is now common practice to abbreviate gibberellin A_n to GA_n and to use GA as a general abbreviation for gibberellin.

However, in this context, GA does not refer to gibberellic acid, which is an alternative name for GA_3, the first gibberellin structure to be elucidated.

The ability of GA_3 to normalise the dwarf phenotype of certain mutants provided the first indication that GAs might be endogenous growth regulators in higher plants, and this was supported by the identification of GAs in seeds of runner bean almost 50 years ago.

Such GA-deficient mutants have been largely instrumental in identifying the myriad developmental processes in which GAs participate, including seed germination, seedling growth, determination of leaf size and shape, stem and root extension, flower induction and development, pollination, seed development and fruit expansion.

Although there was considerable excitement at the discovery of this new growth hormone, particularly in anticipation of its commercial exploitation, the lack of appropriate technology meant that progress in understanding GA signaling in plants was slow.

An exception to this was a-amylase induction in the cereal aleurone, which has long been the best characterised GA response, at least in terms of the downstream events. Although some progress was made in understanding the chemical and biochemical details of the GA-biosynthetic pathways, knowledge of the signal transduction events was sparse.

However, in the last 15 years, spurred on particularly by advances in molecular genetics, our knowledge of GA metabolism and signal trans advanced spectacularly, culminating in the recent identification of a soluble GA receptor.

Furthermore, use of DNA microarrays is allowing the identification of many more downstream gene targets for the GA-signaling pathway and will lead to a clearer understanding of how the developmental consequences of GA action arise.

Our aim in this chapter is to highlight the more recent advances in GA metabolism and signal transduction, which can be considered as parts of a single signaling pathway.

The closeness with which the two parts of the pathway are integrated is evident from feedback regulation of GA biosynthesis, which is mediated by GAsignal transduction.

We will also consider the regulation of GA-signaling by developmental and environmental stimuli, the transcriptional events that are targets of GA action as well as current information on the sites of GA biosynthesis and action.

The Gibberellin Metabolic Pathway

Biosynthesis of Bioactive GAs

The principal growth active structures GA1, GA_3, GA_4 and GA_7 are tetracyclic diterpenoid carboxylic acids possessing a 20-nor ent-gibberel-lane skeleton, a carboxyl group on C-6, a lactone function between C-4 and C-10, and a hydroxyl or other functionality at C-3β. Their biosynthesis, as outlined in Figure elsewhere in this chapter, has been discussed in numerous recent reviews.

Synthesis from the common diterpene precursor geranylgeranyl diphosphate (GGPP) involves the action of terpene cyclases, cytochrome P450 monooxygenases (P450s) and 2 oxoglutarate-dependent dioxygenases (2ODDs). In common with other diterpenes, GAs are produced predominantly via the plastid-localised methylerythritol phosphate

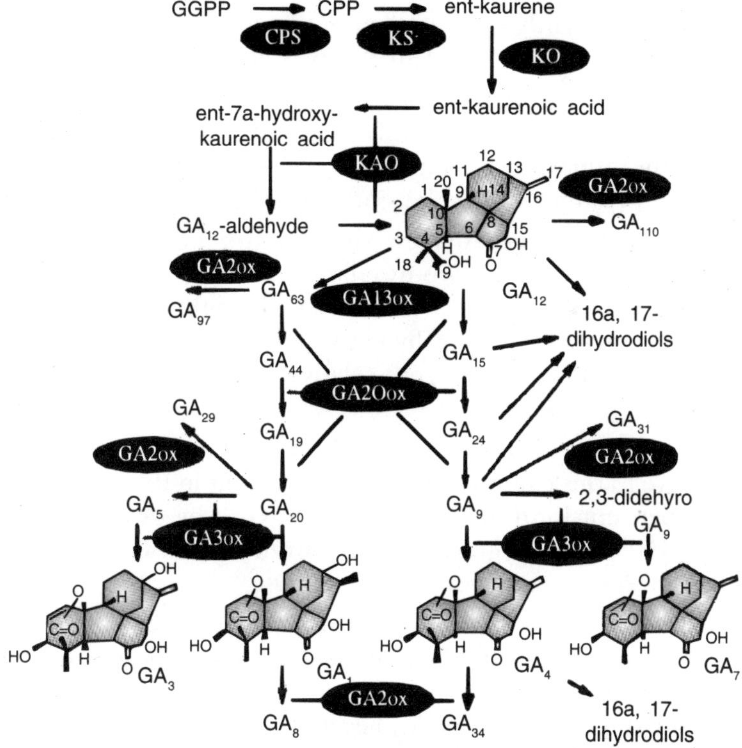

Figure 5.1: Gibberellin biosynthesis and deactivation in higher plants. The scheme illustrates the steps involved in the biosynthesis and deactivation of the bioactive GAs, GA_1, GA_3, GA_4 and GAS. Numbering of the carbon atoms is shown for GA_{12}. The enzymes responsible for catalysing each reaction are indicated by shading. In rice, the conversion of non-13-hydroxylated C_{20} and C_{19}-GAs to GA 16,17-dihydrodiols is catalysed by EUI, a cytochrome P450 monooxygenase (CYP714D1).

(MEP) pathway in vegetative tissues, although there is a small contribution from the cytosolic mevalonic acid (MVA) pathway, presumably because of some movement of isopentenyl diphosphate (IPP) into plastids from the cytosol.

The relative contributions of the MEP and MVA pathways to GA biosynthesis may in fact vary between tissues, depending on the type of plastid present and the permeability of its envelope to IPP. Cyclisation of GGPP to the hydrocarbon intermediate ent-kaurene requires two enzymes, ent-copalyl diphosphate synthase (CPS) and ent-kaurene synthase, which are thought to be located in the plastid.

Surprisingly, it was shown recently that the relatively volatile ent-kaurene is readily released into and taken up from the atmosphere, suggesting facile transport from the plastid, presumably via the endomembrane system.

Although some species, such as the Japanese cedar, *Cryptomeria japonica,* produce large amounts of ent-kaurene that could in theory affect the growth of neighbouring plants, GA concentration is normally regulated late in the biosynthetic pathway so that applied ent-relatively little effect on plant growth.

Nevertheless, ent-kaurene-deficient mutants are extremely sensitive to this compound when it is present in the hea sealed chamber. ent-Kaurene is converted to GA_{12} by two cytochrome P450 monooxygenases, ent-kaurene oxidase (KO) and ent-kaurenoic acid hydroxylase (KAO).

Transient expression of fusions of the enzymes with green fluorescent protein (GFP) indicate that KO is located in the outer membrane of the plastid, while KAO is in the endoplasmic reticulum. GA_{12} lies at a branch in the pathway, being converted by 13-hydroxylation to GA_{53}, and by 20-oxidation to GA_9.

Evidence for both P450 and 2ODD forms of the 13-hydroxylase have been reported but, since no 13-gene has been identified, the nature of this activity is still uncertain. The final reactions of the pathway are catalysed by soluble 2ODDs that are probably present in the cytosol.

GA_{12} and GA_{53} are converted by GA_{20} oxidases (GA20ox) to GA_9 and GA_{20}, respectively, which are further oxidised to bioactive GAs by GA 3-oxidases (GA3ox). The on-13-hydroxylation (from GA_{12}) and 13-hydroxylation (from GA_{53}) pathways run in parallel and it seems likely that their intermediates compete for the GA20ox active site.

The relative amounts of 13-hydroxylated and non-13-hydroxylated GAs, which will depend on the relative strengths of 13-hydroxylase and 20-oxidase activities present, differ between species and between tissues within the same species.

Most species produce major growth active GA in vegetative tissues, although *Arabidopsis* contains more GA_4, and is more sensitive to this GA than to GA_1.

The GA 3-oxidases catalyse the final step in the formation of biologically active GAs. Recombinant GA3ox enzymes *from Arabidopsis* (AtGA3ox1) and pea (PsGA3ox1) were shown to function as strict 3(-hydroxylases, converting GA_9 and GA_{20} to GA_4 and GA_1, respectively, as sole products.

However, some GA 3-oxidases are less regiospecific and oxidise also at C-1 and C-2, resulting, for example, in the formation of GA_5, by desaturation, and then GA_3, by successive oxidation at C-1β and C-3β. In an extreme example of low regiospecificity, a GA3ox from wheat was found to possess 13-hydroxylase activity, which requires that the substrate is turned through 180° at the enzyme active site.

GA Deactivation

Effective regulation of the concentration of the bioactive hormone requires deactivation mechanisms, the best characterised of which is hydroxylation at the C-23 position.

The enzymes responsible for this reaction (GA 2-oxidases) are 2ODDs that fall into three classes on the basis of their derived amino acid sequence: enzymes in the first two classes are specific for C_{19}-GAs, oxidising the active hormones themselves or their non-33-hydroxy-lated precursors, while enzymes of the third class accept only C20-GAs.

One enzyme has been described from spinach that accepts

C_{19}- and C_{20}-GA substrates, although it be first class of GA 2-oxidases. A second deactivation mechanism has been characterised recently in rice.

The *ELONGATED UPPERMOST INTERNODE* gene, a mutant allele of which is used in rice breeding to ensure emergence of the panicle from the flag leaf, was shown to encode a cytochrome P450 that epoxidises the 16, 17-double bond.

The enzyme converts non-13-hydroxylated C_{20}- and C_{19}-GAs to inactive products and may therefore act at several points in the pathway. Although 16, 17-epoxides could not be detected, even when the *EUI* gene was overexpressed, there was accumulation of 16o, 17-dihydrodiols, presumably produced by hydration of the epoxides, either *in planta* or during extraction.

Gibberellin 16, 17-dihydrodiols have been detected in many plants, where they often occur at relatively high concentrations, indicating that epoxidation may be a general deactivation mechanism.

Elongation of the upper internode and an accumulation of GA_4 in the *eui* rice mutants demonstrate this mechanism may serve to control GA concentration in some tissues. Deactivation may also result from GA conjugation, which involve formation of glucosyl ethers and esters.

However, the most abundant glucosides consist of 23-hydroxylated GAs coupled through their 23-hydroxyl group so that their formation cannot have a role in deactivation, although it may serve to sequester GAs in the vacuole.

GENES OF GA BIOSYNTHESIS AND THEIR REGULATION

The availability of complete genome sequences for *Arabidopsis* and rice has enabled the identification of most of the genes involved in GA biosynthesis and deactivation in these species.

However, the list of genes is not complete and genes encoding enzymes with novel functions in GA biosynthesis

Table 5.1: A comparison of GA-metabolic genes in Arabidopsis and rice.

Enzyme	*Arabidopsis*		*Rice*			
	Gene name	*Arabidopsis locus*	*AGI locus identifier*	*Gene name*	*Rice locus*	*Accession number*
ent-Copalyl diphosphate synthase	AtCPS	GA1	At4g02780	OsCPS		AP004872
ent-Kaurene synthase	AtKS	GA2	At1g79460	OsKS		OSJN00255
ent-Kaurene 19-oxidase	AtKO	GA3	At5g25900	OsKO	D35	AP005471
ent-Kaurenoic acid oxidase	AtKAO1		At1g05160	OsKAO		AP000616
	AtKAO2		At2g32440			
GA 20-oxidase	AtGA20ox1	GA5	At4g25420	OsGA20ox1		AC096690
	AtGA20ox2		At5g51810	OsGA20ox2	SD1	AP003561
	AtGA20ox3		At5g07200	OsGA20ox3		AP005840
	AtGA20ox4		At1g60980	OsGA20ox4		AC124836
	AtGA20ox5		At1g44090			
GA 3-oxidase	AtGA3ox1	GA4	At1g15550	OxGA3ox1		AC144738
	AtGA3ox2		At1g80340	OsGA3ox2	D18	AP002523

Table Contd.

or previously unknown classes of the known enzymes are still likely to be discovered.

A common feature is that enzymes catalysing early steps in the pathway are encoded by single or limited numbers of gene 2ODDs are encoded by gene families, the members of which differ in their spatial and temporal patterns of expression.

This is consistent with these later genes being the primary sites of regulation. In *Arabidopsis, CPS, KS* and *KO* are present as single copies, while there are two fully redundant *KAO* genes. Although there are four CPS-like genes in rice, only one, OsCPS1, appears to be involved in GA biosynthesis.

Similarly, mutant studies indicate that only one member from each of the nine-member KS-like and four-member KO-like gene families has a major role in GA production in rice. In contrast to *Arabidopsis,* rice has a single *KAO* gene.

Null mutations in these early genes cause severe pleiotropic phenot-ypic abnormalities, such as extreme stunting, that are characteristic of GA deficiency whereas the effects from loss of a functional 2ODD gene are much less severe, indicating that the paralogues are partially redundant, as a result of overlapping expression patterns or movement of intermediates between tissues.

GA biosynthesis and deactivation are regulated by numerous develo-pmental and environmental factors, much of this regulation acting on the 2ODDs, the activity of which have a major influence on GA content. This is illustrated for the GA 20 oxidase in *Arabidopsis* by work with transgenic plants.

Overexpression of a *GA20ox* gene caused increased GA_4 content, accelerated bolting and longer stems, whereas increasing expression of *CPS* and in higher amounts of ent-kaurene and GA_{12}, but had no effect on the levels of bioactive GAs or the phenotype.

Developmental Regulation

Expression of *CPS,* which encodes the enzyme that catalyses the first committed step in GA biosynthesis and might be expected to control the flux into the pathway, shows strong developmental regulation.

On the basis of experiments with a promoter–GUS reporter gene in *Arabidopsis, CPS* was shown to be expressed most strongly in growing organs or in vascular tissues, consistent with the presence of the enzyme in immature plastids rather than chloroplasts.

Positive regulation within these tissues required the presence of the second intron and the promoter region from -1391 to -997 upstream of the translation initiation site. The expression of *CPS* in vascular tissues is consistent with the findings of Ross *et al.* in 2003 from work with pea seedlings that mature tissues are capable of *de novo* GA biosynthesis.

They suggest that high rates of GA 2-oxidation in such tissues accounts for their low concentrations of biologically active GAs compared with developing tissues. The identification of transcription factors that interact with the promoters of GA-biosynthetic genes is providing clues to the molecular mechanisms by which the spatial and temporal expression of these genes is regulated.

The most extensively studied factors are the KNOTTED1-like homoeobox (KNOX) proteins, which are homoeodomain transcription factors that are implicated in the establishment of meristem identity as well as in determining leaf morphology.

KNOX proteins repress GA biosynthesis by suppressing GA 20-oxidase gene expression. The tobacco KNOX protein NTH15 was shown to bind to *cis* elements within the promoter and first intron of a tobacco *GA20ox* gene, with stronger binding to the intron sequence.

KNOX proteins interact with a second class of homoeodomain proteins, the BEL 1 like proteins, and the two proteins appear to function as heterodimers. Both types of transcription factors suppressed expression of a *GA20ox* gene in potato, while the heterodimer was most effective and bound most strongly to the promoter.

In this case, only the BEL protein bound to the intron.

KNOX genes are expressed in the meristem in vegetative apices of tobacco and *Arabidopsis,* such that *GA20ox* expression is excluded from this region but occurs in the leaf primordia at the flanks of the meristem and in the sub-apical regio *et al.,* 2001a.

In tomato and potato *KNOX* genes are also expressed in the leaf primordia, where they function in the establishment of leaf morphology. KNOX has also been shown to enhance expression of the *Arabidopsis* genes *GA2ox2* and *GA2ox4,* which, on the basis of GUS expression in reporter lines, is located at the base of the meristem and may offer protection from the influx of GAs from surrounding leaves.

Since KNOX proteins also stimulate cytokinin biosynthesis by promoting expression of *IPT* genes, these proteins function by establishing a favourable hormone balance, high cytokinin and low GA, for maintainidentity. The homoeotic gene *AGAMOUS (AG),* which is activated in the meristem after flower induction, induces expression of AtGA3ox1.

This function may serve to increase GA production within the meristem and thereby promote cell differentiation and initiate production of floral organs. The LEC3 and FUS3 transcription factors function to promote embryogenesis in *Arabidopsis.* Both factors were shown to suppress expression of *AtGA3ox2* and thereby reduce GA biosynthesis during early embryo development.

FUS3 bound directly to two RY elements in the promoter of *AtGA3ox2.* Consistent with early embryogenesis requiring a low GA regime, the MADS domain protein Alike 15 (AGL15), which accumulates during embryo development, enhanced expression of a gene, *AtGA2ox6,* involved in GA deactivation.

In this case too it was possible to identify target sites for AGL15 on the *AtGA2ox6* promoter. A bZIP transcription factor from tobacco, known as RSG (repression of shoot growth) was shown to bind and activate the promoter of the *Arabidopsisent-kaurene* oxidase *(KO)* gene.

A dominant negative form of RSG, which retains DNA

binding but no longer activates expression, inhibited GA biosynthesis and stem extension in tobacco consistent with the function of RSG in promoting GA production.

In addition, the dominant negative RSG appeared to interfere with feedback regulation of a *GA20ox* gene so may also bind to the promoter of this gene (Ishida *et al.,* 2004). Gibberellin activity leads to exclusion of RSG from the nucleus via phosphorylation-mediated binding to a 14-3-3 protein that sequesters it in the cytoplasm.

This would provide a mechanism for feedback regulation of *GA20ox* expression, although dominant negative RSG had no effect on the feedback regulation of a *GA3ox* gene and, furthermore, there is no evidence that *KO* is feedback regulated. The physiological function of RSG is still noRSG is still not clear.

Hormonal Regulation

Gibberellin homoeostasis is maintained by regulation of its own metabolism via the DELLA protein-dependent signaling pathway, as discussed elsewhere in this chapter. There is evidence that other plant hormones also modify GA metabolism, allowing integration between different hormone signaling pathways.

The best characterised interaction is with auxin, the action of which results in increased GA concentrations. In some systems, such as pod set and internode elongation in pea, tissue elongation in response to auxin is dependent on GA, which acts as a secondary messenger for the long-distance signal provided by auxin.

Regulation of GA biosynthesis in the pod is specific for 4-chloro-IAA, which originates from the seed and enhances expression of *PsGA20ox1* and *PsGA3ox1* in the pod, while in the stem, IAA from the shoot apex induces PsGA3ox1 expression and suppresses expression of *PsGA2ox1*.

Evidence for auxin regulation of GA biosynthesis in other species suggests that this is a general mechanism, although the targets may vary between species.

On the basis of GA measurements and metabolism experiments it was shown that auxin from the developing barley inflorescence regulated stem elongation by promoting GA 3-oxidation and suppressing 2-oxidation in internodes and nodes, while in tobacco internodes GA 20-oxidase is the major target for auxin from the shoot apex.

In tobacco, auxin also suppresses GA deactivation by 2-oxidation. Evidence for regulation of GA metabolism by other hormones is less convincing.

Although Bouquin *et al.* (2001) found that *AtGA20ox1* expression was increased by application of epibrassinolide to an *Arabidopsis* brassinosteroid-deficient mutant, Jager *et al.* (2005) could find no evidence that brassinosteroids function through altering GA metabolism in pea.

Environmental Regulation

An important function of GAs is to act as intermediaries between environmental signals and resulting changes in growth and developmental patterns.

The induction of developmental processes, such as seed germination, de-etiolation or flower formation in response to light, photoperiod or cold have been shown to involve, at least in part, changes in GA concentration due to effects of the environmental cues on GA biosynthesis and deactivation.

Stimulation of seed germination in lettuce and *Arabidopsis* by red light is associated with increased synthesis of bioactive GAs in the embryo. As well as stimulating the elongation of the radicle and hypocotyl, GA induces the synthesis of enzymes that digest the endosperm and allow the radicle to emerge.

In both species, red light induces expression of *GA3ox* genes, LsGA3ox1 in lettuce and At*GA3ox1* and *AtGA3ox2* in *Arabidopsis.* The induction is reversed by irradiation with far-red (FR) light, indicating the involvement of phytochromes in this process. Although the kinetics of induction of the two *Arabidopsis* genes is similar, their subsequent developmental patterns of expression differ markedly: the increase in *AtGA3ox1* expression is transient, although expression is restored after about 36 h and remains high throughout seedling development, while *AtGA3ox2* expression is associated only with germination, remaining high for about 36 h and then dropping to low levels.

Expression of *AtGA3ox1,* but not that of *AtGA3ox2,* is also enhanced by exposure of imbibed *Arabidopsis* seeds to low temperatures. Stimulation of germination by this treatment, a process known as stratification, is dependent on the presence of *AtGA3ox1,* clearly demonstrating the involvement of GAs in this process.

Recently it was shown tion of *GA3ox* gene expression by light and temperature in *Arabidopsis* seed is mediated by the basic helix–loop–helix transcription factor SPATULA (SPT) in concert with the related protein PIL5.

In contrast to the stimulatory effect of red light on *GA3ox* expression in photoblastic seeds, exposure of dark-grown pea seedlings to red light results in a rapid reduction in PsGA3ox1 expression, accompanied by an increase in PsGA2*ox2* expression.

About 4 h after exposure to light, PsGA3ox1 and *PsGA2ox2* transcripts in the de-etiolating pea shoots return to initial values and there is an increase in *PsGA20ox1* expression, presumably as a response to the reduced GA concentration.

Since GA action suppresses many facets of photomorphogensis reducing GA content is necessary for full de-etiolation. The photoreceptor for suppression of PsGA3ox1 expression in pea is PHYA and possibly also a blue light receptor, whereas photostable phytochromes are involved in *GA3ox* induction in seeds.

A blue light receptor has also been invoked for induction of *GA20ox* expression by light in potato. Higher levels of expression of the *StGA20ox1* gene occur in the light than in the dark.

Lines with reduced PHYB content contained higher levels of *StGA20ox1* transcript suggesting that this receptor may also regulate expression of the gene, although this regulation did not apparently account for the light–dark difference.

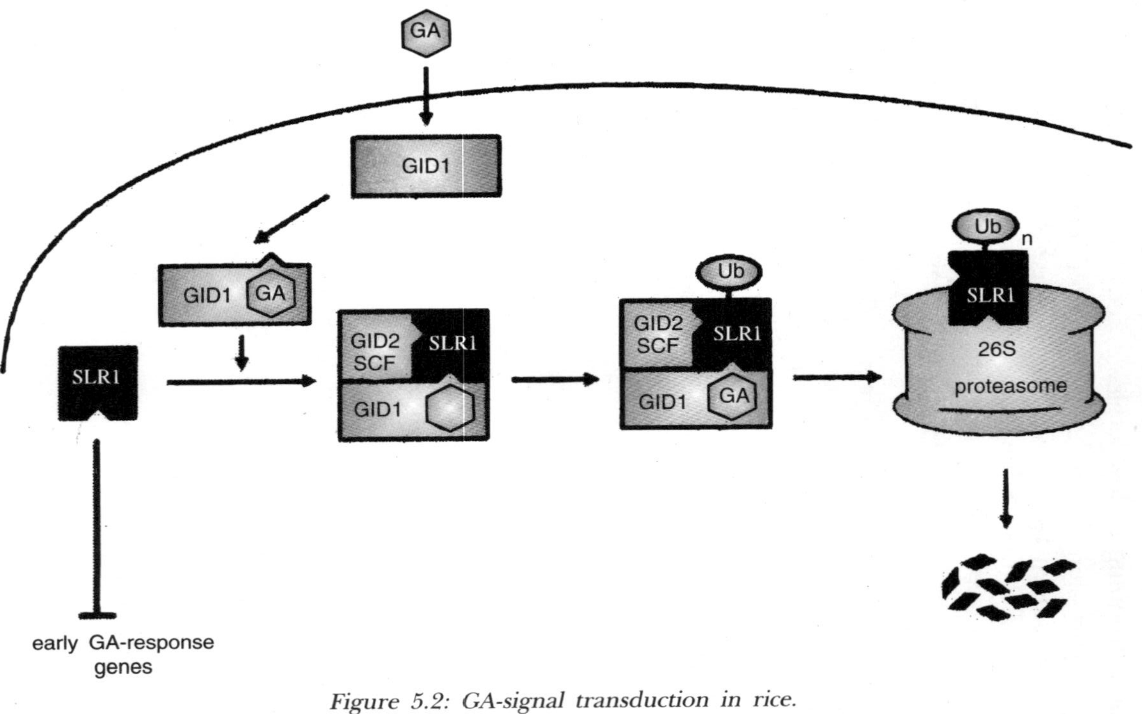

Figure 5.2: GA-signal transduction in rice.

Although tuber formation in potatoes is controlled by photoperiod and is inhibited by GA, the involvement of the light regulation of GA biosynthesis in this process is not clear since there was no difference in *GA20ox* expression or of GA content between plants grown in long (LD) and short days (SD). However, there are several reports of higher expression of *GA20ox* genes in LD compared to SD in rosette species.

Flowering in such species is sensitive to photoperiod and is accompanied by stem extension (bolting), a process that requires GA activity. In spinach, which has an absolute LD requirement for flowering, transfer of plants from SD to LD resulted in increased concentrations of C_{19}-GAs associated with higher levels of expression of *SoGA20ox1,* particularly in petioles and leaf tips.

Expression of a GA 2-oxidase gene, SoGA2ox1 was reduced by LD in young leaves and tips, but increased in petioles, perhaps due to feed forward regulation, so it may not be under photoperiod control in this tissue.

Indeed, the increased expression of *SoGA20ox1* in petioles may be due to light induction rather than circadian regulation since prolonged exposure to light caused high levels of expression regardless of the previous photoperiod.

Petiole elongation in *Arabidopsis* is regulated by two *GA20ox* genes, expression of one of these, *AtGA2ox2,* is strongly induced by FR-rich light via the mediation of PHYB, but does not show diurnal oscillation.

Expression of the second gene *AtGA20ox1* was less strongly increased by exposure to FR, and showed diurnal oscillation so may thus be under circadian regulation. Blazquez *et al.* (2002) showed also that *AtGA20ox1* expression was controlled [b]*dian* clock from work with the circadian mutant tocl.

However, while *AtGA20ox1* expression is indeed higher in LD, the resulting increase in GA production may be related more to the stem extension that accompanies flowering than to the induction of flowering itself.

Balzquez *et al.* concluded that circadian regulation of GA

Table 5.2: A comparison of GA-signaling genes in Arabidopsis and rice.

Signaling	Protein type and function	GA-response Arabidopsis	Rice			
component		regulator	Gene name	AGI locus identifier	Gene name	Accession number
GID1*	HSL-related protein. Soluble GA receptor	Positive			GIDI	AB211399
DELLA	GRAS protein. Putative transcriptional regulator	Negative	RGA	At2g01570	SLRI	AB030956
					GAI	At1g14920
					RGL1	At1g66350
					RGL2	At3g03450
					RGL3	At5g17490
SLY1/GID2	F-box protein. Component of an SCF Ub E3 ligase involved in targeting DELLA proteins for degradation	Positive	SLY1 SNE	At2g24210 At5g48170	GID2	AB100246
SPY	O-G1cNAc transferase	Negative	SPY	At3g11540		
D1/GPA1	Heterotrimeric G-protein a subunit	Positive	GPAI	At2g26300	DI	D38232

biosynthesis and flowering time were independent. *Gibberellins* are, however, essential for flowering under non-inductive conditions.

The grass *Lolium perenne* requires both *vernalisation* and LD for flowering, with the LD requirement, but not that for vernalisation, replaceable by application of GA.

Exposure to LD caused upregulation of the 20-oxidase gene *LpGA20ox1* and increased GA signaling consistent with the photoperiod signal acting through GA in this case.

The involvement of GAs in flower induction in the related species *Lolium temulentum* is discussed elsewhere in this book. Plants have the ability to discriminate between day and night temperatures, a process known as thermoperiodism.

Stem growth is affected by diurnal temperature differences, promoted by positive (higher in the day) and inhibited by negative (higher in the night) differential temperatures, in a GA-regulated process.

It has been demonstrated in pea that the low growth rate differential temperatures was associated with increased expression of the *PsGA2ox2* gene, suggesting a higher rate of GA deactivation.

Plants also reduce their growth in response to stress and there is a negative correlation between GA content and stress tolerance. Evidence is now emerging that stress results in modified GA biosynthesis.

Overexpression of *DDF1,* which encodes an AP2-like transcription factor that is closely related to the DREB (Dehydration Responsive Element Binding protein) factors involved in stress sponses, caused reduced GA content and dwarfism in Arabidopsis.

Expression of DDF1 was strongly induced by salt stress while plants overexpressing this gene had increased stress tolerance.

Based on the effects of DDF1-expression on GA content it was suggested that GA 20-oxidase was the target for DDF1, but this needs to be confirmed.

THE GIBBERELLIN SIGNAL TRANSDUCTION PATHWAY

In recent years there have been impressive advances in our understanding of how the GA-signal is transduced, subsequently leading to changes in GA-responsive growth and development. Studies in this field have in particular emphasised the played by the DELLA proteins, which function as repressors of GA-mediated responses.

However, until recently, the components responsible for perceiving bioactive GAs had remained elusive. An exciting recent study by Ueguchi-Tanaka *et al.* (2005) has now resulted in the identification of a soluble GA receptor from rice.

The current model of GA-signal transduction, based on components identified in rice, is outlined in Figure anywhere else in this chapter. The evidence to support this model is discussed below. Genes encoding signaling components, identified in *Arabidopsis* and rice, are listed in Table elsewhere in this chapter.

The Gibberellin Receptor

Biochemical studies have suggested the presence of both soluble cytoplasmic and plasma membrane-localised GA receptors in plants, but the necessary could not be identified. The identification and characteri-sation of rice *GA-insensitive dwarf (gid)* mutants has proved instrumental in elucidating the GA-signaling cascade.

The gid1 mutants display a severe GA-insensitive dwarf phenotype, including defects in feedback regulation of GA biosynthesis that result in the accumulation of much higher levels of bioactive GAs than wild-type plants.

The gid1 mutations are recessive, indicating that GI*DI* encodes a positive regulator of GA signaling. This is further supported by the demonstration that transgenic plants overexpressing GID1 exhibit a GA-hypersensitive phenotype.

The GID1 gene was isolated by positional cloning and demonstrate a polypeptide of 354 amino acids with significant homology with members of the Hormone Sensitive Lipase (HSL) family.

It appears unlikely that GID1 possesses HSL activity because a histidine residue, essential for HSL activity is replaced by a valine, and indeed recombinant GID 1 lacked HSL activity *in vitro.* Biochemical and genetic evidence indicates strongly that GID1 functions as a GA receptor.

Thus, recombinant GID1 bound a radiolabelled, bioactive GA analogue, 16,17-dihydro[$^{33}H_4$]GA_4, with both high affinity and rapid-binding kinetics. This binding was competed more effectively by bioactive GAs than by inactive compounds.

Furthermore, the three gid1 loss-of-function alleles, *gid1-1, -2 and -3* produce mutant proteins that are no longer capable of binding GAs. Localisation studies suggest that GID1 exists as a predominantly soluble nuclear protein and is thus different from the proposed plasma membrane receptors involved in the induction of o-amylase expression in cereal aleurone cells.

It is possible that there are additional membrane localised GA receptors, although the observation that gid1 mutants are to GA induction of o-amylase expression does not support their existence in rice. Further insights will be provided by the characterisation of GID1 orthologues in other cereals.

DELLA Proteins Act as Repressors of GA Signaling

The use of molecular genetic approaches in monocots and dicots has demonstrated the central role of the DELLA transcriptional regulators in GA-signal transduction.

The DELLA proteins, so-called after a conserved N-terminal domain, act as repressors of the GA-signal transduction cascade, as illustrated by the promotion of GA-independent growth in DELLA loss-of-function mutations.

In contrast, DELLA gain-of-function mutations, which are semi-dominant, produce GA-insensitive dwarf plants due to the formation of constitutively active repressors that are unresponsive to the GA-signal.

The DELLA proteins form a sub-group of the GRAS

(named after the GAI, RGA and SCR members) family of transcriptional regulators. Members of the GRAS protein family have a highly conserved C-terminal domain, which appears to have a functional role.

In the case of DELLA proteins, this is demonstrated by the observations that missense mutations in the GRAS (C-terminal) domain often result in loss-of-function.

The mode of action of GRAS proteins is still unclear, although the demonstration that they are predominantly nuclear localised supports their role as transcriptional regulators, despite not containing a recognisable DNA-binding domain.

The N-terminal domain of DELLA proteins is unique to this sub-group of the GRAS family and defines their role in GA signaling. It contains two highly conserved motifs, which have been designated domains 1 and 2.

In most cases, DELLA gain-of-function mutations result in truncations, deletions or substitutions within these domains, which are, therefore, assumed to have an important regulatory role in GA signaling.

Recent studies have highlighted the conserved role of DELLA proteins in GA signaling. However, a striking difference between monocots and dicots that has become apparent from studies in rice and *Arabidopsis* is the level of redundancy in dicots.

Genome sequencing projects have confirmed that there are five DELLA genes *(GAI, RGA, RGL1, RGL2* and *RGL3)* in *Arabidopsis* whereas rice contains only one, SLR1. Characterisation of the slr1 null alleles indicates that SLR1 represses all GA responses.

Although SLR1 is considered to be the only DELLA gene responsible for mediating GA signaling in rice, searche genome databases have identified two highly homologous sequences, designated *SLR1-like-1* and *-2* (SLRL1 and *-2;* Itoh *et al.,* 2005b).

The C-terminal GRAS domains of SLRL1 and -2 display strong sequence similarities with that of SLRI; however, neither contain the conserved N-terminal DELLA domain. Itoh *et al.* (2005a & b) provide some evidence that SLRL1 may function as a negative regulator of GA signaling in rice.

However, it is clear that further studies, including reverse genetics approaches, are necessary to confirm such a role. The five DELLA *(RGL)* genes in *Arabidopsis* display both overlapping and independent roles in repressing tissue-specific aspects of GA response.

The physiological roles of individual *RGL* genes has been studied by observing the effects of *RGL* null alleles in suppressing the growth defects in the GA-deficient mutant, *gal -3*. GAI and RGA are the predominant DELLAs regulating vegetative development and floral initiation, while RGA, RGL1 and RGL2 are responsible for modulating floral development.

Results on the identity of the DELLA proteins involved in germination are conflicting, although RLG2 appears to have a major role. Neverthe-less, high levels of *RGA, GAI* and *RGL3* transcripts are present in germinating seeds so it is conceivable that RGA, GAI and RGL3 participate in different developmentally or environmentally regulated aspects of seed germination.

Supporting evidence for this hypothesis is provided by a recent study demonstrating that RGL2, RGA and GAI are required to repress germination in the dark. More information on the cellular localisation of the RGL proteins should provide further clues to the developmental processes that they control.

GAs Promote Rapid Degradation of DELLA Proteins

A significant breakthrough in understanding the function of DELLA proteins in GA signaling was the observations that GA promotes their degradation.

The levels of a GFP:RGA fusion protein were rapidly reduced in the roots of transgenic *Arabidopsis* plants after treatment with bioactive GA, while application of the GA-biosynthesis inhibitor, paclobutrazol, increased GFP:RGA levels.

The endogenous RGA protein showed a similar response

to GA treatment, which was not caused by a reduction in *RGA* transcripts. In fact, *RGA* transcript levels are slightly elevated by GA treatment.

The GA-induced destabilisation of DELLA proteins is conserved across plant species and has been demonstrated, for example, in rice and barley. Furthermore, in Arabidopsis, a similar response is observed for the RGA homologues GAI and RGL2.

The kinetics of GA-induced DELLA protein degradation is extremely rapid, with reduction in the levels of SLN1 and RGA being observed in barley and *Arabidopsis,* respectively, within 10min of GA treatment.

Thus the role of GA is to target DELLA proteins for degradation and thereby relieve their repression of growth.

Gain-of-function mutations in DELLA genes have provided some important insights into the functional domains that are responsible for mediating GA-induced degradation.

The best characterised example being the *Arabidopsis gai-1* mutation, which confers a GA-insensitive dwarf phenotype. This mutation results in a 17-amino-acid deletion from domain 1, also known as the DELLA domain, producing a constitutively active repressor of GA signaling that is not inactivated by GA. Overexpression of genes containing analogous DELLA mutations in *RGA* (rga-Δ17) and RGL1 (rgl1Δ17) resulted in GA-insensitive dwarf plants similar to *gai-1*.

Moreover, the rga-Δ17 protein was not degraded in response to GA treatment, confirming the importance of the DELLA domain in GA-induced degradation. In rice, a more detailed functional domain analysis of SLR1 also highlighted the importance of domain 1 as well as that of the adjacent conserved domain 2 in this process.

Based on these studies, it was originally proposed that the N-terminal domain of DELLA proteins is the domain responsible for regulating GA-induced degradation, whereas the C-terminal GRAS domain is the functional domain.

Recent studies now suggest that the GRAS domain may

also play a regulatory role. A semi-dominant GA-insensitive dwarf mutant of *Brassica rapa* (Brrga1-d) with an amino acid substitution in the GRAS domain of the DELLA protein, BrRGA1, accumulated the protein to significantly higher levels than in the wild-type, and the mutant protein was insensitive to GA-induced degradation.

Furthermore, it has now been shown that loss-of-function mutations in the GRAS domain of DELLA genes also prevent GA-induced degradation of the mutant proteins. Thus, there appears to be no clearly defined domain within the DELLA proteins that regulates GA-induced degradation and it is conceivable that these domains have different roles in the degradation process.

SCF$^{SLY/GID}$-mediated degradation of DELLA proteins

Genetic screens for recessive GA-insensitive dwarf mutants in Arabidop*sis* and rice have led to the discovery of GA-signaling components that directly regulate DELLA protein stability in response to the GA-signal.

Plants that are homozygous for the *Arabidopsis* sleepy1 (sly) or rice *GA-insensitive dwarf 2 (gid2)* alleles contain highly elevated levels of DELLA proteins and are unresponsive to GA. Furthermore, genetic analyses demonstrate that DELLA loss-of function mutations are epistatic to sly1/gid2. The SLY1 and *GID2* genes have now been cloned and shown to encode F-box proteins.

The *Arabidopsis* genome contains *a* SLY1 orthologue, designated *SNEEZY (SNE),* which has a related function since it is capable of complementing the sly mutant phenotype. The identification of loss-of-function mutations should help to address such a role for SNE.

Studies in yeast have demonstrated that F-box proteins are a core component of SCF E3 ubitiquitin (Ub) ligases, which are multi-subunit complexes that recognise and poly-ubiquitinate target proteins destined for degradation by the 26S proteasome.

The four main protein subunits of SCF E3 Ub ligases are the Skp1, cullin/Cdc53, Rbx1/Hrt1/Roc1 and F-box components. The F-box subunit provides the substrate specificity of the SCF E3 Ub ligase and is anchored to the Skp1-like subunit of the complex through an N-terminal F-box domain.

The C-termini of F-box proteins are usually required for binding and targeting the substrate for ubiquitination, and often contain a conserved protein-protein interaction domain for this purpose.

In many cases, recognition by the F-box protein requires the target protein to be post-translationally modified, most commonly by phosphorylation, although alternative forms of optional modification have also been shown to promote this association.

The identity of SLY1 and GID2 as F-box proteins, together with the accumulation and GA insensitivity of DELLA proteins in the sly1/gid2 mutants, is consistent with a role in directly regulating GA-induced DELLA degradation as part of a SCF E3 Ub ligase complex. It has recently been confirmed that SLY1 and GID2 are components of the respective SCF^{SLY1} and SCF^{GID2} complexes.

For example, in Arabidopsis, comprehensive yeast two hybrid assays were used to demonstrate that, of the 21 SKP1 homologues, ASK1, ASK2, ASK3, ASK4, ASK11 and ASK13 interacted with both SLY1 and SNE. It was subsequently confirmed *in planta* using co-immunoprecip-itation that SLY 1 interacts with both the ASK2 and AtCUL1 components of the SCF E3 Ub ligase.

In rice, similar experiments have been used to confirm an interaction *in planta* between GID2 and the SCF components OsSkp15 and OsCUL1. Direct interaction between SLY1 and the Arabidopsis DELLA proteins RGA, GAI, RGL1 and RGL3 were demonstrated by yeast two-hybrid assays.

Furthermore, a recombinant glutathione S-transferase (GST) SLY1 fusion protein was capable of interacting with endogenous RGA as well as *in* vitro-translated GAI and RGA protein in pull-down assays.

Similar observations were obtained in rice, when it was

demonstrated that recombinant GID2 interacts with SLR1 isolated from *gid2* plants. Interestingly, in Arabidopsis, *a* SLY1 gain-of-function mutation, sly1-d (formerly *gar2-1),* results in increased GA signaling by reducing the levels of the DELLA protein in plants.

This appears to be caused by an enhanced interaction between sly1-d and the DELLA proteins. An between the DELLA proteins and SLY1/GID2 has yet to be demonstrated *in planta,* although it has been shown that SLY1/GID2 are nuclear localised, consistent with a role in GA-mediated DELLA degradation.

In order to investigate how GA promotes recognition of DELLA proteins by the F-box subunit of the $_{SCF}$SLY1/GID2 E3 Ub ligase, several groups have focused on the potential role of DELLA phosphorylation in this process.

In rice, there was originally strong evidence that phosphorylation of SLR1 may promote its interaction with GID2, because SLR1 exists in the *gid2* background as both phosphorylated and non-phosphorylated forms, with only the phosphorylated form interacting with recombinant GID2 in pull-down assays.

However, the same group have shown recently that, GA-induced the accumulation of both phosphorylated and non-phosphorylated forms of SLR1 in *gid2* with similar kinetics.

Furthermore, they showed that in wild-type cells treated with GA, both forms of SLR1 proteins were degraded with a similar half-life, and, in contrast to their previous results, both phosphorylated and non-phosphorylated forms of SLR1 interacted with GID2 in pull-down assays.

Thus, it appears likely that the phosphorylation status of DELLA proteins is not GA responsive and does not target their degradation, at least in rice. This area clearly requires further study.

By analogy with studies of SCF E3 Ub ligase-mediated degradation in yeast and mammalian cells, it is expected that the interaction of DELLA proteins with the SCFSLY/GID2 complexes would result in ubiquitination and subsequent degradation by the 26S proteasome. This appears to be the case, since GA treatment results in the accumulation of ubiquitinated forms of SLR1 in rice. Furthermore, proteasome-specific protease inhibitors block the GA-induced degradation of some DELLA proteins.

The Role of GID1 in DELLA Degradation

The demonstration that GID1 is involved in the perception of bioactive GAs raises the question of its role in GA-induced degradation of SLR1. Ueguchi-Tanaka *et al.* (2005) provided direct evidence for such a role using both genetic and biochemical approaches.

Firstly, they show that the gid1/slr1 double mutant exhibits the *sir]* phenotype indicating that SLR1 is epistatic to GID1, and secondly, SLR1 protein levels are elevated in gid1 compared to wild-type plants and are insensitive to GA induced degradation.

Furthermore, they demonstrated in yeast two-hybrid assays that GID1 interacts with SLR1 in a GA-dependent manner. Although it is necessary to confirm this interaction *in planta,* this finding provides an important link in the GA-signaling cascade.

The next major step will be to understand whether this interaction plays a role in the recognition of SLR1 by the SCF^{GID2} Ub E3 ligase. It is tempting to speculate that the N-terminal regulatory domain of the DELLA proteins may be necessary for the interaction between SLR1 and GID1, in which case the gain-of-function mutations in domains 1 and 2 of the DELLA proteins may prevent this interaction and render the proteins resistant to GA-induced degradation. Studies aimed at identifying the SLR1 domain responsible for interacting with GID1 should address this possibility.

Additional GA-Signaling Components

The previous sections covering GA signaling describe a relatively simple signal transduction cascade composed of a few core components. It is clear from additional genetic and biochemical studies that this cascade is far more complex and involves other signaling components. In the following sections the potential roles of several of the better characterised components will be discussed briefly.

A role for O-linked N-acetylglucosamine transferases in GA signaling

SPINDLY (SPY) was the first GA-signaling gene to be cloned from *Arabidopsis.* The presence of the spy mutations will partially suppress all of the developmental defects caused by a block in GA biosynthesis, without increasing bioactive GA levels.

The recessive nature of the spy mutations indicates that *SPY* functions as a negative regulator of GA response. Although these studies have illustrated the of SPY in GA signaling, its role currently remains unclear.

The SPY protein has homology with animal O-linked N-acetylgluco-samine (O-GlcNAc) transferases (OGTs), which catalyse the transfer of N-acetylglucosamine to serine or threonine residues of target proteins.

This form of post-translational modification is a dynamic process that has a regulatory role akin to phosphorylation. Although the function of OGTs is less well understood in plants than in animals, *in vitro* assays suggest that SPY has OGT activity, indicating that such activity may have a role in regulating plant development.

In *Arabidopsis, SECRET AGENT (SEC)* encodes a second OGT with significant homology to SPY. It is not clear whether SEC is involved in GA signaling because *sec* mutants do not display any obvious developmental defects.

However, loss of both SPY and SEC activities in the spy/sec double mutant results in embryo abortion, indicating that OGT activity is necessary for embryogenesis.

This observation, together with the demonstration that spy mutants display developmental defects not observed in GA response mutants, indicate that OGTs are also involved in other aspects of plant growth and development.

It seems likely that SPY modulates GA signaling by

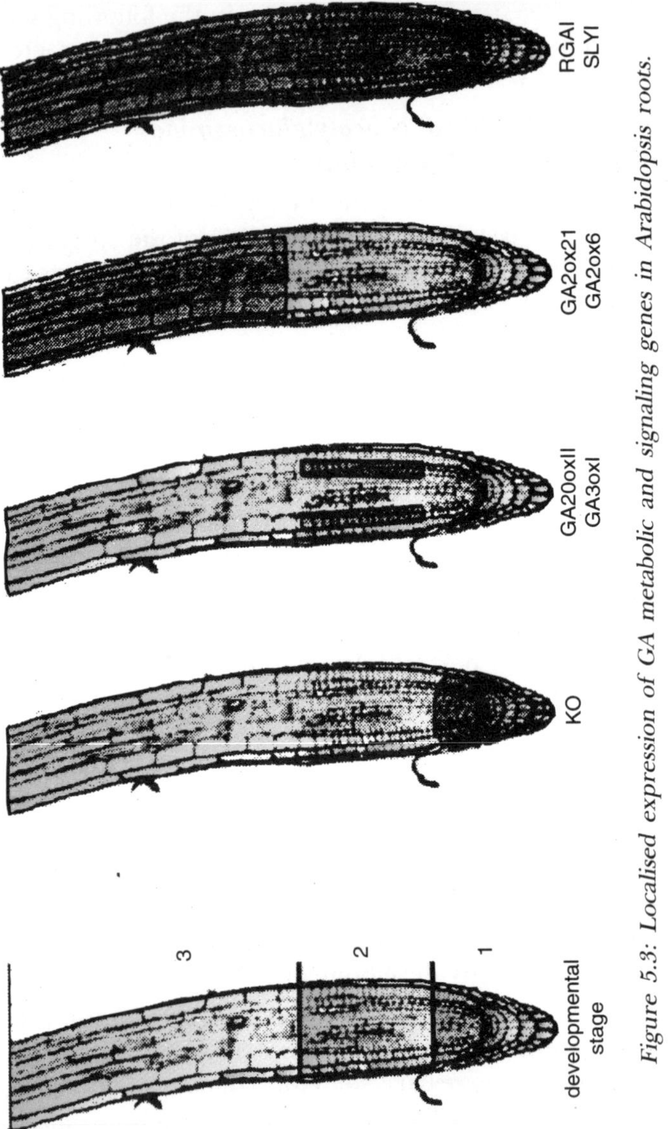

Figure 5.3: Localised expression of GA metabolic and signaling genes in Arabidopsis roots.

catalysing the O-GlcNAc modification of components of GA-response pathway. Considering the importance of DELLA proteins in this pathway, they are obvious candidates as SPY target proteins.

It is conceivable that O-GlcNAc modification could regulate either the stability or activity of DELLA proteins. Biochemical studies aimed at investigating the O-GlcNAc status of DELLA proteins will be necessary to test this hypothesis.

DWARF1 and PHOR1, possible positive regulators of GA signaling

Biochemical and genetic evidence indicating that the Go subunits of heterotrimeric G proteins acts as a positive regulator of GA response has prompted an the potential role of G proteins in GA signaling.

Such a role is most apparent in rice, for which the d1 mutant, which exhibits a GA-insensitive dwarf phenotype, has a defective Go protein.

By analogy with heterotrimeric G proteins in mammalian systems, it is possible that a G protein coupled receptor acts as a membrane-bound GA receptor and transduces the signal through its interaction with the Go.

However, there are now several lines of evidence which argue against this model: firstly, the identification of GID1 as a soluble GA receptor that mediates and is required for all GA responses in rice is not clearly compatible with the heterotrimeric G protein model.

Secondly, in rice and *Arabidopsis* a single gene encodes the Go subunit, but loss-of-function mutations in these genes result in reduced GA responsiveness rather than a complete loss.

Thirdly, Go knock-out mutants also demonstrate defects in several additional signaling pathways that are not commonly observed in well-characterised GA-response mutants.

Therefore, it is currently not clear whether the role of the Ga proteins is to regulate downstream GA responses directly or to modify sensitivity to the hormone.

The identification and characterisation of downstream targets of the Ga subunits should provide further insights into their roles. The photoperiodic control of tuberisation in *Solanum tuberosum* (potato) is mediated, in part, by GAs, which inhibit tuberisation.

A study by Amador *et al. (2001b)* aimed at understanding the photoperiodic induction of tuberisation resulted in the identification of *PHOR1 (PHOtoperiod-Responsive 1),* which encodes an arm repeat protein that may functions as a positive regulator of GA signaling.

Transgenic potato plants with reduced levels of PHOR1 are semid-warf and have reduced GA responses. Gibberellins promoted the relocalisation of a PHOR1–GFP fusion protein from the cytoplasm to the nucleus, in transiently transformed tobacco BY2 cells.

The PHOR1 protein contains a U-Box (UFD2-homology) domain, which is common to a class of E3 ubiquitin ligases, raising the possibility that it regulates GA signaling by promoting the degradation of target proteins through the 26S proteasome.

In *Arabidopsis, the* genes (HIM1, 2 and 3) that share substantial homology to PHOR1. Characterisation of these should provide important clues to the role of PHOR1-related genes in GA signaling.

DOWNSTREAM TRANSCRIPTIONAL EVENTS INDUCED BY GAS

The identification of the genes that are the final targets of the GA-signaling pathway is clearly essential for understanding GA function. Studies of the GA-induced secretion of a-amylase and other hydrolytic enzymes from cereal aleurone cells have been extremely important in understanding how GA regulates gene transcription.

The wealth of information provided by the aleurone system is impossible to cover comprehensively here and the reader is referred to recent excellent reviews of the subject. Much of the recent advances in this field have focused on the involvement of GAMYB transcription factors and this is described in the following section.

Although stimulation of stem extension is one of the classical functions of GAs, this process has been less well studied than the cereal aleurone in terms of the gene targets. Gibberellins promote stem extension by stimulating cell elongation and/or cell division.

There are reports suggesting that GA-induced cell elongation is mediated, in part, through the action of xyloglucan endotransglycosylase/hydrolases (XETs) and expansins, which enable loosening of the cell wall.

Transcript analysis demonstrating GA-induced upregulation of expansin and XET genes has been described for several plants, including *Arabidopsis* and rice. In deepwater rice, which undergoes rapid stem elongation following submergence, GA promotes the expression of *OsEXP4* in internodes within 30 min of treatment, indicating that this is an early GA response gene.

Interestingly, promoter analysis has identified the presence of GA Response Elements (GARE) in some of the rice expansin genes. It will be interesting to see whether the mechanisms of GA-induced expression of *OsEXP4* are similar to those regulating a-amylase.

In addition to promoting cell expansion, the submergence of deepwater rice promotes stem elongation through an increase in cell division in the intercalary meristem.

This cell division activity is induced by GA at the G1 to S phase transition. Further more, GA regulates G2/M phase progression by inducing the expression of genes encoding cyclin-dependent protein kinases, including cycA1;1 and cdc2Os-3.

The availability of DNA microarrays has provided an important tool to dissect the transcriptional changes that promote GA-responsive growth. The potential of this approach has recently been highlighted by the studies of Ogawa *et al.* (2003), who used gene profiling on Affymetrix arrays to investigate the action of GAs in *Arabidopsis* seed germination.

Treatment of ga1-3 seeds with GA for 12 h resulted in

230 GA-upregulated and 127 GA-downregulated genes, with a greater than four fold change in expression. In support of their role in GA-induced germination, the expression profiles of most of these genes were found to change in a similar fashion during the germination of wild-type seeds. Somewhat surprisingly, changes in expression of many of these genes preceded the rise in endogenous GA levels, perhaps indicating response to GA present in the seed before imbibition.

The identities of the GA-responsive genes found in this study is providing new insights into the mechanisms that control GA-mediated germination. For example, many genes that are implicated in cell elongation and cell division were identified, including those encoding for expansins, XETs, aquaporins, a D-type cyclin and a replication protein A.

Interestingly, an ABA-responsive element was overrepresented in the promoters of the GA-downregulated genes, suggesting that it may be also a GARE. Future studies aimed at understanding both the role and regulation of these GA-genes will undoubtedly enhance our understanding of how GAs regulate germination and other developmental processes.

GAMYBs

In barley (Hordeum *vulgare)* activation of o-amylase expression is induced by binding of GAMYB to the GARE of the promoter. It has been demonstrated that GA response mediated through GAMYB is dependent on the DELLA proteins SLN1 and SLR1, in barley and rice, respectively, in which the DELLA proteins act as negative regulators of GAMYB-mediated gene expression.

The expression of *GAMYB* in tissues other than aleurone in barley, rice, *Lolium,* wheat and *Arabidopsis* indicates that it functions in other GA-dependent processes.

Furthermore, the recent characterisation of *GAMYB* knock-out mutants in rice and *Arabidopsis* has provided more conclusive evidence for such roles. In rice, which contains a single *OsGAMYB* gene, mutations in this gene abolished 0—amylase expression in response to GA treatment.

Although the *Osgamyb* plants did not have any obvious

defects in vegetative development, or in the timing of floral transition, they did display abnormalities in floral organ development. For example, there were often dramatic defects in pollen development, resulting in male sterility.

Interestingly, there was a large variation in the severity of the phenotype, which Kaneko *et al.* (2004) suggested was caused by the environmental conditions.

The situation in *Arabidopsis is* complicated by the presence of at least three putative GAMYB genes: *AtMYB33, AtMYB65* and *AtMYB101.*

The findings that each of these three genes is capable of substituting for HvGAMYB in transactivating the barley o-amylase promoter provides support for their roles in GA signaling. Single knock-outs of *Atmyb33* and *Atmyb65* are indistinguishable from wild-indicating functional redundancy, while the *Atmyb33/Atmyb65* double knock-out is male sterile due to defects in pollen development.

This phenotype is consistent with the expression of *AtMYB33,* which is predominantly localised to the anthers in floral tissues. As in rice, the penetrance of the *Atmyb33/ Atmyb65* mutant phenotype is variable and subject to environmental control, low light intensity and high temperatures dramatically enhancing the male sterility of the mutant plants.

Three microRNAs (miRNAs; miR159a, b and c), recently identified in *Arabidopsis,* have high complementarity to the coding region of the three GAMYB genes, in addition to two other AtMYBs.

It was demonstrated recently that miR159 directs the cleavage of *AtMYB33* and *AtMYB65* transcripts. However, if this cleavage is prevented by expression of a mutant *AtMYB33* lacking the miR159 complementary se resulting transgenic plants display pleiotrophic developmental defects.

These severe abnormalities are in contrast to the specific floral defects observed in the *myb33/myb65* double mutant.

The observation that expression of the mutant *myb33 is* increased in additional tissues outside of the anthers provides an explanation for this and supports a role for miR159 in restricting the expression pattern *of AtMYB33.* Although the function of GAMYBs in regulating GA responses in aleurone cells is well defined, it is not clear whether their role in anther development is directly related to GA signaling.

Continuous exógenous treatment of *Arabidopsis* plants with GA does increase *MYB33* transcript levels, but this appears to be independent of the GA signaling status of the plant.

In contrast, the levels of miR159 are induced by GA via opposition of DELLA function, suggesting that miR 159 may function as a GA-response component by regulating GAMYB activity.

It remains to be determined why alterations in miR159 levels found in GA-biosynthetic/signaling mutants do not translate into changes in MYB33 transcript levels. It is conceivable that miR159 regulates MYB33 activity through translational control.

Homoeostatic Regulation of GA Metabolism

It is well documented that plants maintain the levels of endogenous bioactive GAs through the processes of feedback and feedforward regulation of GA metabolism.

Biochemical studies and transcript profiling experiments have demonstrated that the metabolic steps catalysed by the 2-ODDs are predominantly involved in this homoeos-tatic regulatory mechanism.

For example, in *Arabidopsis,* expression of the GA-biosynthetic genes, At*GA3oxl* (formerly GA4) and AtGA20ox1 (formerly *GA5),* are elevated in a GA-deficient back ground and then subsequently reduced following treatment of the plants with bioactive GAs.

In contrast, expression of the GA-inactivating enzymes, AtGA2ox1/2, are elevated when GA-deficient plants are treated with bioactive GAs. The molecular mechanisms that underlie this transcriptional regulation of the 2-ODDs are currently unknown, although, it is apparent that the GA-signal transduction cascade is necessary for this response.

This is illustrated by the findings that feedback regulation is perturbed in GA-response mutants and the direct correlation between the levels of functional DELLA proteins and the expression of the GA-metabolic genes.

For example, in the ga1-3 mutant, DELLA protein and AtG*A3oxl* transcript levels are elevated and then rapidly reduced by bioactive GA treatment, while the DELLA loss-of-function mutant, *gal-3/gai* t6/rga-24, has reduced levels of AtGA3ox1 transcripts compared to ga1-3 and these are unaffected by GA treatment.

Furthermore, DELLA gain-of-function mutations, such as *gai-1* and rga-*0*17, result in constitutively high expression levels of AtGA3ox1 which are unaffected by GA treatment.

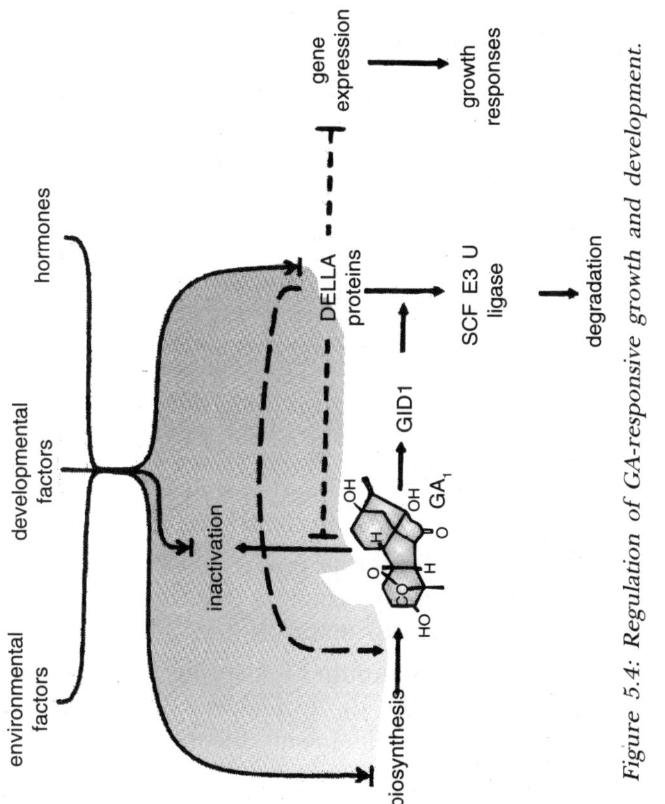

Figure 5.4: Regulation of GA-responsive growth and development.

These observations support a role for DELLA proteins as positive regulators of the 2-ODD genes that are under feedback control.

Feedback regulation of 2-ODD genes are some of the fastest GA responses. Decreases in AtGA3ox1 and AtGA20ox1 transcript levels in ga1-3 are observed within 30 min of treatment with GA.

This raises the possibility that DELLA proteins regulate transcription of these genes directly, despite the absence of a conserved DNA-binding domain within the DELLA protein. It is, indeed, possible that DELLA proteins act as part of a transcriptional complex.

The finding that cycloheximide blocks the feedback regulation of AtGA20ox1 expression indicates the requiremen synthesis in this response, although, this would not necessarily require an earlier round of transcription.

It is clear that one of the next major challenges in this field is to understand the mechanism by which DELLA proteins regulate transcript levels of GA-response genes.

Sites of GA Signaling

A major challenge in our attempts to understand how GAs regulate the many different facets of plant growth and development is to determine the precise sites of GA metabolism and action.

Biochemical studies have proved highly successful in demonstrating that in some cases, most notably in germinating cereal grains, GA acts as a paracrine signal, biosynthesis and response occurring in separate locations.

In contrast, the observations that GA biosynthesis is feedback regulated via the signaling pathway imply that they occur in the same cells in many tissues.

In recent years a number of studies have taken the opportunity provided by the availability of genes encoding GA biosynthetic and signaling components to determine their precise cellular localisation. Several examples are discussed in the following sections.

Germinating Seeds

In germinating cereal seeds, GAs, which are synthesised in the embryo-amylase expression in the aleurone cells. In order to obtain more information on the relationship between these distinct processes and how they control germination, Kaneko *et al.* (2003) investigated the cellular localisation of transcripts encoding GA-biosynthetic enzymes and signaling components in germinating rice seeds.

To determine where bioactive GAs are produced, the expression patterns of four biosynthetic genes, *OsGA20ox1, OsGA20ox2, OsGA3ox]* and *OsGA3ox2* were monitored. Although all of these transcripts were detected in the embryo, there were two distinct expression patterns.

Transcripts of *OsGA3ox]* and *OsGA20ox1* were present exclusively in the epithelium of the scutellum, whereas *OsGA3ox2* and *OsGA20ox2* were expressed also in the developing shoot.

Interestingly, expression of *OsGA3ox2,* but not that of *OsGA3ox1,* in the epithelium appears to be necessary for producing GAs for induction of a-amylase expression. *SLR1,* which encodes a component of GA-signal transduction, was expressed in essentially the same tissues as *OsGA3ox2* and *OsGA20ox2* within the embryo, indicating that bioactive GAs are being produced at their site of action.

However, *SLR1,* but not the GA-biosynthetic genes, was also expressed in the aleur one, confirming that this tissue is dependent on the import of GAs for 0—amylase expression.

Similar studies have been conducted in *Arabidopsis* seed, which require *de novo* GA biosynthesis for germination.

Imbibition of *Arabidopsis* seeds results in the upregulation of expression of multiple genes encoding GA-biosynthetic enzymes.

Results from studies using *in situ* hybridisation and analysis of promoter:GUS reporter lines suggested that GA biosynthesis occurs in two separate locations within the embryo axis; the early steps occurring in the provasculature and the later steps in the cortex and endodermis, where bioactive GAs promote cell expansion. This requires intercellular transport of GA precursors, possibly ent-kaurene.

The transcriptional profiling experiments described in Section 6.5 have uncovered many response genes that are regulated by GA in the germinating *Arabidopsis* seed. The identity of these genes has provided an important opportunity to compare the sites of GA production with those where downstream transcriptional events are occurring.

Analysis of the GA-induced expression profiles of three strongly GA-responsive genes by *in situ* hybridisation indicated that their GA-responsive expression was not restricted to the cortex/endodermal cells where bioactive GAs were produced. This finding supports the movement of bioactive GAs (or a GA-induced signal) within the germinating *Arabidopsis* seeds.

Stems

One of the classical roles of GAs is to promote stem elongation. Although this discovery was made over 50 years ago, the sites of GA metabolism and action in the stem have not been clearly defined. One of the first studies on the site of GA biosyn thesis in stem tissues was by Aach *et al.* (1997), who showed that ent-kaurene synthesis occurred in proplastids within the wheat intercalary meristem.

More recently, Kaneko *et al.* (2003) determined the expression patterns of the GA-biosynthetic genes *OsGA20ox2* and *OsGA3ox2* and signaling component SLR1 in elongating rice stems. On the basis of promoter: GUS reporter lines, they found that expression patterns of these genes were similar and occurred predominantly in the nodes and in the cell division and elongation zones, but not in fully elongated cells of the internodes.

These observations indicate that GA biosynthesis occurs at the sites of its action in the rice stem, in regions that are undergoing cell division and elongation. Similarly, in wheat, the GA-biosynthetic gene *TaGA3ox2 is* expressed in the nodes, internodes and the ear of the elongating stem, with highest expres in the lower part of the internode, where elongation is occurring. However, on the basis of Northern blot analysis, the GA 20-oxidase gene *TaGA20ox1* was shown to be much more highly expressed in the node internode.

This might indicate movement of an intermediate, presumably GA_{20}, from the intercalary meristem to the elongation zone. It is interesting to note that expression of the wheat orthologue of *OsGA20ox2* was not detected in the elongating stem, suggesting that different GA 20-oxidase genes may control stem elongation in rice and wheat.

Flower Initiation and Development

Gibberellins have been implicated in promotion of flowering in several species. The temperate grass, *L. temulentum,* which flowers in response to a single LD exposure, has provided an useful model system for studying GA-induced flowering. Perception of the LD photoperiod occurs in the leaf and a signal is exported to the apex within 24 h.

There is now compelling evidence supporting the role of GAs as this signal. Initially, it was demonstrated that the application of specific GAs can substitute for the LD exposure in promoting flowering in *L. temulentum.*

Interestingly, GA_5 and GA_6 are more effective in floral induction than GA1 and GA_4, which are the most important growth-active GAs. Furthermore, GA_5 and GA_6 levels increase in the leaves following a single LD exposure and a subsequent two-fold rise in the apex is observed 24 h later.

Although GA_1 and GA_4 are detectable in leaves prior to floral induction, they remain undetectable in the vegetative apex. It has been proposed that GA1 and GA_4 are excluded from the vegetative apex by the action of a GA 2-oxidase, which deactivates these compounds, but is ineffective against GA_5 and GA_6.

Support for this hypothesis is provided by studies in rice demonstrating expression of OsGA2ox1 in a ring surrounding the vegetative apex. Expression of OsGA2ox1 is substantially reduced following the phase transition to an inflorescence meristem.

If a similar situation occurs in *L. temulentum* it could

also provide an explanation for the observed increases in GA1 and GA_4 levels at the apex several days after floral induction. It has been suggested that these increases are necessary for promoting inflorescence development.

Further characterisation of GA metabolic and signaling components in *L. temulentum* in combination with reverse genetics approaches in model plants should help to uncover the role of GAs in mediating floral induction.

In addition to their role in promoting flowering, GAs are also involved in promoting development of the floral organs. In many plants the predominant site of GA biosynthesis appears to be the anthers.

It has been proposed that GAs produced in the anthers is necessary for the development of other floral organs. In rice, the study of the sites of GA biosynthesis and signaling by Kaneko *et al.* (2003) provided support for this model.

They demonstrated that the biosynthetic genes *OsGA3ox2* and *OsGA20ox2* were predominantly expressed in the stamen primordia and developed anthers, whereas expression of the signaling component, *SLR1,* was found in additional floral organs.

Although *OsGA3ox2* and *OsGA20ox2* play a major role in producing bioactive GAs in many tissues of the rice plant, OsGA3ox1 and *OsGA20ox1* appear to have more tissue specific roles that were also noted during germination of the seed.

In flowers, both of these genes are specifically expressed in tapetum cells of the anthers.

The Arabidopsis Root

The examples described in the previous three sections illustrate a gene-by gene approach to localisation of GA-signaling elements. The availability of DNA oligonucleotide microarrays provides a high-throughput method to localise the expression of all of these elements by obtaining global gene transcript profiles from individual cell types within an organ.

The potential of this approach has been demonstrated in an elegant study by Birnbaum *et al.* (2003) in which they determined gene expression profiles for specific cell types and developmental stages within the *Arabidopsis* root.

This was achieved using transgenic lines expressing GFP in specific cell populations. Protoplasts prepared from these lines were used to isolate the specific cell types using florescence-activated cell sorting. A combination of the expression profiles from the cell types and distinct developmental stages were used to create a global map of gene expression within 15 zones of the root tip.

Although the function of GAs in regulating *Arabidopsis* root growth is currently poorly understood, the presence of transcripts encoding GA-metabolic enzymes and signaling components in this tissue supports such a role.

Further evidence is provided by the recent findings that the ga1-3 mutants have shorter primary roots than wild-type plants, which are fully rescued by exogenous GA treatment. The DELLA proteins, RGA and GAI, appear to function as the predominant repressors of GA-mediated root growth in *Arabidopsis.*

The global map of gene expression in the *Arabidopsis* root now provides an important opportunity to determine more precisely the cellular localisation of GA-signaling components.

The GA-signal transduction components RGA and SLY] are expressed constitutively throughout the root tip, suggesting that the majority of these cells are capable of responding to bioactive GAs. One intriguing aspect of the root expression data is the apparent localisation of the genes of GA metabolism.

Expression profiles (shaded regions) were determined for: stele, endodermis, endodermis plus cortex, epidermal atrichoblast cells and lateral root cap.

Expression of *GA20ox1* and *GA3ox1* was detected predominantly in endodermis plus cortex at stage 2. Expression of the early biosynthetic gene, *KO,* occurs predominantly in the root tip, developmental stage 1. The later biosynthetic genes, including *GA20ox1* and GA3ox1 are expressed at a later developmental stage.

It is also interesting to note that *GA20ox1* and GA3ox1 display a tissue-specific expression pattern, with their transcripts accumulating predominantly in endodermal cells. In contrast to the biosynthetic genes, expression of the GA-inactivating enzymes, AtGA2ox2 and AtGA2ox6, are predominantly in developmental stage 3, where elongation of the root hairs is complete.

One possible explanation for this expression profile of GA-metabolic components is that biosynthesis of bioactive GAs is required to promote longitudinal expansion within the root elongation elongation is complete, the bioactive GAs are inactivated reducing GA-promoted cell expansion. The characterisation of mutants containing loss-of-function mutations in GA-metabolic genes will provide a useful resource to test this hypothesis.

CONCLUSIONS

Our knowledge of GA signaling has advanced impressively. A simplified model of this pathway, including biosynthesis and signal transduction, is shown in Figure elsewhere in this chapter, which indicates the relationship between signal transduction and metabolism via the feedback/feedforward mechanism.

The recent discovery of a soluble GA receptor has closed several gaps in the model by revealing the signal transduction path way to be much shorter than anticipated, with GA involved surprisingly directly with the turnover of DELLA proteins. Of course, there is still much to learn, including the relationship between the receptor and the F-box protein in targeting DELLA proteins for degradation.

The possible contribution of membrane receptors, for which there is considerable indirect evidence, remains unclear, as does the immediate targets for the DELLA proteins and the mechanism by which they regulate transcription.

A major challenge is the identification of genes that are regulated by GA signaling, directly or indirectly, and to determine how their activity translates into the physiological consequences of GA action.

Knowledge of the identity of most of the components of the GA-signaling path way is enabling progress to be made in our understanding of how this process is regulated by developmental and environmental cues.

Research in this area has focused particularly on the regulation of expression of the GA-biosynthetic and deactivation genes, the results suggesting that control of GA content is of major importance in many plant developmental processes.

However, there has been so far little consideration of the involve-ment of enzyme stability in controlling GA metabolism, although protein degradation plays a pivotal role in GA-signal transduction. This subject clearly deserves more attention despite the technical difficulties associated with measuring the very low abundance of GA-metabolic enzymes in most tissues.

An associated problem, which is receiving attention, is determining the cellular sites of GA biosynthesis and signal transduction. Progress in this area will be facilitated by cell specific transcript profiling using methods such as laser capture micro-dissection and fluorescence-activated cell sorting, whereas the increasing sensitivity of mass spectrometers will allow ever smaller samples to be analysed.

The available evidence, based mainly on transcript distribution or patterns of reporter gene expression, indicates that GAs may be produced and function in the same cells (i.e. they act as autocrine signals).

The existence of a soluble, nuclear-localised receptor and of feedback regulation of GA biosynthesis is consistent with this scenario. However, there are also clear indications of paracrine function in specific cases, such as in the cereal grain.

The regulation of GA signaling via interactions with other hormones is proving an important mechanism for integrating hormone signals. In particular, the accumulating evidence that GA biosynthesis and signal transduction are both stimulated by auxin suggests that GAs may mediate some of the responses of this long-distance messenger locally. Future research will provide further insight into these issues and build on the firm base that has now been established.

6

Chapter

Biosynthesis of Brassinosteroid

In less than a decade, our understanding of plant steroid hormone *biosynthesis* and *signaling* has advanced to the point that this class of hormones can be argued to have one of the best characterised biosynthesis and signaling pathways.

Brassinolide (BL) is the most bioactive form of these hormones, which are generically referred to as *brassinosteroids* (BRs). Genetic approaches have identified dwarf mutants that are defective in BR synthesis and signaling.

The dwarf phenotype, as shown in Figure elsewhere in this chapter, highlights the essential role of BRs in plant development, which involves the regulation of growth, *photomorphogenesis,* fertility and stress resistance.

BR regulation of these physiological functions indicates the importance of maintaining optimal levels of BRs via the coordination of biosynthesis and signaling. Many recent reviews have discussed BR biosynthesis, metabolism and signaling in *model systems* and crops.

Here we aim to provide an account of BR synthesis and signaling, developing a theme of how biosynthesis is regulated by BR signaling. A key concept in this regulation is that homeostatic levels of the hormone are maintained by BR-dependent *transcriptional* control of the genes involved in BR metabolism.

This control mechanism lowers the hormone content when BR levels are too high by reducing the transcription of

Figure 6.1: BR deficiency results in severe dwarf phenotype.

biosynthetic genes and/or increasing the transcription of catabolic genes. This review will therefore include accounts of BR biosynthesis and *metabolism* through to the signaling processes that occur in the presence or absence focus will be on discussing the progress made in the model *plant Arabidopsis thaliana.* Where appropriate, key advances achieved in other species will also be included.

METABOLISM

Biosynthesis

BRs are synthesised from C_{27}, C_{28} and C_{29} *phytosterol precursors* that differ from each other by their *aliphatic*

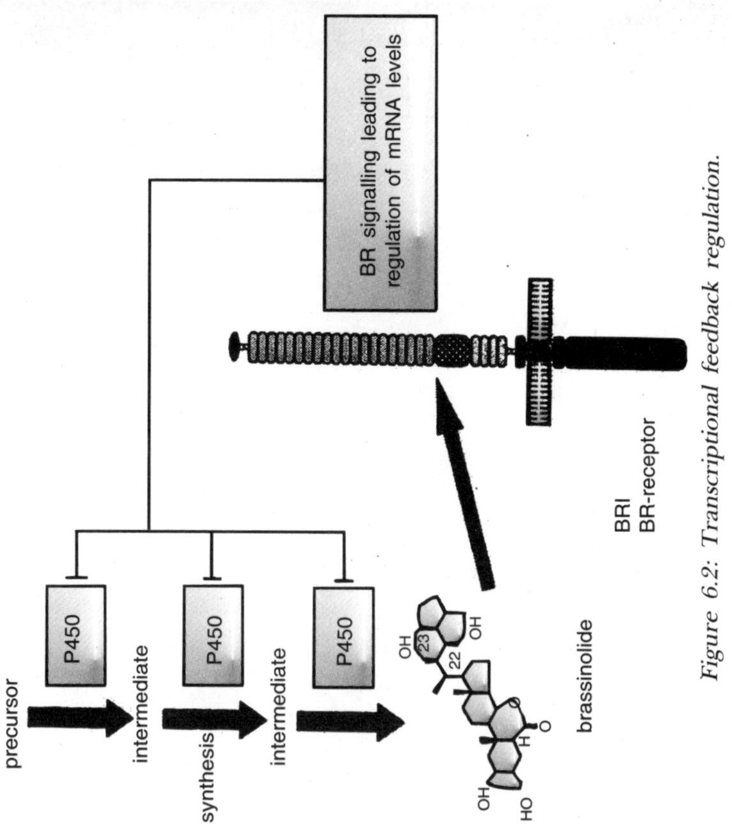

Figure 6.2: Transcriptional feedback regulation.

substituents at the C-24 position. *Campesterol,* a C_{28} sterol is the main precursor for BR synthesis.

Phytosterol synthesis, including that of campesterol, has been reviewed in detail by Fujioka and Yokota, therefore the focus of this section will be on the reactions *downstream* of *campesterol.*

The biosynthetic pathway of BRs has been deduced by the analysis of conversion products obtained from radiolabelled metabolites fed to cell suspension cultures of *Catharanthus roseus.*

These studies revealed that BR synthesis proceeds towards BL via two major routes, namely the early and late C-6 *oxidation pathways.* Subsequently, this model of BR biosynt-

Table 6.1: Genes of BR metabolism.

Genes (alleles)	*Function*	*Species*
BR biosynthesis		
DET2	*5α-reductase*	*Arabidopsis*
LK	*5α-reductase*	Pea
LeDET2	*5α-reductase*	Tomato
PnDET2	*5α-reductase*	*Pharbitis nil*
SAX1	3-oxidase,	*Arabidopsis*
DWF4/CYP90B1	22-hydroxylase	*Arabidopsis*
CPD/CYP90A1 (*CBB3, DWF3*)	23-hydroxylase	*Arabidopsis*
COS10/CYP90A2	23-hydroxylase?	Mung bean
dpy	23-hydroxylase?	Tomato
ROT3/CYP90C1	2-hydroxylase	*Arabidopsis*
CYP90D1	3-oxidase, isomerase?	*Arabidopsis*
D2/CYP90D2	3-oxidase, isomerase?	Rice
CYP90D3	3-oxidase, isomerase?	Rice
DDWF1/CYP92A6	2-hydroxylase?	Pea
CYP85A1	6-oxidase	*Arabidopsis*
Dwarf/CYP85A1	6-oxidase Tomato	
BRD1/CYP85A1	6-oxidase	Rice
CYP85A2	6-oxidase, BL synthase	*Arabidopsis*
CYP85A3	6-oxidase, BL synthase	Tomato
CYP724B1	?	Rice
BR inactivation		
BAS1/CYP734A1	26-hydroxylase	*Arabidopsis*
CHI2/CYP72C1 (*SHK1/SOB7)*	Hydroxylase?	*Arabidopsis*
UGT73C5	UDP-glycosyltransferase	*Arabidopsis*
BNST3 and BNST4	Steroid sulphotransferase SOT	*Brassica napus*

hesis was confirmed in *Catharanthus* and *Arabidopsis.* The isolation of *BR-deficient mutants* and their molecular *genetic* action has been *instrumental* in identifying the genes involved in BR biosynthesis and clarifying the enzymatic role of their products. Currently, most of the biosynthetic genes and their functions have been characterised in *Arabidopsis,* and some of their *orthologues* have been described from other species.

The following provides an account of these enzymes. However, the enzymes responsible for early C-6 oxidation and the *isomerisation* of the C-3 *hydroxyl group* are yet to be identified.

DET2

DEETIOLATED 2 (DET2) was one of the first BR-biosynthetic genes to be identified in *Arabidopsis.* Its lesion results in a typical BR-deficient *phenotype,* characterised by severe *dwarfism,* constitutive *photomorphogenesis,* delayed flowering/senescence and reduced male fertility. *DET2* encodes a steroid 5α-reductase, representing the only known non-cytochrome P450 enzyme (P450) of BR *biosynthesis.*

The enzymatic role of DET2 was determined by *in vivo* feeding assays using deuterated substrates, as well as the analysis of BR intermediates in the *det2* mutant.

These studies revealed that DET2 catalyses one of the initial reactions in the BR pathway, namely the conversion of (24R)-24-methylcholest-4-en-3-one to (24R)-24-methyl-5-alpha-cholestan-3-one. DET2 is an enzyme of relaxed specificity, allowing 5α-reduction of not only BR precursors with C_{28} and C_{27} backbones, but also several animal steroid substrates.

These results and sequence similarities shared with animal 5o-reductases show that DET2 is an ancient enzyme of *steroid biosynthesis.* Genes encoding *orthologues* of *DET2* have also been identified in some other plant species. These include *LK* in pea, *LeDET2* in tomato and *PnDET2* in *Pharbitis nil.*

SAX1

The dwarf phenotype of the ABA- and IAA-*hypersensitive*

sax1 *(hypersensitive to abscisic acid and auxin 1)* mutant of *Arabidopsis* can be rescued by 24cating that the mutation causes BR deficiency. On the basis of rescue assays using intermediates of BR synthesis,

SAX1 was tentatively identified as a steroid C-3 oxidase catalysing the conversion of campesterol to 3-one, immediately upstream of the DET2 reaction.

The sax1 mutation was mapped within an approximately 3.7Mb region at the lower arm of *chromosome* 1, but so far the gene has not been identified.

DWF4

The *dwarf4 (dwf4)* mutant of *Arabidopsis* displays a typical BR-deficient phenotype. *DWF4,* the gene affected by the mutation has been cloned and shown to encode a P450, CYP90B1. In feeding *assays* C-22 hydroxylated BR intermediates rescued the *dwf4* phenotype, indicating that DWF4/ CYP90B1 is responsible for C-22 hydroxylation of the steroid side chain.

Combined gas *chromatography* and mass *spectrometry* (GC-MS) analyses of BR intermediates revealed that plants accumulate very high amounts of *campestanol,* a substrate of DWF4, which suggests that C-22 hydroxylation is one of the rate limiting reactions of BR synthesis.

The importance of this reaction is supported by the results of Choe *et al.* (2001) showing enhanced growth in transgenic *Arabidopsis* and tobacco plants that overexpress *DWF4* under the control of the cauliflower mosaic virus 35S *promoter.*

In addition to its crucial role in BR synthesis, DWF4 is the prime target of the triazole-type BR-biosynthesis inhibitors brassinazole and triadimefon. The natural occurrence of 22-*hydroxycampesterol* and other C-22-*hydroxylated* precursors of 6-deoxocathasterone reveals that DWF4 also catalyses reactions in the early C-22-*hydroxylation* pathway.

Recent ecal studies with *heterologously* expressed DWF4 indicate that campes than campestanol, is the preferred substrate of this enzyme. *DWF4* is expressed primarily in the shoot apex and siliques of *Arabidopsis,* and its mRNA level was found to be very low compared to other BR-biosynthetic transcripts.

High BR levels down-regulate *DWF4* by a transcriptional feed back mechanism that controls the expression of all BR-biosynthetic P450 genes in *Arabidopsis.* In contrast to other genes of this group, *DWF4 activity retains* its responsiveness to the biosynthesis inhibitor brassina zole in a BR-insensitive mutant background.

CPD

Like *dwf4, constitutive photomorphogenesis* and *dwarfism (cpd) is* a T tion mutant with extreme dwarf stature and aberrant skotomorph-ogenesis. *CPD* encodes a P450 (CYP90-A1) that is 43% identical with CYP90B1.

Phenotypic rescue experiments using BR intermediates suggest that CPD is a BR C-23 hydroxylase. *CPD* is the most highly expressed BR-biosynthetic gene, with preferential activity in *cotyledons* and expanding leaves. The high *endogenous* levels of the CPD substrate 6-deoxocath-*asterone* indicate that this is an important enzyme of BR synthesis.

ROT3 and CYP90D1

Compared to *det2, dwf4* and *cpd,* the *rotundifolia 3 (rot3)* mutants of *Arabidopsis* display much weaker phenotypes, with only slightly reduced *elongation.* In contrast, transgenic plants *overexpressing* the ROT3 gene develop elongated leaves and *petals.*

ROT3/CYP90C1 was anticipated to function in BR biosynthesis on the basis of its sequence similarity with CPD/CYP90A1 and DWF4/CYP90B1, as well as its down-regulated expression by BRs. Sequence data revealed that the *Arabidopsis* genome also encodes CYP90D1, another P450 protein sharing 47% sequence identity with ROT3.

CYP90D1 is also transcriptionally down-regulated by BRs, implicating its P450 product in BR biosynthesis, but a *null mutation* in this gene does not have an obvious *phenotypic* effect. By contrast, a cyp90c1cyp90d1 double *mutant* defective in both ROT3 and CYP90D 1 shows the typical BR-deficient dwarf phenotype, suggesting that the two enzymes may have *redundant* functions.

Despite this expectation, Kim, G.-T. *et al.* found that overexpression of *CYP90D1* in the *rot3-1* mutant could not rescue the phenotype. Furthermore, the levels of BR intermediates were affected differently by the *rot3* and *cyp90d1* mutations.

Based on the endogenous BR levels in these mutants, ROT3 was proposed to be a C-2 hydroxylase *catalysing* the conversion of typhasterol to castasterone, whereas CYP90D1 was thought to mediate a reaction upstream of the C-2 hydroxylation, possibly the oxidation of teaterone and 6-*deoxoteasterone* to their respective 3-*dehydro* derivatives.

The BR-deficient *ebisu dwarf (d2)* mutation of rice is caused by a lesion in the *D2* gene encoding CYP90D2, which is 54% identical with *Arabidopsis* CYP90D1 at the amino acid sequence level. Based on the rescue of the *d2* phenotype by BR biosynthesis intermediates and the *endogenous* BR levels dete mutant, CYP90D2 has been proposed to catalyse the conversion of 6-*deoxoteasterone* to 3-dehydro-6-deoxoteasterone.

Therefore, this enzyme is a likely orthologue of the *Arabidopsis* CYP90D1. Genomic sequence data indicate that rice also contains CYP90D3, a likely isoform of CYP90D2 with yet unidentified function.

CYP85A1 and CYP85A2

Mutants at the tomato *dwarf (d) locus* are BR responsive and this gene was transposon tagged using an *engineered Activator transposable* element from maize. The *DWARF* gene was shown to encode CYP85A1, a P450 closely related to the BR-biosynthetic P450s of the CYP90 family. GC-MS analysis of endogenous BRs from dx mutants (a strong allele at the *d locus),* did not detect castasterone, but an *accumulation* of its precursor 6-deoxo *castasterone.*

Overexpression of the *D* gene resulted in the increase of castasterone content at the expense of the 6-deoxocastasterone pool. These results suggested that CYP85A1 catalyses the late

C-6 oxidation reaction converting 6-*deoxocastasterone* to castasterone.

Subsequently, this was confirmed in functional assays in which the yeast-expressed enzyme oxidises 6-dterone to castasterone via a C-6-hydroxylated intermediate. In *Arabidopsis* two *CYP85* genes were identified on the basis of their *homology* to *D*, rather than the *characterisation* of mutants. Sequence analysis of CYP85A1 and *CYP85A2* revealed that they encode closely related P450s sharing 82% amino acid sequence identity.

When expressed in yeast, both enzymes catalysed C-6 oxidation of 6-deoxocastasterone and, to a lesser extent, also 6-deoxotyphasterol and 6-deoxoteasterone. In addition to its C-6 oxidase activity, CYP85A2 also catalysed the conversion of castasterone to BL.

Mutant analyses indicated that these genes have partially overlapping functions, since only double mutants deficient in both CYP85A1 and CYP85A2 displayed the characteristic BR *dwarf phenotype*. The recently discovered CYP85A3 of tomato exhibits both BR C-6 oxidase and BL-synthase activity, thereby indicating that it is an *orthologue* of the *Arabidopsis* CYP85A2.

The analysis of CYP85A3 expression indicates that this enzyme is fruit-specific, which is in good *agreement* with the observation that in tomato BL synthesis is restricted to the fruits. This suggests an important role for BL in *reproductive* development.

Other biosynthetic functions

The exact function of some BR biosynthesis related genes are yet to be clarified. These include:

DARK-INDUCED DWF-LIKE PROTEIN 1 (DDWF1) from pea, which was identified as a specific interactor of the Pra2 dark-induced small GTP-binding protein that is expressed only in *etiolated epicotyls*. The DDWF1 gene encodes CYP92A6, a P450 enzyme that has been proposed to be a BR C-2 hydroxylase.

The importance of this enzyme in BR biosynthesis is not clear because some plants (e.g. *Arabidopsis) lack* CYP92-type P450s. The *dumpy (dpy) mutant* of tomato has reduced BR content and its dwarf phenotype can be rescued by *bioactive* BRs. On the basis of BR content and intermediate *rescue* data, DPY is proposed to function as a C-23 hydroxylase. BRASSINOSTEROID, LIGHT AND SUGAR 1 (BLS1) *of* Arabidops*is* is required for proper BR and light *responsiveness.*

The phenotype of the bls1 mutant can be rescued by BR treatment, a feature shared with BR-*biosynthetic* mutants. The mutation has been mapped within a 1.4Mb region of chromosome 5. DWARF 11 (D11) is a rice P450 enzyme (CYP724B1) related to members of the CYP85 and CYP90 families.

BR analysis and intermediate rescue of the *dl 1* mutant suggest that CYP724B1 is involved in BR synthesis upstream of 6-deoxotyphasterol, but the function of this enzyme remains unclear. Based on sequence similarity, it is likely that the closely related CYP724A1 that has been identified in *Arabidopsis,* also participates in BR biosynthesBR biosynthesis.

Inactivation

Optimal endogenous levels of BRs are maintained by the action of biosynthetic and inactivation enzymes. The biochemical processes of BR inactivation ensure the removal of excess BRs by converting them, reversibly or irreversibly, to biologically inactive forms.

Several types of BR metabolites have been identified by the analysis of steroid-containing compounds produced in explants or cell cultures following feeding with isotope-labelled BRs. Suzuki *et al.* (1993) found that in mung bean BL becomes glycosylated at the C-23 hydroxyl group.

Upon exogenous application the isolated conjugate showed bioactivity, suggesting that *in planta* BL is released from the conjugate. In *Lilium logiflorum* teasterone was shown to form reversible C-3 acylconjugates in a developmentally regulated manner.

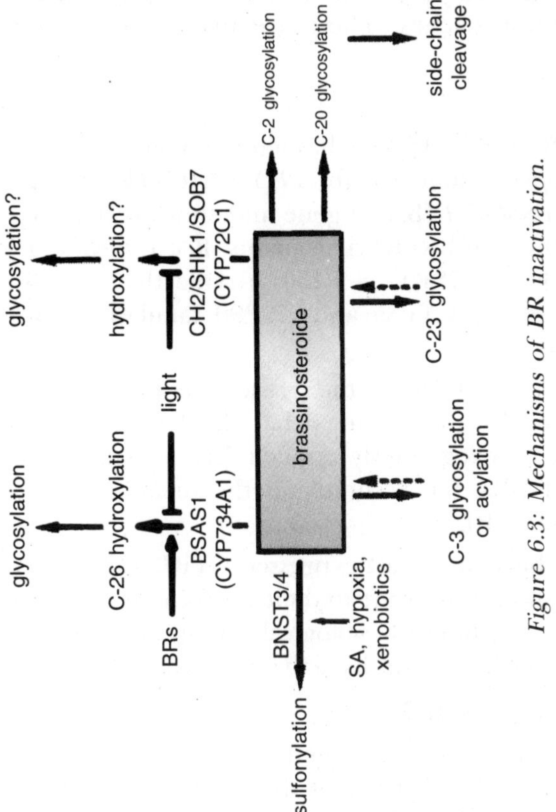

Figure 6.3: Mechanisms of BR inactivation.

Reversible conjugation at the C-23, C-2 and possibly also the C-may play an important regulatory role by allowing temporary removal of bioactive BRs. By contrast, irreversible *inactivation* takes place by P450-mediated hydroxylation and subsequent *glycosylation* of BRs at the C-25 and C-26 positions.

Furthermore, Kolbe *et al.* (1996) reported that hydroxylation at C-20 results in side-chain cleavage, leading to pregnane-type *catabolites*. The biochemical mechanisms of BR inactivation are summarised in Figure elsewhere in this chapter.

Recently, some BR-inactivating functions have been characterised in *Arabidopsis* and *Brassica napus* using molecular *genetic* approaches. These are discussed in the following sections.

BAS1

Neff *et al.* (1999) characterised an activation-tagged *Arabidopsis* mutant °ing the *PHYB4 ACTIVATION-TAGGED SUPPRESSOR 1* (BAS1) gene and showing a similar phenotype to those of BR-deficient plants. BAS1 encodes CYP734A1 (formerly CYP72B1), a P450 enzyme that is only distantly related to the CYP85 and CYP90 families involved in BR biosynthesis.

A role for BAS1 in the irreversible inactivation of BRs is illustrated by the findings that the bas1-D mutant can be rescued by exogenously applied BL, it contains diminished levels of BRs, but accumulates the *biologically* inactive BR, 26-hydroxy-BL.

Furthermore, yeast-expressed CYP734A1 converts bioactive BL and castasterone to their respective C-26-hydroxylated derivatives. Under physiological conditions BAS1 is expressed at very low levels, but its activity is strongly induced by BRs.

CHI2/SHK1/SOB7

Another activation-tagged mutant of *Arabidopsis, chibi 2* (chi2) shows a BR-deficient dwarf phenotype similar to that of bas1-D. This dominant mutation results in *overexpression* of the *CHI2* gene that encodes CYP72C1, a P450 sharing 47% amino acid sequence identity with CYP734A1.

Whereas CHI2/CYP72C1 also utilises castasterone and BL as substrates, the CYP72C1 overexpressing *sob7-D* mutant does not accumulate C-26-hydroxylated BRs, indicating that the inactivation reaction catalysed by this enzyme is different from that of CYP734A1.

In contrast to BAS1, the expression of *CYP72C1* is not induced by BRs. The expression of both *CYP734A1* and *CYP72C1* is light-regulated, and their levels influence *photomorphogenesis* and the accumulation of bioactive BRs.

Therefore, these enzymes seem to play an important role

in the integration of light and *steroid* signaling pathways.

UGT73C5

Recently Poppenberger *et al.* (2005) have reported that UGT73C5, an *Arabidopsis* UDP-glycosyltransferase, *catalyses* 23-O-*glucosylation* of BRs.

Conversion assays carried out with yeast-expressed UGT73C5 revealed that BL and castasterone are the preferred substrates of this enzyme. Transgenic *overexpression* of the UG*T73C5* gene lead to decreased BR content and dwarfness, indicating that 23-O-glucosylation abolishes the bioactivity of BRs. In expression analyses, utilising a promoter-GUS reporter *fusion*, strong *UGT73C5* promoter activity was detected in seedlings, especially in the *elongation* zones of roots and hypocotyls.

BNST3 and BNST4

The *salicylate*-inducible *BNST3* gene of *Brassica napus* encodes a steroid sulphotransferase (SOT) that facilitates the removal of early BR *biosynthesis intermediates* by *sulphonating* them at the C-22 hydroxyl. Although sulphonation by BNST3 could abolish the activity of 24-epi-BL, *in vitro* the enzyme showed pr 24-*epicathasterone*.

Further characterisation of BNST3 and the related BNST4 revealed that in addition to salicylate, the expression of these *Brassica* genes can also be induced by *hypoxia, ethanol* and various *xenobiotics.*

Overexpression of *BNST3* in *Arabidopsis* does not lead to a BR-deficient phenotype, therefore this enzyme may have a role in controlling the pool size of early BR intermediates.

By contrast, BNST4, which is capable of sulphonating a broad range of steroid substrates, has been implicated in stress-related detoxification mechanisms. In *Arabidopsis,* the protein family of SOTs is predicted to comprse 18 members.

Although the functions of most of these enzymes is unknown, one of them participates in *jasmonate inactivation.* It remains to be elucidated whether any of the *Arabidopsis* SOTs are involved in the control of *in planta* BR levels.

Functional Aspects of BR Metabolism

Regulation of biosynthetic genes

Several lines of evidence indicate that transcriptional regulation of the BR-biosynthetic genes plays a crucial role in the control of BR synthesis and, hence, in determining the *endogenous* level of the hormone.

It has been shown that the level of *CPD* mRNA is regulated primarily at the transcriptional level, and that weak CPD expression in the roots of *Arabidopsis* coincides with the *accumulation* of its proposed substrate, 6-*deoxocathasterone.*

Most BR biosynthetic genes are under complex *transcriptional* control that involves multiple regulatory *mechanisms.* One of these mechanisms is the feedback regulation of all P450-encoding *biosynthetic* genes by the action of bioactive BRs.

In *Arabidopsis DWF4, CYP90D1,* CYP85A1 and *CYP85A2* are co-ordinately down-regulated by bioactive BRs, reducing their transcript level to around 10% of the initial value within 2 h of BL atment. Feedback regulation of the *CPD* gene depends on BR signaling initiating at the BRI1 receptor.

It is mediated by the BZR1 transcription factor that binds as a repressor to a specific BR response element present in the *promoter* of *CPD* and all the other feedback-controlled genes of BR synthesis.

In the bri1 BR-insensitive mutant the lack of feedback regulation results in abnormally high levels of BR accumulation. In wild-the activity of BR-biosynthetic P450 genes is partially repressed, allowing either up or down-regulation of their expression through the feedback mechanism at a wide range of *endogenous* BR concentrations.

Therefore, the feed back control is believed to be an important physiological regulator of BR synthesis and accumulation. A further level of transcriptional regulation ensures organ-specific expression.

In contrast to the *ubiquitously* expressed *DET2,* the P450 genes of BR biosynthesis show distinct types of organ specificity. *Spatial* regulation of these genes seems to be important in determining the BR levels in different organs.

The CPD and CYP85A2 enzymes, which catalyse rate-limiting reactions, are expressed more intensely in shoots than in roots of Arabidop*sis* seedlings. This is in good agreement [w]ing that in *Arabidopsis,* tomato and pea, shoots are richer in 6-*deoxocastasterone* and bioactive BRs, whereas roots accumulate 6-deoxotyphasterol and farther upstream BR *intermediates.*

The physiological significance of localised gene expression is highlighted by the reported lack of *in planta* BR transport, which suggests that the expression sites of rate-limiting biosynthetic enzymes coincide with the sites of active BR synthesis.

The transcription of BR-biosynthetic genes is also under developm-ental regulation. In *Arabidopsis* all *CYP85* and *CYP90* genes are strongly expressed ing seeds and young seedlings. This is in good agreement with the role of BRs in hypocotyl elongation and vascular differentiation.

Recent reports have shown light-induced accumulation of castasterone and BL in pea seedlings, indicating the possibility that BR-biosynthetic genes are also activated during *de-etiolation.* The importance of BRs in *photomorphogenic* development is highlighted by the de-etiolated dark phenotypes of severely BR-*deficient* mutants.

Regulation of BR-inactivating genes

Expression levels of BR-inactivating genes are also stringently controlled at the transcriptional level. The gene encoding BAS1/CYP734A1 is BR inducible, indicating that it has a function in the homeostatic regulation of BR content. Choe *et al.* (2001) have shown that this feedforward control requires the BRI1 receptor.

By contrast, the expression of *CYP72C1* is not influenced by BRs. Expression of the CYP734A1 and CYP72C1 genes were found to be down-regulated by light, although in seedlings grown in continuous dark the level of the BAS1/

CYP734A1 transcript was slightly lower than those in continuous white light.

Light regulation of these genes seems to be closely connected to the transition from *skotomorphogenesis* to *photomorphogenesis,* because mutations affecting CYP734A1 or CYP72C1 expression result in altered light *responsiveness.*

This notion is further supported by data showing that white, relight repressed, but far-red induced accumulation of the BAS1/CYP734A1 transcripts and its protein products in the elongation zone of etiolated seedlings.

The expression of the UGT73C5 UDP-glycosyltransferase was also found associated with the *elongating* tissues of seedlings. This localisation suggests that the level of BRs needs to be *stringently* controlled at the sites of BR action.

Conservation of BR synthesis in higher plants

All currently available information indicates a remarkable conserv-ation of BR biosynthesis between plant species belonging to different families. For example, in *Arabidopsis,* pea and tomato there is an accumulation of high levels of 6-deoxocathasterone and 6-deoxocasta-sterone, which are indicative of common rate-limiting reactions in the pathway.

In rice, however, 6-deoxotyphasterol is the most abundant BR intermediate, suggesting that in *monocots* both C-and C-2 hydroxylation can be rate-limiting conversion steps. With the exception of the *Solanaceous* plants *tomato* and *tobacco,* in which no early C-6 oxidation intermediates have been detected, other species seem to synthesise BRs through both the early and late C-6 oxidation pathways.

In each case, however, the late C-6 oxidation route was found to be predominant. Recently, the functional significance of early C-has become uncertain in the light of data showing 6-oxocampestanol accumulation in the cyp85a1cyp85a2-1 *Arabidopsis* mutant deficient in both late C-6 oxidase enzymes.

Shimada *et al.* (2001, 2003) reported that yeast-expressed CYP85A1 and CYP85A2 converted not only 6-deoxocastasterone but also 6-deoxotyphasterol and 6-deoxoteasterone to their respective 6-oxo derivatives.

Other BR-biosynthetic *enzymes* also have relaxed substrate specificities that allow their participation in different subpathways and it therefore seems possible that BRs are synthesised via a network of reactions.

This concept is strengthened by the natural occurrence of 3-epi-6-deoxocathasterone and 2-deoxo-BL, which indicate that C-3 epimerisation or lactonisation of the B ring may precede the C-23 or C-2 *hydroxylation* steps, respectively.

In vitro enzyme kinetic studies are expected to yield valuable information regarding the preferences of DET2 and BR-*biosynthetic* P450s toward their *substrates.*

SIGNAL TRANSDUCTION

At the same time as the advances in our understanding of BR biosynthesis have been made, remarkable progress and insights into BR signaling have occurred.

A key feature of this has been the observation that a functional BR signaling mechanism is required for the transcriptional feedback regulation of BR-biosynthesis genes. The following sections reviewing BR-signaling highlight the success of novel genetic screens and the isolation of mutations/genes in the BR-signaling pathway.

Table 6.2: Key BR-signal transduction genes in *Arabido-psis* Genes/alleles Function.

BRI1	LRR-RLK
BAK1	LRR-RLK
BIN2, DWF12, UCU1	GSK3 like kinase
BSU1	Kelch-repeat-containing phosphatase
BZR1 BZRI	Transcription factTranscription facto
BES1 BEST	Transcription factTranscription facto
BIM1	bHLH transcription factor
BRS1	Serine carboxypeptidase

This genetic approach has been crucial in the rapid advance made, and more recently this has been backed-up with elegant biochemical/molecular data.

This synergy of approaches has enabled a detailed description of the function of these proteins and also the discovery of further factors in the signaling pathway. As an aid to the following sections, a table of the key signaling factors has been provided.

BRI1 and BAK1

When BRs are applied to plants a signaling cascade is initiated at the plasma membrane where BRs bind to a BR receptor, BRASSINOSTEROID INSENSITIVE 1 (BRI1). BRI1 encodes a leucine rich repeat receptor-like kinase and mutants in this gene were first identified in genetic screens for plants exhibiting dwarfism and lacking inhibition to root growth in the pres.

Many experiments have highlighted the importance of BRI1 in BR signaling which has culminated in the recent discovery that BRs bind directly to BRI1 and this leads to a change in state from an autoinhibitory form to a more active kinase.

BRI1 is not the only BR receptor, as other LRR-RLKs similar to BRI1 have been identified that also interact with radio labelled BRs. BRs stimulate *autophosphorylation* of BRI1, and the phosphorylation status of BRI1 is also modulated via the interaction with another LRR-RLK BRASSINOSTEROID-ASSOCIATED KINASE 1 (BAKI).

BAK1 was identified based on its ability to suppress the bri1 dwarfing phenotype when over-expressed, and via a yeast 2-hybrid screen.

It is likely that as in the proposed activation *mechanism* of animal receptor kinase signaling, BRs promote BRI1 and BAK1 to form an activated receptor complex via the change in phosphorylation status of this complex. *Potential downstream* targets of BRI1/BAK1 have been identified, although their exact role in the BR signaling process has yet to be clarified.

TRIP-1 (transforming growth factor beta (TGFI)), a receptor interacting protein has been shown to co-*immunoprecipitate* with BRI1, and it has been demonstrated that the BRI1 kinase can phosphorylate TRIP1.

Antisense TRIP1 plants also exhibit dwarfism and other phenotypic similarities to those of BR-signaling mutants, suggesting that TRIP1 is involved in the BR response.

It remains to be clarified how TRIP1, a component of the eIF3 translation initiation factor, functions in BR signaling. A yeast 2-hybrid screen for other BRI1 substrates using the BRI1 kinas bait has identified a transthyretin-like (TTL) protein.

In vitro experiments indicate that BRI1 phosphorylates TTL, and genetic evidence suggests that TLL is a negative regulator of BR-induced plant growth. The co-expression of TTL with BRI1, and their localisation in the plasma membrane provides further evidence that TTL has a role in BR signaling.

The mechanism, however, by which TTL mediates responses toward downstream signaling components remains a mystery.

BIN2 and BSU1

Genetic screens for mutants insensitive to BRs mainly identified recessive mutations in BRI1. However, careful re-examination of the mutants obtained from such screens also led to the identification of the BR INSENSITIVE *2 locus (BIN2).*

BIN2 was isolated by map-based cloning and shown to have homology to *mammalian Glycogen Synthase Kinase* 3-β (GSK3) and the Shaggy protein kinase of *Drosophila. BIN2* is one member of an *Arabidopsis* gene family comprised of ten genes.

In the *bin2* gain-of-function mutants, increased BIN2 activity resulted in dwarf plants. Genetic and molecular data indicated that BIN2 was acting as a negative regulator of BR synthesis, such that down-regulation of BIN2 activity is required for BR-mediated responses.

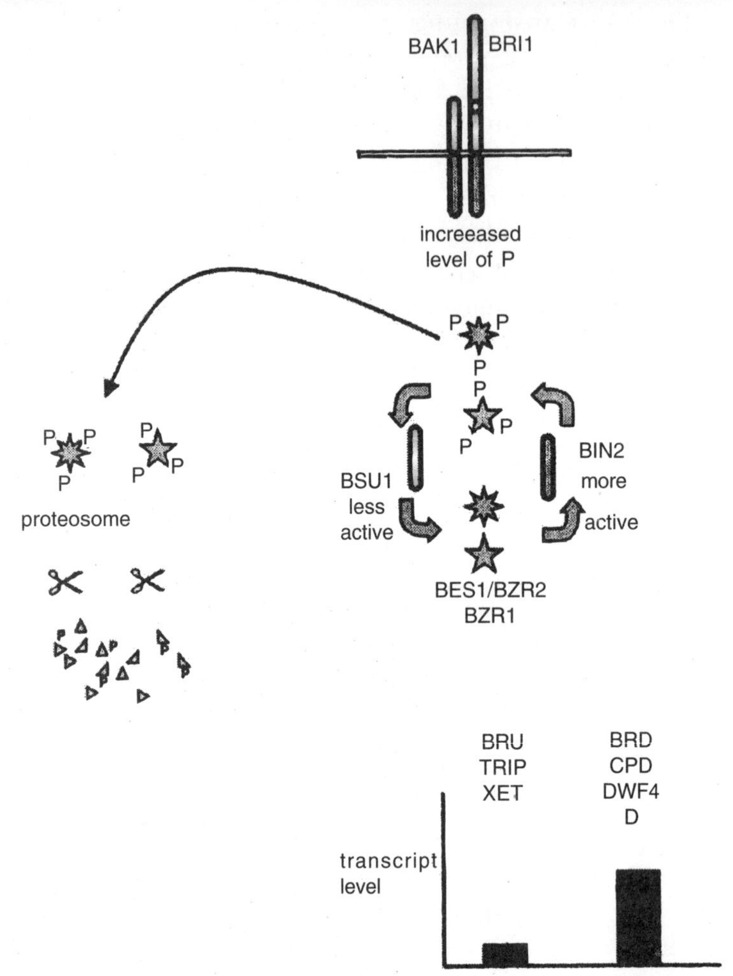

Figure 6.4: Model showing the status of the BR signaling components in the absence of BRs.

An additional mutant at the BIN2 locus (UCUI) was identified at the same time via screens for altered leaf morphology. As mentioned earlier, activation tagging in the bri1 mutant background led to the identification of the bak1 mutation.

A similar screen led to the isolation of an additional suppressor mutant, bsu1 (bri1 *suppressor 1). BSUI* encodes

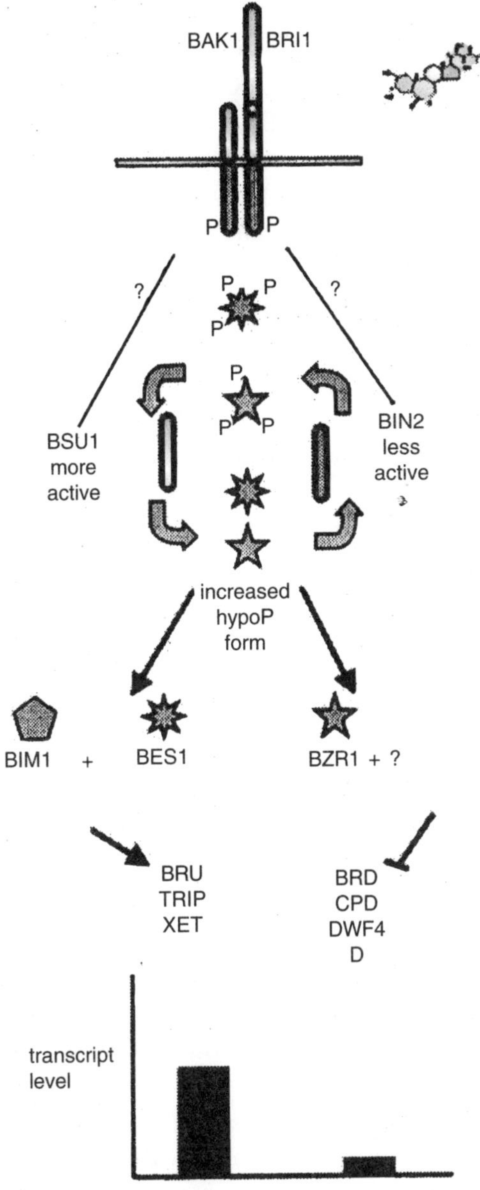

Figure 6.5: Model showing the status of the BR signaling components in the presence of BRs.

an apparently plant-specific phosphatase with N-terminal Kelch-repeat and C-terminal S/T phosphatase domains.

The bsu1 mutation partially suppresses the *bin2* mutant phenotype, and bsu1 RNAi lines exhibit a phenotype similar to the weak alleles of bri1. These results suggest that the BSU1 phosphatase acts antago the BIN2 kinase activity.

This antagonism is apparent in the phosphorylation status of the BIN2/BSU1 substrates, BZR1 and BZR2/BES1, as discussed in the next section.

BZR1 and BZR2/BES1

Brassinazole (BRZ) is a triazole-type inhibitor of BR synthesis developed to specifically interact with the P450 enzymes of the pathway. This inhibitor, when applied at RM to mM concentrations, has been shown to generate dwarfs that are phenotypically similar to the BR-biosynthetic and BR-signaling mutants.

To identify further BR-signaling components mutations that suppress the inhibitor-induced dwarfism in the dark were identified, namely the brassinazole-resistant bzr1 and *bzr2* genes.

The bes1 *(bri1 ems suppressor 1)* mutation was identified in a genetic screen for suppressors of the bri1 mutant phenotype and was found to be allelic to *bzr2.* BZR1 and BES1 are highly homologous and are part of a plant-specific gene family that in *Arabidopsis* has six members.

The *bzrl* and *bes1* mutations are gain-of-function mutations that both lead to a P to L substitution in the proteolysis-linked PEST domain. Although bzr1 and bes1 have similar mutations in their protein sequence and exhibit similar dark-grown phenotypes, their light-grown phenotypes are different.

The bzr1 mutants have a weak dwarf phenotype and increased sensitivity to BRZ, whereas the bes1 mutants have a phenotype similar to lines over-expressing BRI1. This suggested that BZR1 acts as a transcriptional repressor, whereas BES1 as an activator.

The BZR1 and BZR2/BES1 proteins have nuclear localisation sequences, and when fused to FP (fluorescent protein) targeting of these proteins to the nucleus is observed. BZR1 and BES1 over-expression suppresses the bin2 phenotype, indicating that BZR1 and BES1 act downstream of BIN2.

In vitro experiments have shown that BIN2 can phosphorylate BZR1 and BES1, and that in the *bin2* dominant dwarf lines the levels of BZR1 and BES1 are reduced.

The proteasome inhibitor MG132 allowed the accumulation of phosphorylated BZR1, indicating that phosphorylation of BZR1 targets it for degradation. More recent has been the observation that BZR1 and BES1 bind to DNA in distinct manners, with BZRI binding to upstream regulatory sequences of BR down-regulated (BRD) genes, whereas BES1 binds to sequences upstream of BR up-regulated (BRU) genes.

BZRI is therefore a key component in the feedback regulation of BR synthesis, which is consistent with the observed difference between the light-grown phenotypes of the *bzrl* and *bes1* mutants.

BIM1

The discovery that BZR1 and BES1 have DNA binding activity was made at the sametime as that of the bHLH transcription factor BIM1 (BES INTERACTING MYC LIKE 1). BIM1 was identified by screening for proteins that interact with the BES1 C-terminal domain.

The triple mutant defective in BIM1 and those in its close homologues *BIM2* and *BIM3* is dwarfed under light and dark conditions. The over-expression of BIM1 can partially suppress the weak bri1 dwarf phenotype and this causes reduced sensitivity to BRZ.

By contrast, the triple mutant is more sensitive to the inhibitor. These data highlight the fact that BIM1, BIM2 and BIM3 are involved in BR response. Binding assays of BES1 and BIM1 to target gene promoters have shown specific binding to the E-box sequence motif (CANNTG), and a model has been presented suggesting that binding occurs in a heterodimer form. BZR1 also acts as a transcription factor that binds to the CGTG(T/C)G BR-response element (BRRE).

Analysis of microarray data and targets for BZR1 suggests that this transcription factor acts as a repressor that is important both in BR homeostasis and growth responses. It is not yet known, however, if BZR1 forms a heterodimer with a yet to be identified transcription factor.

Signaling Mechanism and other Putative Components

Recent models and reviews of BR signaling have been given by Vert *et al.* (2005), Li (2005) and Li and Deng (2005). Here we summarise these models by showing the process of BR signaling in the absence or presence of BRs.

When BRs are absent, the BRI1 receptor and its co-receptor BAK1 are not activated and this state of the receptor complex does not reduce the activity of BIN2 kinase, or increase the activity of BSU1 phosphatase.

BIN2 phosphorylates BES1 and BZR1, and the phosphorylated forms are targeted for degradation in the proteasome.

This leads to a reduced level of hypophosphorylated BES1 and BZR1 in the nucleus that causes reduced expression of BRU genes and increased expression of BRD genes, for example the BR-biosynthesis genes *DWF4* and *CPD*.

Conversely, in the presence of BRs, BR binds to BRI1 leading to phosphorylation of the BRI1 and BAK1 kinase domains in the receptor complex. By some unknown mechanism, reduction in the activity of the BIN2 kinase and/or increase of BSU1 phosphatase activity occurs.

This results in an increased concentration of hypophosphorylated BES1 and BZR 1 in the nucleus. BES1 with BIM2 bind to E-box sequences to up-regulate a subset of BR responsive genes.

BZR1 binds to BRRE sequences and acts as a repressor, that is feedback regulator, for BR-biosynthesis genes (e.g. *DWF4* and *CPD)* and other BR down-regulated genes. The initial activation of BRI1 is somewhat different from that suggested before, whereby BRs were thought to bind to proteolytically processed sterol binding proteins (SBPs), and these BR-protein complexes were to interact with the LRRs of BRI1 to activate a kinase cascade.

Initial support for the SBP involvement in BR signaling was provided via the isolation of a dominant mutant obtained by activation tagging in the weak bri1-5 background. BRS1 (BRI1 SUPPRESSOR 1), a carboxypeptidase, was found to act upstream of BRI1. Li *et al.* (2001b) postulated that a SBP could be a potential substrate for BRS 1.

Recently there has been further evidence to suggest a role for SBPs in BR signaling, showing that over-expression of MSBP1 (MEMBRANE STEROL BINDING PROTEIN 1) reduces, whereas its under-expression increases growth. This alteration in SBP levels, however, did not affect the expression of BR biosynthetic genes.

Further studies into how BR-signaling processes are affected by BRS1 and MSBP-lines with altered expression will be required to discern the role, if any, of SBPs and BRS in BR-mediated signaling.

FUTURE PROSPECTIVES

Metabolism

The reactions of BR biosynthesis are relatively well known, however the significance of known or yet unknown sub-pathways is yet to be clarified. BRs are synthesised in a complex pathway, and in biosynthetic mutant plants conversion rates and intermediate levels are distorted by the hormonal regulation of both biosynthetic and catabolic enzymes.

Therefore, BR analysis and intermediate rescue data cannot always give conclusive information regarding the enzymatic functions affected in biosynthetic mutants.

Recent progress in *heterologous* expression of functional CYP85s and CYP90s, and their enzymological characterisation seems to be instrumental in understanding the substrate preferences of these P450s.

Because *in vitro* conditions may influence enzymatic

functions, this promising technique can be most powerful when used in combination with the conventional molecular genetic and analytical methods. Detailed characterisation of BR biosynthesis and signaling will greatly benefit from the development of efficient, less time consuming methods capable of quantitating BR levels in different organs and tissues.

Such techniques will be helpful in elucidating if/how organ-specific expression of biosynthetic genes can inflaccumulation of BRs. Future studies are needed to clarify whether any of the BRs or their conjugates are transported within the plant.

Current evidence suggests that bioactive BRs act in paracrine/autocrine manner, with very limited transport between the tissues and organs.

Signal Transduction

Of key importance in BR signaling will be to determine the signaling process by which the activated BRI1/BAK1 kinases lead to the down-regulation of BIN2 kinase activity, and/or increased BSU1 phosphatase activity.

Similarly, clarification of the regulation and mechanism by which the receptor complex becomes deactivated will be of great interest. Endocytosis of the BRI1/BAK1complex has been observed, and this offers an enticing mechanism by which either of the processes above may occur.

Subcellular imaging of where the signaling events take place will also be an exciting area from which greater using of the BR-signaling process will be gained.

One *fascinating* problem is whether the BIN2 kinase can gain access to the nucleus and deactivate the BES1/BZR1 transcription factors.

There are numerous other lines of investigation that will provide highly informative and novel results, for example by determining the structure of the receptor–BR complex, or defining the roles of TTL, TRIP1, BRS1 and MSBP1 in the BR-*signaling* process.

Crops

It will be prudent to utilise our knowledge of BR metabolism and signaling to improve crop performance. *Conceivably*, by altering these process in crops increased yield will be possible through increased biomass or indirectly through greater resistance to stress factors, for example wind damage (*lodging*) and elevated temperatures.

Many advances in our understanding of BR biosynthesis and signaling have been made in *barley*, *cotton*, *pea*, *rice* and *tomato*, through the isolation of BR-related mutants and identification of the genes affected by these mutations.

Further advances in this area will enable better understanding of the conservation of BR related processes and provide methodologies for crop improvement. The adoption therefore of novel breeding strategies, using transgenic or non-transgenic means, are set to yield the desired fruits of BR researchof BR research.

Chapter 7

Plant Hormones Ethylene

The hydrocarbon ethylene (C_2H_4) is a plant hormone that plays an important role in the regulation of many *environmentally* and *developmentally* induced processes, such as *stress resistance, seed germination, fruit ripening, senescence,* and *abscission.*

All tissue types and probably all cells of higher plants produce and liberate ethylene. Many lower plants, such as *liverworts,* mosses, *ferns, lycopods,* and horse tails, also are producers of ethylene, although the biosynthetic route seems to be different.

Tremendous progress has been achieved during the last two decades in the biochemical and molecular characterization of the biosynthetic pathway for ethylene in higher plants. Endogenous ethylene concentrations inside plant tissues depend on the activities of certain enzymes, the rate of *outward* diffusion, and the rate of metabolism.

The rate-limiting reactions of ethylene biosynthesis involve the conversion of S-adenosylmethionine into 1-*aminocyclopropane*-1-*carboxylic acid* (ACC) catalyzed by ACC synthase and the conversion of ACC into *ethylene* mediated by the enzyme ACC oxidase.

Furthermore, ACC can be conjugated into 1-malonyl-aminocyclop-ropane-1-carboxylic acid (MACC) and 1-γ-L-*glutamylaminocyclopropane*-1-*carboxylic* acid (GACC). Ethylene can diffuse rapidly from plant tissues, as demonstrated in an experiment in which shoots of *Rumex palustris* were desubmerged after a *submergence* treatment. Of all the *ethylene* accumulated in the submerged shoot, 90% escaped within 1 min of desubmergence. Furthermore, evidence increases that *aerenchyma* tissue, developed in many wetland plants to facilitate oxygen diffusion to root tips, is also important for outward diffusion of ethylene, thus avoiding growth inhibitory levels of this *phytohormone* in roots.

Higher plants can *metabolize* ethylene into *carbon dioxide, ethylene glycol,* and *ethylene oxide.* Usually <10% of the ethylene produced by plants is *metabolized.* This means that it is highly unlikely that *ethylene metabolism* controls *endogenous ethylene* concentrations in higher plants.

The action of ethylene is not only controlled by endogenous ethylene concentrations in tissues, but also by the tissue sensitivity. It is widely assumed that molecules involved in ethylene perception and in the transduction of the signal probably control how much ethylene is required to evoke a *physiological* response.

It has recently been demonstrated in *Lycopersicon esculentum* and *R. palustris* for various plant processes (fruit ripening, flower senescence, abscission, and flooding-induced shoot elongation) that the expression of genes coding for *putative* ethylene receptors positively correlate to changes in tissue sensitivity.

The first chemical quantification of ethylene was performed more than 60 years ago on ripening apples. In the years thereafter, various techniques, such as *bioassays, gravimetric analyses, manometric techniques,* and *physicochemical colourimetric assays,* were applied to quantify *ethylene* concentrations.

A major breakthrough in ethylene analysis was achieved in the late 1950s, when the gas *chromatographic methodology* was applied for the first time to ethylene. For a more detailed discussion of ethylene quantification by means of gas *chromatography,* the *columns* and *detectors* used, and the potential sensitivity we refer to the methodological review of Bassi and *Spencer.*

Despite the high sensitivity (5–10 nL/L) this gas chromatographical technique still requires accumulation of ethylene to obtain measurable quantities. For this purpose, it is common practice to incubate pieces of tissue for a few hours in small incubation vials.

However, this procedure can disturb the rate of ethylene production because of wounding of tissue, disruption of transport processes, *gravitropical disorientation*, and changes in gas composition around the tissue.

The introduction of artifacts in measuring ethylene production rates with isolated plant tissues is elegantly demonstrated for the effect of plant-water deficit on ethylene production. Cotton leaves, detached from the mother plant and exposed to drying conditions, showed a significant upsurge in the rate of ethylene production compared to detached control leaves.

When intact cotton plants were exposed to drought no increase in ethylene production was observed. The only way to avoid these and other artifacts is to use larger sample chambers in which intact plants can be placed in combination with the use of continuous flow systems, to guarantee a stable gas composition.

If such a setup is in line with a gas *chromatograph*, the concentration of ethylene in the outflowing air is usually below the detection limits of most detectors.

To overcome this problem, ethylene can be concentrated on a cooled column with a high adsorption capacity for ethylene; ethylene released after heating can be measured with gas chromatography. Despite the improvements, this method still has disadvantages, such as the inability to measure fast changes in *ethylene production.*

To follow dynamic processes, it is necessary to measure ethylene directly and nearly continuously in the out flowing air of continuous flow systems. This can be achieved if a flow through system in line with a large sampling chamber is combined with the extremely sensitive laser *photoacoustic detection* technique.

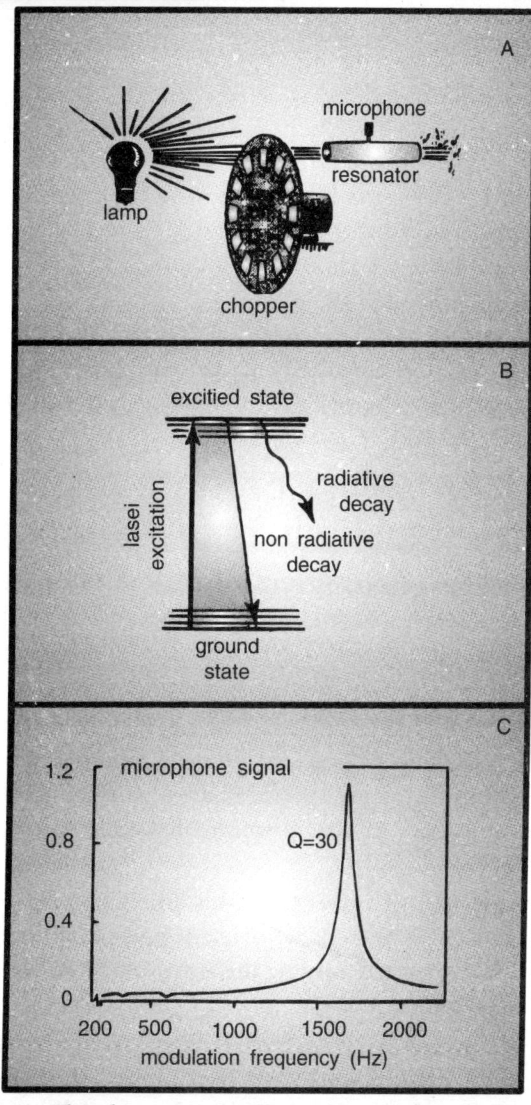

Figure 7.1: (A) The photoacoustic effect, schematically. (B) A light source (sunlight, lamp, or laser) is used to excite the molecules into a higher rotational-vibrational energy level. Because of collisions the molecules return back to their original energy state, releasing heat toward the surrounding gas, resulting in a temperature and pressure increase. (C) The light is mechanically chopped at a frequency that corresponds to the resonance frequency of the acoustical resonator resulting in an enhancement of the photoacoustic effect.

The detection limit of this system is three orders of magnitude better than gas chromatography, i.e., 6 pL/L. Since the 1980s laser photoacoustic *spectroscopy* has been applied to determine ethylene production rates and *concentrations* in studies that *focus* on such processes as *germination, flower senescence, aerenchyma* formation in roots, diffusion through *aerenchymatous* roots, formation of adventitious roots, submergence-induced shoot elongation, and fruit ripening.

In this chapter we describe the setup that allows ethylene detection at the picoliter level (laser-based photoacoustic detector) and an additional setup that makes local, nonintrusive detection of ethylene down to 0.5 nL/L possible (laser-based photothermal detector).

PHOTOACOUSTIC AND PHOTOTHERMAL DETECTION OF ETHYLENE

Photoacoustic *spectroscopy* is based on the conversion of light energy into *acoustic* energy. Alexander Graham Bell described the *photoacoustic* effect for the first time more than 100 yr ago.

He showed that thin *disks* of very different *materials*, such as *selenium, carbon*, and *rubber, emitted* sound when exposed to rapidly interrupted beams of sunlight. In the years thereafter interest in the photoacoustic principle strongly declined.

A renaissance of interest in this phenomenon in physics was initiated by Kreuzer, who used powerful laser light in photoacoustic *spectroscopy* to measure extreme low levels of *pollutants* in gases.

The photoacoustic effect is based on the fact that *molecules* absorb infrared radiation. Thus, they are excited to a higher energy level. Excited molecules fall back to their original ground state either by radiative decay (*fluorescence*) or nonradiative decay (*collisions*).

In the *infrared* region this leads almost exclusively to nonradiative decay. *De-excitation* by *collisional* relaxation increases the kinetic energy and thus the temperature of the

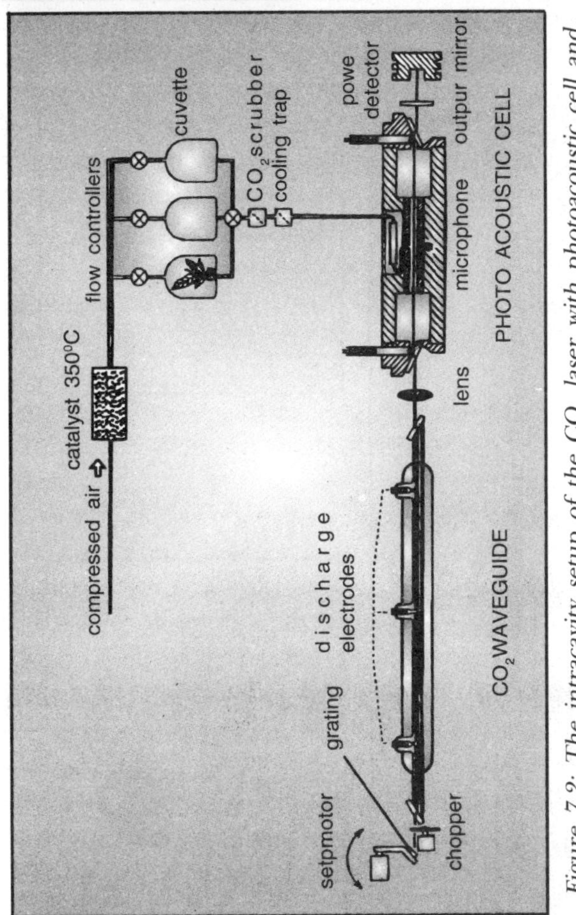

Figure 7.2: The intracavity setup of the CO_2 laser with photoacoustic cell and gas flow system for measuring ethylene production from biological samples. The laser beam is generated in the discharge tube and reflected at one side by the output mirror and at the other side by the grating. The latter is also used for laser line selectivity. The gas flow system flushes the emitted ethylene from sampling cell to photoacoustic cell, passing the CO_2 scrubber and cooling trap

gas molecules around the excited molecules. If this process takes place in a constant volume it increases the pressure (Law of Boyle-Gay Lussac).

A light source modulated at an audio frequency will generate pressure *fluctuations* at the same frequency inside the constant volume (i.e., the *photoacoustic cell*); this can be detected by a microphone. *Photothermal deflection* is based on the same effect and is used to measure specific, local gas emissions at sub-ppb levels under *ambient* conditions.

The difference with *photoacoustic* detection is that the temperature increase itself is detected. This increase in

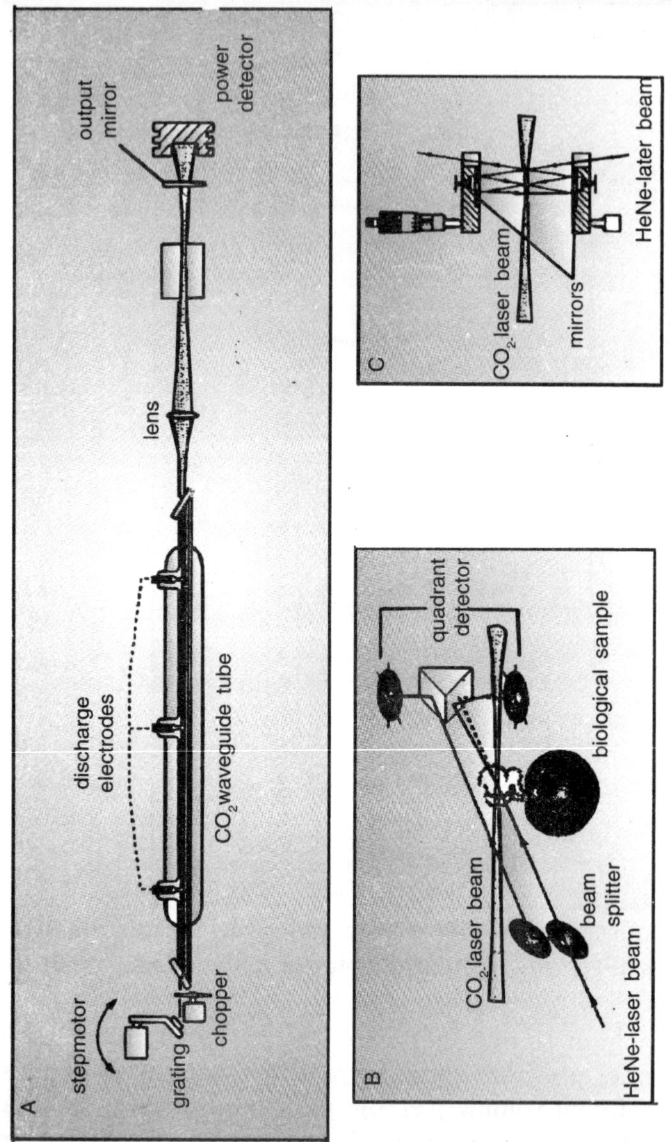

Figure 7.3: The photothermal deflection setup consisting of an intracavity CO_2 laser and a dual He-Ne probe laser beam. The CO_2 laser cavity is similar as to the photoacoustic setup (A). The He-Ne laser beam is split in two parallel beams by a beam splitter from which one is passing the interaction region and the other is used as reference (B).

temperature leads to a change in refractive index in the gas. Because of the spatial gradient of the *refractive* index a second laser beam will be deflected.

The deflection angle of the He-Ne laser beam used is an indication of the amount of molecules absorbing the CO_2 laser radiation. In the *hotothermal deflection setup*, beams of the CO_2 and the He-Ne laser are passing the surface of an intact plant tissue at a distance of just 1.5 mm.

The advantage of this method over the photoacoustic detection is that the experiments can be performed under ambient conditions (open air).

MATERIALS

Photoacoustic Spectroscopy

To gain sensitivity for ethylene, high laser powers (100 W) are necessary. Therefore, a CO_2 laser with an extended cavity to insert a photoacoustic cell is commonly used.

The setup consists of a gas discharge tube (with water jacket) to generate the laser radiation with a high voltage DC discharge through the gas filling of CO_2 (12%), *nitrogen* (23%), and *helium* (65%) (pressure 50 mbar), a grating (PTR 150 L/mm; *Optometrics*, Fakenham, UK) controlled by a stepmotor (Oriel Steppermike; Fairlight, Rotterdam, The Netherlands) to select CO_2 laser lines, and a chopper to modulate the CO_2 laser beam for generation of the signal inside the *photoacoustic cell.*

The ZnSe infrared optics consists of windows (placed at Brewster angle) to seal the discharge tube and photoacoustic cell, a positive lens (f= 35 cm), and output mirror (97% refletivity).

The piezo element (Piezomechanik PST150/5/15/wc; Nema Electronics, Amsterdam, The Netherlands) adjusts the length of the *laser cavity* over 5 μm for optimal laser power and the power *detector monitors* the *outcoupled* laser power.

Additional control and supply units consist of a computer to run the experiment, a lock-in amplifier to filter and amplify the photoacoustic signal, a stepmotor controller, *chopper* controller, high voltage supply, piezo controller, and a laser gas mixing system including valves, mechanical flow controllers, pressure indicators, and vacuum pump to handle the helium, nitrogen, and CO_2 needed for laser action.

A gas-flow system to flush the emitted ethylene from sampling cell to photoacoustic cell consists of a bottle of compressed air (or any other gas mixture), a *catalyst* containing platinized Al_2O_3 pellets (*Aldrich Chemie, Bornem, Belgium*) heated to 400°C to remove all traces of hydrocarbons, a pressure reduction valve, 1/16 in. tubing and connectors, mechanical flow controllers, cuvets with biological sample, a KOH-scrubber between sampling cell and a detector to remove interfering CO_2, a $CaCl_2$-scrubber to remove water, a cold-trap (110°C) to remove ethanol, and a mass flow controller.

Parts not assigned to a company or firm were constructed and assembled at the department of Molecular and Laser Physics, University of Nijmegen, the Netherlands.

PHOTOTHERMAL SPECTROSCOPY

The intracavity CO_2 laser-based photothermal deflection setup consists of a CO_2 laser setup similar to the one described in Subheading 2.1. above. Differences are a ZnSe prism (Laser Power Optics, San Diego, CA) driven by a galvo element to select laser lines and a chopper between 5 and 50 Hz.

The perpendicular placed deflection frame is rigidly coupled to the CO_2 laser frame. It consists of a He-Ne laser, a beam splitter (Melles Griot), a *multipass* arrangement, and two position-sensitive quadrant detectors.

Also for this detector, the parts not assigned to a company or firm were constructed and assembled at the department of Molecular and *Laser Physics*, University of Nijmegen, the Netherlands.

The gas-handling system can be similar to the one discussed for the photoacoustic laser setup; i.e., gas supply, water supply for laser cooling, KOH for CO_2 scrubber, assortment of Swagelok material (1/8 and 1/16 in.), and *Teflon* and *silicon*

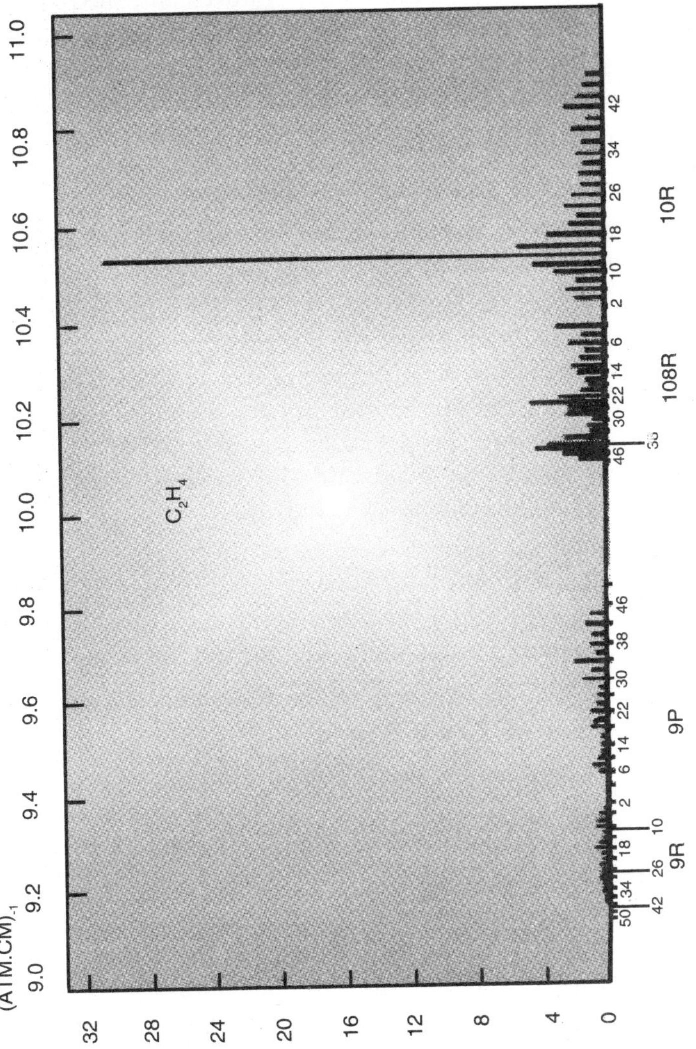

Figure 7.4: The absorption pattern of ethylene at the CO_2 laser lines. The laser generates radiation at about 80 laser lines in a wavelength region between 9 and 11 μm. A distinct pattern appears at these wavelengths with the strongest absorption at the 10P14 line.

tubing material. In addition, temperature-controlled and air-ventilated conditions in the laboratory are *prerequisites.*

METHODS

Photoacoustic Spectroscopy

Alignment and Laser-Beam Generation

Each optical element of the intracavity laser setup is centered around the principal axis. A proper alignment can only be performed by an experienced laser physicist.

An He-Ne laser beam can be used to align all optical elements at this principle axis, either in reflection or in transmission of the He-Ne laser beam. Before switching on the laser discharge, proper laser gas mixture and pressure (50 mbar) should be fixed and the cooling water for the discharge tube should be switched on.

The total gas mass flow through the discharge is about 135 L/h at maximum laser power; the rate can be reduced (by 50%) by adjusting a valve between the gas discharge tube and the vacuum pump; then, the current must also be re-adjusted.

Optimization of Laser Power

Proper alignment, gas mixing, and gas pressure will generate laser power as soon as the DC discharge has been switched on. Be sure that the grating is in a position that one can expect laser radiation (e.g., at the center of the 10P branch at a wavelength of 10.6 μm).

By adjusting the cavity length (i.e., the output mirror) over 5.3 μm (1/2 wavelength), the laser output power can be maximized; this can be done by a *piezo* element converting an applied voltage in a *translation* with high accuracy.

The position of the photoacoustic cell inside the laser cavity can be optimized by moving the cell perpendicular to the laser beam in a vertical or *horizontal* direction. As soon as the outer side of the Gaussian laser beam hits the wall of the acoustic resonator the photoacoustic signal increases and the laser power drops.

To assure proper alignment the cell should be filled or flushed with nitrogen gas to minimize the gas absorption signal (instead of using nitrogen, clean air passing the catalyst, scrubbers and a cold trap can also be used).

The infrared optics should be kept as clean as possible and never be touched by bare hands. Cleaning should only be done with special optical tissues soaked in *methanol.* The grating should never be *cleaned.*

Line Selection and Optimization of Photoacoustic Signal

Laser lines can be selected by using a CO_2 infrared spectrum analyzer (Optical Engineering). However, if this analyzer is not available lines can be selected by adding traces of ethylene gas (e.g., 1 ppm) in the gas flow through the photoacoustic cell.

The CO_2 laser has about 80 laser lines in the 9–11 μm region divided over four branches. Lines in the "10P" branch can be indicated using traces of ethylene, preferably in a flow of nitrogen at standard temperature and pressure (STP); the 10P14 line demonstrates the highest absorption, i.e., six times larger than the neighboring 10P12 and 10P16 laser lines.

To get the maximum photoacoustic signal the chopper has to be tuned to the resonance frequency of the photoacoustic cell. At this frequency an acoustical standing wave is generated in the open resonator.

The speed of sound relates to the modulation frequency with the acoustical wavelength; at resonance frequency half of the acoustical wavelength is equal to the length of the resonator; the nodes of the longitudinal wave are at both ends of the open resonator.

Since the speed of sound depends on temperature and gas content (oxygen, nitrogen, or CO_2 at percentage concentration) the modulation frequency must be adapted to the resonance frequency for maximal signal. Calibration of the system is performed choosing the 10P14 laser line and, subsequently, injecting a specified volume of a certain concentration of ethylene (e.g., certified gas mixture of 1 ppm of ethylene in highly purified nitrogen) into a cuvet, which is flushed with clean air (or nitrogen) at a constant flow.

The area under the obtained curve determines the relation between photoacoustic signal and the total amount of ethylene, i.e., determines the conversion factor.

Flow through System

Starting with compressed air (preferably not too contaminated), the air passes filters (attached to the catalyst) to remove dust and oil droplets. Inside the catalyst carbohydrates are converted to CO_2 and H_2O. The temperature of the catalyst is 400°C.

Check that no water vapor is visible inside the outlet tube of the catalyst; if so, remove the outlet tube and flow air through the catalyst. The outflowing air passes a pressure-valve adjusted at 1.5 atmosphere. Thereafter, the flow is divided into different tubes.

Each of these flows can be adjusted with the help of a flow controller in line. Next, the flow enters the biological sampling cuvet, of which the outlet is led to a three-way valve. One port is connected via a multi-inlet-1-outlet divider to the KOH-based CO_2 scrubber, the $CaCl_2$-based water vapor scrubber, cold trap, photoacoustic cell, and finally a mass flow controller.

The other port acts as additional outlet to prevent stopping the air flow if this specific sample is not connected to the detection cell. To keep the slight overpressure inside the sampling cell, a syringe needle is placed at the second port.

The KOH-based CO_2 scrubber must always be inserted into the flow through system; the $CaCl_2$ is only required if high humidity is used in the sample cuvet and to avoid freezing of the cold trap. The cold trap is used if the production of disturbing components (e.g., ethanol) can be expected.

A typical temperature of the cold trap is –110°C; a lower temperature will liquify the oxygen in the air, a higher temperature will allow partial vapor pressures of interfering gases to pass the trap. Finally, the flow passes a mass flow detector, which monitors the flow rate in L/h.

Depending on the ethylene production of the biological sample and the volume of the cuvet a flow rate of between 0.2 and 5 L/h is installed. The flow rate (L/h) is multiplied by the measured ethylene concentration (nL/L) to obtain a production rate (nL/h). Furthermore, production rates can be normalized to dry or fresh weight of the biological sample to allow comparisons.

Turning Off the System and Maintenance

After finishing an experiment the following sequence of actions safely turns off the system: Turn off the high voltage on the laser discharge tube, close the laser gas supply bottles, close any additional gas valves, and turn off the vacuum pump.

Turn off the catalyst (block the flow through the catalyst approx 15 min after turning off the catalyst) and turn off all other instruments. If any of the ZnSe windows or lenses are contaminated they have to be cleaned with methanol using special lens-cleaning tissues.

Brute force must be avoided to keep from damaging the window surface. Cleaning should only be done by experienced scientists. The grating should never be cleaned or touched.

The Brewster windows, especially onto the laser discharge tube, are polluted frequently on the inside surface; therefore, they must be replaced (e.g., each year at continuous operation). It is preferred to have a small (e.g., 1 L/h) flow of nitrogen gas through the gas sampling system, even when the detector is turned off, to keep it clean.

Measurements

The various parts of the laser-driven photoacoustic setup should be computer controlled, enabling a fully automated sampling of ethylene production rates of biological tissue. The sampling run starts by tuning the grating toward the ethylene-absorbing CO_2 laser line (10P14 laser line at 10.53

μm). Thereafter, the laser power at that laser line is maximized by adjusting the laser cavity length over half a wavelength (5.3 μm) by the piezo, which is mounted to the output mirror holder. Subsequently, the photoacoustic signal and the laser power are alternatively sampled and divided onto each other in a closed loop over (e.g.) 100 times for averaging.

Samples encompassing the 95% confidence interval are used to calculate the mean ethylene signal at this 10P14 line. Hereafter, the position of the grating changes to tune the laser to a non-ethylene absorbing wavelength (i.e., 10P12 laser line at 10.51 μm wavelength).

Again the laser power is optimized and the sample routine is performed. The signals on both laser lines include ethylene absorption and background signal. The latter is generated from wall and window absorption and from interfering gases.

The first two signals can be distinguished quite easily because of their relative wavelengthindependent absorption patterns, which should not change during the experiment. The interfering gases can cause problems in quantifying the amount of ethylene; therefore, they should be removed from the gas flow.

The overall measuring sequence takes approx 1 min; ethylene concentration and background signal are calculated properly by the computer. The next step can be another photoacoustic run on the same cuvet or alternatively, a computer controlled switch to another cuvet that is empty or contains control tissue.

The latter signals should be subtracted from the experiment to extract the pure effect and cancel slow, externally induced variations (e.g., over hours or days).

PHOTOTHERMAL SPECTROSCOPY

Alignment and Laser Beam Generation

The photothermal deflection setup consists of two parts; one frame for the CO_2 laser and another frame for the He-Ne laser. The latter frame should be rigidly fixed to the first one to avoid relative displacement of both laser beams. In principle the CO_2 laser setup is the same as the one described elsewhere in this chapter. above except that here a sharper intracavity focus (waist 0.28 mm) is performed by the combination of a ZnSe lens (f = 75 mm) and a spherical ZnSe outcoupling mirror (inner radius of curvature R = 270 mm).

The distance between lens and mirror is 350 mm, which is the available space to insert a biological sample. Care has to be taken to align the lens and outcoupling mirror properly.

For optimization of the laser power, line selection, flow through system, system shutdown, and maintenance, we refer to the photoacoustic spectroscopy section. Nearly instantaneous detection of trace gases is achieved by implementing a laser-line-selective device in the cavity of a CO_2 laser.

The principle is based on rapidly switching between two laser lines, achieved by installation of a ZnSe prism, mounted on a galvo element, between the grating and discharge tube. The prism is similar to a Brewster window of 1 in.; however, one side is inclined with respect to the other by 2°. The prism is installed at Brewster angle, minimizing power losses to 18% on the strongest laser line.

The angle between the grating and incoming beam is adjusted by rotation of the prism. Using a square wave modulation for the galvo element at a repetition frequency of 10 Hz yields a stable output power at two subsequent laser lines.

Probe Laser Frame

The second frame consists of an He-Ne laser, a beamsplitter, a multipass mirror setup, and two quadrant detectors. All are mounted on a rigid frame to avoid disturbance by mechanical vibrations. The He-Ne laser is chosen for its small beam diameter of 0.79 mm as well as a small divergence angle of 1 mrad.

The beam is divided into two beams, by means of a beam splitter, to decrease the noise caused by air turbulence. The vertical distance between the two beams should be kept small. In this way air turbulence (diameter of vortex ranging from several meters to several millimeters) influences both beams in almost the same way. Both beams are aligned in a parallel fashion. One passes just over the heated region, i.e., at 0.7 mm from the pump beam, and will be deflected; the other, unaffected beam traverses at a distance of 10 mm over the pump beam. The distance of 0.7 mm is chosen such that the deflection will be at a maximum.

The deflection is related to the gradient in refractive index. Using a chopper frequency of 20 Hz and the focused CO_2 laser configuration as described elsewhere in this chapter, the gradient is maximum at an offset of 0.7 mm from the CO_2 laser. The He-Ne probe laser beam is passed over the heated region several times by means of a flat mirror system.

It should be noted that all beams are aligned such that each beam is passing the pump beam with an offset of 0.7 mm. The main multipass system consists of two square flat mirrors (25 × 25 mm) with highly reflective coatings, tilted with respect to each other by a small angle.

The number of passes is a function of this angle and of the angle of the incident He-Ne beam with respect to the mirror. In practice, the beam divergence and the beam waist of the probe beam cannot be neglected.

Thus, the distance between the mirrors should also be taken into account. In our actual setup the optimum number of passes is 31 at a tilt angle of about 1° and a mirror distance of 40 mm. The dimensions of the mirrors determine the interaction length of probe and pump beam and, thus, the spatial resolution of this setup.

Measurements

Within the multipass area a reference cell can be installed. In this way the detector can be calibrated by flushing a standard gas mixture through the cell (e.g., 1 ppm of ethylene in pure nitrogen).

In addition biological experiments can be performed under welldefined conditions. After calibration, CO_2 laser lines can be identified by open-air experiments flushing ethylene, water, or ammonia through the interaction zone of the two laser beams.

All these molecules demonstrate clear fingerprints in the CO_2 laser wavelength region. To identify local trace gas emissions from biological tissue, the tissue needs to be adjusted close to the CO_2 laser beam in the interaction zone of the two beams.

However, care has to be taken to avoid external influences, like heating or burning of the tissue; a typical distance of 1.5 mm between CO_2 laser beam and tissue surface is advised. The deflection of the probe laser beam is measured with a position-sensitive detector, consisting of a diode quadrant detector with a voltage slope of 0.512 V/mm between two quadrant parts.

The reference beam is detected by a separate quadrant detector. The detected signals are subtracted in a lock-in amplifier (time constant of 1 s) yielding an improvement of the sensitivity by a factor of two. This entire experimental setup is computer controlled; in particular the grating adjustment and the piezo optimization necessary to achieve single laser line operation.

The positioning of the biological sample below the crossing of the two laser beams is also adjusted by the computer. Deflection signal and intracavity CO_2 laser power are handled in the same way as for the photoacoustic setup.

PHOTOACOUSTIC SPECTROSCOPY

Acoustic sound from outside the photoacoustic cell will enter the microphone and will induce noise on top of the signal.

Fortunately, one can diminish the surrounding noise by using a lock-in amplifier, which selectively amplifies the photoacoustic signal.

The lock-in amplifier amplifies only within a certain bandwidth (e.g., 1 Hz) and in a small-phase angle around the reference frequency generated by the chopper.

The reminiscent noise can be rejected by constructing the photoacoustic cell of stiff and heavy material (e.g., brass).

The ultimate noise level will be the electronic noise level

from the microphone itself; one should come as close as possible to it. The ratio of generated signal from the sample gas and the acoustic noise level determines the signal-to-noise level and thus the detection limit of the system.

Absorptions generated by the laser beam (window, wall) are in-phase with the modulation frequency and will be seen as a constant photoacoustic signal relatively independent of the laser line.

These background absorptions should not be to high; however, they do not interfere with the sensitivity of the setup.

Another source of noise can arise from the tubing containing the flow though system and will be either flow noise from turbulences of the gas flow (lower the flow rate to check directly on the microphone signal connected to a oscilloscope) or caused by mechanical coupling with, e.g., a vacuum pump or chopper.

Use coaxial cables and connectors to avoid electrical pick-up. Other gases can interfere with the generated signal from ethylene absorption.

They will not have a wavelength-independent signal that is stable over the time period of the experiment; therefore, they have to be removed from the gas flow with a cold trap.

A special case is CO_2; although the vibrational absorption performs only weakly in the 9–11 μm region the individual absorption lines are positioned exactly at the CO_2 laser lines. The fingerprint absorption will appear on these lines as a slowly changing pattern.

In addition, because of the combination of the modulation frequency (>1000 Hz) and the slow collisional relaxation of the absorbed energy by CO_2, the generated photoacoustic signal will undergo a phase shift.

Thus, in combination with the absorption of ethylene the overall signal will be lower and can result in negative (calculated) concentrations. This can be overcome by removing the CO_2 out of the gas flow between sampling cell and detection cell by a KOH scrubber.

PHOTOTHERMAL SPECTROSCOPY

Photothermal deflection is very well suited to detect gases locally, next to those that tend to stick to walls and are reactive. Although less sensitive, because of the open air environment and contact-free detection, this method is advantageous as compared to photoacoustics.

Several sources of noise (at the modulation frequency of 20 Hz) have to be considered and minimized to achieve the sensitivity of 0.5 ppb for ethylene; i.e., instrumental noise, mechanical vibrations, and air turbulence.

To the first group belong the electrical noise of the quadrant detector and the pointing stability of the He-Ne laser. Fluctuations in pointing stability of the CO_2 laser are negligible. The He-Ne laser, multipass system, and detector should be mounted in a rigid frame to minimize mechanical vibrations between the two laser beams.

The entire setup is sustained by soft cushions to uncouple external mechanical vibrations. A low modulation frequency of 20 Hz is preferably to have a maximum gradient of refraction resulting in a maximized signal.

Air turbulences generate the highest noise and are responsible for the detection limit. They can be minimized by shielding the entire setup. For the same reason the chopper is positioned between the grating and the discharge tube, as far away as possible from the detection zone to prevent air turbulence.

Using a double-probe beam setup diminishes the influence of air turbulence. The detection limit of 0.5 ppb ethylene was achieved at 20 Hz, 100 W laser power, pure nitrogen as buffer gas in the detection cell, and 31 passes using the flat-mirror multipass configuration.

The temporal resolution is determined by the slowest step in the pathway from excitation to detection. Excitation is in the order of nanoseconds. For collisional decay the characteristic decay value is below 1 μs for ethylene at standard pressure and temperature.

Thermal conductivity yields the optimum heat profile after a characteristic rise time of 15 ms, whereas probing of the refractive index gradient is determined by the time response of the detector (0.1 ms).

Thus, the temporal resolution is determined by the thermal conductivity. However, to detect low concentrations of ethylene, changes in interfering gases need to be taken carefully into account; these, in contrast to photoacoustics, cannot easily be removed—one needs to switch between several laser lines.

The switching time between two neighboring laser lines, including piezo optimization, is 15 s. This switching time has, however, been reduced to 0.1 s using the oscillating prism. Finally, the signal is fed into a lock-in amplifier; for the fast fluctuation measurements the time constant is 30 ms, for the relatively slow measurements 1 s.

The radial dimensions of the CO_2 laser beam are of importance, considering possible temperature influences on plant tissues. In experiments attention should be paid to external influences on tissues, like heating and burning.

In the wings of the Gaussian beam profile a large amount of laser power is still available. In a control experiment a thermocouple placed inside a tomato just beneath the epidermis showed a temperature rise of 2°C with the tissue 1.5 mm away from the CO_2 laser beam.

Compared to this the temperature rise caused by trace gas absorption is only in the order of a few mK. The most important interfering gases for ethylene detection are CO_2 and H_2O; typical ambient concentrations are 350 ppm and 0.5–2%, respectively.

For CO_2, this results in a concentration equivalent to 60 ppb of ethylene at the 10P14 laser line. For 1.5% water, this value corresponds to 1.4 ppb of ethylene. As mentioned before, CO_2 and H_2O have broad, unstructured absorptions patterns, which in our case is advantageous.

Variations of the concentrations mainly result in a change in background signal. Subtracting the signal from the nonabsorbing, reference laser line from the signal on the absorbing laser line leaves only a small, but still significant, contribution from CO_2.

As difference signal a CO_2 concentration of 350 ppm corresponds to 4.2 ppb of ethylene. Because of the low modulation frequency as compared to photoacoustics (20 instead of 1600 Hz) a phase shift does not occur.

A fluctuation of 10% in absolute CO_2 concentration yields a fluctuation of 0.5 ppb for ethylene. The corresponding value for H_2O is typically smaller by a factor of 10. In experiments with plants, besides CO_2 and H_2O, other gases can be present at high concentrations, e.g., ethanol, an end product of fermentation.

Fortunately, the absorption spectrum of ethanol is also broad, yielding an increase in background signal. Similarly, the role of broadband absorption of other carbohydrates, like propylene, leads mainly to an increase in background.

Some of these components are cryotrapped in photoacoustic measurements; this cannot be applied in open-air photothermal deflection measurements.

GENERAL NOTES

The described ethylene detectors are very sensitive for ethylene; therefore, one should always be aware of unexpected emissions. As an example, the tubing material that contains the gas sample flow may be polluted by ethylene-producing bacteria.

Also UV light (and the UV part of the visible light) will dissociate the polymer tubing, generating traces of ethylene. Both the photoacoustic and the photothermal techniques depend linearly on concentrations over the range of subppb to 100 ppm of ethylene mixed in pure nitrogen.

At higher levels, the intracavity laser power is lowered substantially. Too high laser intensities will lead to saturation effects, giving rise to lower absorption coefficients as compared to literature values. Attention should be paid to this aspect, because both photoacoustic and photothermal detections are using high laser powers and sharply focused laser beams. The CO_2 laser can be replaced by a sealed-off commercial laser. It should be noted that those cannot be used intracavity, which lowers the available power and thus the sensitivity for ethylene.

Implementation of both techniques in the biological field, as well as making use of an additional CO laser, allows one to study various dynamic processes. A list of gaseous compounds being detected at (sub.)ppb level is presented elsewhere.

Because of the complexity of the method additional information should be obtained from the authors. Experience with lasers concerning maintenance is advantageous. In addition, the described methods serve as a user facility at the University of Nijmegen (The Netherlands) and University of Bonn (Germany). To construct these laser-based detectors one should have a close collaboration between laserphysicists and biologists.

ETHENE BIOSYNTHETIC

Antisense and Sense Gene Silencing

Artificial oligodeoxynucleotides, and later RNA complementary to a particular gene, were shown to inhibit the expression of that gene in vertebrate cells.

Transformation of plants with antisense transgenes was first used to block the expression of well-characterized plant genes in 1988 and later it was found that sense transgenes would often similarly block endogenous gene expression.

More recently, it has been shown that a single chimeric gene consisting of coding regions from two endogenous genes can silence the expression of both of the endogenous genes.

This can be very useful if one of the two sequences is from a gene that gives rise to a colour or other visual phenotype. In many cases, genes, or more often cDNAs, may be cloned and sequenced, and little may be learned about the function of the gene product by computer homology searches and other sequence-based predictive methods.

In such cases, antisense transformation may be used to block the expression of the gene to create a null-mutant phenotype. The nature of the phenotype may then indicate something of the nature of the biochemical process in which the gene product is involved.

ACC OXIDASE

The first unknown cDNA to be characterized by antisense transfo-rmation was pTOM13. This was a cDNA isolated by virtue of its induction during the ripening of tomato fruit and subsequently shown to be induced by wounding.

There was no known function assigned to this gene; however, because both of these processes involve ethene production there was circumstantial evidence that this cDNA might be either induced by ethene or involved in ethene biosynthesis.

Elucidation of the actual role came from antisense transformation of tomato to produce plants with a reduced ability to synthesize ethene.

These plants also had a reduced ability to convert the immediate precursor of ethene, 1-aminocyclopropane-1-carboxylic acid (ACC) into ethene when supplied exogenously, indicating that pTOM13 encoded ACC oxidase (ACO), sometimes called ethylene-forming enzyme (EFE).

Historic attempts to purify the ACC oxidase enzyme had always been largely unsuccessful. However, identification of the ACO cDNA allowed sequence comparisons to be made with other enzymes and showed that ACO had amino-acid identity with a flavone-3-hydroxylase of *Antirrhinum majus.*

The knowledge that this hydroxylase requires ascorbate and iron allowed Ververidis and John to purify and assay ACO using the same factors.

Confirmation of the identity of pTOM13 came from experiments where the pTOM13 coding sequence was expressed in yeast, allowing yeast to convert ACC to ethene. This conversion was stereoisomer-specific, and was stimulated by iron and ascorbate.

ACO ANTISENSE PLANTS

The production of ACO antisense plants has had a number of uses. First, the fruit of ACO antisense plants ripen normally but have a much increased shelf life because of inhibition of overripening and reduced mechanical and fungal damage.

The life of cut flowers is similarly extended. Second, the plants have been used to study phenomena thought to be induced by ethene, such as senescence, epinasty, and pathogen attack.

MATERIALS

Gene Construction

1. Plasmid vectors: As source of expression cassette, pDH51.
2. *Agrobacterium* binary transformation vector, pBIN19.

Agrobacterium-Mediated Transformation

1. APM-strep medium: 0.5% (w/v) yeast extract, 0.05% (w/v) casamino acids, 0.8% (w/v) mannitol, 0.2% (w/v) $(NH_4)_2SO_4$, 0.5% (w/v) NaCl, pH 6.6, containing 500 gg/mL streptomycin.
2. APMSS medium: As APM-strep but additionally substituted with kanamycin at 50 gg/mL (or tetracycline at 12.5 gg/mL, as appropriate for the plasmid used).
3. MS medium: 4.4 g/L MS salts, 30 g/L sucrose.
4. MSR3 agar: 4.4 g/L MS salts, 30g/L sucrose, 1 mg/L thiamine HCl, 0.5 mg/L nicotinic acid, 0.5 mg/L pyridoxine HCl, adjusted to pH 5.9 with KOH and autoclaved with 8 g/L agar. For convenience, the thiamine, nicotinic acid, and pyridoxine may be prepared as a 1000 x concentrated solution (R3 vitamins).
5. MS24D medium: As MSR3 without the agar but with 200 mg/L KH_2PO_4, 100 gg/L kinetin, and 200 gg/L

2,4-D and adjusted to pH 5.7.

6. 3C5ZR agar: As MSR3 agar with 1.75 mg/L zeatin riboside and 0.87 mg/L indoleacetyl-DL-aspartic acid added after autoclaving.
7. 3C5ZCK agar: As 3C5ZR agar with 400 mg/L augmentin and 75 mg/L kanamycin sulfate.

Analysis of Plants

1. 10 × PCR buffer: 0.1 *M* Tris-HCl pH 8.0, 0.5 *M* KCl, 20 mM MgCl, 0.01% (w/v) gelatin, 0.5% *(v/v)* Nonidet P-40, 0.05% *(v/v)* Tween 20.
2. dNTP mix: 2.5 mM each of dATP, dCTP, dGTP and TTP, filtersterilized. It is convenient to make up as separate 100 mM stocks.

Ethene Assay and Simple In Vivo ACC Oxidase Assay

1. Subaseal™ caps (W.H. Freeman and Co., Barnsley, UK)
2. Ethene standard (100ppm)
3. ACC solution: 1 mM ACC, 30 mM Na ascorbate, 0.1 mM $FeSO_4$, 0.8 *M* mannitol, 10% glycerol, 0.1 *M* Tris-HCl, pH 7.2.

METHODS

Gene Construction

The main problem with gene construction is the correct choice of vector and coding sequence. We have generally used pBIN19 as the vector in *Agrobacterium tumefaciens* strain LBA4404 and have had good results. pDH51 is the usual source of promoter and polyadenylation site sequences.

In order to produce a fragment with the correct terminal restriction enzyme sites to allow it to be inserted in the correct orientation, several intermediate cloning steps may need to be performed. Fortunately this is not as great a problem as one would assume.

It is not necessary, or even desirable, to use a whole gene

or even a whole cDNA for gene silencing. Fragments of cDNA between 200 and 1000 nucleotides generally work well.

There is no generally accepted way of predicting which fragment will give the most efficient silencing. However, very small fragments are unlikely to work well and very large ones will add to the difficulties of subcloning and transformation.

Complete sequence identity is not necessary and, in the case of multigene families, it is probable that more than one endogenous gene will be silenced by the transgene, as in the case of the highly conserved ACC oxidase genes.

It is not always necessary to use a gene sequence from the same species if the gene in question is highly conserved between species. It is difficult to choose whether to use antisense or sense transgenes. We have found that antisense and sense silencing work similarly in efficiency and perhaps mechanism.

One advantage of using sense transgenes consisting of the full coding sequence is that silencing and overexpression may occur in different plants within the same population of transformants. Over expressers may then be useful controls. Some transgenic plants are mosaics of silenced and nonsilenced cells.

Downregulation of the phytoene synthase gene causes a dramatic change in colour of tomato fruit. Because chimeric transgenes always seem to silence both of the endogenous genes from which they were made, by fusing the Psy coding sequence to part of the polygalacturonase cDNA it was possible to identify those plants that were mosaics and those tissues where the *Pgu* gene was silenced by virtue of the colour change caused by silencing of the Psy gene. It may be possible to use other such systems to identify such mosaic tissues.

Agrobacterium-Mediated Transformation

This is the procedure used in our laboratories for the routine transformation of tomato *(Lycopersicon esculentum Mill.* cv Ailsa Craig) with pBIN19 in *Agrobacterium tumefaciens* strain LBA4404.

In contrast to certain other procedures, such as promoter analysis, antisense or sense gene silencing does not require large numbers of transformants.

This method has worked well in tomato but because transformation procedures are notoriously species-specific, a modification of the procedure or a different procedure altogether may be needed for different types of plants.

Transformation of Agrobacterium

1. To prepare competent cells, strain LBA4404 (which contains a helper Ti plasmid) should be streaked onto an APM-strep agar plate and grown at 29°C for several days in the dark. Subculture the bacteria into APM-strep liquid medium at 29°C overnight in the dark. The following day, dilute 2 mL of the culture into 50 mL of fresh APM-strep medium in a 100-mL flask and grow with vigorous shaking to A600 of 0.5–1.0.
2. Chill the culture on ice, centrifuge, and resuspend the cell pellet in 1 mL of ice-cold calcium chloride (20 mM). Dispense 100-μL aliquots into chilled 1.5-mL microcentrifuge tubes and use for transformation.
3. To an aliquot of competent cells, add 1 μg plasmid DNA, followed by 1 mL of APM medium and incubate at 29°C with gentle shaking for 2–4 h in the dark.
4. Centrifuge the cells (in a microcentrifuge for only 30 s) and resuspend in 100 μL of fresh APM medium. Spread on APMSS plates and incubate the plates at 29°C for several days in the dark until colonies appear.

Transformation of Tomato

1. Inoculate a culture of *Agrobacterium* into APM medium with antibiotics 5 or 6 d before it is to be used and grow as before. This should be diluted 10^{-2} in fresh APM 3 d before use. Dilute 0.2 mL into 10 mL fresh APM again 16 h before use.
2. Surface-sterilize seeds by soaking for 10 min in 50% (v/v) ethanol and 20 min in saturated trisodium orthophosphate, and washing briefly in sterile distilled

water. They should then be soaked for 10 min in 50% (w/v) sodium hypochlorite, rinsed three times in sterile distilled water, and sown (approx 150 per pot) on sterile MSR3 agar. Incubate at 26°C with 16 h light and 8 h dark.

3. Cut cotyledonary explants from 10–12-d-old seedlings and incubate in MS24D medium for 20 min.
4. Place on sterile filter paper laid on 3C5ZR plates. The plates should be sealed with film and incubated in low light (e.g., under a layer of muslin) for 24 h.
5. Centrifuge 25 mL of overnight *Agrobacterium* culture, wash the pellet in APM medium without antibiotics, and resuspend it in MS medium. Prepared cotyledonary explants are added to the culture and shaken very gently for 15–20 min.
6. Remove the explants and blot dry on sterile filter paper, then replace the filter onto the 3C5ZR plates and incubate as in step 4 for 2 d. Transfer the explants to 3C5ZCK plates. Keep in low light for the first week and then transfer to normal light. Continue to transfer the explants to fresh plates every 3 wk until calli and/or shoots appear.
7. At this point, remove dead tissue, divide the callus into approx 1.5 cm^2 sections, and put into 3C5ZCK tubs, which are again subcultured every 3 wk. Shoots should be excised and cultured in MSR3CK tubs until roots form, then grown in compost.

Analysis of Plants

As with any transgene, those used for gene silencing will not always be expressed efficiently. It is generally assumed that this is associated with chromosomal location. In addition, gene silencing is an epigenetic effect and the phenotype is not always stable, especially through meiosis.

In the case of the ACC oxidase antisense plants, it was possible to test for efficient expression of the transgene in the leaves by northern blot because the transgene promoter was constitutive and the promoters of the endogenous genes were not.

In the ripe fruit, RNA from the transgene could not be detected because of the mutual nature of gene cosuppression. Expression of a transgene does not always silence the endogenous genes, so the use of a chimeric transgene containing a visual reporter may be advantageous.

This may also be useful if the object is to silence one member of a multigene family. We have found that it is sometimes possible to silence a gene and obtain a phenotype but still to see bands in northerns because of the continued expression of other homologous genes.

Ultimately, it may be necessary to show that the phenotype obtained cosegregates with the presence of the transgene. The possibility of insertional inactivation may be excluded by demonstrating that the same phenotype occurs in several independent transformants.

PCR

1. Add 50 gL of mineral oil to the open lid of a 0.5 mL microcentrifuge tube.
2. Mix 5 gL 10 x PCR buffer, 4 gL 2.5 mM dNTP mixture, 2.5 gL 20 μM primer 1, 2.5 gL 20 gM primer 2, 30.8 gL sterile H_2O, and 0.2 gL Taq DNA polymerase in the tube.
3. Add 5 gl of template DNA (at about 100–200 gg/mL).
4. Amplify for about 35 cycles in a thermal cycler. The exact conditions for this will depend on the cycler.

Ethene Measurements and ACC Oxidase Assay

Effective assays for purified ACC oxidase are now available. However, we have found that measurements of ethene production or a simple assay of ACC oxidase activity in vitro are normally quite adequate.

Measurement of Ethene Production

1. Cut tissue sections and place in 5-mL glass bottles sealed with selfsealing rubber caps.

2. Remove 1-mL samples of air from the headspace using a gas-tight syringe at regular intervals of 30–90 min and aerate and reseal the bottle after each sampling.
3. Samples should be measured on a gas chromatograph. We use a Pye Unicam apparatus with an alumina column and a flame ionization detector. An ethene source of known concentration should be used as a standard.

ACC Oxidase Assay In Vitro

1. Incubate tissue samples, prepared as described elsewhere in this chapter, in ACC solution for 15 min and discard the solution. 2. Seal the samples into glass bottles and assay as described elsewhere in this chapter.

NOTES

1. Oeller and Gutterson have described a somewhat similar system that is more generally applicable but is less immediate in that it requires a tissue-staining step.

   In their system, a sense *uidA* (GUS) reporter is fused to a sense transgene. In the absence of gene silencing, readily detectable glucuronidase will be formed.

   If cosuppression occurs, not only will the endogenous genes be suppressed, but the transgene message will also be degraded and no glucuronidase enzyme will be made.
2. Incubation of *Agrobacterium* above 29°C or in the light is not recommended because loss of the plasmid is more likely.
3. This is an antiviral treatment.

Chapter 8 Ethylene Signaling

The two-carbon olefin ethylene has fascinated plant biologists for more than a century by its *myriad* of effects on plant growth and development. However, the earliest record of human manipulation of fruit ripening, related to ethylene, goes back to the 8th century B.C., with the prophet *Amos* describing himself as a piercer of *sycamore fig fruits.*

Five centuries later, *Theophrastus*, a Greek philosopher, recognized that the fruits would not ripen unless they were first scraped with an iron claw. This remarkable effect is now known to be associated to the *formation* of wound ethylene, which subsequently stimulates ripening.

The Russian physiologist Dimitry Neljubow was the first to discover that ethylene is a biologically active compound in plants. He demonstrated that ethylene was the component of illuminating gas, which caused *diageotropic* (horizontal) growth of pea seedlings, inhibition of *elongation*, and *swelling*. Others confirmed and expanded Neljubow's observations on the so-called "*triple response*".

The possibility that ethylene was an endogenous growth regulator and its use to manipulate crop growth and development was investigated in the 1920s and 1930s. In 1934, conclusive evidence that ethylene was a natural product from plants, was presented by the English scientist Gane (1934).

A full account on the historical background of the discovery of ethylene as a plant hormone is given by Abeles *et al.* (1992). The subsequent *biochemical* dissection of the ethylene biosynthesis pathway further strengthened its acceptance as a true plant hormone, despite the fact that strictly *speaking*, a gaseous hormone is not *translocated* and hence does not comply with the original definition of a *hormone.*

The chemical properties of ethylene are important in understanding its biology. The diffusion coefficient of ethylene in air is approximately 10,000 times that in water. Furthermore, ethylene is about 14 times more soluble in lipids than in water.

Like other *olefins*, ethylene binds to metals through a *co-ordination* bond. Among the metals reported to bind to ethylene are Cu(I) and Ag(I). Copper ions serve as a critical cofactor in *high-affinity* ethylene binding to the receptors.

Application of silver ions can displace copper ions from the receptor proteins and, consequently, block ethylene perception. Physiological effects of ethylene are *detectable* at *ambient* levels as low as 0.1 μl/l. Ethylene is particularly known as a ripening hormone.

Yet, it has profound effects on plants at most developmental stages. The effects range from stimulation of *germination, triple response* in dark-grown *dicotyledonous seedlings*, impairment (in most species) or stimulation (in aquatic and semi-aquatic species) of cell *expansion, over-induction* of flowering in *bromeliads*, to leaf and petal *senescence*, and *abscission*.

Furthermore, the production of ethylene is tightly regulated by internal signals during development and in response to environmental stimuli, both biotic and abiotic, including *pathogen attack, wounding, hypoxia, ozone, chilling*, or *freezing*.

However, the most significant advances in the functional analysis of ethylene in plant physiology have occurred in the past 15 years with thorough studies of the model plant *Arabidopsis*.

Exploitation of the most conspicuous effect of ethylene in *Arabidopsis*, the induction of the triple response in the dark characterized by an *exaggerated* apical hook, a short

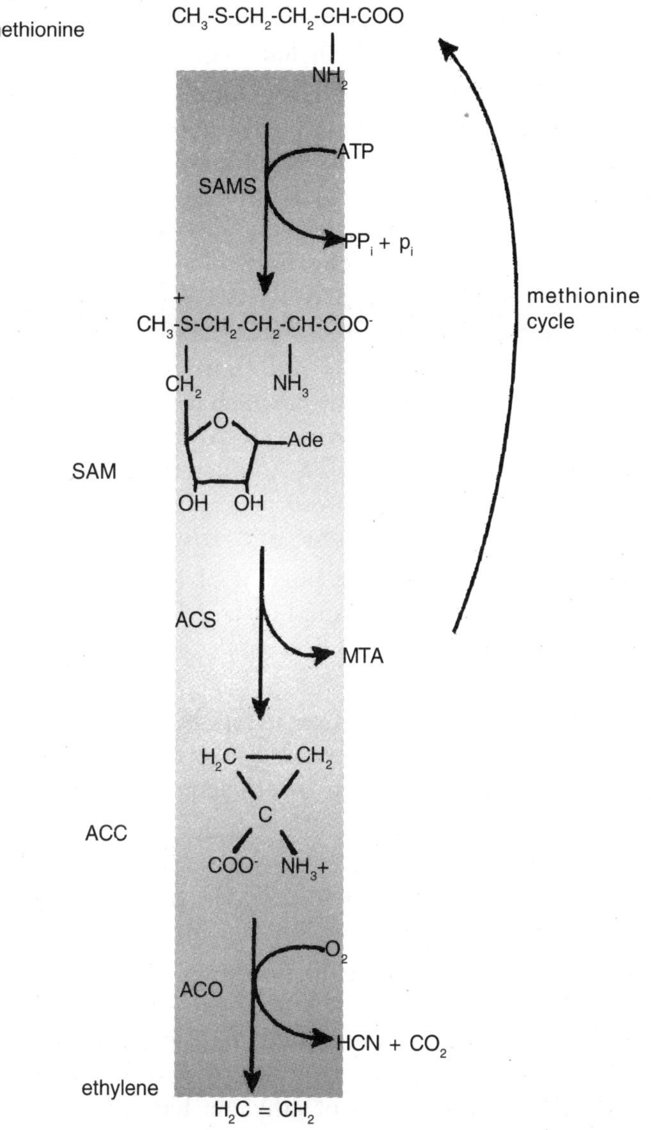

Figure 8.1a: Overview of ethylene biosynthesis. (a) Methionine is converted to S-AdoMet by SAMS. SAM is subsequently used by ACS to yield ACC and MTA. MTA is recycled to methionine in the methionine cycle. ACO oxidizes ACC, resulting in ethylene production. The last step also releases hydrogen cyanide (HCN) and CO_2 as by-products.

and thick hypocotyl, and a short root led to the *identification* of mutants with defective ethylene signaling.

The characterization of these mutants enabled cloning and functional analysis of nearly all components in the chain of ethylene *biosynthesis* and signaling. The intent of this review is to briefly highlight major findings in ethylene biology and further focus on more recent discoveries that shaped our current view on ethylene *biosynthesis* and signaling.

ETHYLENE BIOSYNTHESIS

In the late 1970s, Yang and co-workers elucidated the ethylene biosynthesis pathway in which methionine is converted to *S-adenosyl-methionine* (*S-Adomet*) by S-Adomet synthetase (*SAM synthetase*). S-Adomet is the major methyl donor in plants and is involved in a number of biochemical pathways, including *polyamine* and ethylene biosynthesis.

However, only a minor portion of cellular S-Adomet is used for 1-aminocyclopropane-l-carboxylic acid (ACC) production; hence, the levels of S-Adomet do not limit ethylene production.

S-Adomet synthetase action is followed by two regulated steps. ACC synthase (ACS), which converts S-Adomet to ACC, is the first rate-limiting step in ethylene biosynthesis.

In addition to ACC, it also produces 5'-*methylthioadenosine* (MTA), which is subsequently recycled to *methionine*. This pathway, known as the Yang cycle, preserves the methyl group for another round of ethylene production.

The second point of regulation involves the oxidation of ACC by ACC oxidase (ACO) to form ethylene, CO_2, and *cyanide*. The latter is detoxified to (3-cyanoalanine by 3-cyanoalanine synthase to *prevent toxicity* of accumulated cyanide during high rates of ethylene biosynthesis.

Alternatively, ACC can be conjugated by either *malonylation* (MACC) or *γ-L-glutamylation* (GACC), which is regarded as a way to exclude ACC from the ethylene biosynthesis pathway.

However, there are some indications that *conjugation* is

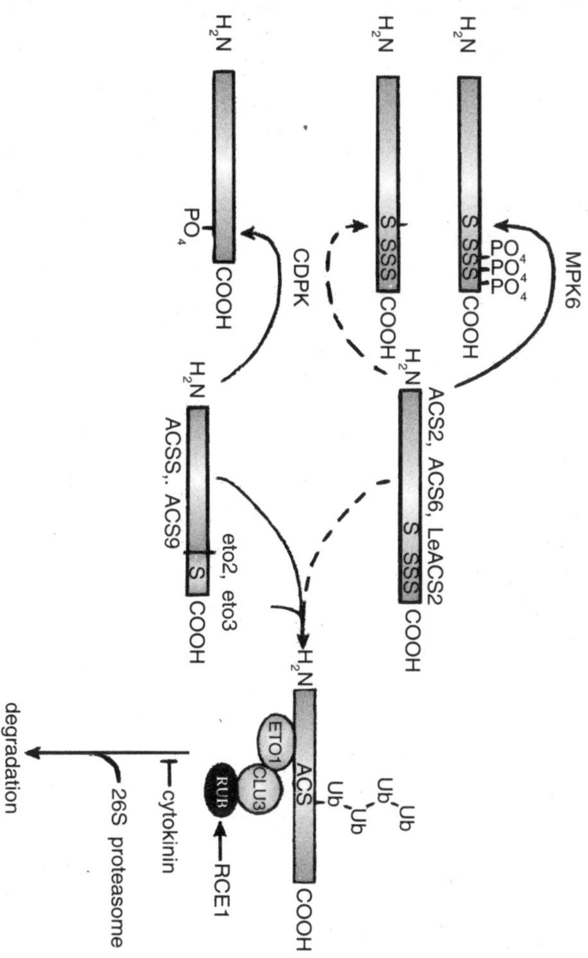

Figure 8.1b: Model for regulation of ACS enzyme stability. Phosphorylation on C-terminally located serine residues by either CDPK or MPK6 leads to increased stability. When dephosphorylated, this serine-rich region is necessary for stimulation of ubiquitination and eventual protein degradation. Mutations in that region, like eto2 or eto3, increase protein stability. ETO1 serves as an adaptor for ACS to associate with Cullin3, which is part of an E3 ubiquitin ligase. The activity of this ligase is regulated by rubylation and derubylation through RCE1. Cytokinin inhibits degradation of ACSs by the 26S proteasome.

not *irreversible* and under certain conditions MACC may serve as a pool for ACC. We will limit further discussion to the two committed steps in ethylene biosynthesis: ACS and ACO.

ACC synthase

In all studied plant species, ACSs are encoded by a multigene family, with high divergence. Biochemical characterization of ACS purified from *zucchini, tomato,* and *winter squash* led to the cloning of the first ACS genes.

Due to the release of these sequences a wealth of knowledge on ACS genes was developed shortly thereafter, including that of the ACS family of both dicot and *monocot* model systems, *Arabidopsis* and rice.

With the sequencing of both *genomes,* the number of identified ACS genes has substantially increased, and in expression studies using RNA gel blot *hybridization,* cross-hybridization may have occurred due to extremely high homology within certain clades (e.g. *At-ACS4* and *At-ACS8* have over 80% *nucleotide* identity).

The structure of ACSs resembles that of the subgroup I family of pyridoxal 5'-phosphate (PLP)-dependent aminotransferases. In *Arabidopsis,* the ACS gene family has 12 members, two of which are functional only as aminotransferases *(ACSIO* and *ACS12)* and two others that encode ACS proteins without a proven enzymatic activity *(ACSI* and *ACS3). In vitro* activity assays indicate large differences in enzymatic *efficiency* among the isoforms, with K_m values for AdoMet *ranging* from 8 to 45 μM and k_{cat} values varying from 0.19 to 4.82 per s and per *monomer.*

Moreover, the proteins can *heterodimerize,* suggesting a vast array of complexes with different enzyme activities, which may add to the fine-tuning of ethylene biosynthesis. The fact that the rate of *ethylene* biosynthesis is tissue specific and is influenced by environmental factors, implies the presence of a tight regulatory mechanism.

The expression of *ACS* genes is specifically regulated in various tissues and *modulated* by environmental and developmental factors. The overlapping patterns of expression of different ACS family members may reflect a *combinatorial* code for functional heterodimers.

The *ACS8* gene is particularly strongly regulated at the transcript level and its activity is controlled by *auxins, light intensity, circadian rhythms,* and by negative feedback by ethylene. *ACS4* and *ACS7* expression are also highly influenced by *endogenous* factors, including auxin, and external factors.

Recently it was *demonstrated* that ACS enzyme activity is also regulated by protein stability. Attenuation of this process results in mutant *phenotypes.* All characterized mutations that specifically lead to ethylene over-production in *Arabidopsis (eto mutants*) are the result of *stabilization* of ACSs.

The *eto2* mutant produces an ACS5 protein with a modified *C-terminus,* which renders it hyperstable. A missense mutation in the *C-terminal* region of the closely related *ACS9* gene leads to the ethylene overproduction in *eto3,* suggesting that both mutations confer disruption of a similar *post-translational* control.

Mutations in the *ETOI* gene also result in ethylene overproduction. Wang *et al.* (2004) showed that *ETOI encodes* a protein that directly interacts with ACS5/ETO2. Being a BTB (Broad complex-Tramtrack-Bric-a-Brac) domain-containing protein, ETO1 also interacts with CUL3 (cullin3), a subunit of E3 *ubiquitin-ligase* complexes.

Thus, ETO1 links *ubiquitin-mediated* protein *degradation* to ethylene biosynthesis and could serve as an adaptor for and a positive regulator of ACS5 breakdown.

The mutated form of ACS5 in *eto2* does not contain the binding site for ETO1 and, as a consequence, it is not recognized for ubiquitin-mediated protein breakdown. Further evidence that *ACS5* is *post-transcriptionally* regulated came from the analysis of the *cin* mutants (*cytokinin insensitive*).

Low doses of *cytokinin* (0.5-10 μM) stimulate ethylene production in etiolated seedlings of *Arabidopsis,* inducing *morphological* changes resembling the triple response upon ethylene treatment in darkness. This was *exploited* to identify mutants that fail to increase ethylene in response to cytokinin. *CIN5* was found to correspond to *ACS5*.

However, since cytokinin-mediated ethylene production does not correlate with an accumulation of *ACS5* mRNA, it can be concluded that cytokinin increases ACS5 function primarily by a post-transcriptional mechanism. It was demonstrated that *eto2* does not alter the specific activity of the enzyme, but increases the half-life of the ACS5 protein.

In addition, cytokinin treatment increased the stability of ACS5 in the *eto2* background, indicating a mechanism that is at least partially independent of the *eto2* mutation. Another clade of the *ACS* family consists of the closely related ACS2 and ACS6 proteins.

Like ACS5 and ACS9, these enzymes share a common regul mechanism, being phosphorylated by *mitogen-activated* protein kinase 6 (MAPK6) on three C-terminal serine residues that are not present in other active ACSs of *Arabidopsis*.

Moreover, this *phosphorylation* increased the stability of the ACS6 protein. A related tomato isoform, Le-ACS2, can be phosphorylated on yet another *serine* residue in its *C-terminal* region by a *calcium-dependent* protein kinase (CDPK).

Interestingly, a maize CDPK could phosphorylate the corresponding Ser residue of a C-terminal peptide of the *Arabidopsis* ACS5. Thus, depending on the species or protein, phosphorylation is brought about by different mechanisms and is probably the basis for stimulation of protein stability.

The four *Arabidopsis ACS* isoforms that share a highly conserved C-terminal sequence (ACS4, ACS5, ACS8, ACS9) may therefore be regulated by CDPK in a similar manner.

ACC oxidase

Biochemical characterization of ACOs progressed well only after cloning of the first gene. Hamilton *et al.* (1991) over-expressed antisense pTOM13 in tomato, a gene with similarity to flavanone-3-hydroxylases, resulting in much reduced ethylene levels. The ACO enzyme requires iron, ascorbate, and CO_2 for its activity. In *Arabidopsis,* like ACSs, ACOs are encoded by a multigene family, albeit with limited divergence. On the basis of sequence similarity, the family has at least 17 members in *Arabidopsis.*

Enzyme assays for each of these genes have not been performed yet, making it difficult to speculate on the specific role in the plant. However, it is generally accepted that in ethylene biosynthesis, ACC oxidation is most often not the rate-limiting step, since the activity is present in most vegetative tissues.

However, it has been suggested recently that ACO activity can regulate ethylene production in seedlings. This activity is dependent on the intactness of RCE1 (RUB CONJUGATING ENZYME), also linking ACO activity to protein stability. In contrast to vegetative tissue highly regulated during fruit ripening, leaf senescence, and upon wounding and ethylene treatment. Few reports have been made on the expression of *ACO* genes in *Arabidopsis.*

ACO2 has been studied in most detail, and being ethylene induced in a feed-forward mechanism, the gene serves as a positive control for ethylene responses.

Microarray studies have revealed that more ACOs are subject to (auto)regulation at the transcript level. Expression of three ACOs and one ACO-like gene was modified by ethylene.

The differential expression of multiple ACOs supports a complex auto-regulatory mechanism in ethylene biosynthesis.

Ethylene Signal Transduction

Apart from the discovery of *eto* mutants, the classical triple response screening has led to the isolation of various mutants with defects in genes involved in ethylene signaling, including *ethylene resistant (etr),* ACC and *ethylene insensitive (ain/ ein),* and *constitutive triple response (ctr)* mutants.

Subsequently, the triple response screening was refined towards identification of mutants that display an enhanced ethylene response at low *concentrations* of the hormone.

Using this screen, the *enhanced-eethylene-response 1 (eerl)* mutant was isolated.

Furthermore, seven other components *(weil-wei7)* have been identified by a low-dose screen for weak ethylene-insensitive mutants. In parallel, other *screening* methods were applied. One method used responsiveness to an *antagonist* of ethylene (a compound that interacts with the receptor but acts as an inhibitor of ethylene responses).

The *responsive to antagonist (ran)* mutant was isolated using trans-cyclooctene (TCO). A second method exploited the phenotype of ethylene/ACCtreated light-grown *Arabidopsis* seedlings, which display an elongated hypocotyl in the presence of ethylene on a low nutrient medium (LNM), a response that is absent in the *etr/ein* mutants and constitutively present in the *ctrl* mutant.

Using this response, *alhl (ACC-related long hhypocotyl)*, *eer2*, and *slol (slow)* were isolated. Identification of most of the genes affected in these mutants has enabled modelling of a quite complete ethylene-signaling chain. The first ethylene receptor gene to be cloned and characterized was from *Arabidopsis*.

Subsequently, putative ethylene receptor *orthologs* have been discovered in many plant species, including *Rumex*, *melon, tomato, carnation, peach,* and rice. In *Arabidopsis,* ethylene is perceived in the *endoplasmic reticulum* (ER) membrane by a five-membered family of receptors, named ETR1, ETR2, ERS 1, ERS2, and EIN4.

The receptor proteins have similarities to two-component regulators of *bacteria* and *yeast*. These proteins typically consist of a *sensor*, with a *transmembrane* input domain and a *transmitter domain* with *histidine kinase* (HK) *homology*, and a response *regulator*.

The latter contains a receiver domain with a conserved Asp residue, receiving a phosphate from the sensor and further acting by phosphotransfer (a *phosphorelay mechanism*) to an output domain (usually with transcription factor activity).

Three of the *ethylene receptor* proteins (ETR1, ETR2, and EIN4) have a receiver domain covalently attached at the carboxyl terminal of the *sensor*, and are therefore considered to be *hybrid protein kinases* (HPKs). In contrast, ERS1 and ERS2 lack a receiver domain and may thus function in with a response regulator.

With respect to their predicted enzymatic function, only ETR1 and ERS1 have the conserved residues typical for HK. This *characteristic* groups them in subfamily I; while ETR2, EIN4, and ERS2 lack these residues and form subfamily II. Nevertheless, only ETR1 has been shown to possess HK activity. The other receptors have Ser/Thr kinase activity.

A role for HK activity in ethylene signaling has been question ETR1 without HK activity could rescue the etr1 ers1 loss-of-function (subfamily I) double mutant. This leads to the conclusion that canonical HK activity is probably not required for ethylene receptor signaling. A possible role for the HK activity in ETR1 was proposed by Hass *et al.* (2004) and Qu and Schaller (2004).

The *Arabidopsis* response regulator 2 (ARR2) was identified as a signaling component functioning downstream of ETR1 in ethylene signaling. It was shown that an ETR1-initiated *phosphorelay* regulates the transcription factor activity of ARR2. This *mechanism* could constitute a novel signal transfer route from the ER-associated ETR1 to the nucleus for the regulation of ethylene-responsive genes.

In conclusion, ETR1 may have a dual functional role in the initiation of ethylene-signal transduction: (1) over a CTR1-dependent pathway (negatively regulated), (2) over an ARR2-dependent pathway (positively regulated). Retention of the HK activity in subfamily I receptors may also provide fine-tuning of the signaling pathway. Recent work indicates that the His kinase domain of ETR1 plays a role in repression of ethylene responses.

Moreover, Binder *et al.* (2004) demonstrated that receiver domains play a role in the recovery from growth inhibition since the *ers]-2 ers2-3* loss-of-function double *mutation* had no effect on recovery rate after ethylene was removed, while loss-of-function mutations in *ETR1, ETR2,* and *EIN4* significantly prolonged the time for *recovery.*

Analogous to the assay applied by Neljubow (1901), who identified ethylene by making use of its affinity to copper, the ethylene receptors use *copper ions* as a *cofactor* for binding ethylene.

The copper ions in ETR1 are co-ordinated by two amino acid residues, Cys65 and His 69. The copper transporting P-type ATPase, RAN1, is responsible for delivery of copper to the receptor molecules.

The ethylene receptors function as homo- and/or heterodimers that are connected by a disulphide bond in the amino terminal region. Studies using *heterologous* expression of the ethylene receptors in yeast showed that ethylene binds to the *receptors* with a *dissociation* constant of 0.04 μl/1 with a binding half-life of 12 h.

These values match with the rates observed in ethylene binding/response assays in plants. The receptor mutations first isolated on the basis of conferred ethylene insensitivity are all *dominant* gain-of-function *alleles* that introduce a novel or *persistent* function to the receptor protein.

Single loss-of-function receptor mutants do not display a phenotype. *Interestingly,* of all receptor double mutants produced, only the etr1 ers1 combination showed a phenotype. The latter mutant and any triple or *quadruple* loss-of-function mutants displayed constitutive ethylene responses.

It was deduced that the ethylene receptors are negative regulators of the ethylene response in the absence of ethylene. Conversely, ethylene must be a negative *regulator* of receptor function, implying that when *ethylene* is bound, the receptors are *inactivated.*

This means that the pathway is de-repressed by the hormone, thus leading to ethylene responses. A mutant that lacks the *capability* of ethylene binding (as is the case for some of the dominant-insensitive mutations) remains constitutively active and its kinase activity represses ethylene respo-nses.

In addition, the model is consistent with higher ethylene sensitivity in the triple and quadruple loss-of-function mutants because less ethylene is necessary to deactivate the remaining functional receptors. Considering that there is differential expression of the receptors, further modulation of ethylene signals may be achieved by altering the relative abundance of each receptor, even though the expression patterns overlap.

The differential regulation of the receptor gene family may provide a mechanism to achieve differential sensitivities. Furthermore, ethylene up-regulates expression of the ERS1, ERS2, and ETR2 receptor, which may be a desensitization response to prevent toxic effects of high levels of ethylene.

Yeast two-hybrid screens and *in vitro* binding assays have shown that both the kinase (transmitter) and the receiver domain of ETR1 and the kinase domain of ERS 1 can directly interact with the downstream component CTR1.

Physical interactions of the subfamily II ETR2 transmitter domain were also demonstrated, but are much weaker than those reported for ETR1 and ERS1. These findings provide an explanation for the observation that subfamily I receptors play a particular role in ethylene signaling.

They suggest that the difference between type I and type II receptors may lie in the strength of their physical interaction with CTR1, which would also explain why only etr1 *ers]* double loss-of-function mutants have a phenotype. Moreover, from studies of the missense ctr1–8 mutant, it was concluded that the N-terminal region of CTR1 is necessary for interaction with the ethylene receptor ETR1, but has no detectable effect on the kinase activity of CTR1.

Formation of an ETR1–CTRL signaling complex was also observed *in planta,* where both proteins associate with the *endoplasmatic reticulum.* It was *demonstrated* that plants defective in multiple receptors cause detachment of CTR1 from the membrane.

Moreover, the severity of the *constitutive ethylene* response in combined loss-of-function receptor mutants is correlated with the quantity of CTR1 present at the ER membrane.

Considering the *homology* of CTR1 with MAPKKKs, its identification prompted the suggestion that an MAPK cascade may reside downstream of CTR1, and there are indications that such a cascade exists. Ouaked *et al.* (2003) showed that the MAPKK SIMKK specifically mediates ACC-induced activation of MAPKs in Medicago.

Two MAPKs, SIMK and MMK3, were activated by ACC in this species, and two MAPKs are also activated in *Arabidopsis,* one of which is MPK6 and the second is a 44-kDa protein, which is probably MPK13. MPK6 may be a central player in ethylene-signaling downstream of CTR1.

However, Liu and Zhang (2004) found that MPK6 affected ACS stability, rather than ethylene signaling. Although CTR1 is highly important, ethylene-signal *transduction* is not entirely dependent on its activity.

The ctr1 null mutants are still capable of responding to ethylene, and plants containing loss-of-function mutations in four ethylene receptors display a more severe phenotype than ctr1 loss-of-function mutations. This leaves the way open for an additional branch in the pathway.

The results of Hass *et al.* (2004) suggest that ARR2 may be part of an additional regulatory route. There may also be CTR1 homologues involved. Further downstream EIN2 comes into play, as a positive regulator of ethylene signaling. Null *ein2* mutants cause strong ethylene *insensitivity*.

The protein is similar to N-ramp metal transporter proteins with 12 membrane spanning domains. Metal uptake in yeast could not be elicited by EIN2 expression, while this was the case for other N-ramp proteins. EIN2 is a component shared with several other signaling routes, including those for cytokinin, *abscisic acid* (ABA), and *senescence*.

EIN2 appears to be a single copy gene in a number of plant species, including rice, petunia, maize, and tomato. From EIN2, the ethylene signal is transferred to the *nucleus*. At this point, there remains a hole in the *maze*. Although it has been shown that over-expression of the soluble *C-terminus* of EIN2 provokes a constitutive *triple response*, it is not clear how the signal is passed from EIN2 onto the downstream nuclear components, which include the EIN3, EIN3-like (EIL), and ERF transcription factors.

The level of the EIN3 protein is efficiently regulated by ethylene in an ubiquitin-dependent proteolysis process. In the absence of ethylene, EIN3 is degraded through an ubiquitin/proteasome pathway mediated by the F-box proteins EBF1 and EBF2 (EIN3-binding F-box protein 1 and 2).

Over-expression of EBF1 resulted in ethylene insensitivity. In addition, *ebf] ebf2* double loss-of-function mutants showed constitutive ethylene responses, and in the case of strong alleles, growth arrest. The stability of EIN3 is a point for cross-talk with glucose signaling. Whereas ethylene inhibits the degradation of EIN3, glucose enhances it.

Of the five EILs, only EIL1 has a functional overlap with EIN3. EIN3 is a transcription factor that forms the first step in a transcriptional cascade. The EIN3 proteins act as dimers, and bind the promoter of Ethylene Response Factor *1 (ERFI)* on a primary ethylene response element (PERE), with consensus sequence AYGWAYCT. Up until now and in spite of the identification of various *ERFI homologues*, the *ERFI* promoter is the only known EIN3 target.

ERF1 itself is a member of a large family of Ethylene-Responsive Element-Binding Protein (EREBP) transcription factors. However, only few of these EREBPs are ethylene regulated. It is therefore not surprising that they were found to function in a variety of processes.

ERFI binds a secondary ethylene-responsive element (SERE) in promoters of target genes involved in pathogenesis, such as plant defensins *(PDF).* Moreover, ERF1 is a common signaling component for another defence-related plant hormone, *jasmonic acid* (JA). Large-scale transcriptome studies have added to the inventory of ethylene-regulated genes.

In a genome-wide expression study, using an Affymetrix chip representing 22,000 *Arabidopsis* genes, Alonso *et al.* (2003b) identified four AP2 and B3 domaincontaining proteins that were inducible by ethylene. They were designated *Ethylene response DNA-binding Factors* (EDF). Other microarray studies focused on different aspects of *ethylene biology*. Ethylene-regulated gene expression in *Arabidopsis* leaves was investigated using a cDNA *microarray* containing about 6000 unique genes.

In this study, the emphasis was on relatively long-term (24 h) ethylene regulation. For identification of genes involved in the very early phase of ethylene response, De Paepe *et al.* (2004) performed a kinetic analysis of the *transcriptional* cascade by means of cDNA-AFLP and *cDNA-microarray technology*.

They determined the major *ethylene-regulated* classes of genes. In particular, a large number of genes involved in *cell rescue*, *disease*, and defence mechanisms were identified as early ethylene-regulated genes, confirming the important role of ethylene in *defence* and *stress responses*.

A Complex Network

The current detailed view on ethylene biosynthesis and signaling pathways and their regulation paved the way to test *interactions* of specific players within these pathways with other *endogenous* or *environmental* cues.

In recent years, evidence has accumulated that both ethylene biosynthesis and signaling are integrated in a broad network, in which some signals operate master switches while care of fine-tuning the output. *Multiple hormones* influence ethylene biosynthesis. Cytokinin treatment increases the stability of ACS5 so that many of the growth defects attributed to cytokinins are the result of ethylene over production.

In addition, auxin stimulates ethylene *biosynthesis* by raising ACS transcript levels. In mung bean, an extra increase in *VrACS6* and *VrACS7* mRNA was shown in response to brassinosteroid treatment, while VrACS1 was down-regulated.

This suggests that ethylene biosynthesis is regulated by a delicate *hormone* dependent mechanism. Besides specific *screens* for ethylene mutants, alleles of mutations in ethylene signaling have also been recovered from screens for resistance to *auxinhibitors* or to cytokinins, or for *suppressors* and enhancers of ABA-related mutants, or to uncover regulators of *sugar metabolism.*

In addition to inter actions with glucose and ABA at germination, ethylene is often part of a network of hormonal interplay during vegetative plant development. Auxin and ethylene co-ordinately regulate several developmental programmes in plants. For example, in *Arabidopsis* both hormones regulate *root growth, root hair elongation,* and *hypocotyl phototropism.*

Nevertheless, it is often unclear whether developmental effects attributed to auxin are solely due to this hormone or rather mediated by ethylene, or resulting from a *synergistic interaction* between both hormones. Other developmental and growth response involves cross-talk betwe and *gibberellins* (GAs).

The opposite response of terrestrial and *semi-aquatic* plants to ethylene is explained by the effect of ethylene on GA biosynthesis and signaling. Ethylene reduces cell elongation in dark-grown seedlings even in the presence of a high concentrations of GA.

Molecular analysis demonstrated that cell elongation is inhibited by the presence of a high level of RGA, a negative regulator of the GA-signaling pathway belonging to the family of DELLA proteins. *Ethylene* appears to modulate the GA signal by enhancing RGA stability.

Root growth is also repressed by DELLA proteins, which are removed from the nucleus in the presence of the growth-promoting signals auxin or GA, presumably due to enhanced degradation.

This process is counteracted by ethylene, which stabilizes DELLA repressors in the nucleus, thus inhibiting root elongation. Bipartite hormone interactions are most simple to consider, but may not reflect the actual situation *in planta.*

More complex hormonal interactions have been demonstrated for the *regulation* of shoot *meristem* activity. In addition, a classical *auxin-ethylene* interaction, the formation and maintenance of the *apical hook* in *Arabidopsis,* was recently *re-evaluated.*

A higher level of complexity was demonstrated, involving GAs and *brassinosteroids,* besides the previously defined players. The current model suggests that ethylene stimulates *brassinosteroid* biosynthesis at the outer side of the *apical hook.*

Brassinosteroids could regulate the transport of auxins to the inner side of the hook, thus creating *supra-optimal* levels of auxins. GAs are the most downstream components determining the severity of response. *Cross-talk* with ethylene biosynthesis and signaling pathways also occurs in the *pathogen* defence response with JA and *salicylic acid* (SA).

A *microarray* analysis suggested the co-ordination between these three signaling pathways, supported by a big overlap in gene expression, especially between *jasmonate* and *ethylene.* Previous studies have shown that both ethylene and JA are required for the induction of the defensin gene *PDF1.2* in response to the avirulent *fungal pathogen Alternaria brassicicola.*

Furthermore, it was demonstrated that ethylene and *jasmonate* pathways converge at ERFI, the expression of which can be activated *rapidly* by ethylene or *jasmonate,* but also *synergistically* by both hormones.

Moreover, blocking either pathway by mutations prevents *ERFI* induction by the two hormones either alone or in combination; therefore, both signaling pathways are required concurrently for the induction of *ERFI* expression and the activation of its *target gene PDF1.2.*

These results suggest that ERFI acts downstream of the intersection between ethylene- and *jasmonate-signaling* pathways and that this transcription factor is a key element in the integration of both signals for the *regulation* of defence response genes.

In conclusion, almost all steps of ethylene biosynthesis and signaling are specifically controlled throughout development and serve as *cross-roads* with other signaling routes.

An *integration* with the glucose, jasmonate, auxin, cytokinin, GA, and ABA pathways, but also with light and *circadian clock signaling* has been illustrated. The *puzzle* of plant life is yet to be completed.

9 Chapter Extraction and Purification of Enzyme

The advent of genetic *engineering* has provided a means to manipulate the biosynthesis of plant hormones to the advantage of *agriculture*. Such *manipulation* is very dependent on a detailed knowledge of the *biosynthetic* pathways involved in the production of the hormones, and more *precisely* about the enzymes involved in this *biosynthesis*.

The knowledge of enzymes assists, but is not always a *prerequisite* for, the isolation of the genetic material, usually cDNAs, used as the *genetic* tools to *manipulate* hormone synthesis. The first such example of the manipulation of hormone *biosynthesis* by the application of genetic engineering was for the hormone ethene.

The biosynthetic pathway for ethene was first described in apples by Adams and Yang. Methionine was found to be the precursor of this hormone in plant tissue and is converted via *S-adenysyl-methionine* (SAM) into the unique compound 1-amino-1-*carboxyl cyclopropane* (ACC).

The conversion of SAM into ACC is carried out by a key biosynthetic enzyme, ACC synthase, and the subsequent conversion of ACC into ethene is carried out by a second enzyme, namely ACC oxidase. These two enzymes have been extensively studied and cDNAs for both identified, although by completely different methods.

ACC oxidase cDNA was initially identified by a process of differe-ntial screening of a tomatoripening cDNA library. This technique was used to identify cDNA clones from a library made from ripe tomato, which are exclusively expressed in a ripe fruit but not a green fruit.

Since the biosynthesis of ethene was known to be ripening specific, it was postulated that at least some of any clones identified would encode biosynthetic enzymes. The technique identified several *clones*, one of which, pTOM13, appeared to have expression closely correlated with *ethene synthesis.*

The use of this cDNA to transform tomato plants with an antisense gene resulted in genetically manipulated plants with lowered ethene production and a correspondingly reduced ability to convert ACC to ethene.

It was thus postulated that the pTOM13 cDNA encoded the enzyme ACC oxidase, a conclusion further supported by the observation that *yeast genetically* engineered with pTOM13 cDNA acquired the ability to convert ACC to ethene.

The sequence analysis of the pTOM 13 cDNA suggested a close relationship between the ACC oxidase and flavonone oxidase enzymes. This information enabled Ververdis and John to successfully extract the ACC oxidase enzyme and carry out its *purification* and *characterization.*

The isolation of a cDNA encoding *ACC synthase* was achieved by a different route. In this instance the enzyme itself was first extracted and partially purified, and then an antibody was raised against the *protein.*

Using this antibody a cDNA expression library was screened and the corresponding cDNA isolated. The identity of the cDNA was confirmed by the expression of ACC synthase activity in *Escherichia coli* transformed with the cDNA.

This cDNA has been used to construct an *antisense gene,* which has in turn been used to silence members of the *endogenous* ACC synthase gene family and bring about a marked reduction in ethene synthesis in *transgenic plants.*

The resultant plants showed <0.5% of normal ethene production and since this was *achieved* in tomato, the fruit showed markedly inhibited ripening. This technique of gene silencing could easily be used to reduce the synthesis of any or all plant *hormones* given sufficient knowledge of the *biosy-*

nthetic pathways involved and the genetic tools, i.e., cDNAs, for key *biosynthetic enzymes.*

The enzyme step(s) must be chosen with care to influence hormone synthesis exclusively. For instance, in the case of ethene the two target enzymes—*ACC synthase* and *ACC oxidase*—appear to be exclusively involved in the *biosynthesis* of this hormone and are not involved in any other key *metabolic pathways.*

In contrast, had the enzyme converting *methionine* to SAM been the target for *genetic manipulation,* a more unpredictable *phenotype* may have *arisen.* This is because SAM is a key intermediate in several biosynthetic pathways, including those for cell walls (SAM provides the *methyl groups* for the *esterification* of *pectin*) and *polyamines.*

The general biosynthetic routes for several of the major plant hormones are fairly well established. Auxin (indole-3-acetic acid) has close structural similarity to *tryptophan* and *tracer* studies have identified *tryptophan* as a *precursor* for this auxin.

However, the precise biosynthetic route is not clear. Several pathways have been *postulated* involving intermediates, such as indole-3-acetaldehyde and indole-3-acetamide.

The gibberellins are all derived from the diterpenoid precursor *geranyl–geranyl pyrophosphate,* the over 70 naturally occuring gibberellins being the result of a complex branched biosynthetic pathway.

The cytokinins are *N-substituted adenines* and as such could arise from the turnover of tRNA species or directly from *adenine metabolism.* In all these cases cell-free systems have been reported that may retain at least part of the biosynthetic chain in an active state.

Thus, for auxin, cell-free extracts have been demonstrated that can convert tryptophan to indole-3-acetic acid via the *intermediates* indole3-pyruvic acid and indole-3-acetaldehyde.

For gibberellins an enzyme—ent-kaurene synthase—has been identified that catalyzes the conversion of geranyl-geranyl pyrophosphate to *ent-kaurene,* which in turn can be oxidized and rearranged to give GA_{12} *-aldehyde*. For cytokinins a cell-free system has been isolated from the slime mold *Dictostelium discordeum,* which can use adenosine monophosphate (AMP), and the *isopentenyl group* from *isoprenyl pyrophoshate*, to synthesize *trans-zeatin*. The final major plant hormone is abscisic acid (ABA), and again much is known concerning the biosynthesis of this compound.

ABA is a *sesqueterpenoid* with close structural similarities to the terminal rings of several *oxygenated carotenoids* (*xanthophylls*), such as *violaxanthin*. An ABA-deficient mutant of *Arabidopsis thaliana* was shown to be impaired in the epoxidation of *zeaxanthin* to form violaxanthin. This gene was subsequently *cloned* and a tomato *homolog* has recently been obtained.

This provides strong evidence that ABA is biosynthesised from *xanthophyll* precursors. Further evidence has been provided by a transposoninduced ABA-deficient mutant of maize (the *vp-14 mutant allele*). This gene has been cloned and a fusion *protein* expressed in E. *coli.*

The enzyme was shown to carry out the oxidative cleavage of 9-cis xanthophylls to form the first C_{15} intermediate in the ABA pathway, an *aldehyde* known as xanthoxin. A tomato homolog of this has recently been obtained and it has been shown that mRNA levels are upregulated by water stress.

Cell-free systems can be produced that carry out the conversion of xanthoxin to ABA. The *penultimate* precursor of ABA has been shown to be *ABA-aldehyde* (AB-CHO) and the enzyme carrying out this conversion can thus be called ABA-aldehyde oxidase (AAO).

The gene encoding this enzyme has yet to be cloned. In this chapter the extraction and purification of AAO will be used as an example to illustrate the general principles involved in the *isolation* of key enzymes involved in *hormone* synthesis.

The extraction described is based on that of Sindhu and Walton. Although precise methods will be given for the extraction and assay of AAO it is obvious that these will not be directly applicable to other hormone systems. Indeed, it is very difficult to predict the conditions required for the extraction and assay of any enzyme.

The purification methods described, apart from the affinity chromatography, are obviously generic and can be applied to any enzyme system.

Again, however, the conditions required would need to be determined by experiment for each individual case. Some general considerations are given in *Notes 1–6*. Several excellent texts cover in detail the considerations required in protein purification.

MATERIALS

Extraction and Assay

1. Plant tissue: Leaf tissue used in these experiments was obtained from tomato plants *(Lycopersicum esculentum,* Mill cv. Ailsa Craig). The experimental material was grown in a glasshouse. Supplementary lighting was supplied to give a light period of at least 16 h and a dark period of no less than 8 h. The age at which the plants were harvested was determined by the number of true leaves. Plants having between four and 10 true leaves were harvested. In any one extraction there was a range of tissue ages.
2. Extraction and assay buffer: 0.2 M KH2PO4, 7.5 mM dithiothreitol adjusted to pH 6.5 with 0.1 M KOH. 3. Substrate: 0.1 mg/mL^{-1} c-(RS)-AB-CHO in acetone.
4. Partitioning of ABA: Diethyl ether. Rotary evaporator, Howe Gyrovap (Banbury, UK).
5. High performance liquid chromatography (HPLC) analysis of ABA.
   a. Equipment: Perkin-Elmer (Beaconsfield, UK) series 10 Liquid Chromatograph, Perkin-Elmer LC-95 UV/Visible Spectrophotometer Detector, and Perkin-Elmer LCI-100 Laboratory Computing Integrator.

   b. Column: Analytical reverse-phase either a 10 μm Techsil C18 ODS bonded column (250 × 4.6 mm id) or a Bio-Rad (Hemel Hempstead, UK) Rsil C18 ODS bonded column (250 × 4.6 mm id).
   c. Eluent: 45% aqueous methanol (Romil, UK) acidified with 1% ethanoic acid de-gassed *in vacuo.*
6. GC-MS analysis of ABA:
   a. Equipment: Hewlett Packard (Palo Alto, CA) 5890A series gas *chromatograph* linked to a Hewlett Packard 5970 series mass selective detector. Grob type *splitless* injector (1 μL sample volume). BP-1 WCOT 25 m × 0.22 mm id column.
   b. *Diazomethane* reagent: React 10.7 g diazald (Aldrich Chemical Company Ltd., UK) in 65.mL diethyl ether with 5 g potassium hydroxide (KOH) dissolved in 33 mL of 68% aqueous ethanol at 40°C. Collect the resultant *diazomethane* in diethyl ether at 0°C.

Affinity Chromatography

1. Sepharose 6B support with an epoxy-activated 12-atom spacer (Sigma Chemical Company Ltd, UK).
2. (RS)-cis-ABA.
3. Column buffer: Eluent from ultrafiltration buffered with 50 mM Tris-HCl, pH 7.5.
4. 42 μM AB-CHO in column buffer.

Protein Determination

1. Bio-Rad protein determination kit.
2. Bovine serum albumin (Sigma).
3. Spectrophotometer.

SDS Gel Electrophoresis

Preparing and Running the Gel

1. 30% Acrylamide, 0.8% NN'-methylenebisacrylamide (BDH, UK) made up in distilled H_2O and filtered through a Whatman No. 1 filter paper.

2. Tris-HCl, pH 8.8 (at 20°C).
3. 1% SDS (sodium dodecyl sulfate) (Fisons, UK).
4. N,N,N',N'-*Tetramethylethylanadiamine* (TEMED) (*Sigma*).
5. Freshly prepared 5% (w/v) *aqueous ammonium persulfate*.
6. 1M Tris-HCl, pH 6.8 (at 20°C).
7. Electrode buffer: 0.192 *M* glycine, 0.025 *M* Tris base, 0.1% (w/v) SDS pH 8.8. This was prepared fresh for each run.
8. Sample buffer: 10% (w/v) SDS, 20% (v/v) glycerol (Fisons, UK), 0.04% (w/v) bromophenol blue (Fisons), 125 mM Tris-HCl, pH 6.8, and 100 mM iodoacetamide (Sigma).
9. Pharmacia minigel system (Pharmacia, Sweden). Gallekamp Biomed E250 power pack (Fisons, UK).

Staining Gel with Coomassie Blue

1. 45% (v/v) Methanol (Fisons), 10% (v/v) ethanoic acid, and 0.1% (w/v) Coomassie Brilliant Blue R-250 (Fisons).
2. 45% (v/v) Methanol, 10% (v/v) ethanoic acid
3. 20% (v/v) Methanol, 10% (v/v) ethanoic acid

Silver Staining the Gel

1. 50% Ethanol (Fisons); 10% ethanoic acid (Fisons).
2. 25% Ethanol; 10% ethanoic acid.
3. 10% Ethanol; 0.5% ethanoic acid.
4. 11 mM silver nitrate ($AgNO_3$) (Fisons).
5. 95 mM Methanol (Fisons); 750 mM NaOH (Fisons).
6. 10% Ethanoic acid.

METHODS

Extraction and Assay

1. Leaf tissue (typically 5–20 g), including cotyledons, was harvested and weighed. The tissue was blended

in a blender (Moulinex, France) using 3 mL cold extraction buffer per gram fresh weight of leaf tissue. The *homogenate* was filtered through four layers of muslin and *centrifuged* at 20,000g for 30 min at 4°C. The supernatant was retained and the pellet discarded.

2. Crude extract was concentrated using a *stirred* cell *ultrafiltration* unit (Amicon, UK), fitted with a filtration membrane with a mol wt cut-off of 1000 kDa (PM10 membrane, Amicon, UK). The sample was filtrated under nitrogen at a pressure of 60 psi. Ultrafiltration was carried out over ice. Both the eluent and retentate were retained.
3. Crude extract (0.3–0.5 mL) was made up to a total volume of 0.7 mL with assay buffer and 0.75 mL of eluent from the ultrafiltration added. The requirement for eluent is discussed in Note 4.
4. Fifty microliters of substrate was added to give a final substrate concentration of 8.06 μM. The assay mixture was briefly mixed (1 s) using a *Whirlimixer* and to determine c-ABA concentration at time = 0, a 0.5-mL aliquot was taken and *frozen* immediately in liquid *nitrogen.*
5. The remaining 1 mL of assay mixture was incubated for 60 min at 32°C, then frozen in liquid nitrogen. The samples were stored at –20°C until extraction of ABA for analysis and quantification.
6. The samples were defrosted and the pH was adjusted to pH 3.0 by the addition of 10% aqueous HCl. The samples were then partitioned against a fivefold excess of diethyl ether. The aqueous phase was discarded.
7. The organic phase was taken to dryness at 30°C *in vacuo,* using a rotary evaporator.
8. The samples were redissolved in 500 μL methanol (Romil Ltd., UK) and transferred to a 900 μL microinsert. The samples were taken to dryness at 20°C *in vacuo* using a Howe Gyrovap. The samples

were stored at 4°C until analysis by HPLC.

9. The samples were redissolved in 50 μL methanol. A 20-μL aliquot was injected onto the HPLC column, using a fixed volume sample loop, via a Rheodyne 7125 valve. Analytical reverse-phase HPLC was carried out on either a 10 μm Techsil C18 ODS bonded column (250 × 4.6 mm id) or a Bio-Rad Rsil C18 ODS bonded column (250 × 4.6 mm id). The column conditions were 45% aqueous methanol acidified with 1% ethanoic acid. The eluent was degassed *in vacuo.* An isocratic system was used. The solvent flow rate was 2 mL/min, delivered by a Perkin-Elmer series 10 Liquid Chromatograph. Eluted compounds were detected at 260 nm using a Perkin-Elmer LC-95 UV/ Visible Spectrophotometer Detector, and the peak area and peak height calculated by a Perkin-Elmer LCI-100 Laboratory Computing Integrator.
10. Confirmation of the identity of the cis-ABA peak was carried out by comparison of retention time with the peak obtained from an authentic external standard. In addition, validation of the peak identity was carried out by both gas chromatography-mass spectroscopy (GC-MS) and ultraviolet (UV) scan.
11. Confirmation by GC-MS was carried out by taking the peak from the HPLC, which eluted at the retention time of authentic c-ABA standards. This was taken to dryness at 35°C *in vacuo* using a rotary evaporator. The sample was redissolved in methanol and transferred to a 900-μL microinsert. The sample was then taken to dryness at 20°C *in vacuo* using a Howe Gyrovap.
12. The sample was derivatized by methylation (to give 1-methyl-ABA ester (Me-ABA). One milliliter of diazomethane solution was added to the sample. The sample was left at room temperature (in a fume cupboard) and allowed to react for 2 h. The sample was dried at 20°C *in vacuo* using a Howe Gyrovap,

and redissolved in 20 μL of 10 μg/mL Et-ABA for quantification by GC-MS.

13. GC-MS was performed on a Hewlett Packard 5890A series gas chromatograph linked to a Hewlett Packard 5970 series mass selective detector. Sample aliquots of 1 μL were injected via a Grob type splitless injector onto a BP-1 WCOT 25 m × 0.22 mm id column. The carrier gas was helium, at a flow rate of 1 mL/min. The temperature program started at 135°C and was maintained for 2 min before being increased to a final temperature of 265°C at a rate of 10°C/min. Mass spectra for eluted compounds were recorded over the range m/z 40–320; scan time was 0.5 s. Confirmation of the identity of the cis-ABA was by comparison of mass spectra obtained from authentic standards and published data.

Purification

Many methods are available for the purification of proteins and no generic method can be described. A very powerful and specific purification method, however, is affinity chromatography.

It is not always applicable but given the availability of a suitable ligand often provides a useful single-step purification. The construction and use of an affinity column for the purification of AAO will be described here.

1. Both *cis-* and *trans-diol* isomers of 1',4'-ABA-diol (1',4'-ABA-cis/ *trans-diol)* were used as the ligand. This was synthesized from (RS)-cis-ABA (Lancaster Synthesis, UK) by reduction of the 4'-keto group by sodium borohydride, using the method described by Milborrow: 0.775 g (2.93 mmol) (RS)-c-ABA was dissolved in 16 mL methanol.

   To this 2 g sodium borohydride was added, dissolved in 8 mL H_2O. The reaction mixture was kept on ice for 30 min, and the reaction stopped by the addition of 95% ethanoic acid. The methanol was evaporated off at 30°C *in vacuo.*

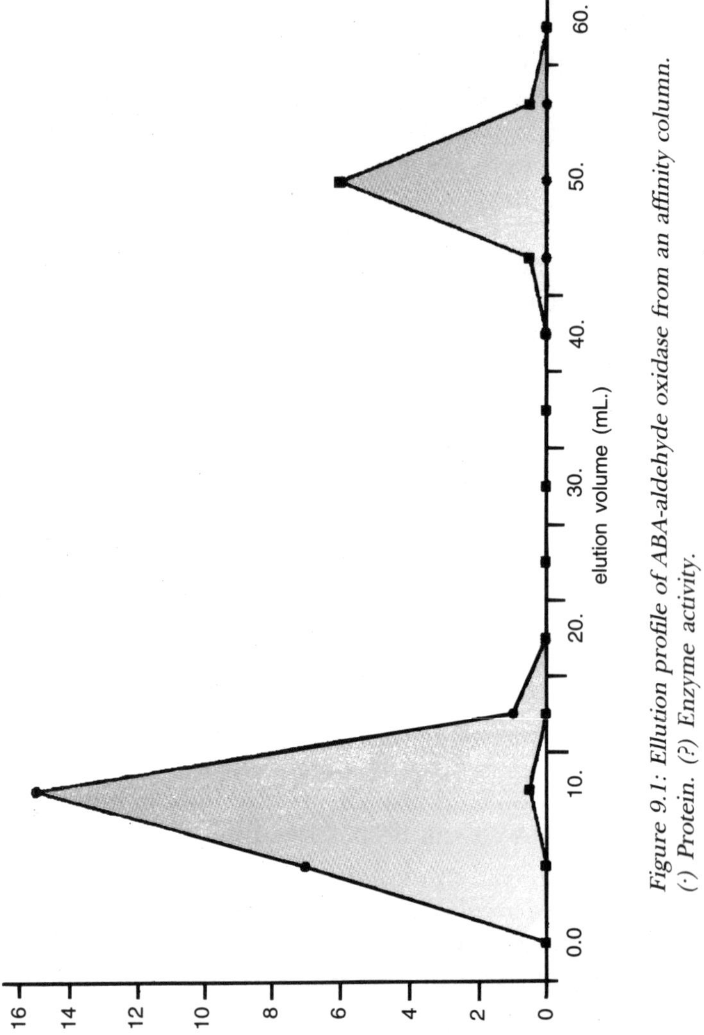

Figure 9.1: Ellution profile of ABA-aldehyde oxidase from an affinity column. (·) Protein. (?) Enzyme activity.

The aqueous phase was partitioned against a twofold excess of diethyl ether. The organic phase was retained and taken to dryness at 30°C *in vacuo.* All reactions were carried out under dimmed lighting conditions to prevent isomerization of the 2,3-C double bond.

2. The matrix used was a Sepharose 6B support with an epoxy-activated 12-atom spacer. Five grams of epoxy-activated Sepharose 6B (285-600 μmol activated sites) were hydrated overnight in 20 mM Na_2HPO_4, adjusted to pH 10.75 using 2 M NaOH. The matrix was washed with 100 mL of the hydration buffer and allowed to drain to remove excess buffer.
3. For coupling the ligand to the matrix, the 1',4'-ABA-diol was redissolved in 2 mL acetone. To this was added 58 mL of 20 mM Na_2HPO_4, adjusted to pH 10.75 using 2 M NaOH. The hydrated matrix was added to the mixture, and the coupling reaction was allowed to proceed for 16 h at 35°C, with continuous shaking.
4. The slurry was transferred to a GF/A filter and washed with 300 mL dH_2O, 500 mL 100 mM sodium carbonate-bicarbonate buffer, pH 8.0, and 500 mL of 100 mM sodium acetate-ethanoic acid buffer, pH 4.
5. To block any nonreacted sites, the gel was then reacted with 1 M ethanolamine for 4 h at room temperature, at pH 9.0, using a Na_2HPO_4 buffer adjusted to pH 9.0 using 2 M NaOH. The slurry was then washed as above before being equilibrated with 200 mM Tris-HCl, pH 7.5, and packed into a column. The affinity gel matrix was stored at 4°C.
6. The affinity column was equilibrated with a column buffer (Eluent from ultrafiltration buffered with 50 mM Tris-Cl, pH 7.5). One milliliter of extract was applied and washed through with column buffer. ABA oxidase activity was eluted by the application of 42 μM AB-CHO in column buffer. Fractions were collected and assayed for enzyme activity and protein content.
7. A typical elution profile from the affinity column is shown in Figure elsewhere in this chapter. The specific activity of the crude extract was approx 4 nmol ABA/hr/mg protein and of the affinity purified enzyme about 230 nmol ABA/hr/mg protein.

Protein Determination

Protein determination was carried out using a Bio-Rad protein assay microassay procedure.

1. Protein samples were diluted with 20 mM Tris-HCl buffer, pH 7.5, to give a concentration within the range of 1–20 μg/mL.
2. E_{595} was measured on a Pye Unicam SP8-400 UV/ visible spectrophotometer.
3. Standard calibration curves were constructed using a concentration range of bovine serum albumin (Sigma) of 0–25 μg/mL.

SDS Gel Electrophoresis

Denaturing, discontinuous sodium *dodecyl sulfate-polyacrylamide* gel *electrophoresis* (SDS-PAGE) was used for analysis of protein purity and for estimation of M_r of subunits. SDS-PAGE was performed with a *Pharmacia minigel* system.

Preparing and Running the Gel

1. For the main gel and gel plug, a solution (solution A) of the following constituents was made up: 3.67mL 30% acrylamide/0.8% *NN'*methylenebisacrylamide, 4.18 mL Tris-HCl, pH 8.8 (at 20°C), 1.1 mL 1% SDS (sodium dodecyl sulfate), and 2.05 mL H_2O (distilled). The solution was de-gassed in vacuo.
2. Two milliliters of solution A were taken. To this was added: 4 μL N,N,N',N'-tetramethylethylanadiamine (TEMED) and 0.1 mL freshly prepared 5% (w/v) aqueous ammonium persulfate. This was poured into the gel mold and allowed to set to give a plug that acted as a seal at the bottom of the gel.
3. To the remainder of solution A was added: 4.4 μL TEMED and 0.2 mL freshly prepared 5% (w/v) aqueous ammonium persulfate. The gel was then poured. The exposed surface of the gel was covered with a layer of water after pouring, to prevent dehydration and to give a flat surface. The gel was allowed to set for at least 45 min.

4. For the stacking gel, a solution of the following solution was made up: 0.66 mL 30% acrylamide/0.8% NN'-methylenebisacrylamide, 0.5 mL 1 M Tris-HCI, pH 6.8 (at 20°C), 1 mL 1% SDS, 6.04 mL $_{H20}$ (distilled), 2 μL TEMED, and 0.1 mL freshly prepared 5% (w/v) aqueous ammonium persulfate.
5. The water was removed from the surface of the set main gel and replaced with stacking gel solution. A suitable gel comb was inserted and the stacking gel allowed to set. Prior to sample loading the comb was removed and sample wells were flushed with 50 μL of electrode buffer to remove any nonpolymerized polyacrylamide. The electrode tanks were then filled with electrode buffer.
6. The protein samples for SDS-PAGE were added to an equal volume of sample buffer. The protein samples were then heated for 5 min in a boiling water bath. The samples were spun at 8400g for 5 min to precipitate any particulate matter resulting from the heat treatment.
7. Protein samples (20-50 μL) were loaded into the wells. The gel was run at 30 mV until the blue tracker dye had passed into the plug.

Staining the Gel

Coomassie blue staining

1. The following aqueous solutions were made up:
   A. 45% (v/v) Methanol (Fisons), 10% (v/v) ethanoic acid, and 0.1% (w/v) Coomassie Brilliant Blue R-250.
   B. 45% (v/v) Methanol and 10% (v/v) ethanoic acid.
   C. 20% (v/v) Methanol and 10% (v/v) ethanoic acid.
2. Fixing and staining of the proteins after electrophoresis was accomplished by immersing the gel in solution A for 4 h.
3. Destaining (removal of background stain) was carried out by immersing the gel in solution B for 24 h. Two

changes of solution B were used to enhance the destaining process.

4. The gel was stored in solution C.

Silver staining

1. The following aqueous solutions were made up:
   A. 50% Ethanol and 10% ethanoic acid.
   B. 25% Ethanol 10% ethanoic acid.
   C. 10% Ethanol and 0.5% ethanoic acid.
   D. 11 mM silver nitrate.
   E. 95 mM Methanol and 750 mM NaOH.
   F. 10% Ethanoic acid.
2. Proteins were fixed in the gel by immersing the gel in solution A for 1 h.
3. Rehydration of the gel and partial removal of ethanoic acid was achieved by immersing the gel in solution B, followed by solution C, both for 30 min.
4. The gel was immersed in solution D for an additional 1 h.
5. The gel was then rinsed rapidly (2 × 45 s) in distilled water to remove unbound $AgNO_3$ from the gel surface.
6. Colour development was carried out by immersing the gel in solution E until bands were visible.
7. The reaction was stopped by immersion of the gel in solution F.
8. The gels were stored at 4°C in solution B.

NOTES

1. During the extraction, enzyme stability can be influenced by many parameters. These need to be determined experimentally for each specific enzyme. However, there are some general precautions. The ionic strength within a cell is typically within the range of 0.15–0.2 M.

It is thus normal to use this ionic strength to solubilize cytoplasmic proteins. However, the cell wall can act as a strong ion-exchange medium and many basic proteins can adhere to the wall remnants following homogenization.

These can often be desorbed using higher ionic strength (1 M) and neutral pH. Similarly hydrophobic proteins, and those proteins that are intrinsically membrane associated, can often be solubilized by the addition of a nonionic detergent, such as Triton X-100 (0.1%–3%) or by the use of chaotropic agents, such as 1 M LiCl. It should be noted, however, that these reagents can themselves result in enzyme inactivation.

2. The extraction solution should also be buffered. Typical buffers include 50 mM phosphate and 0.1 M Tris-HCl. The normal pH range within a cell is between 6.5 and 7.5, and this pH range is a good starting point for any extraction.

   It should be noted that the pH of many buffer systems, in particular Tris, will vary with temperature. Thus, storage of extracted enzyme at low temperature can sometimes induce adverse pH changes, resulting in inactivation of the enzyme.

3. The active site of an enzyme can be modified by many factors, including oxidation and heavy metals. Oxidation is normally prevented by the addition of reducing agents, those commonly employed being (3-mercaptoethanol (5%), cysteine (10 mM), or dithiothreitol (DTT) (5-10 mM).

   However, all three of these reducing agents will oxidize rapidly in solution and should always be used fresh. Of the three, DTT is perhaps preferred since this does not form mixed disulfides with proteins.

   It is often necessary to include a chelating agent in the extraction buffer. Ethylenediamine tetra-acetic acid (EDTA) at between 1 and 5 mM is commonly used.

4. For many enzymes, essential cofactors are often required both for activity and to retain stability during purification. These may include metal ions, such as copper and iron. For instance, ACC oxidase requires Fe^{2+} and ascorbate.

   The requirement of ABA oxidase for eluent from the initial ultrafiltration of the crude extract probably indicates the presence of an essential cofactor.

   This has not been identified but could be molybdenum since it is postulated that ABA oxidase contains a molybdenum cofactor.

5. During extraction it is often necessary to protect the enzyme from proteolytic activity. A range of protease inhibitors can be employed, including phenylmethylsulfonyl fluoride (PMSF). In addition, the inclusion of a chelating agent may also serve to limit some forms of protease.

6. Dilute enzyme solutions tend to lose activity more rapidly than concentrated solutions. It is thus advisable to concentrate the samples following each purification step as quickly as possible. Several methods are available for concentrating proteins.

   These include ultrafiltration, salting out with ammonium sulfate, and precipitation with organic solvents, such as ethanol. It is also a common practice to stabilize very dilute proteins by the addition of bovine serum albumin (0.1-10 mg/mL) or glycerol (20-30%).

   Glycerol can be used at up to 50% but under these conditions becomes too viscous to handle. However, it is common to use 50% glycerol in solution to be stored at low temperature and under these conditions the effect on the retention of activity can be very dramatic.

7. The affinity column gave best recovery when the column buffer was made using the eluent from the initial ultrafiltration step. The reason for this is unclear but may indicate the presence of a limiting cofactor.

The nature of this cofactor was not determined. However, since it has been suggested that ABA oxidase may require a molybdenum cofactor, this may be involved.

8. Ionic strength of the column buffer may influence the efficiency of both binding and elution from the affinity column. ABA, rather than AB-CHO, was equally effective at eluting the enzyme from the column.

   However, in this case the residual ABA in the fractions can interfere with subsequent assay. Fractions in this case would thus need desalting using spun G-25 columns prior to the assay.

9. Several methods are available for protein determination. The BioRad microassay is sensitive and, unlike some of the other methods, does not appear to be unduly effected by the reagents commonly used for enzyme extraction, such as Tris, DTT, and ammonium salts.

   However, it has been noticed with several plant enzymes that the absolute protein content as determined with the Bio-Rad system is often much lower than that determined by the Lowry method. Thus, it is important to realize that these assays can often only provide a relative measure of protein content and are not absolute.

10. Coomassie staining is linear up to around 20 μg/cm but intensity varies between individual proteins. Silver staining is 10–20 times more sensitive than Coomassie staining but this again depends on the type of protein.

    In a crude extract it is normal to load between 50 and 100 μg of protein for Coomassie staining and between 10 and 25 μg for silver staining.

11. The silver staining method is also very prone to the appearance of false bands. The reason for this is unclear but may be caused by keratin or the gel chemistry. The incorporation of iodoacetamide in the sample loading solution minimizes this problem.

10

Chapter

Oxylipins

Plants have to adapt to the environment due to their sessile lifestyle. Consequently, constant monitoring of abiotic factors of the environment, such as light, *oxygen, water, osmotic pressure, salt, temperature, nutrients* (e.g. *glucose, nitrogen* and *phosphate*), gravity, wind, touch or chemicals have to be performed by independent *perception* and *transduction* pathways.

In many cases, however, factors reach *unfavourable* levels corresponding to stress. Furthermore, biotic interactions between plants and *pathogenic* or symbiotic *microorganisms* and *herbivores* or between different plants may occur.

Due to the high number of herbivorous insects and pathogenic micro-organisms, there are numerous complex interactions. In the past 15 years, *jasmonic acid* (JA) and *metabolites,* such as its *methyl ester* (MeJA) or amino acid *conjugates* of JA, all of them commonly named *jasmonates* were recognized as important *signals* in plant responses to *biotic* and *abiotic stress.*

Jasmonates originate from the common precursors 12-*oxophytodienoic acid* (OPDA) and dinor-OPDA (dnOPDA), which are collectively called *octadecanoids.* These JA precursors are formed within the *lipoxygenase* (LOX) pathway, which is initiated by *oxygenation* of free or *esterified polyunsaturated fatty acids* (PUFAs) leading to many different products collectively named oxylipins.

More recently, octadecanoids and some other *oxylipins*

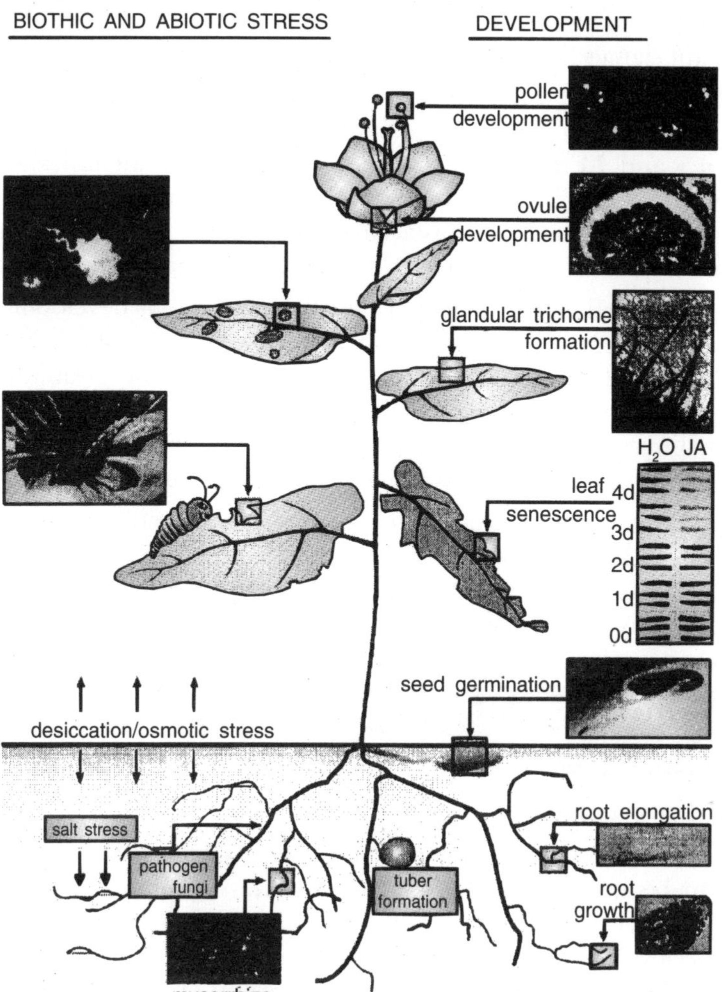

Figure 10.1: Scheme showing biotic and abiotic stress responses and developmental processses that are known to be jasmonate dependent.

were recognized to be JA-independent signals in plant stress responses. Beside analysis of biosynthesis of all these oxylipins, increasing interest is given to their perception and signal *transduction.* Here, transgenic approaches and analyses of mutants led to fundamental knowledge on JA signaling, including a remarkable *cross-talk* with signaling pathways of other plant signals (hormones), such as *salicylate, ethylene* or *abscisic acid.*

In *Arabidopsis thaliana,* a common phenotype of *JA deficiency* and *JA insensitivity* is male sterility. Since identification of the first *JA-insensitive* male sterile mutant in 1994 increasing knowledge has accumulated on the role of *jasmonates* and other oxylipins in distinct developmental processes.

These data led to deeper insights into various developmental processes, such as root growth or senescence for which JA was already recognized as a stimulatory or inhibitory effector by *physiological experiments* in the 1980s. This chapter will cover recent aspects of biosynthesis, signal transduction and action of jasmonates and other oxylipins.

As usually in a field of high interest, constantly appearing reviews are available on specific aspects. Here, I review recent progress in biosynthesis, signal transduction and role of oxylipins. (I apologize for references not cited due to space limitation.)

α-DIOXYGENASE, PHYTOPROSTANES AND ELECTROPHILE COMPOUNDS

α-Dioxygenase

In saturated and unsaturated fatty acids molecular oxygen can be inserted at the C-2 by an a-dioxygenases (α-DOX), first shown for tobacco, and later described for several plant species including pea, *Arabidopsis* and rice. The tobacco α-DOX catalyzes the stereo-specific insertion of oxygen leading to unstable 2-*hydroperoxide derivatives.*

The α-*DOX* expression is up-regulated upon bacterial infection of tobacco leaves, and metabolic profiling of tobacco leaves infected with an incompatible strain of *Pseudomonas syringae* revealed strong rise in accumulation of α-DOX products and decrease in LOX products indicating role of α-DOX in plant pathogen interactions, *oxidative stress* and cell death.

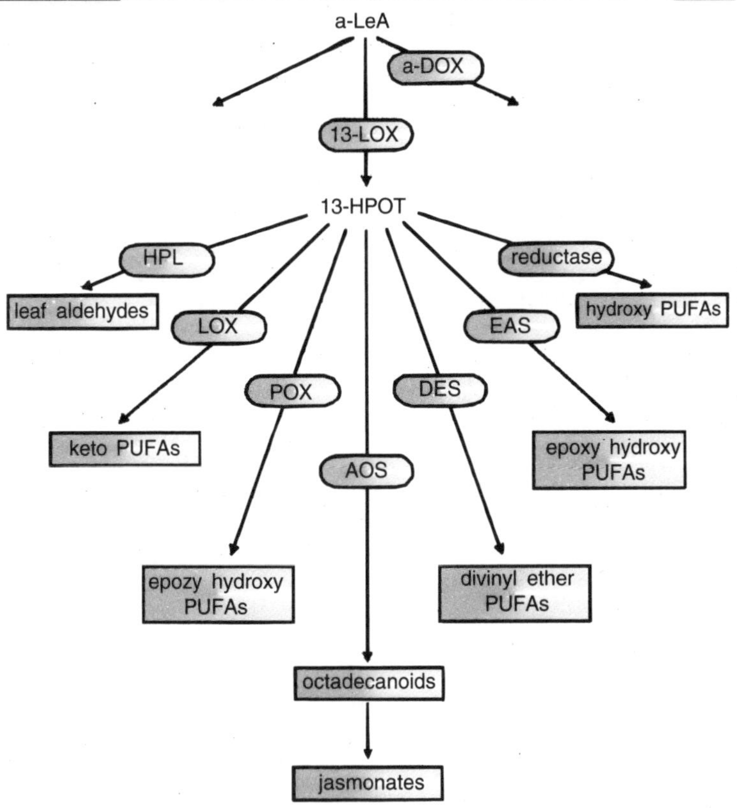

Figure 10.2: The different branches of the LOX pathway. Metabolism of α-LeA by non-enzymatic formation of dinorisoprostanes, a-dioxygenase (a-DOX)-catalyzed formation of α-hydroxy-PUFAs and 13-lipoxygenase (13-LOX)-catalyzed formation of the 13-hydroperoxide of α-LeA (13-HPOT). 13-HPOT can be the substrate of a reductase, an EAS, a DES, an AOS, a POX, an LOX and an HPL.

Phytoprostanes and Electrophile Compounds

The plant-specific JA biosynthesis from a-linolenic acid (α-LeA) is homologous to prostaglandin biosynthesis from *arachidonic acid* in animals. Detailed inspection of degradation products of lipid membranes revealed the occurrence of *numerous prostaglandin*-like oxylipins called *phytoprostanes.*

Phytoprostanes are formed non-enzymatically by action of free *radicals.* First products are 9(R, S)-, 12(R, S)-, 13(R, S)-

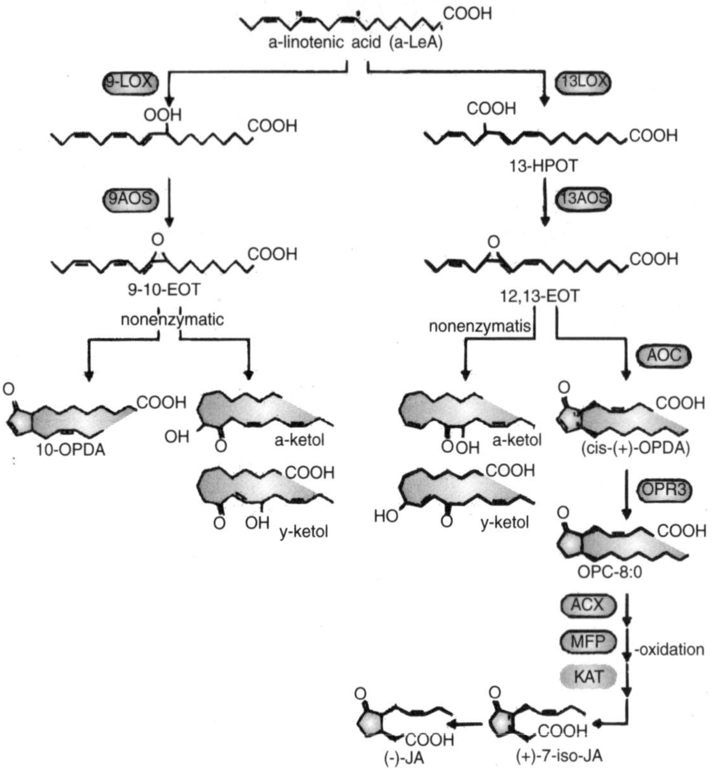

Figure 10.3: Metabolic scheme showing formation of 9-LOX and 13-LOX products from α-LeA. In both pathways LOX products are used by AOSs with positional specificity. The corresponding epoxides are spontaneously hydrolyzed to α- and —ketols, as well as racemic OPDA, whereas in the presence of AOC cis-(+)-OPDA is formed. EOT: epoxyoctadecatrienoic acid.

and 16(R, S)-*hydroperoxy fatty acids,* whereas the *enzymatically* (LOX)formed compounds are 9(S)- and 13(S)-*hydroxyperoxy* fatty acids.

Most of these phytoprostanes are esterified in membranes and increase upon oxidative stress. Some of them were shown to be short-lived stress metabolites that mediate expression of genes known to function in stress *protection* and *apoptosis.* Although most of lipid peroxidation is assumed to occur by LOXs and α-DOX, *phytoprostanes* and *non-enzymatically* formed oxylipins are *permanent* constituents with *significant* amount in extracts of healthy *plant tissues.*

Wound- and pathogen-induced *accumulation* of fatty acid *degradation* production with a ketodiene or ketotriene structure led to the concept that these types of compounds, for example *malondialdehyde* (MDA), represent reactive *electrophile* species with activity in *plant-defense gene expression.*

Transcriptome and *metabolome analyses* with *Arabidopsis* revealed remarkably different properties among the various *electrophile species* such as MDA and small *vinyl ketones.* Whereas MDA seems to act as a *crosslinking/modifying* agent thereby contributing to express in response to *abiotic stress,* the vinyl ketones strongly activate genes in response to biotic stress.

It will be interesting to see how the *biological* relevance of these reactive *carbonyl* compounds can be dissected by use of *mutants.* First *indication* came from analysis of the JA-deficient opr3 mutant of *Arabidopsis.*

Here, the ketodiene-containing OPDA accumulated in response to pathogen attack suggesting role of OPDA but not JA in some plant pathogen interactions. *Transcriptome* analysis following wounding or treatment with OPDA, JA or MeJA revealed a remarkable number of genes that were specifically *up-regulated* by OPDA.

THE LOX PATHWAY

PUFAs are constituents of membrane lipids, which are permanently altered in their composition and turnover. Following release of PUFAs *hydroperoxidesized* by different forms of LOXs. The *LOX pathway* covers all *LOX-catalyzed* reactions, and the subsequent steps lead to different groups of *oxylipins.*

The LOX

LOXs (linoleate: oxygen oxidoreductase, EC 1.13.11.12) catalyse the regio- and stereo-specific *insertion* of oxygen in PUFAs containing a (1Z,4Z)-*pentadiene* system, for example linoleic acid (18:2, LA) or a-*linolenic acid* (18:3, α-LeA).

Oxygen insertion takes place either at C-9 (9-LOX) or at C-13 (13-LOX) of the carbon backbone leading with a-LeA as substrate to (9S)-*hydroperoxyoctadecatrienoic acid* (9-HPOT) or (13S)-*hydroperoxyoctad-ecatrienoic acid* (13-HPOT).

The exclusive formation of the *S-isomer* indicates enzymatic synthesis, whereas concomitant presence of the R-form is indicative for *non-enzymatic* synthesis. LOXs constitute a large gene family of non-heme iron-containing *dioxygenases.*

Beside classification of plant LOXs according to positional specificity (9-LOXs, 13-LOXs), they can be grouped by their primary structure. LOXs lacking a transit *peptide* and exhibiting high-sequence similarity (>75%) are *grouped* as type1-LOX*s,* whereas LOXs with a putative *chloroplast* transit peptide *sequence* and low overall sequence similarity (-35%) are classified as *type2-LOXs.*

All *type2-LOXs* identified so far are 13-LOXs. In respect to the reaction mechanism of LOXs, the space within the active site and the orientation of the substrate were identified to be important factors for positional specificity. In the case of the cucumber lipid body 13-LOX, site-directed mutagenesis of the histidine residue within the substrate binding pocket led to a 9-LOX activity.

In contrast to higher plants, lower plants such as algae or the moss Physcomitrella *patens* carry LOX enzymes with less substrate specificity and even a multifunctional LOX was found recently in *P. patens.* This enzyme is a 12-LOX with arachidonic acid and a 13-LOX with LeA as substrate and even C_{12}-C_{22} fatty acids are partially tolerated.

Surprisingly, this LOX is also a *hydroperoxide* lyase which allows *P. patens* to generate a broad spectrum of defense compounds by a single enzyme. This dual function of a single enzyme is reminiscent to a *dual-oxylipin metabolism* of red *algae*, where animal-like (*eicosanoid*) and plant-like (*octadecanoid*) oxylipins seems to be components of defense reactions.

The available sequence data allowed *phylogenetic* tree analysis which led to individual groups for all type1- and *type2*- as well as all 9- and 13-LOXs including distinction of monocotyledonous and dicotyledonous LOXs within these *subgroups.*

The clear distinction between LOXs of their regiospecificity is seen also with respect to expression pattern, intracellular location and substrate utilization.

Furthermore, conversion of 9-LOX as well as 13-LOX products by enzymes specific for one of these products led to the concept that oxylipins are formed in discrete 9-LOX and 13-LOX pathways.

The 9-LOX and subsequent reactions seem to have an essential role in plant defense. Initially, an enhanced susceptibility to infection with Phytophthora *parasitica* was observed in tobacco plants with *antisense* expression of a specific 9-LOX.

The potato homologue was activated upon infection of leaves, and is also activated in elicitor-treated potato cells grown in suspension including elevation of 9-LOX products.

Interestingly, in infected potato plants deficient in *9-LOX* expression high level of non-enzymatically formed 9-LOX products were found, whereas wild-type plants contained 9-LOX-derived compounds, indicating that the hypersensitive response appearing in both plant types was independent of the source of lipid hydroperoxides.

Beside the obvious role of 9-LOX products in plant defense, developmental programmes seem to be controlled by a 9-LOX. A 9-LOX of rice is specifically expressed in germinating seeds and a tuber-specific *9-LOX* (StLOX1) is expressed during tuber initiation.

Tuber development was disrupted in plants with antisense expression of this 9-LOX. Among the potato and tomato 13-LOXs the potato LOXH3 and its tomato homologue *TomloxD* function in wound-induced defense signaling, whereas the *TomloxC*, a homologue of potato LOXH1, is highly expres and functions in generation of *volatile* C_6 flavour compounds.

HPOT/HPOD: the Branch Point in the LOX Pathway

The majority of LOXs are 13-LOXs, which are localized in chloroplasts. The 13-LOX product 13-HPOT formed by oxygenation of a-LeA (18:3), and the 18:2 fatty acid oxygenat 13-hydroperoxyoctadeca-dienoic acid (13-HOPD) are substrates of at least seven different enzymes, which initiate individual branches within the LOX pathway:

(*a*) The allene oxide synthases (13-AOSs) leading to octadecanoids and jasmonates.

(*b*) The hydroperoxy lyases (13-HPLs) leading to w-oxo fatty acids and alcohols.

(*c*) The peroxygenases (POXs) forming epoxy hydroxy-PUFAs.

(*d*) The divinyl ether synthases (DESs) leading to divinyl ether-containing PUFAs.

(*e*) LOXs catalyzing the formation of keto-PUFAs.

(*f*) The epoxyalcohol synthases (EASs) forming epoxyhydroxy-PUFAs.

(*g*) The reductases leading to hydroxy PUFAs.

The corresponding reactions can take place with the 9-LOX products 9-HPOT and 9-HPOD. Consequently, a remarkably high number of oxylipins exist. Since the various PUFAs, preferentially 18:2 and 18:3, and many of their oxygenation products occur in free and esterified form, a metabolite profiling of oxylipins to describe lipid peroxidation and lipid-derived signals requires large scale high performance thin-layer chromatography (HPLC) analysis including separation of enantio-meric forms. So far, only few laboratories can perform such a large-scale metabolite profiling.

Many oxylipins generated by the different branches of the LOX pathway are antifungal and antimicrobial, for example the POX-generated epoxy and hydroxyl derivatives. This might be linked to a role of POX in cutin formation.

Also divinyl ethers generated by DES are elevated upon pathogenic attack and are thought to possess antimicrobial activity. Antifungal activity was also detected for EAS products of 9-HPOT. DES together with AOS and HPL are highly related members of the CYP74 family of P450s.

They are characterized by lack of a requirement for O_2 and an external redox compound. Based on sequence identity and enzymatic properties including substrate specificity, CYP74 enzymes are grouped in the subfamilies A, B, C and D. AOSs and HPLs using 13-hydroperoxides as the substrate belong to the subfamily A and B, respectively, CYP74C enzymes are HPLs accepting 9- or 13-hydroperoxides, whereas CYP74D enzymes are DESs with specificity for 9-hydroperoxides.

The role of HPLs in defense reactions has been repeatedly shown. Whereas 13-HPL-derived C-6 volatiles exhibit antimicrobial activity and performance, 9-HPL-derived nonenals may lead to a broad resistance to herbivores and pathogens. Interestingly, the moss *P. patens* contains not only a 9-LOX with HPL activity as mentioned above, but also a HPL which converts 9-hydroperoxides of C-18 fatty acids and the corresponding 11-*hydroperoxides* of arachidonic acid, a constituent of *P. patens.*

This may explain the natural broad resistance of *P. patens* against pathogens. It will be interesting to discover how the regulatory interplay between the HPL branch and the AOS branch determine the diverse patterns of *oxylipins* which could allow the plants to respond specifically to various *environmental* factors occurring under stress in nature.

The AOS Branch: Jasmonate Biosynthesis

The AOS

The initial reaction in the JA-forming branch of the LOX pathway is catalyzed by AOS. This enzyme, which was cloned first from flax, is a cytochrome P450-type (CYP74A), but is independent of *molecular oxygen* and NADPH, and exhibits low affinity to CO.

In the AOS-catalyzed reaction, the hydroperoxide group of LOX products is used as the source of reducing equivalents and of oxygen leading to a highly unstable epoxide, which degrades spontaneously to a-ketol and y-ketol or *racemic* 12-OPDA.

In the AOS gene family about 15 members have been cloned so far. *Phylogenetic analysis* indicates clear separation of the 9-AOSs specific for 9-*hydroperoxides* and the 13-AOSs specific for 13-hydroperoxides, supporting the above mentioned concept of discrete 9-LOX and 13-LOX pathways.

The 9-pathway was demonstrated for tulip bulbs, potato, and tomato. Its activity is increased upon pathogen attack accompanied by increased generation of oxylipins, such as 10-oxo-11,15-phytodienoic acid (10-OPDA).

Among the various plant species, the number of genes encoding AOSs is different. Whereas *Arabidopsis* has a single copy gene, there are three AOS genes in barley, potato. One of the three AOSs of tomato is a root specific 9-AOS.

The potato *9-AOS* is also expressed in roots, and additionally in tubers and sprouting eyes, and the encoded protein located in the envelope of young amyloplasts catalyzes formation of a-ketols (Stumpe *et al.,* unpublished information).

This suggests a new role for this type of hydroperoxide degradation products which was overlooked so far due to missing analytical methods. The barley AOSs exhibit either preference for 13-hydroperoxides, or accept 9- and 13-hydroperoxides. Obviously, in some plants defined by substrate *and* tissue specificity which is of regulatory impact.

Due to the single AOS in *Arabidopsis,* the AOS-knockout mutant is JA deficient, lacks wound induced accumulation of JA and JA-responsive gene expression and is male sterile, the characteristic phenotype of JA deficiency.

Except for the guayule AOS in rubber particles, all AOSs analysed so far were localized in chloroplasts, immunocytochemically and by import studies. Furthermore, with the exception of the barley AOSs, they all exhibit a putative chloroplast target sequence.

Upon wounding the *AOSs* are expressed locally and systemically in tomato, *Arabidopsis* and tobacco. In contrast, *Arabidopsis* plants treated locally with OPDA, JA and their molecular mimic coronatine exhibited only local activation of the *AOS* promoter.

The *AOS* promoter analyses in Arabido*psis* showed also developmental regulation. High *AOS* promoter activity, detected in the anther filament and early stages of carpel development, points to role for JA in anther development, as clearly indicated by JA-biosynthesis mutants and JA-insensitive mutants.

This accords with the tissue-specific occurrence of high amounts of various oxylipins, including JA, in tomato flower organs. First indications for regulatory elements upstream of the *AOS* promoter are given by the cas1 mutant of *Arabidopsis* which exhibits elevated levels of AOS mRNA, AOS protein, JA and OPDA leading to constitutive expression of JA inducible genes.

So far, CAS1 is not might be a negative regulator of *AOS* expression. First transcription factors of JA-responsive gene expression were identified for *Catharanthus ros* AP2-domain transcription factors, such as ORCA3. It will be interesting to see whether there are ORCA homologues in *Arabidopsis* which activate genes of *JA biosynthesis* such as *AOS.*

The allene oxide cyclase

The spontaneous decomposition of the AOS product is by-passed by allene oxide cyclase (AOC)-catalyzed formation of cis-(+)-OPDA. AOC establishes the enantiomeric structure of the naturally occurring cyclopentenones and cyclopentanones, such as JA.

Since the first cloning of AOC from tomato, more than 58 sequences are available, indicating the occurrence of gene families of different size. In contrast to the single copy gene of *AOS,* there are four AOCs in *Arabidopsis,* whereas in tomato the inverse situation occurs, a single copy gene for AOC and three *AOSs.*

Further differences among the various plant species are given by tissue specificity. Whereas LOX, AOS and AOCs of *Arabidopsis* occur in all leaf tissues, the tomato AOC is confined to vascular bundles, the surrounding parenchymatic

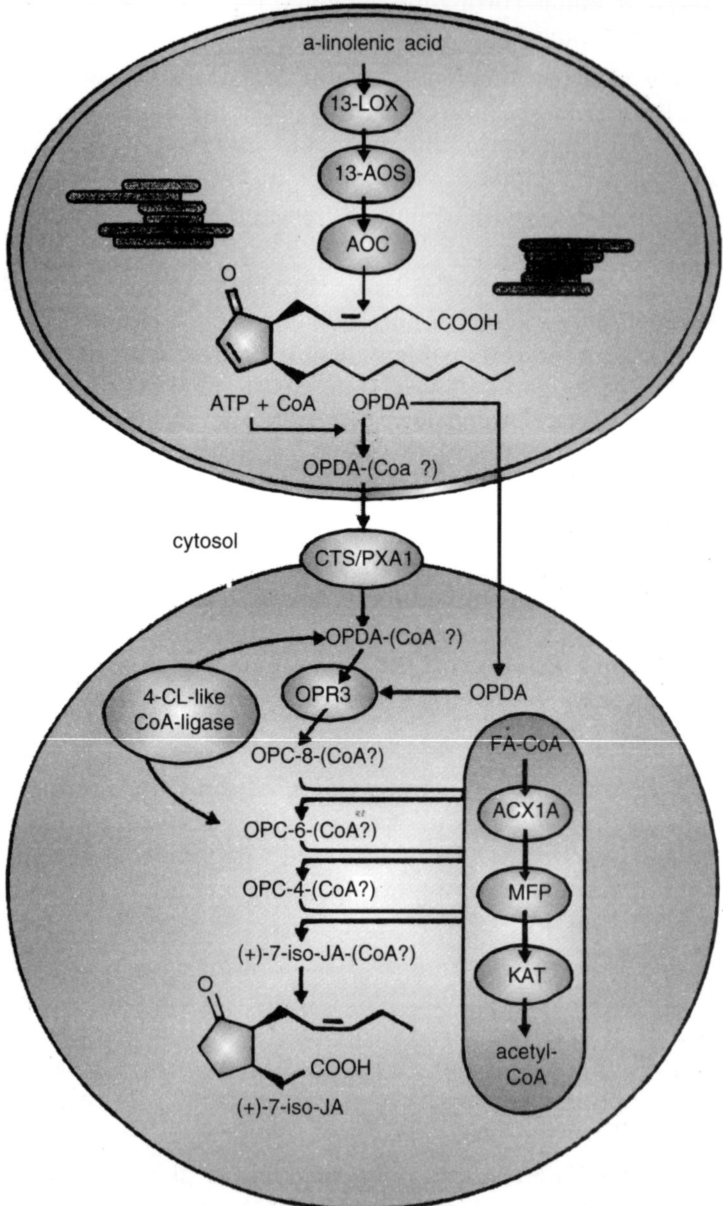

Figure 10.4: Intracellular loacation of JA biosynthesis.

cells and the ovules of flower buds suggesting regulatory role. In fact, the high abundance of AOC in ovules of tomato flowers is correlated with high amount of octadecanoids and jasmonates in pistils. In all species analysed so far, the AOCs are expressed upon wounding or other stimuli, such as glucose, osmotic stress or JA treatment.

Interestingly, salt tolerance is given by a 70 amino acid extension of the mangrove AOC, which is up-regulated under salt stress. Less understood is the light dependency of JA formation. AOC might be a target of phytochrome regulation.

During development of roots and flowers the four AOCs of *Arabidopsis* are expressed in a spatially and temporally distinct, non-redundant manner (Stenzel *et al.,* unpublished information).

OPR3

The conversion of cyclopentenones into cyclopentanones is catalyzed by the OPDA reductase (OPR). This enzyme is encoded by small gene families in A*rabidopsis* and tomato. Interestingly, among the three OPRs of both species, only OPR3 exhibits specificity for cis-(+)-OPDA, whereas the other OPRs seem to convert unspecifically α-,β-unsaturated carbonyl compounds.

The specificity of OPR3 is strongly supported by identification of the JA-deficient lines *opr3* and dde1 with mutations in *OPR3,* indicating that OPR1 and OPR2 cannot substitute the OPR3 function. OPR3 carries a peroxisomal target sequence and was shown to be localized in peroxisomes.

OP*R3* expression is induced by numerous stimuli, such as wounding, and correlates with the accumulation of JA. Due to the location of AOC in chloroplasts and the peroxisomal location of OPR3, transport of OPDA or its CoA ester is required between these organelles.

Indeed, there is evidence for the import of OPDA or its CoA ester by the ABC transporter COMATOSE (CTS), als PXA1. *CTS* mutants are JA deficient, but not male sterile indicating that the CTS function can be bypassed possibly by ion trapping of OPDA^{H}.

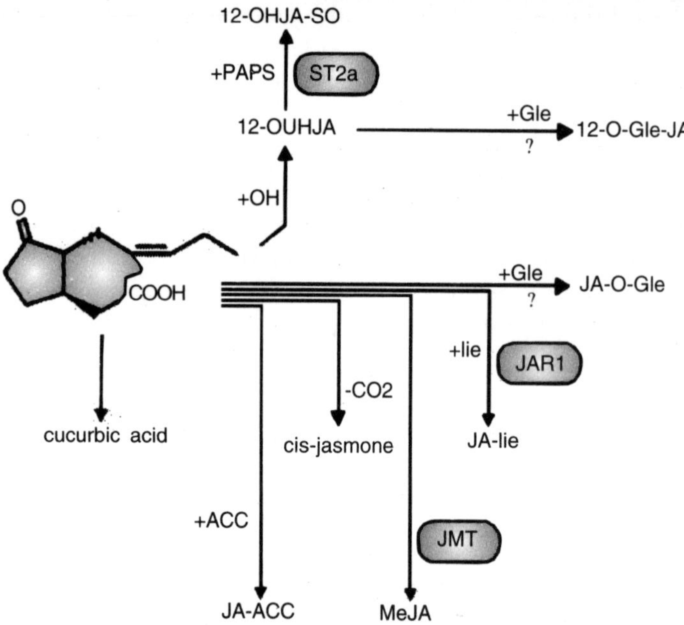

Figure 10.5: Metabolism of JA. The carboxyl group can be glucosylated, conjugated with amino acids, methylated, decarboxylated and conjugated with the ethylene precursor ACC. The pentenyl side chain can be hydroxylated and subsequently glucosylated or sulphated. The pentanone ring can be reduced to form cucurbic acids. So far the enzymes JA methyltransferease (JMT), JA conjugate synthase (JAR1) and 12-OHJA-sulphotransferase (ST2a) have been cloned from Arabidopsis.

β-oxidation in JA biosynthesis

The final steps in JA biosynthesis require shortening of the carboxylic acid side chain of 12-oxophytoenoic acid (OPC-8). Feeding experiments with OPC-derivatives carrying different lengths of the carboxylic acid side chain revealed that only even numbered OPC derivatives are converted to JA suggesting (-oxidative side chain shortening.

Recently, genetic evidence indicated that, similar to auxin biosynthesis, the final steps of JA biosynthesis take place *via* fatty acid β-oxidation steps. Fatty acid β-oxidation requires the activity of an acyl-CoA synthase, an acyl-CoA oxidase (ACX), a multifunctional protein (MFP) and a L-3 ketoacyl

CoA thiolase (KAT). The *antisense* expression of *ACX1* and *KAT2* led to JA deficiency upon wounding. Cloning of ACX1A of tomato revealed its role in wound-induced JA biosynthesis, herbivore resistance and generation of a systemic wound signal.

Interestingly, one of the 4-coumarate:CoA ligase-like enzymes of *Arabidopsis* is located in peroxisomes and can activate OPDA to the CoA ester. At present, two different scenarios are suggested:

(*a*) OPDA or its CoA ester is transported into the peroxisomes by the ABC transporter CTS/PXA1 located in the peroxisomal membrane and further converted by OPR3, ACX1, MFP and KAT.

(*b*) OPDA is transported into peroxisomes by ion trapping, directly reduced or activated by a 4-Cl-like enzyme before being reduced by OPR3 and β-oxidized by ACX1, MFP and KAT.

JA biosynthesis is thought to be regulated by three different factors:

(*a*) Substrate availability

(*b*) Positive feedback

(*c*) Tissue specificity.

The importance of substrate availability is indicated by the fact that transgenic plants, such as those of *Arabidopsis,* tobacco and tomato, over-expressing *AOS* or AOC constitutively, generate JA only upon wounding.

This burst in JA precedes transcriptional activation of JA-biosynthetic genes. Furthermore, fully developed *Arabidopsis* leaves contain abundant LOX, AOS and AOC activities, but form JA only upon external stimuli such as wounding.

Positive feedback in the regulation of JA biosynthesis was shown by:

(*a*) Up-regulation of JA-biosynthetic genes following treatment with JA.

(*b*) Up-regulation of AOC expression in mutants with constitutively elevated JA levels.

(*c*) A down-regulation of AOC expression in JA-deficient mutants such as *opr3.*

Finally, tissue-specific occurrence of JA-biosynthetic enzymes may affect the capacity to form JA. In tomato, AOC, but not LOX and AOS, is confined to vascular bundles while there is preferential formation of JA in this tissue upon wounding.

In *Arabidopsis,* the single-copy gene product AOS gives specificity for the AOS branch, but the four AOCs may allow the plant to generate OPDA and JA in a spatially and temporally distinct manner during development.

As mentioned above, the four AOC promoters exhibited spatially and temporally different, non-redundant activities in root and flower development.

Jasmonate metabolites

Accumulation of JA is usually taken as a first indicator for its role in any JAdependent process under study. JA homeostasis, however, is influenced by at least six metabolic conversions most of them not well understood:

(*a*) Methylation at the carboxylic acid group by a JA-specific methyl transferase.

(*b*) Decarboxylation to cis-jasmone.

(*c*) Adenylation at the carboxylic acid side chain by an AMP transferase followed by conjugation to an amino acid.

(*d*) Hydroxylation at C-11 or C-12 of the pentenyl side chain followed by O-glucosylation or sulphation.

(*e*) Formation of jasmonoyl-1-β-glucose, jasmonoyl-β-gentiobiose and hydroxyjasmonoyl-1-β-glucose.

(*f*) Reduction of the keto group of the cyclopentanone ring leading to cucurbic acids.

Methylation of JA by its methyl transferase is counteracted by unspecific esterases. Plant tissues contain much more JA than methyl jasmonate (MeJA).

Constitutive over-expression of the JA-specific methyl

Table 10.1: Mutants and genes functioning in JA biosynthesis and JA signaling in Arabidopsis and tomato.

Mutants	*Phenotype*	*Gene product*
JA biosynthesis		
dad1	Reduced filament elongation, delayed anther dehiscence JA deficient in flowers	Phospholipase Al
fad3–2fad7–2fad8	Male sterile, delayed anther development, altered α-LeA level	ω-7-fatty acid desaturase
spr2	Deficient in a-LeA and JA levels, no wound response suppressed prosystemin expression	ω-7-fatty acid desaturase
aos	JA deficient, decreased resistance to pathogens	AOS
dde2–2	Male sterile, delayed anther development,	AOS
opr3	JA deficient, decreased resistance to pathogens, reduced filament elongation	OPR3
dde1	JA deficient, reduced filament elongation, delayed dehiscence1	OPR3
acx1	JA deficient reduced wound response	ACX
aim1	Anther development	MFP1
comatose	Reduced JA content	COMATOSE/ PXA1 ABC transporter
Constitutive JA response		
cev1	Constitutive expression of vegetative storage proteins	Cellulose synthase CeS3
cet1-9	Constitutive expression of thionins, increased JA levels	?
cex1	Constitutive root growth inhibition, constitutive expression of JA-responsive genes	?

Table Contd.

Mutants	*Phenotype*	*Gene product*
cas1	Constitutive expression of *AOS*	?
joe1	Increased expression of *LOX2*, increased accumulation of anthocyans	?
joe2	Reduced inhibition of root growth, increased expression of *LOX2*	?
Others		
ore9	Delayed leaf senescence	F-box protein
cos1	Suppressor of JA-dependent defects in coi1 (root growth, senescence, defence)	Lumazine synthase
Reduced sensitivity to JA		
coi1	Reduced root growth inhibition, male sterile, reduced filament elongation, enhanced sensitivity to necrotrophic pathogens	F-box leucine reach repeat (LRR) COI1
jai1	Female sterile, altered trichome development, increased sensitivity to pathogens, decreased wound response	Tomato homologue of COI1
jar1/jin4/jai2	Reduced root growth inhibition by JA, increased sensitivity to necrotrophic pathogens	JA amino acid conjugate synthase
jin1/jai1	Reduced root growth inhibition	AtMYC2 (bHLHzip transcription factor)
jai3	Reduced root growth inhibition in *ein3* background	
jue1-3	Reduced expression of *LOX2*	?
oji	Enhanced sensitivity to ozone,	?

Table Contd.

Mutants	*Phenotype*	*Gene product*
	reduced root growth inhibition	
mpk4	Dwarf phenotype, altered expression of JA- and SAresponse genes	AtMPK4
rcd1	Reduced sensitivity to JA, ethylene and ABA, impaired in ozone signaling	RADICAL INDUCED CELL DEATH1
axr1	Reduced root growth inhibition by JA enzyme	RUB-activating
jai4/sgt1b	Reduced root growth inhibition in the *ein3* background	AtSGTlb

transferase increased MeJA content without affecting that of JA, and was accomp-anied by a specific gene expression pattern and increased pathogen resistance. This may indicate that under specific conditions the methyl ester is the active form of JA. Formation of the volatile cis-jasmone by decarboxylation is accompanied by resistance to insect feeding.

Possibly, this is a direct and an indirect defense mechanism by cis-jasmone-induced emission of volatiles, repelling attracting aphid antagonists. Similar to auxin amino acid conjugates, JA amino acid conjugates are formed by an enzyme which activates JA at the carboxylic acid group by adenylation followed by exchange of the AMP residue with any amino acid, but preferentially isoleucine (Ile).

The JA conjugate synthase is affected in the jar1 mutant. This type of enzyme is encoded by a large gene family-containing members, such as auxin conjugate synthase, or 4-CL-like ligases.

The predominant activity of JA conjugate synthase with Ile as the amino acid substrate accords with the preferential occurrence of JA–Ile among the JA amino acid conjugates in several plant species. JA-Ile is the most abundant oxylipin in tomato flowers. Although in some species JA-Ile exhibits biologindependent of JA, hydrolytic enzyme activity has been detected in some cases.

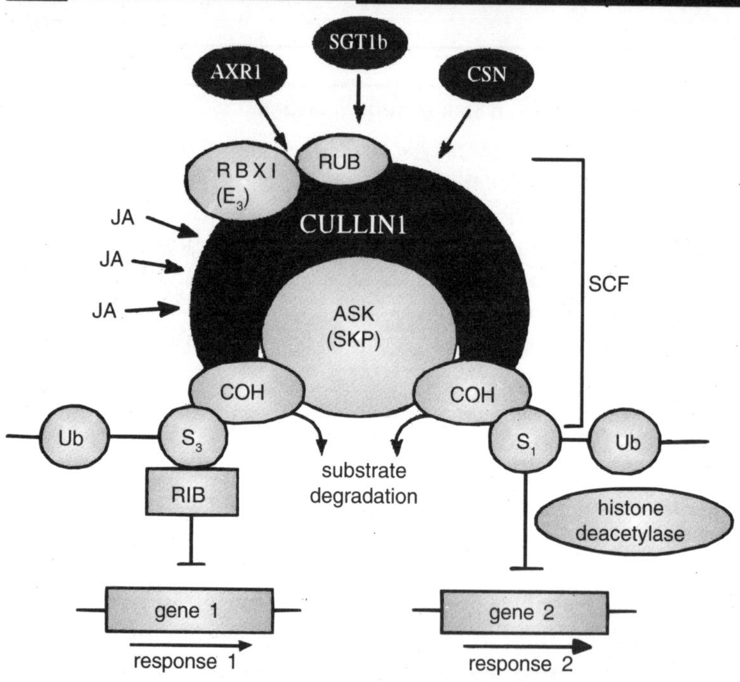

Figure 10.6: Model of the SCF complex in JA signaling.

Thus, for JA amino acid conjugates a similar situation seems to exist as for auxin conjugates, where auxin homeostasis is regulated by auxin conjugate synthase and various auxin conjugate hydrolases. Initially, hydroxylated JA and its O-glucoside were found exclusively in solanaceous species.

12-OH-JA was called tuberonic acid due to tuber-inducing properties, whereas its glucoside seems to be the transport form. 12-OH-JA synthesized in the leaves accumulates in tuber-forming stolons under short day conditions.

More recently, 12-OH-JA and its sulphated derivative have been found in *Arabidopsis*, while screening of many different dicotyledonous and monocotyledonous plants revealed the accumulation of 12-OH-JA in many species. In immature soybean seeds the 12-OH-JA level exceeds that of JA by up to 275-fold.

Unlike JA, 12-OH-JA does not inhibit growth or tendril coiling and does not induce JA-responsive genes, such as

THIONIN2.1 in *Arabidopsis*, *PIN2* in tomato or a set of JA-inducible genes of barley. These data suggest that hydroxylation of JA might be a type of inactivation in JA signaling, at least for a subset of genes.

For *Arabidopsis,* a sulphotransferase was cloned which converts specifically 12-OH-JA. Sulphation of hydroxylated compounds is a well-known mechanism in animal systems to inactive hormones, suggesting hydroxylation of JA followed by sulphation as a route of complete inactivation of JA signaling.

The glucose ester of JA has been detected in cell cultures of tomato. Detailed inspection of the tobacco BY-2 suspension culture revealed accumulation of 12-OH-JA, jasmonoyl-jasmonoyl-1-β-gentiobiose and hydroxyjasmonoyl-1-β-glucose. Interestingly, these esters did not inhibit the G2 phase of the cell cycle, as has been shown for JA which blocks B-type cyclin-dependent kinase accumulation as well as CYCLINB1;1 expression. This points again to inactivation of JA signaling by metabolism.

It will be interesting to see whether or not these observations with cell suspension cultures can be confirmed with whole tissues. Initial data indicated a stimulatory effect of JA in meristematic tissues, and high *AOC* promoter activity was found in meristemic cells of the root tip.

MUTANTS IN JA BIOSYNTHESIS AND IN JA SIGNALING

Mutants in JA Biosynthesis

Ten years ago the first mutant altered in JA biosynthesis was isolate mutant *fad3-2fad7-2fad8 is* affected in the final step in the formation of α-LeA, the substrate for JA biosynthesis. Due to the unique occurrence of α-LeA in the tapetum of anthers, α-LeA deficiency leads to JA deficiency.

Consequently, the pollen fail to develop and dehisce properly leading to a male sterile phenotype. Subsequently, most of the *Arabidopsis* mutants affected in JA biosynthesis, including *aos, dde2-2, opr3, dde1* and aim1, were found to be male sterile. In contrast, dad1 and *comatose* plants are fertile due to residual JA formation.

A characteristic phenotype of JA-deficient mutants of *Arabidopsis,* such as dad1 and *opr3* is also an insufficient filament elongation at stage 12 of anther development. Consequently, pollination occurs only upon JA treatment before stage 12.

Expression analyses during anther development revealed up-regulation of *LOX2,* known to function in JA biosynthesis, and JA-responsive promoters are active in filaments.

Possibly, the auxin response factors ARF6 and ARF8 are involved in JA induction of filament elongation. A common phenotype of JA-deficient mutants is increased sensitivity to insects and pathogens, since both processes are JA dependent.

Differential gene expression between *opr3* and wild-type plants has allowed identification of OPDA-dependent genes. The tomato mutants *spr2* and acx1 were found in a screen for suppressors of prosystemin expression, an essential component of the wound-response pathway. These mutants are affected in the final step of α-LeA biosynthesis by the ω-7-fatty acid desaturase and in the ACX.

Mutants in JA Signaling

Mutants in JA signaling may lead to the following:

(*a*) Reduced sensitivity or even insensitivity to JA or

(*b*) Constitutive JA responses.

In the first group there is the most prominent member of JA-signaling mutants, coi1. Isolated in a screen for insensitivity to coronatine, a molecular mimic of JA, the affected gene was shown to code for an F-box protein with function in ubiquitin-dependent protein degradation. Large-scale expression analyses with wild-type and coi1 plants revealed the central role of COI1 in JA-dependent gene expression. Together with data from the *opr3* mutant, genes were shown to be expressed COI1 dependently, COI1 independently, OPDA dependently, OPDA independently, JA dependently or JA independently.

The coil plants are both male sterility and JA deficient. JA deficiency might be partially caused by the positive feedback regulation in JA biosynthesis. The tomato mutant jail, in which a gene homologous affected, is female sterile and altered in trichome development, which indicates different functions of COI1 in *Arabidopsis* and tomato.

A screen based on root growth inhibition by JA led to isolation of several jar1 mutants, which are allelic to *jin4* and ja*i2*. Cloning of JAR1 revealed that JAR1 is homologous to adenylate-forming enzymes of the firefly luciferase family. JAR1 adenylates JA leading subsequently to conjugation with amino acids.

JAR1 can also conjugate JA to the ethylene precursor 1-aminocy1-carboxylic acid (ACC) suggesting a type of co-regulation in JA and ethylene availability. Interestingly, another allele of jar1 encodes and is defective in auxin-amino acid synthase *activity*.

Cloning of the gene affected in jin1 revealed that JIN1 encodes the bHLHzip type transcription factor AtMYC2. AtMYC2 is a positive regulator of JA-dependent, wound-induced expression of genes such as *VSP, LOX, Thi2.1* and a negative regulator of pathogen-defense genes, such as *PLANT*

DEFENSIN 2.1, which are positively regulated by the ethylene-dependent transcription factor ERF1. Due to this antagonistic action of MYC2 and ERF1, plants can respond differentially to pathogen attack and wounding. In development, AtMYC2 is a positive regulator of lateral root formation downstream of COI1.

A cross-talk between JA-dependent and salicylic acid (SA)-dependent signaling was found with *mpk4. MPK4* codes for the MAP kinase 4 which activates some JA-dependent defense genes and represses SA-dependent PR genes.

The auxin-insensitive mutant *axrl* revealed the first cross-talk of JA- and auxin-signaling at the level of Pmediated protein degradation. AXR1 encodes a RUB-activating enzyme which function in the SCF complex.

Another member of these proteins was identified by the JA-insensitive mutant *jai4* screened in an ethylene-insensitive background. JAI4 encodes a SGTlb and interacts like AXR1 with SCF subunits. Mutants with *constitutive JA response* were screened in plants carrying JA responsive promoter reporter constructs.

All these mutants exhibit constitutive or elevated JA responses. In the case of cas1, a regulatory gene upstream of the *AOS* promoter seems to be affected. So far only the gene affected in *cevl* could be cloned. CEV1 is the cellulose synthase gene *CeSA3,* which is preferentially expressed in roots, mid veins and anthers.

Two other mutants (or*e9* and *cos1)* could be identified: ORE9 encodes an F-box protein, which delays senescence, whereas COS1 encodes a lumazine synthase functioning downstream of COI1.

Proteasome-Mediated JA Signaling

In 1998, the COI1 gene was identified as 67 kDa protein with 16 leucine reach repeats (LRRs) and an N-terminal F-box motif (Xie *et al.,* 1998). F-occur ubiquitously in eukaryotic kingdoms and are known to recruit regulatory proteins for ubiquitin-dependent degradation in the proteasome.

F-box proteins give the specificity for binding of the substrate which will be degraded upon ubiquitinylation by the other components of the SCF complex. The SCF complex is composed of SKP1 (ASK1 in plants for Arabidopsis SKPI), CULLIN and RBX1 (for ring box1) as well as the F-box protein and functions as an E3 ligase.

All these SCF members occur in gene families, for example 19-SKP 1-like proteins (ASKs) and about 700 potential F-box proteins. CULLIN1 interacting with SKP1 (ASKs) seems to function as a backbone and is modified with an ubiquitin-related protein 1 called RUB1.

This modification is similar to the ubiquitinylation, and is catalyzed by RBX1, which functions as a RUB-specific E3 ligase; CUL1 conjugated with RUB1 binds to ASK.

This model is discussed for ubiquitin-mediated protein

degradation in developmentally regulated processes such as embryogenesis, hormone signaling and senescence, and in response to changes in the environment, such as light (circadian clock, photoperiod).

The SCF complex functioning in auxin signaling is very well studied and led recently to the identification of its F-box protein (TIR) as the auxin receptor. The principle functions of the SCF components were also identified for JA signaling.

Role of COI1 as an F-box protein could be identified by its physical interaction with CUL1, RBX1 and ASK1/ASK2 *in vitro* and *in vivo* and by the requirement of a functional F-box motif. Furthermore, deficiency in any SCF component impairs JA signaling.

A histone deacetylase (RPD3b) was identified as a putative target of COI1. Another histone deacetylase (RPD3a) was shown to function in JA and ethylene signaling. Histone deacetylases are transcriptional repressors.

In this scenario gene expression is induced by targeting negative regulators to protein degradation. Whereas the numerous SCF-mediated responses can be explained in terms of the large number of F-box proteins, it is still unclear, how the numerous *COI1* dependent processes are orchestrated.

Beside a modular activity within the SCF complex, components upstream and downstream of COI1 could allow individual COI1-dependent responses. Regulation upstream of COI1 could occur by COP9.

The COP9 signalosome (CSN), together with COP1 and COP10 is a key component of light-signal transduction occurring in photomorphog-enetic processes.

Surprisingly, CSN interacts also with E3 ligases, such as SCF^{COI1}, and reduction in CSN functions affects JA signaling, suggesting a link between JA and light signaling. CSN seems to affect also the amount of RUB1 conjugated to CULLIN1, as known for auxin signaling.

An example of a component downstream of COI1 is coronatine-insensitive suppressor 1 (COS1), which is a lumazine synthase, a critical component of riboflavin biosynthesis. Consequently, critical cellular processes using redox cofactors are affected in *a* cos1 mutant.

However, some coi1-related phenotypes (esterility) are restored in the mutant, suggesting that COS1 (RIB) acts [d]of COI1 and attributes to suppression of a negative regulator (substrate of SCF^{cou}). A link between JA signaling and components of plant responses to pathogens was found recently.

The *jai4* mutant is affected in a gene coding for SGT1b, which interacts with SCF complex components in yeast. SGT1b is a pleiotropic effector with roles in JA, auxin and pathogen signaling. Similarly, AXR1, a positive regulator of auxin responses, affects SCF activity via CULLIN1/RUB1 and leads to pleiotropic effects in JA signaling.

Consequently, the *axr1* mutant exhibits reduced root growth inhibition by JA. These examples highlight the central role of the ubiquitin-SCF-mediated protein degradation in orchestrating signaling pathways.

Whereas COI1 acts specifically in JA signaling, other components allow cross-talk. Due to similarities in the function of SCF^{TIR} and SCF^{COI1} it is tempting to speculate, since TIR was identified as an auxin receptor, that COI1 functions as a JA receptor.

JA, OPDA and Related Compounds in Plant-Defense Reactions

Plant–Microbe Interactions

Plants have to cope with a great variety of microorganisms during their life-cycle. The interactions can be beneficial or deleterious for the plants. Symbiontic interactions occur by fungi leading to mycorrhiza or by bacteria, for example the nitrogen-fixating *Rhizobium spp.* interacting with legumes.

Furthermore, there are non-pathogenic rhizobacteria which promote plant growth. In pathogenic interactions plants develop resistance by activation of a resistance gene (R) following recognition of an avirulence (AVR) gene product or by local restriction of pathogen growth (hypersensitive

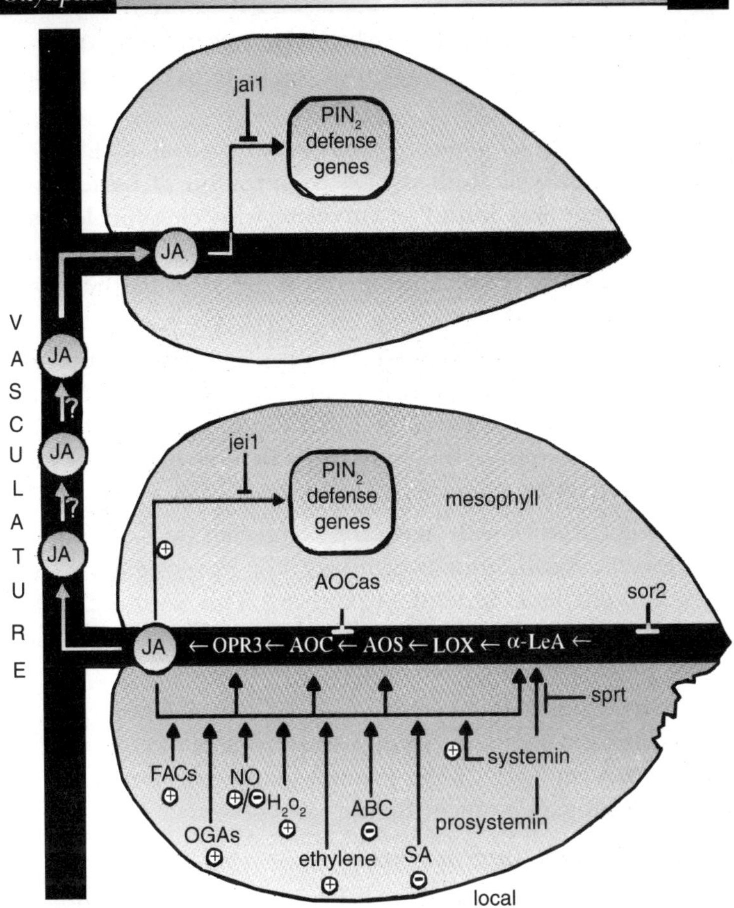

Figure 10.7: The wound-response pathway in tomato. Local wounding of a leaf activates systemin processing and genes encoding enzymes of JA biosynthesis in the vascular bundles. Beside a positive feedback by JA, numerous signals act synergistically (+) or antagonistically (–) in JA generation. PIN expression is induced locally and systemically in the mesophyll cells. The systemic signal might be JA. Mutants known for totmato are indicated.

response, HR). In all these plant-microbe interactions JA was recognized to function as a signal.

Symbiontic interactions

The formation of N_2-fixing nodules in legumes by *Rhizobia* and the intracellular growth of fungi preferentially of the order *Glomales* defined as arbuscular mycorrhiza (AM) are two extensively studied symbiontic interactions between plants and microbes.

Although *NOD* genes of *Rhizobia are,* a role of JA in N_2-fixation is not well studied. AM colonization of barley roots by the fungus was found to correlate with elevated levels of JA and expression of *AOS* within the arbuscule-containing cell, whereas upstream components of the LOX pathway were not altered by AM.

Suppression of *AOC* in hairy roots of *Medicago truncatula* reduced JA levels and the degree of AM with *Glomus intraradices* indicating role of JA in the establishment of AM symbiosis. The non-pathogenic rhizobacteria stimulates plant growth and induces systemic resistance (ISR).

Genetic studies with *Arabidopsis* infected by *Pseudomonas fluorescens, Xanthomonas campestris* or P. *syringae* revealed a JA- and ethylene-dependent pathway. This SA-independent ISR seems to be caused by enhanced sensitivity of the affected tissue to JA and ethylene, called "priming".

Apart from a basal resistance, JA and ethylene elevate the expression of many JA/ethylene-inducible genes such as *DEFENSIN* and HEVEIN. Primed plants are more effective in establishing resistance to the pathogen.

Plant pathogen interactions

Plants can be attacked by a great *diversity* of pathogens. These are biotrophic, if living cells are required for pathogenic growth, or necrotrophic, if the att cell is killed and used as the nutrient source for growth of the pathogens.

Plants respond to biotrophic pathogens often by a hypersensitive response (HR), a SA-dependent response in which the attacked cell is killed by programmed-cell death (PCD) thus restricting pathogen growth. The various forms of establishment of plant innate immunity are ultimately linked with JA, SA and ethylene, although roles for ABA, brassinosteroids and auxins have also been shown. Obviously, the different resistance strategies have been evolved *via* a combinatorial use of these signaling compounds.

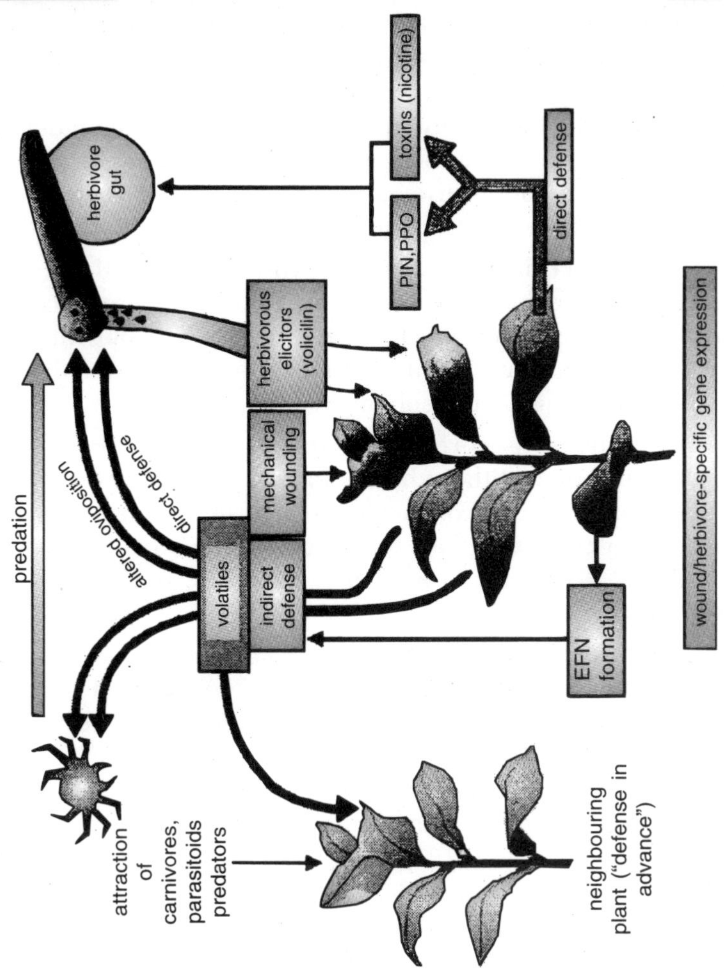

Figure 10.8: Direct- and indirect-defense mechanisms.

Beside being active in ISR, JA has a role together with ethylene in resistance against necrotrophic pathogens, such as the fungi *Alternaria brassicicola, Bothrytis cineria, Pythium sp.* and *Fusarium oxysporum,* and the bacteria *Erwinia carotovora.*

This could be clearly shown by mutants of JA biosynthesis and of JA signaling. JA-deficient *Arabidopsis* mutants, such as *fad3-2fad7-2fad8* exhibit increased susceptibility to *Pythium mastophorum* which could be compromised by JA treatmen. Similar data for the JA-insensitive mutants coil and jarl support the JA dependence of the interactions. Beside *JA-deficient* and *JA-insensitive* mutants, JA-accumulating mutants show altered response to necrotrophic pathogens. Increased resistance and constitutive expression of defense genes were found in cevl and cetl plants.

There is a common action of JA and ethylene in the response to many necrotrophic pathogens. An exception is *E. carotovora,* elicitors from which induce tryptophan biosynthesis and formation of its terminal product, the 3-indolylmethylglycosinolate, in a JA-dependent manner.

Consequently, coil plants are more sensitive to this pathogen, but not the ethylene-insensitive mutants. Similar to the common action of JA and ethylene in response to many necrotrophic pathogens, both signals act coordinately in response to abiotic stress, such as ozone exposure and wounding.

The ozone-induced cell death of *Arabidopsis is* sustained by a mutual antagonism of ethylene and JA. An rcdl mutant affected in H_2O_2 and ozone signaling is less sensitive to JA, ethylene and ABA, and was identified as a member of the ADP-ribosyl transferase domain-containing subfamily of the WWE protein—protein interaction domain protein family.

Thus, RCD1 may function in post translational modifications as an integral mode in hormone signaling related to regulation of stress-responsive genes. Other reactive oxygen species, such as singlet oxygen ($^1O2$) are also linked to PCD and *ethylenaling*.

In contrast to the JA-induced suppression of H_2O_2/superoxide-dependent PCD, JA promotes singlet-oxygen-induced PCD in the *flu* mutant, but is antagonized by OPDA. Phytopathogenic bacteria, such as *X. campestris* and *P. syringae* contain numerous genes that encode potential virulence factors.

Interestingly, one of these factors, coronatine, is a molecular mimic of JA and leads to similar, but not identical gene expression profiles in the host. Recently, it was shown that coronatine, together with the *P. syringae* type III effectors, promotes parasitism by augmenting a COI1-dependent pathway in the host. In tomato this coronatine-mediated, increased bacterial virulence is

JAI1-dependent and suppresses PR1 gene expression. In nature, plants are attacked simultaneously by various pathogens and insects. Many of them were shown to activate the JA-signaling pathway suggesting its dominant role in the establishment of resistance against diverse pathogens.

Cross-talk between JA, SA, ethylene and ABA

Analyses of numerous *Arabidopsis* mutants revealed existence of two distinct signaling pathways in response to biotrophic and necrotrophic pathogens.

Whereas plants activate PR gene expression by a SA dependent pathway in response to biotrophic pathogens, expression of defense genes, such as *DEFENSINS* and *THIONINS* is activated in a JA- and ethylene-dependent manner in response to necrotrophic pathogens.

Thever, clear evidence for cross-talk between these signaling pathways by antagonistic and synergistic interactions. A mutual antagonism seems to occur preferentially.

This can be a negative effect of SA on JA biosynthesis, and of cytosolic NPR1 on JA signaling. Furthermore, the WRKY70 transcription factor has been identified as a node of convergence for the SA- and JA-mediated signaling pathways.

Without affecting SA or JA levels, WRKY70 acts positively in the SA-mediated pathway downstream of NPR1, and negatively in the JA-mediated pathway downstream of COI1.

Furthermore, the negative effect of SA on JA signaling could be demonstrated in mutants impaired in SA accumulation, such as *eds4* and *pad4,* or SA-accumulating mutants, such as *cpr6.*

A negative effect of JA on SA signaling was shown in mutants, such as *mpk4,* ss*i2* and *coil* that have enhanced or constitutive SA-dependent defense. Few examples exist on synergistic action of SA and JA in response to pathogens and a recently performed detailed inspection revealed antagonistic and synergistic action depending on the concentrations used.

Possibly metabolic conversion of JA and/or SA may influence their signaling properties, for example loss of a SA-specific methyl transferase function influences the response to pathogens.

A recent transcriptional profiling of *Sorghum bicolour* treated with SA, JA or an ethylene precursor revealed numerous genes expressed synergistically, whereas others were antagonistically activated.

This large-scale approach provided indications of how molecular switches in the SA- and JA-dependent signaling pathways might be orchestrated.

As in the wound response, JA and ethylene function coordinately in the host reactions to pathogens. In contrast to the mutual antagonism of JA and ethylene in the plant response to ozone, which seems to occur by protein—protein interactions, their action in response to necrotrophic pathogens and wounding might be sustained at the level of transcription factors.

The recently cloned JIN1 affected in the JA-insensitive mutant jin1 codes for the transcription factor AtMYC2, which antagonizes ERF1, and both of them function down stream of COI1. The JA/ethylene pathway is also activated during non-host interactions. An interesting sequential action of JA, ethylene and SA was shown for tomato responding to *X. campestris*, in a manner clearly different from that in *Arabidopsis*.

Whereas R-gene-mediated resistance was not affected, the extent of HR was controlled sequentially by all three signals. In nature biotic stress by pathogens and abiotic stress, such as desiccation, may occur simultaneously. In *Arabidopsis* these responses to pathogens and stress are orchestrated by the antagonistic action of ABA on the JA/ethylene-signaling pathways.

The Wound-Response Pathway

Many insects and other animals take nutrients from plant leaves or roots, which is accompanied with wounding. Plants respond with local and systemic formation of defense proteins, such as proteinase inhibitors (PINs), defense compounds, such as nicotine or volatiles influencing plant–plant and plant–insect interactions.

In all these wound responses JA is an essential signal. The wound-response pathway is the best-studied JA-signaling pathway, particularly in tomato and other solanaceous species, in which the accumulation of PINs upon wounding was first observed.

In the early 1990s, work in Ryan's laboratory revealed that airborne MeJA can induce *PIN* expression, and the 18-amino acid peptide systemin was an upstream signal.

Meanwhile, a tremendous amount of data has accumulated, but the JA receptor is still missing. In tomato, JA perception seems to occur at the plasma membrane, where applied labeled JA was localized. Herbivorous insects wound leaves.

Mechanical wounding if applied alone is qualitatively similar to wounding by herbivores in terms of local and systemic responses. Herbivory, however, is accompanied by oral secretions from the feeding larvae containing a complex mixture of elicitors, including fatty acid amino acid conjugates (FACs). Among FACs the α-LeA glutamine conjugate (volicitin) was identified as highly active compound.

FACs amplify wound signaling. Systemin is locally processed from a prosystemin precursor, which is encoded by a gene expressed in parenchymatic cells of vascular bundles. Subsequent systemin perception occurs at the systemin receptor, characterized as a protein of 160kDa (SRI 60), but not yet localized.

SR160 is a leucine-rich repeat receptor kinase with dual function in systemin and brassinosteroid perception. Systemin perception may occur in neighbouring cells of the *PROSYST-EMIN-expressing* parenchyma cells, for example the companion cells, where JA-biosynthetic enzymes, such as AOC and its mRNA accumulation were localized.

Indeed, AOC expression in tomato is systemin dependent. Intracellular steps between systemin perception and AOC expression in the local tissue are documented by findings, such as wound-induced PLA_2 activation, α-LeA accumulation, elevated Ca^{2+} levels and activation of MAPKs.

AOC expression may lead to amplification in wound signaling due to the JA dependent *PROSYSTEMIN* expression and systemin-dependent AOC expression.

Most of these data were drawn from transgenic approaches covering sense and antisense expression of *PROSYSTEMIN* and AOC, and from mutants affected in JA biosynthesis, JA signaling and systemin perception. Upon local wounding a transient burst of JA occurs in the first hour followed by late events, which include expression of JA-biosynthetic genes and plant-defense genes, such as *PINs*.

Obviously, *PIN* expression is triggered spatially and temporally: whereas signals, such as JA and systemin are formed in vascular bundles, *PIN* expression occurs only in mesophyll cells of a leaf.

Since JA and systemin are assumed to be insufficiently mobile, additional signals may attribute to *PIN* expression upon local wounding. One candidate is H_2O_2, which is highly mobile in the apoplast between vascular bundles and mesophyll cells and induces *PIN* expression.

Although the preferential and direct function of JA in local wound signaling has been substantiated by many studies, several other signals may modulate *PIN* expression indirectly. Apart from systemin and FACs, these include ethylene, cell wall oligogalacturonides (OGAs), ABA, SA, NO, ROS.

For ethylene and JA a synergistic action in the wound response was shown initially in tomato, and has subsequently been observed in many other plants. Analyses of ABA-deficient tomato mutants revealed that ABA is also a signal of the wound response, presumably acting upstream of JA. SA was shown to inhibit wound-induced JA formation and *PIN* expression, but may also act downstream of JA formation. Synergistic and antagonistic action between these signals, depending of the plant system has been observed. OGAs were among the first signals identified to function in the wound response and seem to be generated by the wound-inducible polygalacturonase.

The role of the immobile OGAs in the generation of the mobile H_2O_2 was shown. NO may negatively modulate the wound response in tomato. This could be linked to the wound- and JA-inducible expression of *ARGINASE,* which in turn antagonizes NO production. Furthermore, UV light leads to *PIN* expression *via* the octadecanoid pathway.

The complex network in wound signaling is illustrated by the fact that these signals act sequentially, synergistically and antagonistically. Furthermore, some wound-induced genes are expressed JA-independently.

This fact highlights the flexibility of plants to respond on one external stimulus by expression of individual sets of genes. Recent large scale expression analysis in *Arabidopsis* revealed that a large group of wound-induced genes were expressed in an OPDA- but not JA- or COI1-dependent manner, whereas others dependent on JA and COI1.

A characteristic feature of the wound response is an activation of plant-defense genes in systemic leaves distant from the wounded site. Several scenarios have been proposed for the nature of the systemic signal and the question, whether or not *de novo* signal generation occurs in the systemic leaves.

Systemin, JA and/or related compounds, electric currents, or turgor pressure were suggested to act as systemic signals in tomato. Elegant reciprocal grafting experiments of G. Howe's laboratory led to strong arguments for JA as an essential component of the systemic signal.

Using mutants affected in JA biosynthesis, such as def1, *spr2,* and acx*l,* in JA signaling, such as jai1, and in systemin-signaling, such as spr1, it could be shown that the response in the systemic leaf does not require JA biosynthesis, OPDA perception and systemin perception, but JA perception is essential. Consequently, JA may be the mobile amplified generation of JA in vascular bundles (see above), the occurrence of LOX, AOS and AOC in sieve elements and the timing in the transport of phloem-mobile compounds support this assumption. Similar grafting experiments with the coil and *opr3* mutants suggest also a systemic activity of JA for *Arabidopsis*.

Direct and Indirect Defense

Despite numerous physiological and chemical data on "allelopathic" interactions between plants this concept was treated with scepticism for a long time.

However, the number of studies showing such interactions, as for example, altered leaf chemistry in trees neighbouring a wounded tree or induced formation of PINs in tomato leaves by airborne MeJA, has grown exponentially.

Chemical communication between plants is now well accepted as a strategy for defense and fitness. Defense responses of plants, induced for example by piercing, chewing or sucking insects, can be established by formation of the following:

(*a*) Proteins, such as PINs that are deleterious for the feeding insects

(*b*) By synthesis of phytoalexins, such as nicotine

(*c*) By formation and release of volatile organic compounds (VOCs) that attract parasitoids and predators

(*d*) By formation and release of green leafy volatiles (GLVs)

(*e*) By extra-floral nectar (EFN) formation

(*f*) By a mechanical strategy such as increased cell wall thickness.

Consequently, these defense responses can be divided into direct and an indirect defense. In both cases, JA acts as an essential signal. Direct defense is established following herbivore attack by formation of deleterious proteins, such as PINs or polyphenol oxidase, and formation of toxic quantities of secondary metabolites, such as nicotine or glycosinolates.

Both of thes are JA inducible. Although the nitrogen-intensive synthesis of compounds, such as nicotine may seem costly, plants are permanently monitoring the relative costs and benefits. Under field conditions the inducible-defense system established by jasmonates depends on herbivore pressure.

In contrast to green house experiments, several JA-inducible defense responses are constitutive in plants grown under field conditions. Furthermore, plants can recognize specific herbivores and can switch off the costly JA-inducible direct-defense mechanism, for example *Manduca sexta* larvae attacking *Nicotiana attenuata* release volicitin into the wound site leading to transcriptional down-regulation of direct-d up-regulation of indirect-defense marked by release of volatile compounds.

The indirect defense is given by release of a specific blend of volatiles, which attracts predators, such as parasitoids and carnivores, and the essential role of JA and SA in this process has been shown also for *Arabidopsis*. The emitted volatiles can be LOX-pathway-derived GLVs, such as leaf aldehydes, leaf alcohols or numerous monoterpenoids, sesquiterpenoids and diterpenoids.

The specific pattern of compounds allows parasitoids to find their host. Such volatile emission correlating with high JA levels is elevated under nitrogen deficiency suggesting that plants are more sensitive to establish defense during lack of nutrients.

In case of GLVs, neighbouring plants can be primed against insect attack ("defense in advance"). Spider mite-induced emission of volatile terpenoids and methyl salicylate is mediated by JA. In the case of stem-boring insects on conifers, a similar but not identical pattern of terpenoids compared to that upon JA-treatment was found indicating a role of JA in resinosis and conifer defense.

An interesting and intensively studied aspect of direct

and indirect plant-defense strategies is how plants cope with the diversity of insects and how they orchestrate general and specific responses.

On the one side, insects with completely different dietary strategies (specialists and generalists, such as *Spodoptera* and Pie*ris,* respectively) induce a highly similar set of genes.

On the other hand, herbivores can monitor intactness of host-defense signaling pathways.

As shown with LOX-deficient plants in the native environment, *N. attenuata* was more sensitive to its specific herbivore, but also attracted novel herbivore species.

This indicates that the composition of the herbivore community is dependent on the plant-signaling pathway in induced-defense responses.

Besides the emission of VOCs and GLVs, EFN formation is a mechanism by which plants establish indirect defense. Again, this strategy is mediated by the taxonomically conserved octadecanoid pathway. Symbiontic ants live on glands of the leaf stalk in many plants leading to resistance of the plant against herbivores.

Interestingly, a phylogenetic analysis of the genus *Acacia* and closely related genera revealed constitutive EFN formation in those species on which ants are an obligate symbiont.

Obviously, inducible EFN formation has evolved to be constitutive by modified functional demands. These plant–plant and plant–insect communications mediated by JA on the exhibit a remarkable phenotype plasticity in the natural environment.

JA IN DEVELOPMENT

Inhibition of germination and seedling development as well as leaf sene among the first physiological effects observed for JA applied to plants.

Subsequently, mutant analyses revealed a role of JA in root growth and flower development. Tendril coiling and tuberization are further processes affected by JA or its metabolites.

Seedling Development and Root Growth

Initial data on the role of JA in seedling development came from treatment with JA. Inhibitory effects appeared in non-dormant seeds, whereas seed germination of dormant seeds was stimulated by JA.

Dry seeds and young seedlings exhibit high levels of JA. Interestingly, its metabolite 12-OH-JA can accumulate to much higher levels than JA.

During seedling development, levels of jasmonates decline within a few days. So far the role of jasmonates in seedling development is not clear. They might be involved in

(*a*) Growth and development by cross-talk with other hormones such as auxin, ethylene and ABA

(*b*) Mobilization of reserve compounds

(*c*) Increased defense status by direct action via their antimicrobial activity or by expression of defense genes.

Inhibition of root growth was one of the first physiological effects observed for MeJA and has been used to isolate JA-insensitive mutants. Stunted roots following MeJA treatment correspond to the root phenotype of JA-accumulating mutants, such as cev1 and cet1.

The molecular mechanism of root growth inhibition by JA is unclear. It might be based on the inhibitory effect of JA on auxin-induced cell elongation. Interestingly, the auxin-insensitive mutant axr1 exhibits reduced root growth inhibition by JA supporting the cross-talk of auxin and JA *via* the SCF complex.

Furthermore, the *auxin-inducible AXR2/IAA7* gene which encodes a negative regulator of auxin signaling is repressed by MeJA treatment. Consequently, generation of JA in the elongation zone, where *AOC* promoters are active would enhance auxin signaling by down-regulation of *AXR2/ IAA7.*

Lateral root formation seems to be JA dependent. AtMYC2 which is affected in the mutant jin1 is a key player in JA-induced gene expression. *AtMYC2* is transiently up-regulated by JA in a COI1-dependent manner and is a positive regulator of lateral root formation. Correspond-ingly, lateral root primordia exhibit high-AOC promoter activity.

Tuber Formation

Tubers of potato are formed under short-day conditions and cool night temperature. The complex developmental programme from growing stolons to the swelling tubers is clearly affected by JA and its metabolite 12-OH-JA, called tuberonic acid.

Consequently, a role of a tuber-specific StLOX1 in tuber formation has been shown. Elevated levels of JA and 12-OH-JA formed in the leaves and transported to the stolons may induce cell expansion, a known phenomenon for jasmonates. Under long-day conditions, there is no tuber formation, and 12-OH-JA levels are undetectable.

The tuber formation is dependent on *CONSTANS (CO)*, the key player in the photoperiod-dependent pathway in flowering time control. Interestingly, transgenic approaches revealed that flowering time control in *Arabidopsis* is linked to CO-regulated conversion of 12-OH-JA to its inactive sulphated derivative suggestin leaf-generated signal for both photoperiod-dependent morphogenic processes.

Flower Formation

Clear evidence for the role of JA in flower formation came from identification of the JA-insensitive mutant coi1 and the JA-deficient mutants *fad3-2fad7-2fad8,* dad1, *opr3* and dde1 as well as from the AOS-knockout mutant of *Arabidopsis.*

Except for dad1, all of these mutants are male sterile. Interestingly, the COI1 homologue of tomato affected in the JA-insensitive mutant jai1 is female sterile suggesting different JA-dependent processes in fl$_{o}$wer development between these species.

Further evidences for the role of JA in flower formation is given by distinct expression of JA-biosynthetic genes in flower organs, such as ovules correlating with elevated levels of jasmonates, and by the fact that flower organs exhibit a distinct oxylipin signature. The ratio as well as total amount of oxylipins in different flower organs can be shifted by constitutive over-expression of the AOC.

The AOC expression and the elevated JA levels in ovules and pistils, respectively, of tomato flowers correlated with expression of defense genes, such as *PIN2* or threonine deaminase.

Also flowering time control, well defined by a sequential and concerted activity of genes orchestrated in different pathways, seems to be affected by jasmonates. The level of 12-OH-JA, regulated in a COI1-dependent manner, affects the onset of flowering.

Although not clearly understood, mutant and expression analyses of JA-induced genes suggest a role for JA and related compounds in the following processes of flower formation and functions:

(*a*) Anther development and dehiscence
(*b*) Female organ development
(*c*) Increased defense status of a sink tissue, such as ovules
(*d*) emission of volatiles to attract insects for pollination
(*e*) Formation of deterrent alkaloids and glycosinolates
(*f*) Formation of secondary metabolites functioning in colour formation of petals.

An interesting new aspect on cross-talk between JA and auxin in flower maturation was found recently. The auxin-response factors ARF6 and ARF8 were shown to promote JA formation leading to proper filamen and pollen release of anthers.

Correspondingly, in the double mutant *arf6-2arf8-3* genes encoding JA biosynthesis enzymes are under-expressed. This corresponds well to the phenotype of JA-deficient mutants.

The role of JA in anther development is indicated by male sterility of JA-deficient mutants and by microarray analyses of developing anthers showing up-regulation of JA-inducible genes in stage 12 of flower development, when anthers become mature.

Senescence

Senescence is the terminal phase in the development of plant organs, accompanied by a dramatic reprogramming of the anabolic and catabolic capacity.

More than 100 genes, including those encoding nucleases, proteinases, lipases and chlorophyllases, are specifically up-regulated during leaf senescence (senescence associated genes, SAGs). A large-scale screen for genes up-regulated in *Arabidopsis* in response to ABA, SA, JA or stress revealed a subset of JA-responsive genes containing many *SAGs.*

SAG12 encoding a cyste is a marker for the onset of senescence. SAG101 was shown to code for an acyl hydrolase with a significant role in senescence.

Interestingly, SAG 101 is an essential component of plant innate immunity against biotrophic pathogens by interacting with ENHANCED DISEASE SUSCEPTIBILITY1 (EDS1) and PHYTOALEXIN DEFICIENT4 (PAD4).

During senescence endogenous content of JA is augmented, and expression of many JA-biosynthetic genes is up-regulated. Correspondingly, transgenic barley constitutively over expressing the barley *LOX2* gene known to function in JA biosynthesis exhibited a senescent phenotype.

Leaf senescence does not occur in the JA-insensitive mutant coi1, affected in an F-box protein, while mutation of another F-box protein, ORE9, resulted in delayed senescence. There is an antagonistic and synergistic overlap in the activity of genes related to photosynthesis, stress responses and senescence.

Recent microarray analyses revealed which metabolic pathway of carbon partitioning and nitrogen remobilization is preferentially activated during senescence.

Among the transcription factor gene families such as *WRKYs, NACs, bZIPs,* and *ERFs,* several members are associated with senescence. How coordinate activity of transcription factors may regulate senescence- and defense-related gene activity was shown for WRKY6.

Transcriptome analysis of senescent *Arabidopsis* leaves was recently combined with a metabolome analysis using early senescing and late senescing lines. Interestingly, Glu, Asp, Leu and Ile could be identified as chemical markers of the degree of senescence.

It will be interesting to see how JA is linked to this metabolic reprogramming during leaf senescence. In case of chlorophyll degradation, the first visible symptom of senesenescence-promoting effect of JA known from the1980s, may occur by induction of chlorophyllase.

CONCLUDING REMARKS

In the past two decades an exponential increase in the number of publications appeared showing an impressive increase in knowledge on the formation and action of jasmonates.

After elucidation of the biosynthetic pathway and several physiological effects in the1980s, a shift to molecular-genetic analyses of biosynthesis, signaling and action of jasmonates appeared in the 1990s. A breakthrough was the identification of mutants affected in JA biosynthesis and signaling combined with transgenic approaches.

These tools allowed questions on the function of JA in plant–microbe interactions and many other stress responses as well as its role in developmental programmes, such as flower development and leaf senescence to be addressed.

At the same time, it became clear that JA formed part of a signaling net work involving other molecules, such as SA, ethylene, and ABA. New tools for the analyses of JA and related compounds of the LOX pathway, the oxylipins, led to a much broader perspective, leading to questions on which of the compounds is most active in a particular signaling pathway.

Currently, analyses of the transcriptome, proteome and metabolome are improving our understanding of metabolic links and gene activities occurring in processes in which JA is involved.

Future work will address questions on JA and oxylipin

perception, *cis*- and transacting factors regulating JA-responsive promoters, MAP kinases active in JA signaling, cross-talk of JA with other signals and diversity of action of JA in the plant–plant and plant–microbe interactions under natural conditions. Analyses of cell- and organ-specificity of action of jasmonates will improve our understanding on their role in developmental processes.

Cytokinins

The *Cytokinins* were discovered as a result of efforts to find factors that would stimulate plant cells to divide. Subsequently, they were shown to affect many other *physiological* and *developmental* processes.

These effects include the *delay* of senescence in detached organs, the *mobilization* of nutrients, *chloroplast maturation*, the expansion of *cotyledons*, and the control of morphogenesis. Cell division is not necessarily a component of these other responses.

In the case of chloroplast maturation, *delay of senescence*, and mobilization of nutrients, cell division does not even occur during the cytokinin-induced response. In other words, cytokinins have a number of different, apparently unrelated regulatory roles in higher plants.

Nevertheless, the control of cell division is the process by which the cytokinins are defined, and it is of considerable significance for plant growth and development.

For these reasons, we will present what we know about the cytokinins after first learning about how cell division is regulated in plants and how the ability to culture cells and tissues outside the whole plant has contributed to our understanding of the factors regulating plant cell division.

CELL DIVISION IN PLANT DEVELOPMENT

Mature plant cells generally do not divide. They are formed as a result of cell divisions in a primary or secondary meristem, and they enlarge and differentiate after they are formed.

However, once they assume their function, whether it be *transport, photosynthesis,* or support, they normally do not divide again during the life of the plant. In this respect they appear to be similar to animal cells, which are said to exhibit terminal differentiation.

However, many examples could be cited to show that this similarity to the *behaviour* of animal cells is only *superficial.* Virtually every type of plant cell that retains its *nucleus* at maturity has been shown to be *capable* of dividing.

Differentiated Plant Cells Can Resume Division

Under some *circumstances* mature, differentiated plant cells may resume cell division. This can occur in the normal course of development of some types of cells or in response to external stimuli, *demonstrating* that plant cells are not terminally *differentiated,* except, of course, when they are dead at maturity.

In many species, some mature cells of the *cortex* and/or phloem resume division to form secondary *meristems,* such as the vascular *cambium* or the *cork cambium.*

The abscission zone at the base of a leaf *petiole* is a region where mature parenchyma cells begin to divide again after a period of *mitotic inactivity. Wounding* plant tissues induces cells near the lesion to divide. Even highly *specialized* cells, such as phloem fibers and guard cells, may be stimulated by wounding to divide at least once.

Wound-induced mitotic activity typically is self-limiting; after a few divisions the derivative cells stop dividing and do not divide again. However, when the soil-dwelling bacterium *Agrobacterium tumefaciens* invades a wound it can cause the plant *neoplastic* (*tumor-forming*) disease known as crown gall, which provides dramatic natural evidence of the mitotic potential of mature plant cells.

Crown gall affects most dicots. Without *Agrobacterium*

infection, the woundinduced cell division would *subside* after a few days and some of the new cells would differentiate as a protective layer of cork cells or vascular tissue. However, *Agrobacterium* changes the character of the cells that divide in response to the wound so that they become *cancerlike*.

They do not stop dividing, but continue to divide throughout the life of the plant to produce the *unorganized* mass of tumor tissue that is called a gall. We will have more to say about this important disease later in this chapter.

Diffusible Factors May Control Cell Divison

The above considerations suggest that *mature plant* cells that have stopped dividing do so because they no longer receive some signal, possibly a hormone, that is necessary for the initiation of cell division.

The idea that cell division may be initiated by a *diffusible* factor is derived from the work of Gottleib Haberlandt, who, before World War I, demonstrated that vascular tissue contained a soluble substance or substances that would stimulate the division of wounded potato tuber tissue.

The effort to determine the nature of this factor (or factors) led to the discovery of the *cytokinins* in the 1950s.

Plant Tissues and Organs Can Be Cultured

Biologists long have been *intrigued* by the possibility that organs, tissues, and cells could be grown in culture on a simple nutrient medium, in the way that *microorganisms* are *cultured* in test tubes or on *Petri dishes*.

In the 1930s Philip R. White demonstrated that tomato roots could be grown indefinitely in a simple nutrient medium containing only sucrose as an energy source, *mineral salts* essential for plant nutrition, and a few vitamins.

These isolated roots continued to grow in culture for many years, with periodic subculturing. The cells of the apical and lateral *meristems* divided *repeatedly* and the derivative cells differentiated, just as they would have done in the intact plant to produce the cells and tissues of the roots, but they did so without stems or leaves attached. In contrast to the behaviour of roots, isolated stem tissues *exhibit* very little growth in culture on simple media.

Some growth may occur if auxin is added to the medium, but usually it is not sustained. Frequently this auxin-induced growth is due to cell *enlargement* only.

With most plants, no growth will occur on the simple medium lacking hormones even if the cultured stem tissue contains apical or *lateral meristems*, at least until adventitious roots are formed.

Once the stem tissue has rooted, growth resumes, but now as an *integrated*, whole plant.

These observations tell us that there is a difference in the regulation of cell division in root and shoot *meristems*. They also suggest that some *root-derived* factor(s) may regulate growth in the shoot.

Crown gall tissue is an exception to these *generalizations*. After a gall has formed on a plant, the *bacterium* that incited gall formation can be killed by heating the plant to 42°C. The plant will survive and its gall tissue will continue to grow as a *bacteria-free* tumor.

Tissues removed from these bacteria-free tumors grow on simple, chemically defined culture medium that would not support the *proliferation* of normal stem tissue of the same species. However, these stem-derived tissues are not *organized*. Instead they are a mass of cells, growing without *recognizable* organs as a tissue called *callus*.

Callus tissue sometimes develops on plants in response to wounding, or in graft unions where stems of two different plants are joined. *Crown gall tumors* are a type of callus, whether they are growing attached to the plant or in culture.

The finding that crown gall callus tissue could be cultured *demonstrated* that mature stem cells were capable of *proliferating* in culture and that contact with the bacteria may have caused the cells to produce cell division-stimulating factors.

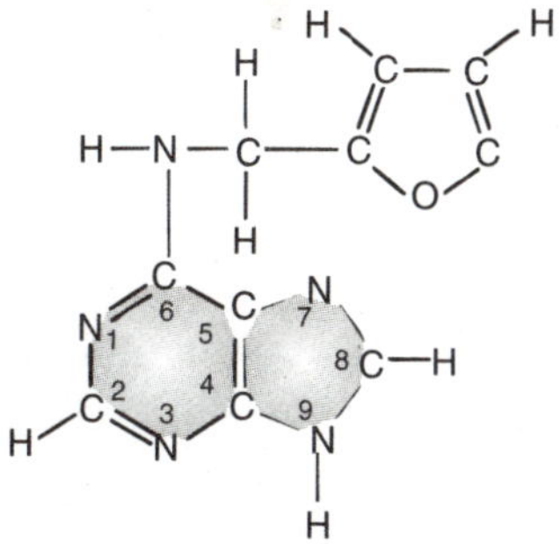

Figure 11.2: The chemical structure of kinetin.

THE DISCOVERY AND IDENTIFICATION OF CYTOKININS

A great many substances were tested in an effort to initiate and sustain the *proliferation* of normal stem tissues in culture. Materials ranging from yeast extract to *tomato juice* were found to have a positive effect, at least with some tissues.

However, the most dramatic stimulations occurred when the liquid endosperm of coconut, also known as *coconut milk* or water, was added to the culture medium. White's nutrient medium supplemented with an auxin and 10-20% coconut milk will support the division of mature, differentiated stem cells from a wide variety of species and their continued *proliferation* to form callus tissue.

This indicated that coconut milk contains a substance or substances that *stimulates* mature cells to enter and remain in the cell division cycle. Many attempts were made to determine the chemical nature of the substance in coconut milk responsible for initiating cell proliferation.

Ultimately, coconut milk was shown to contain the cytokinin zeatin, but this did not occur until several years after the discovery of the cytokinins.

The Discovery of Kinetin, a Synthetic Cytokinin

Folke Skoog at the University of Wisconsin tested many substances for their ability to initiate and sustain the prolifer-

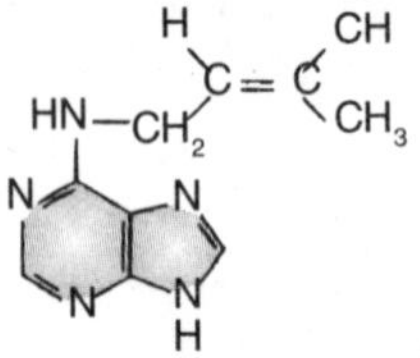

trans-zeatin

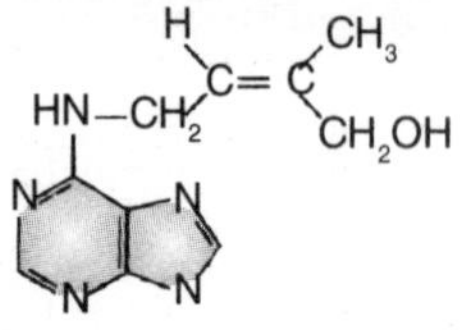

cis-zeatin

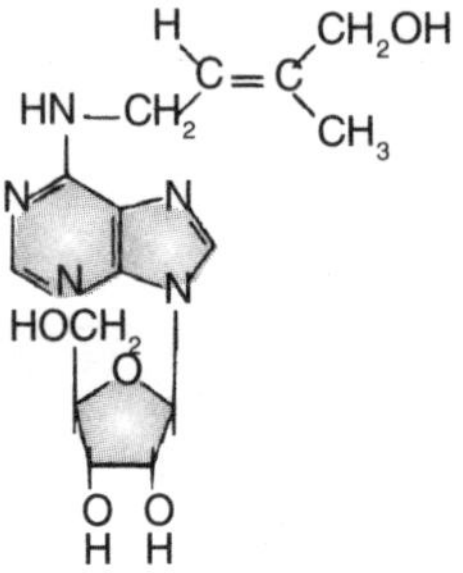

ribosylzeatin(zeatin riboside)

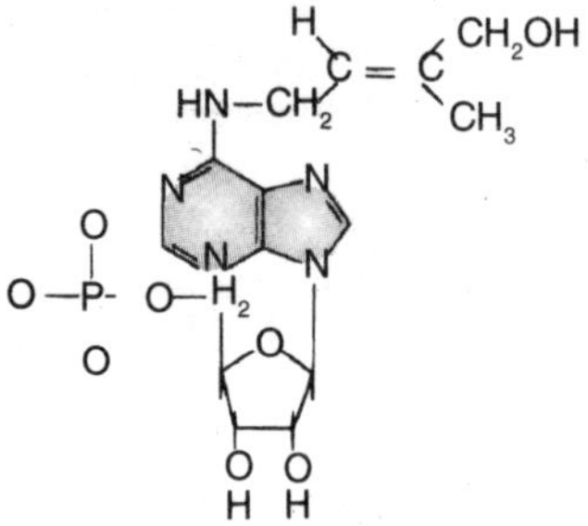

ribosylzeatin-5'-monophosphate(zeatin ribotide)

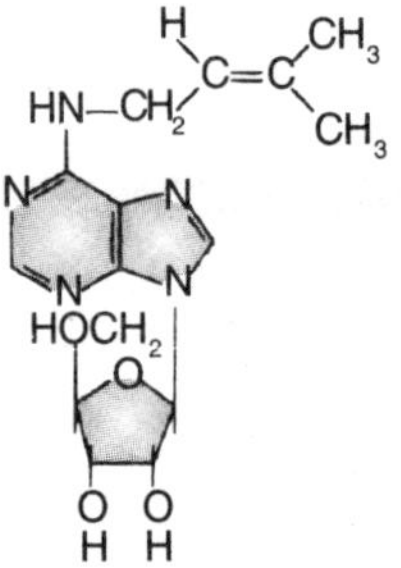

N6-(2-Isopentenyl)-adenosine(i6Ado)

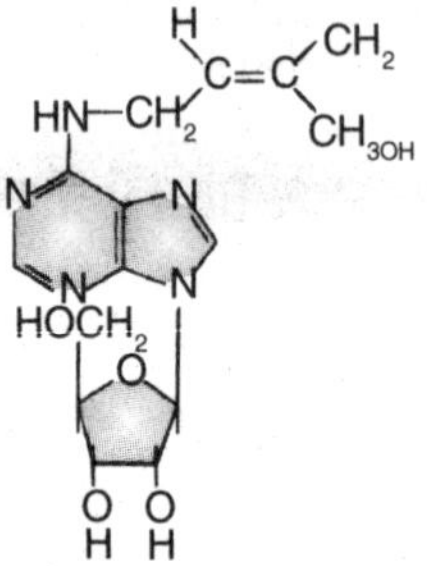

cis-ribosyleatin

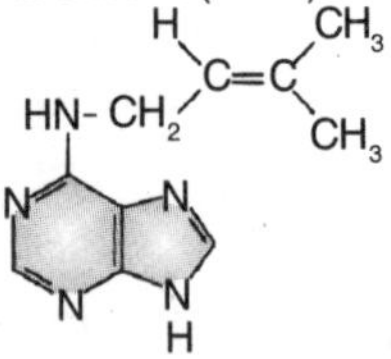

N6-(2-Isopentenyl)-adenosine(i6Ado)

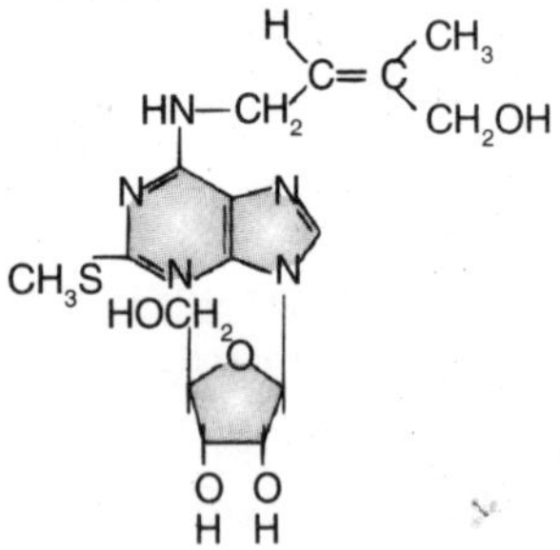

2-methylthro-cis-ribosylzeatin (beacterial)

Figure 11.2: The structures of some naturally occurring cytokinins.

ation of cultured tobacco pith tissue. He had observed a slight promotive effect of the nucleic acid base *adenine*, so he tested the possibility that nucleic acids would stimulate division in this tissue.

Surprisingly, autoclaved herring sperm DNA had a powerful cell division-promoting effect. A single chemical substance was isolated from the heat-treated DNA that would, in the presence of an auxin, stimulate tobacco pith *parenchyma tissue* to *proliferate* in culture. This substance was identified as 6-*furfurylaminopurine* and named *kinetin.*

Kinetin stimulated cell division in tobacco pith when it was cultured on a medium containing an auxin. No cytokinin-induced growth occurred in the absence of an auxin.

Kinetin is not a naturally occurring plant growth regula-

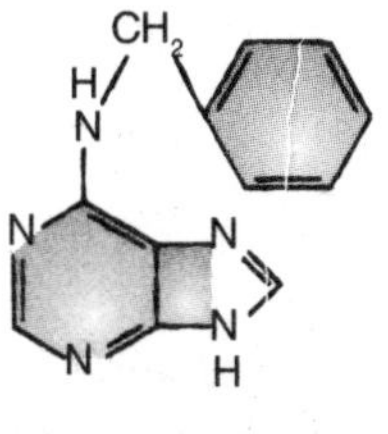

benzyladenine (benzylaminopurine)
(BAP)

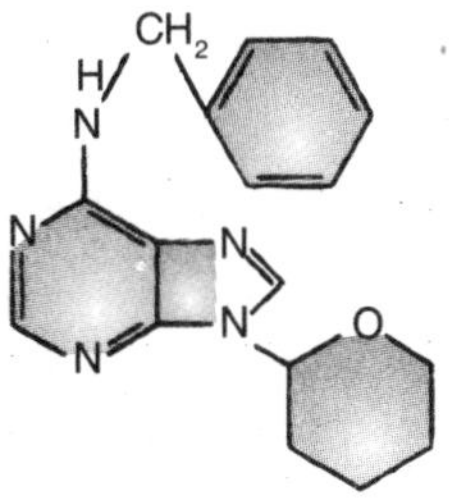

tetrahydropyranylbenzyladenine

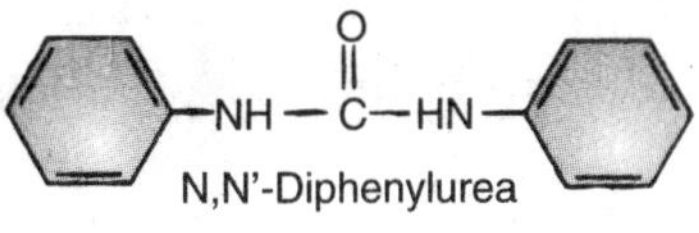

N,N'-Diphenylurea

(a) synthetic cytokinins

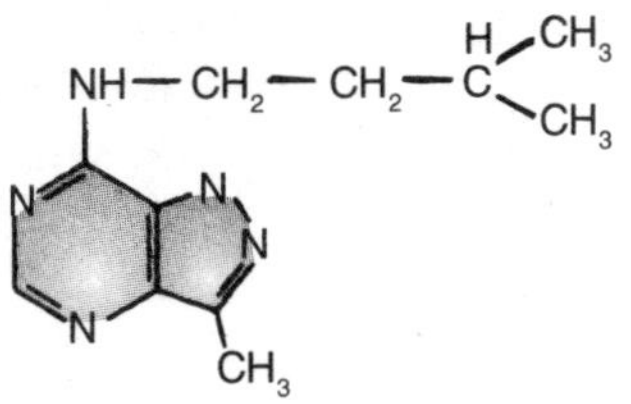

3-methyl-7-(3-methylbutylamino)pyrazolo[4,3-d]pyrimidine

Figure 11.3: The structures of some synthetic cytokinins.

tor, and it does not occur as a base in the DNA of any species. It is a by-product of the heat-induced *degradation* of the DNA in which the *deoxyribose* sugar of *adenosine* is converted to a furfuryl ring and shifted from the 9 to the 6 position on the adenine ring.

The discovery of kinetin was important because it demonstrated that cell division could be induced by a simple chemical substance. More important, when a *synthetic molecule* initiates a *biological response*, frequently it does so because the synthetic molecule has many of the same properties as naturally occurring molecules that regulate that response in the organism.

Thus, the discovery of kinetin suggested that naturally occurring molecules with a structure similar to kinetin may regulate cell division activity within the plant. Of course, this proved to be correct.

Zeatin is the Naturally Occurring Cytokinin of Most Plants

Several years after kinetin's discovery, Carlos Miller in the United States and D. S. Letham in Australia independently demonstrated that extracts of the immature endosperm of corn *(Zea mays)* contained a substance that had the same biological effect as kinetin.

It stimulated mature plant cells to divide when added to a culture medium along with an auxin. Letham isolated the molecule responsible for this activity and identified it as 6-(4hydroxy-3-methylbut-trans-2-enylamino) purine, which he called *zeatin*. Clearly, its structure is similar to that of kinetin.

The two *molecules* have different side chains, but both are adenine or *aminopurine* derivatives with a side chain attached to the N^6 nitrogen. Because the side chain of zeatin has a double bond, it can exist in either the cis or the trans configuration.

The naturally occurring free zeatin of higher plants has the trans configuration, although both the cis and trans forms of zeatin are active as cytokinins. Since its discovery in immature maize *endosperm*, zeatin has been found in many plants

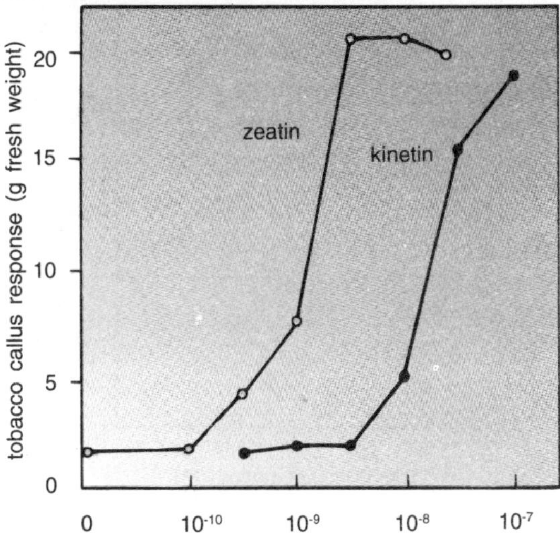

Figure 11.4: Cultured tobacco tissues are dependent on cytokinin for their growth in culture. Cultured tobacco callus was transferred to fresh medium that contained an auxin and either zeatin or kinetin at the indicated concentrations. The tissues were weighed after growing for 1 month on the various media.

and in some bacteria. Zeatin is the most prevalent cytokinin in higher plants, but other substituted *aminopurines* active as cytokinins have been isolated from many plant and *bacterial* species.

These differ from zeatin in the nature of the side chain attached to the N^6 nitrogen or in the attachment of a side chain to carbon 2.

In addition, each of these can be present in the plant as a riboside (a ribose sugar is attached to the N^9 nitrogen of the purine ring), a ribotide (the *ribose sugar moiety* is esterified with *phosphoric acid*), or a *glucoside* (a *glucose sugar molecule* is attached to the N^7 or N^9 nitrogen of the purine ring).

Antagonize Cytokinin Action

A large number of chemical compounds have been synthesized and tested for cytokinin activity. Analysis of these compounds provides insight into the structural requirements

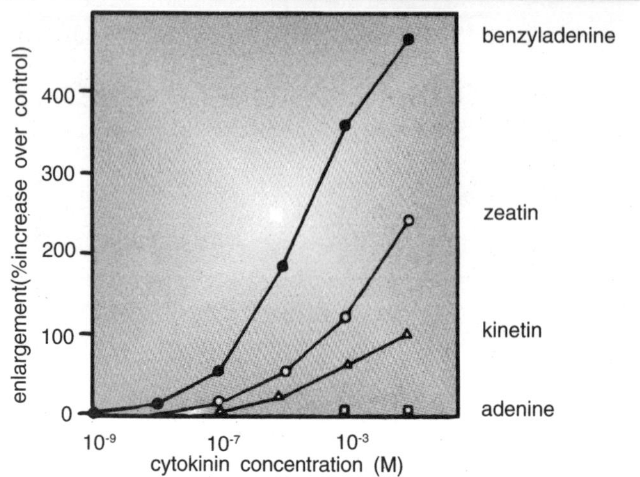

Figure 11.5: Cytokinins stimulate the enlargement of cocklebur (Xanthium) cotyledons.

for activity. Nearly all compounds active as cytokinins are 6-substituted *aminopurines*. Certainly all the naturally occurring cytokinins are *aminopurine* derivatives. *Benzylaminopurine* (BAP), which has found uses in agriculture, is an example of a synthetic 6-substituted *aminopurine cytokinin.*

Of course, kinetin itself is a synthetic 6-substituted aminopurine cytokinin. The only exceptions to this generalization are certain *diphenylurea* derivatives that show weak cytokinin activity. These diphenylurea derivatives are *synthetic cytokinins* but they are not 6-substituted aminopurines, and it is not clear why they are active.

One suggestion is that they may stimulate the biosynthesis of the native cytokinins in plant tissues that respond to these compounds.

In the course of determining the structural requ-irements for cytokinin activity, some molecules were found to act as *cytokinin antagonists.*

These molecules are able to block the action of cytokinins, and their effects may be overcome by adding more of the cytokinin. One of the most potent cytokinin *antagonists* is 3-methyl-7-(3methylbuty-lamino)pyrazolo[4,3-d]pyrimidine.

Methods Used to Assay for Cytokinins

The naturally occurring molecules with cytokinin activity may be detected and identified by a combination of methods, including chemical methods such as highperformance *liquid chromatography* and mass *spectroscopy, immunological methods,* and *bioassays.*

As discussed in other chapter of this book, introduction of combined gas *chromatography* and *mass spectroscopy,* along with the use of *isotopically labeled cytokinins* as internal standard', has resulted in a major advance in measurement of cytokinin levels in plants.

Historically, bioassays were the only methods for the identification of cytokinins. Cell proliferation bioassays continue to be important because a cytokinin is defined *operationally* as a compound "which, in the presence of optimal auxin, induces cell division in tobacco pith or similar tissue cultures".

In addition to *tobacco* pith tissue, *carrot tap root phloem* requires a cytokinin for its proliferation in culture. Also, some continuously cultured callus tissues of tobacco and soybean will not grow in culture without cytokinin.

These cytokinin-requiring tissues all exhibit a linear increase in growth with increasing cytokinin concentration over a very broad range. The disadvantage of cell *proliferation* assays is that it takes nearly a month to see the results.

Therefore, a number of alternative bioassays, some of which can be performed in a few days, were developed for the detection of cytokinins in plant extracts. Other *cytokinin stimulated* physiological and developmental responses have been adapted as cytokinin bioassays.

For example, in some organs cytokinins induce cells to enlarge without dividing. Bioassays based on this effect were devised using the cytokinin-dependent expansion of radish (*Raphanus*) or cocklebur *(Xanthium)* cotyldeons and radish leaf disks.

Cytokinins also delay the senescence of detached leaves, and a bioassay based on the retention of chlorophyll in detached oat *(Avena)* leaves has been used to estimate cytokinin levels in plant *extracts.*

The advantage of these alternative assays is their speed. However, they must be used with care, since substances that are not cytokinins also may evoke the response or interfere with it. *Immunological methods* may also be used for cytokinin measurement.

Antibodies against cytokinins can be produced by injecting rabbits or mice with cytokinin ribosides conjugated to a protein. Some of the antibodies that the animal produces to this complex will be directed against the cytokinin.

These antibodies can be used to quantitate the amount of a cytokinin in a sample by means of a radioimmunoassay. Plant extracts are first fractionated, usually by high performance liquid chromatography (HPLC), and the cytokinins in the fractions are detected and their concentrations determined by means of the *radioimmunoassay.*

The cytokinin antibodies can also be used to isolate the hormone from extracts by immunoaffinity chromatography. These immunological methods hold great promise for the identification and quantification of naturally occurring cytokinins because the antibodies are highly specific and more sensitive than most bioassays. Furthermore, these immunological methods are very fast.

Cytokinins are Both Free and Bound

The naturally occurring cytokinins are found as free molecules (not covalently attached to any macromolecule) in plants and certain bacteria. Cytokinins also exist as modified bases in certain transfer RNA molecules of all organisms.

Free cytokinins have been found in a wide spectrum of angiosperms and probably are universal in this group of plants. They have also been found in algae, diatoms, mosses, ferns, and conifers.

Their regulatory role has been demonstrated only in angiosperms, conifers, and mosses, but they may function to regulate the growth, development, and metabolism of all plants. Zeatin is usually the most abundant naturally occurring free cytokinin.

In addition to *zeatin, dihydrozeatin* and *isopentenyladenine* (i^6Ade) are commonly found in higher plants. Numerous derivatives of these three cytokinins have been identified in plant extracts. Transfer RNA (tRNA) contains not only the four nucleotides used to construct all other forms of RNA but also some unusual nucleotides in which the base has been modified.

Some of these "*hypermodified*" bases act as cytokinins when the tRNA is hydrolyzed and tested in one of the cytokinin bioassays. Some tRNAs of higher plants contain zeatin as a hypermodified base, although it is usually the cis isomer instead of the trans form found as free cytokinin.

Higher plant tRNAs may also contain a derivative of zeatin in which a methylthio group is attached to the purine ring (2-methylthio-cis-ribosylzeatin) or may contain N^6(A^2-isopentenyl) adenosine (i^6 Ado). In addition to tRNAs that participate in cytoplasmic protein synthesis, plants have a different set of tRNAs for protein synthesis within chloroplasts.

These two classes of tRNA contain different cytokinins. Cytokinins are not confined to plant tRNAs. They are part of certain tRNAs from all organisms, from bacteria to humans. In bacteria, methylthio-i^6 Ado is the main hypermodified base with cytokinin activity, while i^6 Ado is the principal cytokinin of animal tRNAs.

Some Bacteria also Secrete Free Cytokinins

Some bacteria and fungi are intimately associated with higher plants. In many cases these microorganisms produce and secrete substantial amounts of cytokinins and/or cause the plant cells to synthesize plant hormones, including cytokinins.

The cytokinins produced by microorganisms include zeatin, i^6Ade, cis-zeatin, and their ribosides. Infection of plant tissues with these microorganisms can induce the tissues to divide and, in some cases, to form special structures such as mycorrhizae, in which the microorganism can reside in a mutualistic relationship with the plant. As we saw earlier, some pathogenic bacteria may stimulate plant cells to divide. In addition to the crown gall bacterium *Agrobacterium tumefaciens,* these include *Corynebacterium fascians,* which is a major cause of the growth abnormality known as witches'-broom.

The shoots of plants infected by *C. fascians* begin to resemble an old-fashioned straw broom after the infection has proceeded for several months because the lateral buds, which normally would remain dormant, are stimulated to grow by the *bacterial cytokinin.*

BIOSYNTHESIS, METABOLISM, AND TRANSPORT OF CYTOKININS

The side chains of naturally occurring *cytokinins* are chemically related to rubber, carotenoid pigments, the plant hormones gibberellin and abscisic acid, and some of the plant defense compounds called *phytoalexins.* All of these are constructed, at least in part, from units of isoprene. *Isoprene* is similar in structure to the side chain of zeatin, 2-i^6Ade, and other cytokinins.

These cytokinin side chains are synthesized from an isoprene derivative. In the case of rubber or the carotenoids, large molecules are constructed by the *polymerization* of many isoprene units, whereas cytokinin contains just one of these units.

The precursor for the formation of these *isoprene* structures is mevalonic acid. *Mevalonic acid* is converted to A^2-*isopentenyl pyrophosphate* (A^2IPP) by a series of enzymatic reactions known as the mevalonic acid pathway.

Cytokinin Synthase Catalyzes the First Step in Cytokinin Biosynthesis

An enzyme that synthesizes cytokinins has been found in plants. It is called A^2-isopentenyl-pyrophosphate: AMP A^2-isopentenyltransferase, or cytokinin synthase. It is a type of prenyltransferase, similar to the prenyltransferase enzymes active in the synthesis of other isoprenoid compounds.

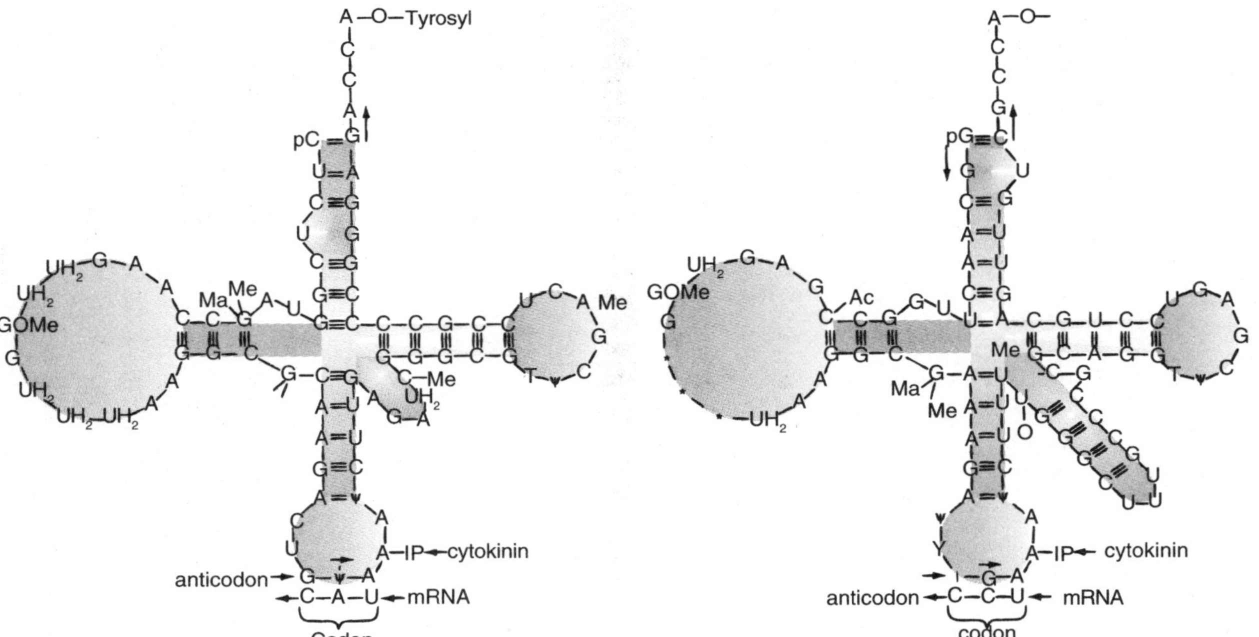

Figure 11.6: The structure of yeast tRNAs for tyrosine and serine, both of which contain a cytokinin. The cytokinin in either case is i⁶Ado, indicated as A-IP in the figure. Note that the cytokinin is the base next to the 3' end of the anticodon, a position in which the side chain could be expected to play a role in codon-anticodon recognition.

The prenyltransferase active in cytokinin synthesis catalyzes the transfer the *isopentenyl* group of A^2-IPP to *adenosine monophosphate.* The product of this reaction, the ribotide of i^6Ade, is not a major higher plant cytokinin. However, it is active as a cytokinin in bioassays and is readily converted to zeatin and other cytokinins.

Modification of the Polymerized Base Produces the tRNA Cytokinins

The synthesis of the tRNA cytokinins takes place by an entirely different route. Free cytokinins are not used to any significant extent in the synthesis of the *cytokininactive* bases in tRNAs. Instead, tRNAs are made from the four conventional nucleotides during the *transcription* of the genes encoding their sequences.

The first product is a tRNA precursor that lacks the *hypermodified* bases and is somewhat larger than the final product. This *precursor* is processed, much as messenger RNA is processed, to yield the *functional* tRNA molecule. In this processing, specific adenine residues of some of the tRNAs are modified to give the *cytokinin.*

As with the free cytokinins, O^2-isopentenyl groups are transferred to the adenine molecules from A^z-*isopentenyl pyrophosphate* by a prenyltransferase. This enzyme is unlikely to be the same transferase that was involved in the synthesis of the free *cytokinins.*

The transferase that synthesizes the tRNA cytokinins must be able to *recognize* a specific base sequence in the tRNA and transfer the *isopentenyl group* to the *adenosine nearest* the 3' end of the *anticodon.* It is unlikely that it would also utilize free AMP as a substrate, but the enzyme has not been isolated and characterized.

Cytokinins Synthesized in the Root are Transported to the Shoot in the Transpiration Stream

Root apical meristems are major sites of synthesis of the free cytokinins in whole plants. The cytokinins synthesized

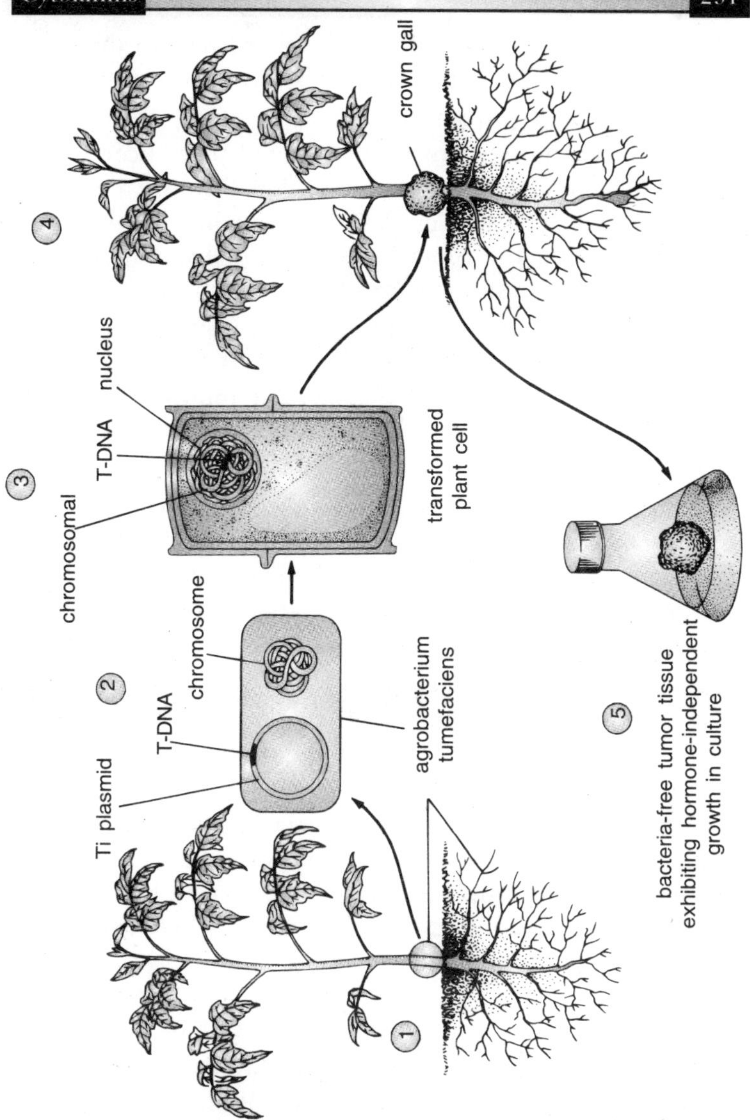

Figure 11.7: Tumor induction by Agrobacterium tumefaciens. The tumor is initiated when bacteria enter a lesion, which is usually near the crown of the plant (the junction of root and stem), and attach themselves to cells (1). A virulent bacterium carries, in addition to its chromosomal DNA, a Ti plasmid (2). The plasmid's T-DNA is introduced into a cell and becomes integrated into the cell's chromosomal DNA (3). Transformed cells proliferate to form a crown gall tumor (4). Tumor tissue can be "cured" of bacteria by incubation at 42°C. The bacteria-free tumor can be cultured indefinitely in the absence of hormones (5).

in roots appear to move through the *xylem* into the shoot. This movement has not been proved, but there is circumstantial evidence to support it.

When the shoot is cut from a rooted plant near the soil line, the xylem sap may continue to flow from the cut stump for some time. This xylem exudate contains cytokinins. If the soil covering the roots is kept moist, the flow of *xylem exudate* can continue for several days.

Since its cytokinin content does not diminish, the cytokinins found in the exudate may be synthesized by the roots. Also, environmental factors that interfere with root function, such as water stress, reduce the cytokinin content of the xylem exudate.

Using antibodies raised against zeatin riboside and *isopentenylad-enosine*, it has been shown by *immunocytochemical* staining methods that cytokinins are concentrated in the apical *meristems* of both roots and shoots of tomato.

The staining pattern also showed a *basipetally* decreasing gradient of cytokinins along both the root and stein. This observation suggests that tomato shoots may produce much of their own cytokinins. Thus, the importance of root-derived cytokinins for shoot development remâins to be elucidated.

Based on their cytokinin content and behaviour in culture, embryos may be sites of cytokinin biosynthesis. Unlike the shoot apical meristem, embryos removed from the plant will continue to grow and develop normally when cultured in medium lacking hormones.

It is not clear exactly where in embryonic development cytokinin autonomy begins, although it is probable that very young embryos lack the ability to synthesize cytokinins since this would explain the high cytokinin levels present in *immature endosperm tissue.*

Cultured Cells Can Acquire the Ability to Synthesize Cytokinins

When cultured normal callus tissues of many species have been *subcultured* repeatedly over a long period, they may become hormone *autonomous*; that is, they will grow on culture medium lacking an auxin or a cytokinin.

This phenomenon is known as habituation. Most likely, a plant tissue becomes *habituated* because it acquires the capacity to synthesize its own hormones. Habituated callus tissues have been shown to contain cytokinins.

Frederick Meins and his colleagues in Basel, Switzerland, have shown that different tissues of tobacco plants exhibit different capacities to synthesize cytokinins in tissue culture. Tobacco pith tissue is *cytokinin-dependent* but capable of being *habituated.*

In contrast, tissues cultured from the cortex of the stem are *cytokinin-autonomous*; they can be cultured indefinitely on medium containing auxin as the only hormone supplement. Finally, tobacco leaf tissue has an absolute requirement for cytokinins and cannot be habituated.

These observations indicate that the ability to synthesize cytokinins can be switched on or off during development and that the on and off states can be stably maintained during cell divisions. Such developmental control of cytokinin synthesis may have important effects on *morpho-genesis.*

Cytokinin Synthesis by Crown Gall Tissues Results from Genetic Transformation of Plant Cells

Bacteria-free tissues from crown gall tumors proliferate in culture in the absence of any hormone additions to the culture medium. Substantial amounts of free cytokinins, in addition to auxins, are found in these crown gall tissues.

Furthermore, when radioactively labeled adenine is fed to periwinkle *(Vinca rosea)* crown gall tissues, it is incorporated into both zeatin and zeatin riboside, demonstrating that active cytokinin biosynthetic machinery is present in the gall tissue.

Control stem tissue, which has not been associated with the crown gall organism, does not incorporate labeled adenine into cytokinins. During *Agrobacterium tumefaciens* infection, plant cells incorporate some DNA from the bacteria into their chromosomes. The virulent strains of *Agrobacterium* contain a large plasmid known as the Ti plasmid. Plasntids are circular pieces of extrachromosomal DNA that are not essential for the life of the bacterium. However, plasmids frequently contain genes that enhance the ability of the bacterium to survive in special environments.

A small portion of the Ti plasmid, known as the T-DNA, is incorporated into the host plant cell's nuclear DNA. The T-DNA contains genes necessary for the biosynthesis of *transzeatin* and auxin, as well as a member of a class of unusual nitrogen-containing compounds called *opines.*

Opines are not synthesized by plants except after crown gall transformation. The T-DNA gene involved in *cytokinin* biosynthesis encodes a *prenyltransferase* that uses AMP as its substrate, similar to the cytokinin synthase that was identified in normal tobacco tissue.

The T-DNA also contains two genes encoding enzymes that convert tryptophan to the auxin indoleacetic acid (IAA). The pathway of *tryptophan* conversion differs from that in untransformed cells and involves indoleacetamide as an intermediate.

None of these T-DNA genes are expressed in the bacterium, but when they are inserted into the plant chromosomes the cells begin to produce *zeatin*, *auxin*, and an *opine*. The bacterium can utilize the opine as a *nitrogen* source, but higher plant cells cannot.

Thus, by transforming the plant cells, the bacterium provides itself with an expanding environment (the *gall tissue*) in which the host cells are directed to roduce a substance (the opine) that only the bacterium can utilize for its nutrition.

There are important differences between the control of cytokinin biosynthesis in crown gall tissues and that in normal tissues, since the T-DNA genes for plant hormone synthesis are expressed even in cells in which the native plant genes for cytokinin *biosynthesis* are completely shut down. The regulation of the expression of the T-DNA gene encoding crown gall cytokinin synthase may be very different from that of the native higher plant gene for the *analogous* enzyme.

Cytokinin Nucleotides are the Predominant Form in the Xylem

Cytokinins are passively transported from roots into the shoot through the xylem. They move through the plant with the transpiration stream, along with water and minerals taken up by the roots. Since the cytokinins present in the xylem exudate are *predominantly nucleotides,* it has been suggested that the nucleotides may be the form in which cytokinins are transported.

Once they reach the leaves, the nucleotides may be converted to the free base or to glucosides. Cytokinin glucosides accumulate to high levels in leaves, and substantial amounts may be present even in senescing leaves.

Although the glucosides are active as cytokinins in bioassays, they appear to lack hormonal activity after they are formed in leaf cells, possibly because they are compartmentalized in such a way that they are unavailable.

Compartmentalization may explain the confli fiting observations that cytokinins are transported readily by the xylem but that radioactive cytokinins given to leaves in intact plants do not appear to move from the site of application.

The different chemical forms of the cytokinins are rapidly metabolized by most plant tissues. Cytokinin bases, when given to many plant tissues, are converted to the respective nucleotides: zeatin to zeatin ribonucleotide, i^6Ade to i^6Ade ribonucleotide, and so forth.

They also may be converted to their glucosides. Many plant tissues have been found to contain the enzyme cytokinin oxidase, which converts zeatin, zeatin riboside, and i^6Ade to adenine or its derivatives. This enzyme may be responsible for the inactivation of the hormone, possibly as a mechanism for preventing its accumulation to toxic levels.

The Free Base is Probably the Active Form of the Hormone

The active form of cytokinin is not known, although circumstantial evidence suggests that it is the free base. For example, excised radish cotyledons grow when they are cultured in a solution containing the synthetic cytokinin base benzylaminopurine.

The cultured cotyledons readily take up the hormone and convert it to various BAP glucosides, BAP ribonucleoside, and BAP ribonucleotide. When the cotyledons are transferred back to a medium lacking a cytokinin, their growth rate declines, as do the concentrations of BAP, BAP *ribonucleoside,* and BAP ribonucleotide in the tissues.

However, the level of the BAP glucosides remains constant. This suggests that the glucosides cannot be the active form of the hormone.

In cultured tobacco cells, growth does not occur unless cytokinin ribosides supplied in the culture medium are converted to the free base. Thus, the free base is the most likely candidate for the active form of the hormone.

THE BIOLOGICAL ROLE OF CYTOKININS

Plant hormones do not seem to work alone. Even in cases in which a response can be evoked by application of a single hormone, the tissue may contain additional endogenous hormones that contribute to the response. In some cases we know that a response is evoked by two or more hormones.

However, until we have a way to block the action of the endogenous hormones, we cannot be certain that the actual regulation of the phenomenon being studied is as simple as it appears to be.

Nevertheless, the cytokinins can evoke a variety of *physiological, metabolic, biochemical,* and developmental processes when they are applied to higher plants, and it is probable that they play an important role in the regulation of these events in the intact plant.

Some of these responses were mentioned in connection with the bioassays used to detect cytokinins. Here we will outline some of the major biological roles of the cytokinins, but the reader should be aware that there are more.

The Cell Cycle in Plants has Two Control Points

As discussed in other chapter of this book, the cell cycle in *eukaryotes* is a complicated process that involves a number of distinct biochemical and cytological events, all of which are *integrated* in some manner. In a dividing cell population, such as an actively growing meristem, the average cell size remains constant.

This means that, after it is formed, each cell approximately doubles its cytoplasmic mass, including all of its organelles, before it divides again. Most of the growth in *cytoplasmic* mass occurs in the G1 phase of the cell cycle, whereas the replication of the DNA and other components of the nucleus as well occurs in the S phase.

In the *mammalian cell cycle* there is a key regulatory point somewhere early in G1. At this point the cell becomes committed to the initiation of DNA synthesis. Once a cell has initiated DNA synthesis, it is irreversibly committed to completing the cell cycle through mitosis and *cytokinesis.*

After the cell has completed mitosis, it may initiate another complete cycle (G1 through mitosis) or may leave the cell cycle and differentiate. This choice is made at the critical G1 point, before the cell begins to replicate its DNA.

DNA replication and mitosis are deterministically linked in mammalian cells. The regulation of the plant cell cycle appears to be more complex. Plant cells can leave the proliferative cycle either before or after they have replicated their DNA.

This suggests that there are two control points in the plant cell cycle, one regulating the initiation of DNA replication and the other *governing* the initiation of *mitosis*.

As a consequence, whereas most animal cells are diploid (having two sets of chromosomes), plant cells frequently become polyploid (having more than two sets of chromosomes) because they may go through one or more cycles of nuclear DNA replication without mitosis.

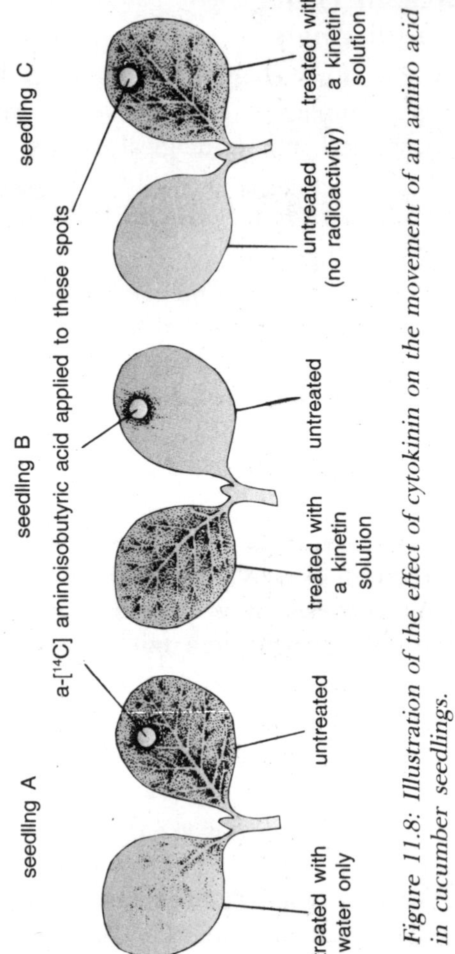

Figure 11.8: Illustration of the effect of cytokinin on the movement of an amino acid in cucumber seedlings.

Hormones May Regulate the Plant Cell Cycle

Earlier in this chapter we saw that cytokinin triggers cell proliferation in tissues that contain or are supplied with an optimal level of auxin.

There is evidence that both hormones participate in the regulation of the cell cycle, but that auxin may regulate events leading to DNA replication while cytokinin regulates events leading to mitosis. Cultured tobacco tissue, when treated with auxin alone, may initiate DNA synthesis, but the cells do not divide unless they also are given a cytokinin. Similarly, in tissues treated with cytokinin alone, a few cells that had previously replicated their DNA will be stimulated to divide.

Both hormones are necessary for the cells to remain in the cell cycle. These observations do not mean that auxin directly *triggers* DNA replication or that cytokinin directly initiates mitosis in G2-phase cells. We do not know enough about either the plant cell cycle or the mechanism of hormone action to do more than note that these hormones permit the respective processes to occur.

This caveat holds for all the other responses that are evoked by cytokinin as well. The state of our knowledge is such that we rarely can do more than make correlations between the application of the hormone and the appearance of a given response.

The Auxin/Cytokinin Ratio Regulates Morphogenesis in Cultured Tissues

Shortly after the discovery of kinetin, it was observed that cultured tobacco pith segments or tobacco callus tissues produce roots or shoots, depending on the ratio of auxin to cytokinin in the culture medium.

High levels of auxin relative to kinetin stimulated the(formation of roots, whereas high levels of the cytokinin relative to auxin led to the formation of shoots.

At intermediate levels the tissue grew as an undifferentiated callus. More recently, investigators have used molecular genetic methods to investigate the significance of the auxin/ cytokinin ratio in regulating morphogenesis in crown gall tissues.

Mutations have been made in the T-DNA of the *Agrobacterium Ti* plasmid to observe the effects of different T-DNA genes on the growth and development of tumors. In some cases, bacteria containing Ti plasmids with mutated T-DNA genes induced the formation of a mass of proliferating shoots or roots instead of the usual tumors.

These partially differentiated tumors are said to be *terato-*

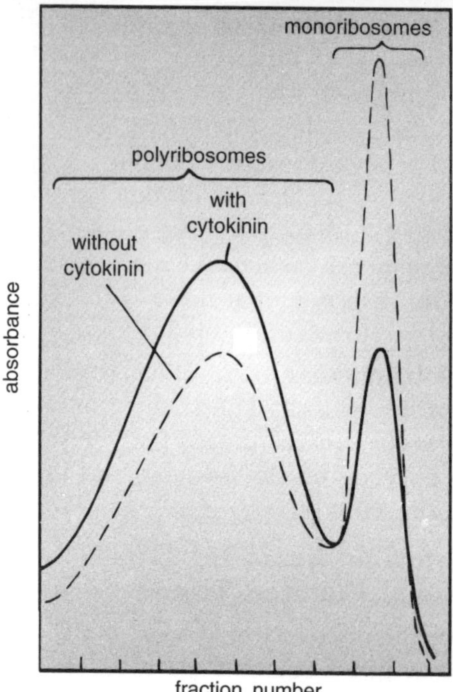

Figure 11.9: Cytokinin stimulation of polyribosome formation in cultured soybean tissues.

mas. When the *mutations* occurred in one region of the T-DNA, the teratomas consisted of an abnormal proliferation of roots.

Mutations in a different region of the T-DNA resulted in an *abnormal proliferation* of shoots. The first class of mutants were said to be "*rooty*," while the second were called "*shooty*."

Subsequently it was proved that shooty mttations had inactivated genes necessary for the synthesis of the auxin IAA. Similarly, the rooty mutants lost the function of the T-DNA gene necessary for the synthesis of zeatin.

Tissues transformed by rooty Ti plasmids contained high levels of auxin relative to cytokinin, whereas those transformed by shooty mutant plasmids had high levels of cytokinin and low levels of auxin. These findings further demonstrate the importance of the auxin/cytokinin ratio in regulating *morphogenesis.*

Cytokinins Delay Senescence and Stimulate Nutrient Mobilization

Leaves detached from the plant slowly lose chlorophyll, RNA, lipids, and protein, even if they are kept moist and provided with minerals. This programmed aging process, leading to death, is termed *senescence*. Leaf senescence is more rapid in the dark than *jri* the light.

Treating isolated leaves of many species with cytokinins will delay their senescence. Although cytokinins do not prevent senescence completely, their effects can be quite dramatic, particularly when the cytokinin is sprayed directly on the intact plant.

If only one leaf is treated, it remains green after other leaves of similar developmental age have yellowed and dropped off the plant. Even a small spot on a leaf will remain green if treated with a cytokinin, while the surrounding tissues on the same leaf begin to senesce.

In an effort to account for this phenomenon, investigators have studied the effect of cytokinin treatment on the movement of nutrients into treated leaves. *Radioisotope-labeled* nutrients (sugars, amino acids, etc.) are fed to the plants after one leaf or part of a leaf is treated with a cytokinin.

By subjecting the leaves to autoradiography, the pattern of movement and the sites at which the nutrients accumulate can 6e determined. Experiments of this nature have demonstrated that nutrients are preferentially transported to and accumulate in the cytokinin-treated tissues.

It has been postulated that the hormone causes nutrient mobilization by creating a new source-sink relationship. The metabolism of the treated area may be stimulated by the hormone so that nutrients move toward it.

However, it is not necessary for the nutrient itself to be metabolized in the sink cells, since even nonmetabolizable substrate analogs are mobilized by cytokinins.

Cytokinins Promote the Maturation of Chloroplasts

Although seeds can germinate in the dark, the morpho-

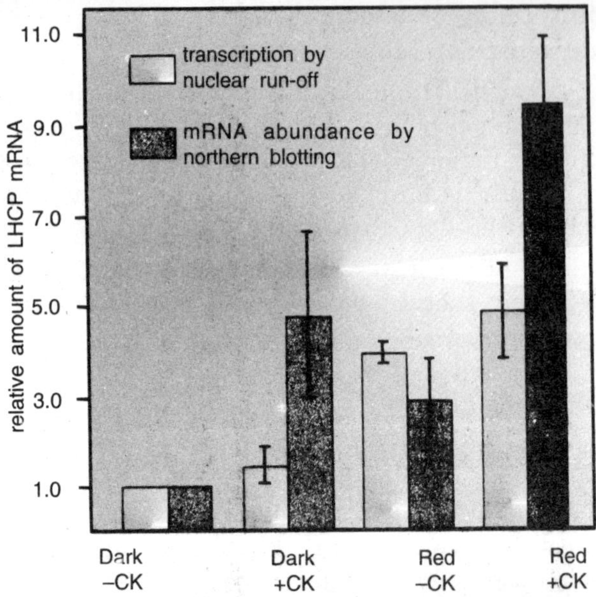

Figure 11.10: Comparison of the effects of a cytokinin (benzyladenine) and dim red light on the transcription versus total abundance of LHCP mRNA in Lemna gibba.

logy of dark-grown seedlings is very different from that of light-grown seedlings. Dark-grown seedlings are said to be etiolated.

The internodes of etiolated seedlings are more elongated, leaves do not expand, and chloroplasts do not mature. Instead, the proplastids of *darkgrown* seedlings develop into etioplasts, in which the inner membranes form a compact, highly regular *lattice* known as the *prolamellar body*. Etioplasts contain some carotenoids, which is why the etiolated seedlings appear yellow, but they do not synthesize *chlorophyll* or most of the enzymes and structural proteins required for the formation of the chloroplast *thylakoid* system and *photosynthetic* machinery.

When seedlings are germinated in the light, chloroplasts mature directly from the proplastids present in the embryo, but etioplasts also can mature into chloroplasts when etiolated seedlings are illuminated. If the etiolated leaves are treated with cytokinin before they are illuminated, they form chloroplasts with more extensive grana.

Also, chlorophyll and photosynthetic enzymes are synthesized at a greater rate after illumination. Cytokinin cannot promote these changes in the dark, but the stimulation of light-initiated chloroplast maturation by cytokinin is quite pronounced. These results suggest that cytokinins promote the synthesis of photosynthetic proteins.

Cytokinins can Stimulate Cell Enlargement

Cytokinins can promote cell enlargement in certain tissues and organs. This effect is most clearly seen in dicots with leafy cotyledons, such as mustard, cucumber, and sunflower. The cotyledons of these species expand as a result of cell enlargement during seedling growth. Cytokinin treatment promotes additional cell expansion with no increase in the dry weight of the treated cotyledons.

Cleon Ross and his colleagues at Colorado State University have shown that cytokinin stimulated the growth of the cotyledons by increasing the plasticity of the cell walls without changing their elasticity. At noted in the discussion of auxins, the plasticity of the wall is a measure of its ability to be stretched permanently by turgor pressure.

Leafy cotyledons expand to a much greater extent when the seedlings are grown in the light instead of the dark. However, cytokinins promote the growth of cotyledons in both the light and the dark. Superficially, at least, this cytokinin-promoted growth appears to be similar to the auxin-induced promotion of stem cell elongation.

However, cytokinin did not increase plasticity by acidification of the cell wall, as auxin appears to do. In addition, neither auxin nor gibberellin promotes cotyledonary cell expansion. These observations illustrate an important point about plant hormones: their effects are not universal.

Instead, a given hormone elicits a specific response from a specific tissue in a particular species or group of species when the hormone is applied under carefully controlled conditions. In a different species the same response may be elicited only under different conditions, or it may be elicited by a different hormone. For example, we usually think of auxins and gibberellins as hormones that regulate stem elongation.

However, cytokinins promote the elongation of young wheat coleoptiles and water-melon hypocotyls, in both cases by increasing cell elongation with only a minor effect on cell number.

In both cases this effect was observed only when the cytokinin was applied under specific circumstances: only at an early stage of development in the wheat coleoptiles, and only when applied to the roots or to the shoot tip of intact watermelon seedlings.

Most other studies of the effects of applied cytokinins on stem elongation have used isolated stem segments, in which cytokinins have a strong inhibitory effect on auxin-promoted cell elongation, as in the case of soybean hypocotyls.

THE MECHANISM OF CYTOKININ ACTION

As noted in earlier chapters, it is generally assumed that plant hormones interact with specific receptors that reside either on the cell surface or within the cytoplasm. In animal systems in which they have been characterized, hormone receptors are proteins to which the hormone binds with high affinity.

Binding of a steroid hormone to its cytoplasmic receptor produces an active hormonereceptor complex that moves into the nucleus, where it binds preferentially to particular DNA sequences and leads to the expression of specific genes.

As we discussed in other chapter of this book, the receptors for nonsteroid animal hormones, such as insulin, are found on the cell surface, usually as integral proteins in the plasma membrane.

In this case, the binding of the hormone to its receptor may stimulate the formation in the cytoplasm of a second messenger that alters some aspect of cellular metabolism.

The hormone-receptor complex need not enter the cell to trigger the formation of the second messenger and a biological response. These two models for animal hormone action are useful in designing experiments to examine plant hormone action, but so far there has been little direct evidence that the cytokinins act by a mechanism similar to either of these models.

Plant Cells Contain Cytokinin-Binding Proteins

Specific cytokinin binding sites have been identified in some plants, and cereal grains contain factors that bind cytokinins. In the case of a protein factor called CBF-1 (CBF = cytokinin-binding factor), this binding has the expected characteristics of hormone-receptor binding.

The binding sites can be saturated by increasing concentrations of the hormone, cytokinins bind to CBF-1 with moderately high affinity, and the binding is specific for the cytokinins. The CBF-1 was obtained from salt washes of ribosomes, suggesting that it may be a ribosomal protein.

Although no function was proposed for the CBF-1-cytokinin complex, the location of the binding factor suggests that the complex may regulate protein synthesis.

Cytokinins Regulate Protein Synthesis

There is good evidence that cytokinins play a role in regulating protein synthesis. Polyribosomes are the protein synthetic machinery. They consist of messenger RNA molecules to which numerous ribosomes are attached.

Each ribosome is in a different stage of translating the mRNA into a polypeptide. When cultured soybean cells are treated with cytokinin, within 15 min there is an increase in the polyribosome content of the cells. This increase comes about as a result of the movement of free monoribosomes (monosomes) into polyribosomes (polysomes).

Cytokinin can not only increase the rate of protein synthesis but also change the spectrum of proteins made by plant tissues. This has been demonstrated by labeling the proteins synthesized by cultured soybean cells with [^{35}S] methionine and separating them by polyacrylamide gel electrophoresis.

Autoradiograms of the gel show that cytokinin treatment enhances the synthesis of certain proteins while inhibiting the synthesis of others. Tobacco tissues treated with cytokinin also show altered patterns of protein synthesis, suggesting that the hormone is necessary for the synthesis of some proteins and inhibitory to the synthesis of others.

The specific nature of the proteins whose synthesis is enhanced or suppressed by cytokinin is not known in either of these tissues.

Cytokinins Affect a Posttranscriptional Step in *Lemna*

Elaine Tobin and her colleagues at the University of California-Los Angeles have studied the role of cytokinin in chloroplast maturation in the small aquatic duckweed *Lemna gibba. Lemna* can be grown heterotrophically in the dark for long periods of time by adding sucrose to the culture medium.

When green *Lemna* plants are placed in the dark, the nuclear-encoded mRNAs for two important chloroplast proteins-the small subunit of ribulose-1,5-bisphosphate carboxylase (SSU) and the major chlorophyll a/b-binding polypeptide of light harvesting complex II (LHCP)-decrease in abundance over a week.

As a result, the synthesis of SSU and LHCP drastically decreases. However, the decrease in abundance of these mRNAs can be itihibited either by a pulse of dim red light or by the addition of cytokinin to the culture medium 24 h prior to harvest.

The abundance of LHCP mRNA, for example, is about 5-fold greater in the cytokinin-treated plants than in the controls. The combination of cytokinin and red light caused a 9.5-fold increase relative to the controls.

How does cytokinin prevent the decrease in these two important mRNAs in the dark? To determine whether cytokinin treatment influences the LHCP mRNA levels by increasing the rate of transcription or by decreasing the rate of mRNA turnover, Flores and Tobin (1988) analyzed the transcripts produced by nuclei isolated from cytokinin-treated and control *Lemna* in nuclear run-off experiments. Briefly, isolated nuclei are allowed to extend their tr.anscripts (initiated in vivo) in the presence of ^{32}P-labeled nucleotides.

The labeled RNA is then hybridized to filters containing cloned LHCP sequences. The amount of radioactivity bound corresponds to the amount of transcript synthesized.

As shown in Figure elsewhere in this chapter, cytokinin caused only a 1.5-fold enhancement of transcription while a 1-min exposure to red light stimulated transcription 4-fold. When cytokinin was given along with red light, a 4.9-fold increase in transcription was observed. These results suggest that transcription of the gene is mainly under the control of the phytochrome system.

Cytokinin appears to increase the abundance of LHCP mRNA at a posttranscriptional level, possibly by making the mRNA more stable.

The Cytokinins in tRNA May Regulate Protein Synthesis

The relationship between the free cytokinins and the cytokinin bases in tRNA is unknown. There is no evidence that the free cytokinins act through a mechanism that involves the tRNAs. Indeed, the strongest argument against such a mode of action is that the cytokinins of tRNA are synthesized by the addition of a side chain to the polymerized base, rather than by the direct incorporation of free cytokinin.

Nevertheless, the tRNA cytokinins could play an important role in protein synthesis. In the tRNAs that contain them, cytokinins occupy a critical position adjacent to the anticodon, where they may influence the binding of the tRNA to mRNA.

There are different tRNA molecules for each amino acid, the number of tRNAs varying from two to six, depending on the amino acid. Each tRNA has a different anticodon, consisting of a three-base sequence complementary to the three bases of the codon that specifies it.

In the bacterium *Escherichia coli,* only the tRNAs whose anticodons recognize codons beginning with the letter U have been found to contain cytokinins. The tRNAs that contain a cytokinin may require it for proper codon-anticodon recognition. Different proteins have quite different codon usages.

One protein may use the codon CUU to specify leucine while another uses the codon UUA to specify the same amino acid. If the cytokinin-containing leucyl tRNA responding to the UUA codon was not present or was inactive because the adenosine base next to the codon had not been modified to make it a cytokinin, the second protein would be made and the first would not, even though the mRNAs for these two proteins had the same abundance.

Thus, the tRNA processing step could play an important regulatory role in determining the nature of the proteins that are made by a cell. Finally, although most of the free cytokinins in plants are thought to be synthesized as the free molecules, it is possible that turnover of tRNA can contribute to the total cytokinin activity of cells.

Cytokinins Regulate Calcium Concentration in the Cytosol

One of the many biological effects of the cytokinins is stimulation of bud formation from the protonemata of the moss *Funaria hygrometrica.* The protonemata grow at their tips to form a one-cell-thick filament of cells. Bud formation begins with an asymmetric division of a target cell several cells back from the tip.

This step is initiated by cytokinin-binding to an unidentified receptor within the target cell. The new bud begins as protuberance at the basal end of the cell, and its further development requires the continuous presence of cytokinin.

Secretory vesicles accumulate at the site of the new bud. Cytokinin is ineffective in inducing moss bud formation in calcium-freemedium, however, and the calcium ionophore A23187 can substitute for cytokinin to initiate bud development.

Ionophores are molecules that insert into membranes,

opening pores through which specific ions may freely pass, either alone or in exchange for another ion. Most cells maintain a cytosolic calcium concentration between 0.1 and 1.0 μM by actively pumping calcium outside the cell or into the vacuole.

The calcium concentrations of the vacuole and the cell wall are on the order of 1000 times greater than that of the cytosol. The calcium ionophore A23187 increases the cytosolic calcium concentration by exchanging external Ca^{2+} for internal hydrogen ions.

These experiments with the moss *Funaria* indicate that cytokinin may act, at least in part, by increasing the cytosolic concentration of calcium ions by promoting calcium uptake from the medium (since external Ca^{2+} is required).

How, then, does a change in the concentration of cytosolic calcium bring about bud initiation? As we discussed in other chapter of this book, calcium can affect the cytoskeleton, which can regulate exocytosis. In addition, calcium ions have been shown to act through the regulatory protein calmodulin.

Each calmodulin has four high-affinity calcium binding sites. Calmodulin alone is inactive as an regulator, but the calmodulin-calcium complex can bind to and activate a number of enzymes including protein kinases-enzymes that add phosphorus to the serine or tyrosine hydroxyl groups of proteins. The phosphorylation of enzymes can change their activity.

Thus, the calcium-calmodulin complex would be in a position to act as a master switch regulating alternative metabolic pathways within the cell. The finding that calcium ions play a role in cytokinininduced responses does not provide us with the mechanism of action of the hormone. For example, buds initiated by treatment with calcium and A23187 fail to develop normally in the absence of cytokinin.

The results do demonstrate that calcium ions may act as a second messenger, transforming the hormonal signal into a biochemical switch regulating the initial stages of bud formation. Further development of the bud almost certainly involves changes in protein synthesis, possibly via cytokinin-induced alterations of transcription, mRNA stability, or translation.

12

Chapter

Seed Development and Germination

In higher plants, seed dormancy and germination are complex physiological processes that are influenced by many genetic and environmental factors.

Many lines of genetic, physiological and biochemical evidence have illustrated the importance of two plant hormones, abscisic acid (ABA) and gibberellin (GA), in the regulation of seed dormancy and germination.

Antagonistic actions of ABA and GA during seed development and germination have been thought to be achieved through alterations in sensitivities and/or endogenous levels of these hormones.

In addition to the roles of ABA and GA, there is emerging evidence to suggest some roles of other hormones in controlling seed germination. During the course of seed development, the embryo remains attached to the mother plant for a long period of time, even after it completes morphogenesis and acquires the ability to germinate.

This association with the mother plant enables the seed to accumulate reserves, acquire desiccation tolerance and establish dormancy. When the mature seed are dispersed and then imbibed, the seed have to decide "to stay dormant" or "to germinate".

This decision is determined by sensing various environmental factors, such as light, temperature and nutrients. These external signals often alter metabolisms and sensitivities of plant hormones. In particular, the antagonistic actions of ABA and GAs are known to be an important determinant for seed germination.

In this review, we summarize recent advances in understanding the regulation of hormone metabolisms and actions, especially ABA and GA, both of which are tightly linked to developmental and environmental factors. We also discuss the crosstalk of ABA, GA and other hormones during seed development and germination.

HORMONAL CONTROL OF SEED DEVELOPMENT

Recent molecular genetic analyses have revealed that the actions of ABA and GAs are modulated directly by developmental regulators, which are know"space" or "timing" of embryo development. Importantly, these regula"balancer" of the metabolism and sensitivities of these two hormones that in part explains the antagonistic actions of ABA and GAs.

These findings also suggest that the hormone itself plays an indispensable role in regulating developmental processes more deeply than we have thought.

In this section, we first introduce developmental phases and regulators for seed development, and then summarize current knowledge on the interaction of ABA and GAs in terms of both metabolism and signaling.

Developmental and Physiological Phases

Developmental and physiological phases are defined by expression of phase specific genes, thus the phase transition requires both down-regulation of genes for the former phase and up-regulation of genes for the latter phase.

Galau (1987) and his colleagues isolated a large number of genes that are differentially expressed during seed development and germination in cotton *(Gossypium hirsutum).*

They defined five phases in seed development and germination of dicotyledonous plants by the marker gene expression as well as by the timing of physiological and morphological processes.

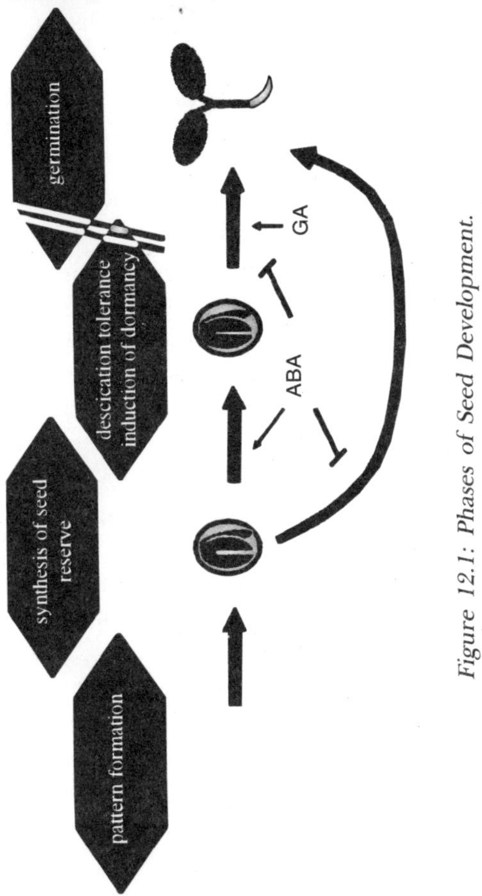

Figure 12.1: Phases of Seed Development.

Recent molecular genetics and transcriptome analyses from various plants suggest that these phases are similar in angiosperms. In general, developmental processes in seed development are largely divided into two phases: pattern formation (morphogenesis) and seed maturation.

The seed maturation is further divided physiologically into two phases: based on before or after abscission, here designated as mid maturation stage and late embryogenesis, respectively.

The mid maturation stage is characterized by expression of genes for seed reserve synthesis especially seed storage protein genes, while the late embryogenesis by the expression of late embryogenesis abundant (Lea) protein genes.

Lea proteins are hydrophilic proteins and are structurally divided into at least six groups. Although their specific function is still unclear, several lines of evidence indicate that they are involved in the acquisition of desiccation tolerance, which occurs in late embryogenesis.

Mature dry seed contains a large amount of mRNAs that is thought to be utilized after imbibition. The presence of these transcripts was illustrated by Nakabayashi *et al.* (2005) using microarray analysis on dry and imbibed Arabidopsi-study, using oligonucleotide-based microarrays representing approximately 22,000 genes, revealed that more than 10,000 mRNA species were detected both in dry and imbibed seeds.

Furthermore, it was demonstrated that proximally located genes are often co-regulated in imbibed seeds; thus, the up-regulated genes or down-regulated genes constitute 3 to 5 gene "expression clusters" on the chromosome.

This coregulation of gene expression is consistent with the finding that the genes for stored mRNAs expressed at high levels are often located in tandem on the chromosome. Rajjou *et al.* (2004) reported that *Arabidopsis* seeds can germinate in the presence of α-amanitin, an inhibitor of polII-mediated transcription, although it is delayed compared to the untreated controls.

In contrast, the treatment of seeds with a translational inhibitor, cycloheximide, abolishes germination completely. Somewhat surprisingly, a subset of proteins is newly synthesized prior to germination even when the transcription is blocked.

These proteins include seed storage proteins and Lea proteins, for which mRNAs are abundant in dry seed. These findings suggest that both stored mRNAs and *de novo* synthesized mRNAs are necessary to initiate early events after seed imbibition and allow successful germination. Plant developmental and physiological phases are loosely separated, such that the phase transitions occur gradually.

Consequently, there is considerable overlap between the processes of late embryogenesis and germination. In cotton, oilseed *(Brassica napus),* and *Arabidopsis,* a subset of germination-associated genes is expressed in late embryogenesis.

Conversely, a subset of transcripts for late embryogenesis-associated genes is present during seed germination. The heterochronic mutations in *Arabidopsis* alter the timing of such gene expression: precocious expression of the latter (germination-associated) genes and down-regulation of gen for maturation and late embryogenesis.

Notably, these heterochronic mutations render phase transition more gradual, suggesting that multiple checkpoints exist between the phases.

Developmental Regulators

Defects in the regulators of maturation stage and late embryogenesis lead to reduced accumulation of seed reserves, improper acquisition of seed dormancy and desiccation intolerance.

These mutants often exhibit precocious germination on the mother plants and produce desiccation intolerant seeds. They are also conditional lethal, but can be rescued when immature seeds are harvested and sown prior to desiccation.

Such non-dormant mutants are reported in various plant species, especially Arabidopsis and maize. In Arabidopsis, four transcription factors (LEAFY COTYLEDON 1 (LEC1), LEAFY COTYLEDON 2 (LEC2), FUSCA 3 (FUS3) and *ABSCISIC ACID-INSENSITIVE 3 (ABI3))* have been identified genetically as important developmental regulators of seed development.

In maize, many mutations that result in vivipary occur in the genes necessary for the biosynthesis of ABA or its intermediate carotenoids. In addition, the *VIVIP*AROUS 1 (VP1) gene encodes a transcription factor that is the orthologue of ABI3. Consistent with their role as regulators of seed development, the *Arabidopsis lec1, fus3, lec2* and *abi3* mutants exhibit severe defects in the maturation stage and late embryogenesis.

These mutants produce desiccation intolerant seeds with a reduced amount of seed reserves. The *LEC1, FUS3, LEC2* and *ABI3* genes are essentially considered to be specific regulators of seed development and germination, because the mutants do not exhibit dramatic developmental defects in

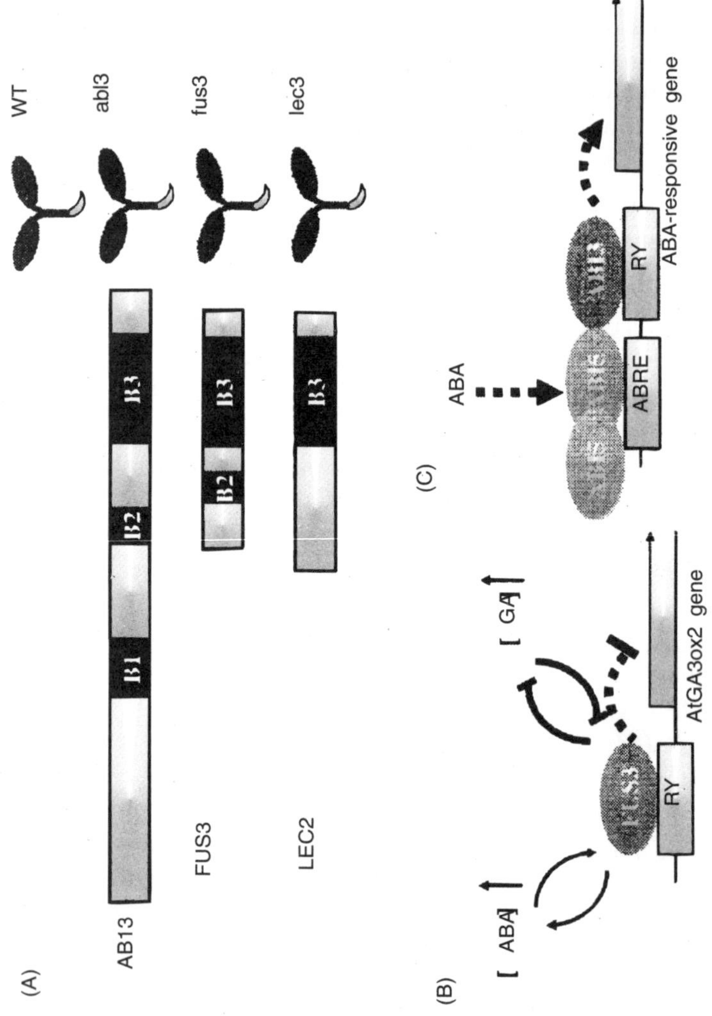

Figure 12.2: Comparison of structures and funcitons of B3 transcription factors.

vegetative and reproductive growth. The *abi3* mutant also demonstrates a strong resistance to ABA-mediated inhibition of seed germination, indicating a role in regulating ABA *sensitivity*. In contrast, mutants of the LEC1, FUS3 and *LEC2 loci* show relatively normal sensitivity to ABA, although the lec1 mutant shows reduced sensitivity to ABA.

A common defect of the lec1, *lec2* and *fus3* mutants is the presence of trichomes on their cotyledons. In *Arabidopsis,* wild-type plants form trichomes only on true leaves, but not on cotyledons. Such a phenotype in these mutants is interpreted as the result of a loss of cotyledon identity. LEC1 encodes a HAP3 subunit of a CCAAT-box-binding factor that is widely conserved among eukaryote transcription factors.

The CCAAT box is postulated to be involved in the expression of a particular set of co-regulated genes, such as nitrogen metabolism and non-fermentable carbon-inducible genes in yeast and cell-cycle-regulated genes in higher eukaryotes.

The expression pattern of the LEC1 is seed specific, which probably reflects a specific role in seed development. It is interesting to note that ectopic expre LEC1 transforms the true leaves into cotyledon-like organs, indicating that LEC 1 is sufficient to confer the cotyledon identity.

The maize VP1 gene was shown to encode a transcription factor that contains a conserved B3 basic domain. In addition to the B3 domain, VP1 has three other conserved domains: one acidic domain (A1) and two basic domains (B1 and B2). The truncated VP1 protein, containing the B3 domain, binds specifically to an Sph element including the seed-specific enhancer RY repeat, which is highly conserved in the promoters of seed protein genes of both monocots and dicots.

However, the B3-deleted vp1 allele still retains some residual function in seed development, indicating that VP1 can also function via the B3 independent manner.

The *Arabidopsis ABI3* gene was shown to be an orthologue of VP1. Ectopic expression of the *ABI3* can induce the expression of seed protein genes in vegetative tissues of transgenic *Arabidopsis* plants, when exogenous ABA is applied to these plants.

This indicates that ABI3 is sufficient to elicit seed-specific expression. In addition to ABI3/VP1, both FUS3 and *LEC2* encode B3 domain-containing proteins. However, they do not contain the conserved B1 domain.

The B3 domains of the ABI3 and FUS3 are structurally similar and both transcription factors bind to the RY repeat *in vitro.* Ectopic expression of FUS3 or LEC2 in transgenic plants transforms vegetative leaves to cotyledon-like organs, suggesting that these components are also required for the specification of cotyledon identify.

The developmental regulators, LEC1, *LEC2* and FUS3, are co-ordinately regulated in embryonic and post-embryonic development. In *pickle (pkl)* mutants, expression of these genes is up-regulated during post-embryonic development.

The *pkl* mutants were identified based on the mis-expression of embryonic traits in the root. The *pkl* phenotype is exaggerated when ABA or a GA biosynthesis inhibitor, uniconazole-P, is applied.

The *PKL* gene encodes a chromatin remodelling protein that belongs to CHD3 family. These findings suggest that the expression of LEC1, *LEC2,* and FUS3 is repressed epigenetically during post-embryonic development.

Further evidence demonstrating co-ordinated regulation of LEC/FUS3/ABI3 expression is provided by ectopic expression experiments. The over-expression of LEC1 using an inducible promoter caused simultaneous induction of *ABI3* and FUS3 expression in seedlings.

Similarly, short-term induction of LEC2 leads to ectopic expression of LEC1, FUS3 and *ABI3.* Further research will be needed to clarify the regulatory interaction of these key developmental regulators, which is essential for the understanding of molecular aspects of seed development.

Regulators of ABA Responses in the Seed

The use of genetic approaches has been highly successful

in identifying loci involved in ABA responses in the seed. Among the *Arabidopsis abi (abscisic acid-insensitive)* mutants, *abi3, abi4* and *abi5* show remarkable ABA insensitivity, most specifically in germinating seeds. *abi3* null alleles produce desiccation intolerant seeds, whereas *abi4* and *abi5* seeds display a similar tolerance to wild-type seeds.

Orthologues of ABI3, ABI4 and ABI5 have been identified from various plant species including cereals and crops, indicating that these regulatory mechanisms are common in higher plants. The *ABI5* and *ABI4* genes encode bZIP and AP2-type transcription factors, respectively.

The ABI5 protein is capable of binding to G-box-like ABA-responsive elements (ABREs), whereas ABI4 and maize ortholog ZmABI4 bind to the coupling element1 (CE1) that acts cooperatively with ABREs.

The contribution of these elements to determining *Arabidopsis* transcriptomes of stored mRNAs was recently shown using microarray analysis.

Statistical analysis indicated that the G-box-like ABREs are over-represented most significantly in upstream regions of genes whose transcripts accumulate in dry seed.

The over-representation of this element is indeed alleviated in the *abi5* dry seeds, indicating that these G-box-like elements act as ABREs *in vivo.* In addition, the RY repeat and CE1 tend to co-exist with ABRE in the genes whose transcripts are highly accumulated in dry seeds.

This is consistent with the previous finding that ectopic expression of maize *VP1,* in *Arabidopsis,* causes up-regulation of ABRE containing genes.

Collectively, these results demonstrate that ABI5, which acts cooperatively with ABI3 and ABI4, is the key determinant for the stored mRNA transcriptome composition in *Arabidopsis* dry seeds.

ABA and GA Metabolism Genes

During seed development, the levels of ABA and bioactive GAs are thought to be correlated negatively, as is shown in developing cereal grains. An increase in seed abortion in the pea *(Pisum sativum) lh-2* mutant indicates that GA is essential for embryo growth in this species. The *lh-2* mutation was recently shown to be a single base substitution in the ent-kaurene oxidase gene.

A prominent role of GAs in embryo growth has also been shown in *Arabidopsis,* where over-expression of a GA-deactivation enzyme gene (pea GA 2-oxidase2) in *Arabidopsis* increases the proportion of seed abortion.

Concomitant with the reduction of bioactive GA levels, ABA levels increase when the maturation phase is initiated. It appears that there are two peaks of ABA accumulation in the mid and late stages during seed development.

The first peak of ABA is synthesized in both zygotic and maternal tissues. On the other hand, ABA at the second peak is derived from the zygotic tissues. This zygotic-derived ABA is thought to be essential for the induction and maintenance of seed dormancy.

In contrast, the maternal-derived ABA is involved in the inhibition of precocious germination and processes of seed maturation in tomato, tobacco and *Arabidopsis.* In recent years, almost all of the genes necessary for the biosynthesis and deactivation of ABA have been identified in *Arabidopsis.*

These genes have provided the opportunity to study the molecular basis of hormone metabolisms during seed development and germination. In the ABA biosynthetic pathway, the oxidative cleavage of 9-cis-epoxycarotenoids catalyzed by 9-cis-epoxycarotenid dioxygenases (NCEDs) is an important regulatory step.

The *Arabidopsis* genome contains five possible *AtNCED* genes. Recent work has shown that AtNCED6 and AtNCED9 ar isoforms involved in regulating *Arabidopsis* seed development.

Loss-of-function of these genes lead to a decrease in ABA levels in dry seed, and the double mutant exhibits reduced seed dormancy. On the other hand, ABA 8'-hydroxylation catalyzed by CYP707As is a key regulatory step in the ABA deactivation in various physiological processes. In *Arabidopsis,* four members of CYP707A (CYP707A1 to CYP707A4) are recently shown to encode ABA 8'-hydroxylases. These genes are expressed differentially during seed development through to germination, suggesting that each CYP707A plays a distinct role in each physiological process.

CYP707A1 and *CYP707A3* are expressed predominantly during seed development, whereas CYP707A2 is responsible for regulating ABA levels after seed imbibition. In contrast to the active ABA metabolism in seed development, GA biosynthesis appears to be more active in the early stage of seed development.

An important regulatory step in the production of bioactive GAs is catalyzed by GA 3-oxidases. In *Arabidopsis,* there are four GA 3-oxidase genes, AtGA3ox1 to *AtGA3ox4.* Kim *et al.* (2005) reported that the expression of AtGA3ox1 and *AtGA3ox4* was induced transiently in early immature seeds.

The *AtGA3ox4* expression appears to be localized in outer integuments and the epidermal layer of embryos. Loss-of the *AtGA3ox4 leads* to defective seed coat development, which is rescued by application of GA. On the other hand, expression of AtGA3ox1 and AtGA3o*x2* throughout embryogenesis appears to be restricted to the apical and basal meristem, respectively. *AtGA2ox6* encoding a GA deactivation enzyme, GA 2-oxidase, is shown to be highly expressed in the embryo during early embryogenesis as well as seed germination. It has been shown that expression of the *AtGA2ox6 is* directly regulated by a MADS box transcription factor AGAMOUS like 15, a regulator of embryo development. The loss-of-function of the *AtGA2ox6* leads to an enhanced germination capacity, indicating that AtGA2ox6 is a regulatory isoform of GA 2-oxidase during seed germination.

Regulation of Balancing ABA and GA Levels

Recent reports have demonstrated that ABA and GA biosynthesis during seed development are regulated by common factors in an opposite manner.

The *FUSS* gene has been shown to regulate the levels of both ABA and GA during seed development. Gazzarrini *et al.* (2004) found that the ectopic expression of F*USS,* driven by an epidermis-specific *AtML1* promoter, transforms vegetative organs to those that are embryo-like, by a non-cell-autonomous process.

The FUS3-induced transformation is alleviated by the introduction of an ABA-deficient mutation, *aba2,* or the application of bioactive GA. Moreover, the transient induction of *FUSS* resulted in ABA accumulation and repression of the GA-biosynthetic genes, *AtGA20ox1* and AtGA3ox1.

These findings indicate that FUS3 acts as a positive regulator of ABA levels and a negative regulator of GA levels during seed development. Consistent with these roles for FUS3, the *fus3-3* mutant exhibits delayed ABA accumulation during the seed maturation stage.

Importantly, FUS3 protein levels appear to be regulated by ABA and GA in a positive and negative way, respectively. These regulatory loops support a role for FUS3 as a metabolic switch that regulates ABA and GA levels.

A better understanding of the mechanisms by which these heterochronic genes regulate GA biosynthesis has come from the finding that FUS3 directly regulates the expression of GA-biosynthetic genes.

Initially, Curaba *et al.* (2004) reported that bioactive GAs levels increased in the immature seeds of the *fus3* and *lec2* mutants. The immature embryos of these mutants were subsequently found to have higher levels of *AtGA20ox1* and *AtGA3ox2* transcripts than those of wild-type plants. In these mutants, the mis-expression of *AtGA3ox2* was observed in the epidermis of embryo axis and vascular tissues, which coincide with the localization of the FUS3 expression.

Furthermore, FUS3, but not LEC2, interacts physically with the RY repeats located in the *AtGA3ox2* promoter, presumably to repress *AtGA3ox2* expression.

It is worth noting that the *fus3* and *lec2* mutants differentially over-accumulate the bioactive GAs, GA1 and GA_4, suggesting that FUS3 and LEC2 regulate GA biosynthesis through distinct mechanisms.

Regulation of ABA and GA Action

Hormone sensitivity is regulated differentially in a particular developmental and physiological process. The molecular interaction between ABA signaling components and developmental regulators was initially demonstrated in rice. (1999) screened for protein interactors with OsVP1, the rice VP1/ ABI3 ortholog.

One of the interactors that specifically binds to the truncated OsVP1, harbouring B1 and B2 domains, was TRAB1, a bZIP-type transcription factor. TRAB 1 was shown to bind to ABRE and transactivate ABRE-mediated transcription synergistically with OsVP1.

Accordingly, the developmental regulator VP1/ABI3 controls ABRE-mediated transcription in the seed *via* direct interaction with the ABRE binding protein TRAB1. In *Arabidopsis,* ABI3 and ABI5 were shown to interact in yeast two-hybrid assay.

The B1 domain of ABI3 appears to be responsible for the interaction with ABI5. In contrast, other B3 proteins, FUS3 and LEC2, do not contain the B1 domain, and it is unlike interact with ABI5.

This might reflect the phenotypic difference between *abi3* and *fus3/lec2* mutants in ABA sensitivity. In contrast to the role of ABA, much less is known concerning GA signaling in seed development. Nevertheless, the antagonistic actions of ABA and GA, that are well-characterized in germinating seeds, are also apparent during seed development.

The maize ABA-insensitive vp1 mutants show defects in seed reserve accumulation, acquisition of desiccation tolerance and induction of seed dormancy.

Concomitant with such defects in seed maturation processes, a set of processes that are normally observed upon wild-type germination are precociously expressed during vp1 seed development, including precocious induction of GA responsive α-amylase gene expression.

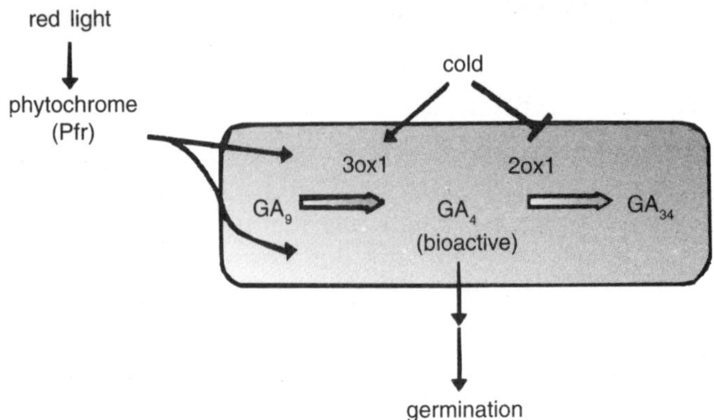

Figure 12.3: Environmental regulation of GA biosynthesis and deactivation in imbibed Arabidopsis seeds.

Transient introduction of VP1 into immature vp1 seeds can repress the precocious induction of a-amylase gene, suggesting that GA action is suppressed by VP1 during seed development in maize.

HORMONAL CONTROL OF SEED GERMINATION AND POST-GERMINATIVE GROWTH

Regulation of GA Levels in Imbibed Seeds

Non-dormant seeds germinate upon water uptake when they are exposed to favourable light, temperature and nutrient conditions. There is accumulating evidence to indicate that the regulation of seed germination by environmental signals is, in part, mediated by hormones, particularly by GAs. Here, we summarize our current under standing on light- and temperature-regulation of GA biosynthesis and response pathways.

Light-regulation of GA Biosynthesis

Seed germination is light-dependent and under phytochrome control in some small seeded plants, such as lettuce, tomato and *Arabidopsis.* Light-regulated seed germination was first recognized in dark-imbibed lettuce seeds, where red (R) light induces, but far-red (FR) light reversibly inhibits germination. In dark-imbibed lettuce seeds, endogenous GA, (the major bioactive GA in lettuce seeds), but not its immediate precursor GA_{20}, increases in abundance after R-light treatment.

The effect of R-light on the GA1 level is cancelled when FR is irradiated following the R-light treatment, suggesting the involvement of phytochrome. Since the precursor GA20 accumulates at a high level (about 100 times that of GA1) in dark-imbibed lettuce seeds, the conversion of GA_{20} to GA1 is likely to be the limiting step for the production of GA1.

Consistent with these observations, the level of *Ls3h* transcript, encoding a GA 3-oxidase that catalyzes the conversion of GA_{20} to GA1, increases in response to R-light. In contrast, transcript levels of two GA 20-oxidases are induced by imbibition alone regardless of the light regime.

A slight reduction in the level of *LsGA2ox2* transcript by R-light treatment suggests that GA deactivation might also be regulated by phytochrome in lettuce seeds. In *Arabidopsis,* five genes encoding phytochromes, *PHYA* to PHYE, have been identified.

Among them, PHYB is the major family member that is stored in seeds at maturity, and is responsible for the tpical photoreversible response shortly after the start of imbibition. In dark-imbibed *Arabidopsis* seeds, transcript accumulation of the AtGA3ox1 and *AtGA3ox2* genes, both of which encode GA 3-oxidase, is elevated by a brief R pulse, and the effect of R-light is reversed by FR-light.

In the *phyB* mutant, *AtGA3ox2* expression is not increased by R-light, indicating a primary role of PhyB in mediating the R-light induction of *AtGA3ox2.* It is still unclear which phytochrome species is responsible for R-induced AtGA3ox1 expression.

In *Arabidopsis,* GA 3-oxidases are encoded by at least four genes. The non-germinating phenotype of the digenic atga3ox1/atga3ox2 mutant shows that the phytochrome-regulated AtGA3ox1 and *AtGA3ox2* genes encode major GA 3-oxdases necessary for seed germination.

So far, phregulation of GA biosynthesis has been studied only in the classical photoreversible response to R- and FR-light pulses given immediately after imbibition, which is mainly mediated by PHYB in *Arabidopsis.*

However, additional phytochromes are in fact involved in sensing a variety of light regimes (wavelength, duration and intensity) in imbibed *Arabidopsis* seeds. For example, PHYA accumulates in the seed during a long period of dark-imbibition (e.g. 48 h), and plays a role in the irreversible response to irradiation with extremely low fluence light in a wide range of wavelength (very low fluence response).

In addition, both PHYA and PHYE are required for germination in continuous FR-light. It is therefore likely that multiple phytochromes play distinct and overlapping roles in sensing light in natural conditions.

It will be valuable to examin of GA biosynthesis by such phytochrome species in defined light conditions to better understand how light signals control seed germination through changes in hormone levels.

Recently, a phytochrome-interacting basic helix–loop–helix protein, PIL5, has been shown to function as a negative regulator of seed germination.

Investigations into the relationships between such light signaling components and GA biosynthesis genes may help to uncover the molecular mechanisms for phytochrome-regulation of GA biosynthesis.

Temperature-regulation of GA biosynthesis

Temperature is another important environmental factor that controls seed germination. Exposure of imbibed seeds to cold temperature (stratification) accelerates the release from seed dormancy in many plant species.

Due to its positive effect on seed germination, cold treatment (pre-incubation at cold temperature in the dark) has been studied as a potential regulator of GA biosynthesis in several plant species.

In *Pyrus malus* (apple), *Corylus avellana* (hazel) and

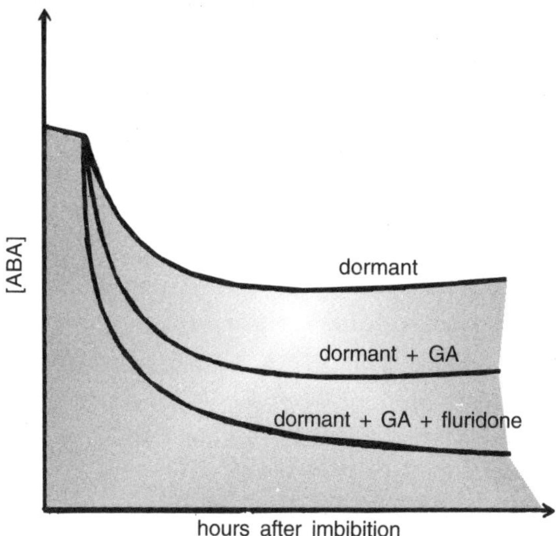

Figure 12.4: Changes in endogenous ABA levels after seed imbibition. ABA levels decrease rapidly after seed imbibition. This reduction in ABA levels is completed within 6–12 h after imbibition depending on plant species. Dormant seed maintains a higher ABA level compared with that of non dormant imbibed seed. GA and fluridone treatments reduce ABA levels and permit seed germination.

Arabidopsis, cold treatment improved the ability of seeds to synthesize bioactive GAs during seed germination.

More recently, the effect of cold temperature on the GA biosynthesis pathway has been investigated in detail in dark-imbibed *Arabidopsis* seeds. During dark-imbibition at 4°C (after an FR-light pulse to inactivate pre-existing phytochrome), the level of *AtGA3ox*] mRNA increases to a high level, while it remains low during dark-imbibition at 22°C.

In contrast, the level of *AtGA2ox2* transcript is much higher at 22°C than at 4°C in seeds imbibed in the dark. These results suggest that the synthesis of bio-active GAs is activated, while GA deactivation is suppressed, by cold temperature.

In agreement with these notions, the levels of GA_4 and GA_1 in dark imbibed seeds are elevated at 4°C compared to those at 22°C. Among four *AtGA3ox* genes in *Arabidopsis,* only AtGA3ox1 is induced by cold temperature in dark-imbibed seeds.

The increase in the amounts of bioactive GAs, cold-induction of GA-up-regulated genes and cold stimulated seed germination did not occur in the atga3ox1 mutant, demonstrating that AtGA3ox1 is required for mediating the temperature signal.

GA response components in germinating seeds

In recent years, several GA signaling components have been identified by genetic approaches utilizing mutants with increased or decreased GA response, and their roles in various aspects of plant growth and development are being studied extensively.

Here, we cover the GA response pathway with focus on its relation to environmental regulation of seed germination in *Arabidopsis.* Light modulates the apparent sensitivity of seeds to exogenous GA during germination in multiple plant species.

In *Arabidopsis,* GA sensitivity is photoreversibly altered by R and FR-light, suggesting the involvement of phytochrome. DELLA proteins form a subfamily in the GRAS family of putative transcription factors, and act as negative regulators in the GA response pathway. GA de-represses its signaling pathway by inducing proteolysis of the DELLA proteins through the ubiquitin-26S proteasome pathway.

Among five *DELLA* genes (RGA, *RGL2* and *RGL3)* in *Arabidopsis, RGL2* has been shown to encode the major negative regulator during seed germination; loss-of-function *rgl2* mutations, but none of the *rga, gai, rgl1* and *rgl3* single mutations, are able to suppress the non-phenotype of the GA-deficient ga1-3 mutant, although other members are also expressed in germinating seeds.

Interestingly, rga/rgl1/rgl2 and gai/rgl1/rgl2 triple knockout mutations confer GA dependent germination in the light, but not in the dark, whereas *a rga/gai/rgl2* triple mutation allows germination of ga1-3 seeds regardless of the light condition. These results imply that RGA and GAI may be involved in alterations of the GA response pathway by light in imbibed seeds. It is also intriguing that RGA is present at a higher level than RGL2 in imbibed seeds, in spite of the genetic evidence that RGL2 plays a more prominent role than does RGA in suppressing seed germination.

Detailed time-course analysis indicates that down regulation of *RGL2* mRNA accumulation is not essential for seed germination, as it occurs at a post-germinative phase.

Altogether, current experimental evidence suggests the importance of investigations into the role of DELLA genes in seed germination at the protein level, including the cell-type specificity in seeds (see below) and regulation by environmental signals.

Cold treatment decreases the amount of exogenous GA necessary for inducing germination of GA-deficient mutant seeds in *Arabidopsis*. Therefore, a change in sensitivity to GA might also play a role in the stimulation of seed germination by cold temperature. At present, molecular mechanisms underlying this phenomenon are unknown.

Regulation of ABA Levels in Imbibed Seeds

De novo ABA biosynthesis and deactivation are involved in regulation of ABA levels

In general, mature dry seed contains a significant amount of ABA. The ABA level decreases rapidly after seed imbibition, and is then maintained at a particular level that is determined by environmental and developmental factors.

There have been many reports using various plant species, demonstrating the release of seed dormancy following a pretreatment with an inhibitor of ABA biosynthesis, fluridone.

This implies that after seed imbibition, the ABA level is determined by a balance of *de novo* biosynthesis and deactivation, but not by deactivation alone.

Light, high temperature, and GA regulation of ABA metabolism

ABA levels have been analysed during photoreversible

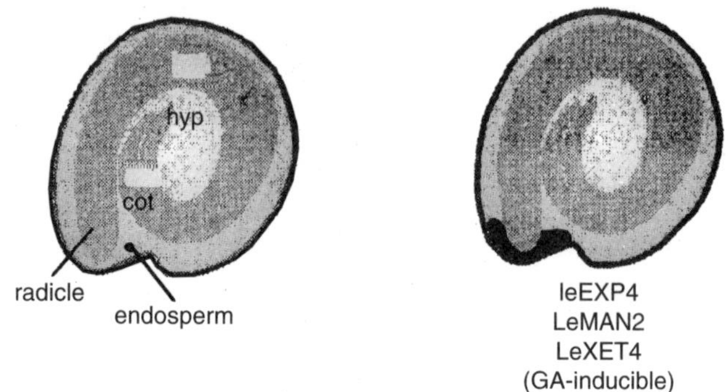

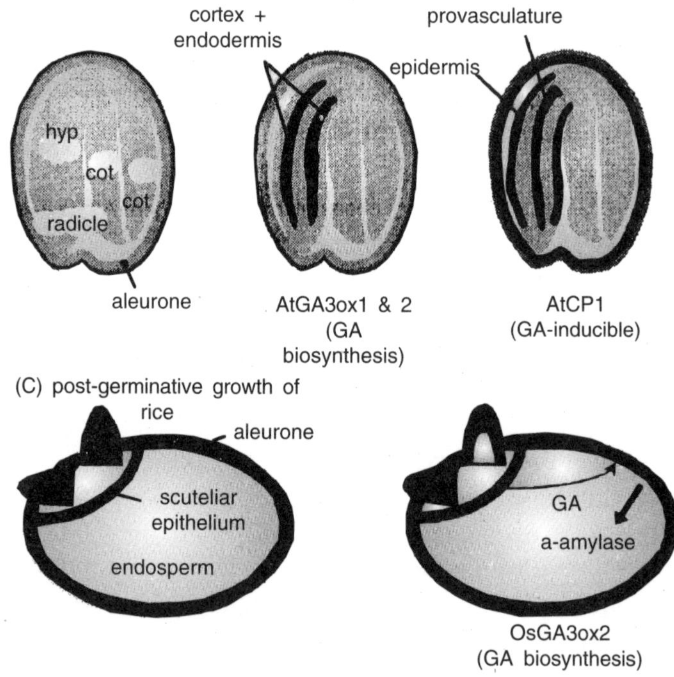

Figure 12.5: Sites of GA biosynthesis and response in germinating seeds.

seed germination in lettuce. In lettuce *(Lactuca sativa L.* cv Grand Rapids), seed germination is strictly regulated by light and temperature.

In dark-imbibed lettuce seeds, germination is prevented by a FR-light pulse irradiation, whereas a subsequent R-light pulse treatment or GA application acts to promote it.

The FR-treated seed maintained a high ABA level and the R treatment or GA application elicit a rapid reduction in ABA levels, which occurs prior to seed germination. Lettuce seed germination is also blocked when imbibition occurs at a high temperature (33°C) in darkness.

The effect of this thermoinhibition is alleviated partially when fluridone and GA are co-applied exogenously. The high-temperature treatment results in the imbibed seeds accumulating higher levels of ABA compared with those incubated at room temperature.

Treatment with fluridone or GA alone leads to a decrease in ABA levels prior to germination, and an additive effect of co-application of these chemicals to decrease the ABA levels was observed prior to germination.

Since the GA treatment increases the levels of phaseic acid (PA) and dihydrophaseic acid (DPA), compared with those of ABA conjugates, one of the effects of GA action in this response is likely to enhance the rate of ABA 8'-hydroxylation.

In *Arabidopsis,* changes in endogenous ABA levels during dormancy release has been studied in the Cape Verde Islands (Cvi) ecotype, which exhibits prominent seed dormancy. The dormancy of Cvi seeds is released by after-ripening, stratification, and by treatment with nitrate or fluridone.

GA treatment has little effect on breaking dormancy in this accession. Imbibed dormant seeds maintain higher ABA levels compared to non-dormant seeds especially after 3 days of imbibition.

These findings indicate that high levels of ABA are important for maintenance of seed dormancy after imbibition. The recent identification of genes encoding ABA 8'-hydroxylases reveals that CYP707A2 is responsible for the rapid decrease in ABA levels after seed imbibition.

The *CYP707A2* expression is induced after seed imbibiti of-function of this gene leads to hyperdormancy of the seeds.

Sites of GA biosynthesis and response in imbibed seeds

The tomato GA-deficient mutant, *gib-1* requires exogenous GA treatment for germination to occur. However, removal of the endosperm and testa layers around the radicle tip will bypass this requirement.

Likewise, when the structure covering the *Arabidopsis* embryo (aleurone and seed coat) is mechanically removed, the GA-deficient ga1-3 embryos can grow into dwarfed seedlings.

Therefore, GA has been thought to play a role in overcoming the physical constraint of the surrounding structure, endosperm or seed coat or both, by inducing their weakening. Weakening of the endosperm and testa during germination was estimated by measuring the puncture force needed to break through these layers at the micropyler region (where the radicle protrudes) in tomato seeds.

In wild type seeds, the puncture force decreases before radicle emergence. However, in *gib-1* seeds a reduction in the necessary puncture force is only observed in the presence of exogenous GA.

When isolated endosperm and testa (embryo-less half seeds) of the *gib-1* mutant are incubated with isolated wild-type embryos, the puncture force decreases significantly.

These results suggest that the weakening of the endosperm and testa is dependent on GA produced in the embryos. Although actual movement of GA from the embryo to the endosperm has not been demonstrated, this hypothesis is consistent with the expression of GA biosynthesis genes in the embryos of germinating *Arabidopsis* seeds.

There is evidence to suggest that GA weakens the endosperm and testa by increasing the levels of cell wall

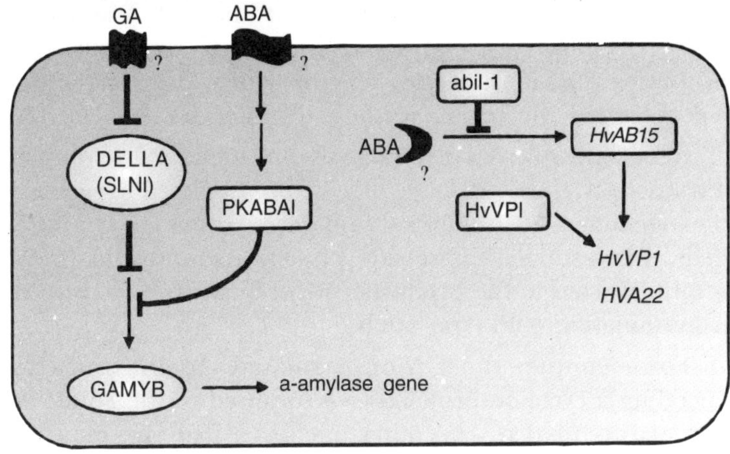

Figure 12.6: Crosstalk between ABA and GA action in barley aleurone.

modifying enzymes. This is illustrated in tomato seeds where GA-dependent breakdown of the endosperm cell wall results in the release of mannose, and endo-(-mannanase activity is detected exclusively in the micropylar endosperm prior to germination.

In agreement with this observation, *LeMAN2* mRNA, encoding an endo-(-accumulates specifically in the micropylar endosperm before radicle protrusion. Expansins are involved in cell wall extension, possibly by disrupting hydrogen bonding between the cell wall components.

The *LeEXP4* gene, encoding an expansin, is specifically expressed in the micropylar endosperm cap prior to radicle protrusion in a GA-dependent manner.

A gene encoding xyloglucan endotrans *glycosylase, LeXET4,* exhibits a similar GA-dependent, tissue-specific expression pattern. Tissue-specific expression of these GA up-regulated genes identify the micropylar endosperm cap as a site of GA action, and supports the role of GA in facilitating the weakening of the mechanimposed by the tissues surrounding the embryo.

Sites of GA biosynthesis in seeds have been studied in *Arabidopsis* by analysing the expression of GA biosynthesis genes at cellular resolution. In light-imbibed *Arabidopsis* seeds, AtGA3ox1 and *AtGA3ox2* transcripts are localized to the cortex and endodermis of embryonic axes, suggesting that these are the major synthesis of bioactive GAs.

GeneChip microar ray analysis has identified a number of transcripts, the abundance of which is regulated in response to exogenous GA_4 in imbibed non-germinating ga1-3 mutant seeds. Interestingly, expression of some GA-inducible genes is not restricted to the predicted site of bioactive GA synthesis in germinating wild-type seeds.

For example, the GA-up-regulated *AtCP1* transcript (encoding a cycteine proteinase) is localized to the epidermis and provasculature of embryonic axes and the aleurone (endosperm) layer, whereas transcripts for the major GA 3-mainly detected in the cortical and endodermal cell layers.

These observations suggest that GA itself, or GA signal(s), might be transmitted across different cell layers in germinating *Arabidopsis* seeds. In germinating cereal grains, aleurone cells play a role in assisting the mobilization of nutrients stored in the seed by secreting hydrolases that degrade starch, protein and lipid.

In imbibed *Hordeum vulgare* (barley) grains, the major increase in GA content occurs after the start of radicle emergence, and a necessity for GA for germination of cereal grains has been elusive, unlike the cases with *Arabidopsis* and tomato.

However, it is clear that the synthesis of bioactive GA is required for the production of hydrolases in the aleurone in imbibed cereal grains. Measurements of ent-kaurene accumulation in imbibed wheat grains treated with paclobutrazol (an inhibitor for ent-kaurene metabolism) indicate that the scutellum and the shoot are the major sites of *de novo* GA biosynthesis.

In rice, GA 3-oxidase is encoded by two genes, OsGA3ox1 and *OsGA3ox2*. In germinating rice seeds, *OsGA3ox2,* plays a dominant role in o-amylase gene expression in the aleurone. The *OsGA3ox2* transcript accumulates specifically in the scutellar epithelium and the apical region of growing shoots.

The synthesis of bioactive GAs in the epithelium is important for o-amylase induction in the aleurone, because an embryonic mutant defective in shoot formation, but not a mutant defective in epithelium development, is able to induce 0-amylase gene expression.

Taken together, *OsGA3ox2* expressed in the epithelial cells is likely to be responsible for *de novo* GA synthesis necessary for 0-amylase induction in the aleurone.

GA and ABA Action in the Cereal Aleurone

Over the past few decades, the cereal aleurone of germinating grains has been a valuable system to study GA and ABA signaling using well-characterized hormone responsive genes as molecular markers.

Pharmacological studies using hormone responding protoplasts and the use of effector and reporter constructs in transient gene expression analysis have contributed to the identification of components in the ABA and GA signaling pathways in cereal aleurone.

Recently, genes originally identified by molecular genetic analysis using GA/ABA response mutants have proven to be common signaling components in the aleurone system as well.

Although GA and ABA antagonism has long been studied as an important factor controlling seed dormancy and germination, our knowledge is still limited on how molecular interactions between GA and ABA response pathways are achieved.

Cereal aleurone serves as an advantageous system in which to pinpoint nexus(es) of the signaling pathways, as it consists of a single cell type. Several review articles have described the GA and ABA signaling pathways in cereal aleurone in detail.

In this section, we start with our current understanding on the hormone perception in cereal aleurone cells, and then describe some major components in the GA and ABA signaling pathways to highlight briefly how these two hormones interact to regulate gene expression.

GA and ABA perception

There are two lines of circumstantial evidence that suggest that GA is perceived at the outer surface of the plasma membrane in the cereal aleurone.

First, Sepharose beads covalently bound with GA_4 is able to induce o-amylase gene expression in aleurone protoplasts of wild oat, despite the fact that they are not permeable through the plasma membrane.

Second, GA does not stimulate α-amylase gene expression when it is micro-injected into barley aleurone cells, unlike the case with exogenous GA in the incubation media.

Recently, a soluble GA receptor has been identified through characterzation of a recessive GA-insensitive dwarf mutant of rice, gid1.

In germinating gid1 mutant seeds, α-amylase activity is undetectable even at a high concentration of exogenous GA. This observation indicates that GID 1 is required for GA-induced α-amylase expression in the aleurone, in which GA is thought to be recognized at the plasma membrane.

Therefore, a role of GID1 in GA perception in cereal aleurone cells remains to be investigated further. Microinjection of ABA into GA-treated barley aleurone protoplasts is not effective in inhibiting a-amylase gene expression, while ABA in the incubation media is.

Therefore, the ABA inhibition of GA action in the aleurone system is likely to be mediated by ABA perception at the plasma membrane.

Interestingly, induction of an ABA-up-regulated *Em* promoter occurs when ABA is micro-injected into aleurone protoplasts, suggesting that this ABA response is mediated by ABA perception inside the protoplast.

Thus, cere cells appear to have two sites of ABA perception, although the identity of these ABA receptors is currently unknown.

Crosstalk between GA and ABA action

An MYB transcription factor, HvGAMYB, is a GA-up-regulated transcriptional activator of a-amylase gene expression in barley aleurone cells.

HvGAMYB is able to transactivate a-amylase and other GA-responsive promoters in the absence of exogenous GA. HvGAMYB, is not only sufficient, but also necessary for the GA induction of a-amylase in barley aleurone, as proved by transiently expressed RNA-interference in protoplast assays.

GA causes a 2-fold increase in the rate of HvGAMYB transcription, and this effect can be partly blocked by ABA. A DELLA protein, SLN1, which is the product of the Slender1 locus of barley, is necessary for repression of HvGAMYB in barley aleurone cells, which indicates that SLN1 acts upstream of HvGAMYB.

GA treatment rapidly decreases SLN1 protein levels before the increase in HvGAMYB levels. GA-induced SLN1 degradation is not blocked by ABA, indicating that ABA acts downstream of SLN1 to block GA signaling.

Transient over-expression of an ABA-inducible Ser/Thr protein kinase, PKABA1, represses the GA induction of α-amylase and HvGAMYB expression, but not GAMYB-transactivated α-amylase gene expression.

Constitutive GAMYB and α-amylase expression in *sln1* aleurone cells is also repressed by PKABA. It is therefore likely that PKABA1 mediates ABA suppression of α-amylase expression at a point that is upstream of the formation of GAMYB and downstream of the site of SLN1 action in the GA response pathway. However, suppression of PKABA1 by RNA-interference does not inhibit the negative effect α-amylase gene expression, suggesting that a PKABA1-independent pathway may also exist.

Exogenous ABA induces expression of the HVA1 and *HVA22* genes, both of which are normally expressed at high levels during late embryogenesis, in the aleurone of germinating barley grains.

The ABA induction of HVA1 and *HVA22* gene expression is inhibited by a mutated version of protein phosphatase 2C, encoded by the dominant abi1-1 mutant gene that blocks

ABA responses in *Arabidopsis*. However, the abi1-1 gene product (abi1-1) does not affect the ABA suppression of GA-inducible α-amylase gene expression. Interestingly, PKABAI, which suppresses GA-inducible o-amylase genes, has little effect on the ABA induction of HVA1 and *HVA22* genes.

Therefore, it there are two separate ABA signaling pathways; one inhibited by abil-1 and the other regulated by PKABA1. A bZIP transcription factor, HvABI5, recognizes the ABA response promoter complexes (ABRC) of the *HVA12* genes, and is capable of trans-activating ABRC-reporter genes in barley aleurone cells in the presence of HvVP1.

Activation of the *HUAI* and *HVA22* genes by HvABI5/ HvVP1 is not inhibited by abi1. Therefore, HvABI5 and HvVP1 are necessary for the ABA-up-regulation of *HVA12* genes, but are dispensable for the ABA suppression of GA-inducible α-amylase gene expression.

Other Hormones

Ethylene

Ethylene is known to be a positive regulator for seed germination in many species. Ethylene can induce germination of *Arabidopsis* ga1 mutant in the light in the absence of exogenous GA.

However, this is not the case for the tomato *gib-1* mutant. On the other hand, ethylene antagonizes ABA in *Arabidopsis* seed germination. Beaudoin *et al.* (2000) reported that genetic screening of the enhancer and suppressor of ABA-insensitive germination of the ab*il-1* mutant were allelic to ctr1 and *ein2,* respectively.

Ghassemian *et al.* (2000) also found that ABA-hypersensitive *era3* mutants were *ein2* alleles. The ethylene signaling components, CTR1 and EIN2, are negative and positive regulators, respectively.

The etr1 mutants that are defective in an ethylene receptor show similar phenotypes, indicating that ethylene and ABA signaling pathways interact antagonistically, rather than CTR1 and EIN2 play a specific role in the crosstalk.

Ethylene insensitive mutants show hyper seed dormancy, which is canceled by stratification or by after-ripening. This suggests that ethylene acts independently from stratification-induced events during germination.

It is also noteworthy that ethylene-insensitive mutants of *Arabidopsis* display Active root growth, suggesting that the mode (or component) of crosstalk between ethylene and ABA signaling pathways is tissue specific.

Crosstalk between ethylene and ABA during germination is not restricted to signaling, but is also evident with respect to ABA metabolism.

Chiwocha *et al.* (2005) quantified hormone levels in dry and imbibed etr1 seeds. The etr1-2 dry seed contained approximately 10-fold higher ABA levels relative to the wild type.

After imbibition, the etr1-2 seed maintained 2- to 3-fold higher ABA levels compared with the wild type. In the etr1-2 imbibed seed, levels of dihydropha catabolite from ABA 8'-hydroxylation), 7'-hydroxy ABA, and ABA glucose ester were lower than those in the wild type, suggesting that ABA deactivation is down regulated in the etr1-2 mutant.

In addition, the most significantly down-regulated catabolite in the etr1 mutant was ABA glucose ester. Based on this obse authors claimed that ABA glucosylation plays an important role in ethylene mediated regulation of ABA metabolism.

Brassinosteroids

Brassinolide (BL) is also known to positively regulate seed germina-tion in several plant species. In *Arabidopsis,* application of BL partially rescues germination of the non-germinating GA-deficient mutants.

BL treatment also alleviates partially ABA-mediated inhibition of *Arabidopsis* seed germination. In addition, ABA-hypersensitive germination was evident in the BL deficient and insensitive mutants, *det2* and bri1, respectively.

Tobacco seed germination is also accelerated by application of BL. The effect of BL application is distinct from that elicited by GA application. Exogenous BL accelerates endosperm rupture in light-imbibed seed, which is not observed after GA treatment.

On the other hand, BL fails to release dark-imbibed photodormancy nor induce endosperm-specific class I 1,β-glucanase activity that is stimulated by GA application. Based on the differences,

Leubner-Metzger (2001) proposed that BL promotes tobacco seed germination through enhancing growth potential of the embryo, which is distinct from the dual functions of GA on seed germination of enhancing embryonic growth potential and weakening the micropylar endosperm.

The BL action on seed germination is also suggested to act in a GA-independent manner in *Arabidopsis,* although both of BR and GA actions require heterotrimeric G-proteins.

CONCLUSIONS AND PERSPECTIVES

In this chapter, we have highlighted recent advances in our understanding of hormonal regulation of seed dormancy and germination. Identification of ge biosynthesis and deactivation pathways of ABA and GA are allowing researchers to study regulation of the concentrations of these two hormones in seeds at the cellular resolution, in relation to specific developmental phases and under defined environmental conditions.

Evidence has been provided that well-characterized developmental regulators, such as FUS3 and LEC2, play a (direct) role in modulating hormone levels in developing seeds.

Identifications of additional key regulators of ABA and GA levels will increase our knowledge on how cellular concentrations of antagonistic hormones are balanced during seed development and germination.

The molecular basis of crosstalk between ABA and GA actions is beginning to be uncovered in the cereal aleurone, and this system will continue to be useful to dissect the ABA and GA antagonism at the molecular level and to place additional components in respective hormone signaling pathways.

Applications of the newly available large-scale transcriptome and proteome technologies to seed biology will be powerful aids in developing our understanding of the exact roles of each hormone in seed dormancy and germination.

Such genome wide analyses in combination with the use of molecular genetic tools will allow us to reveal unidentified molecular links among different hormones as well as connections between a hormone and a developmental or environmental regulator during seed dormancy and germination.

13 Chapter Reproductive Hormones

Similar to other essential processes in plant growth, reproductive development consists of a highly regulated series of decisions that control the timing, the spatial distribution and the morphology of newly arising organs.

Hormones are an integral part of this signaling network, and there are multiple examples to support the view that the participation of hormones in these regulatory events provides plasticity and robustness in the response to environmental and endogenous cues.

In this chapter, we will review and discuss our current knowledge on how the different hormones affect the diverse aspects of reproductive development, with emphasis in the molecular aspects of the mechanisms involved.

FLOWERING TIME

The transition from vegetative growth to reproductive development is a complex but well-organized process that involves changes in gene expression, physiology, metabolism and architecture of the plant.

The transition between these developmental programmes is executed through a change in the nature of the shoot apical meristem, transforming leaf-into-flower-type primordia.

These events are tightly regulated and the resulting onset of flowering is controlled by endogenous cues and environmental factors. Both endogenous and exogenous factors regulate flowering time through different well-characterized pathways.

The main environmental factors controlling flowering are light and temperature, and the corresponding inputs are driven through the photoperiod-dependent, vernalization and thermosensory pathways.

In addition, endogenous cues, including age- or size-related factors and the activity of hormones and carbohydrate-related metabolites, also control the transition to flowering.

These factors exert their regulation through the autonomous and the gibberellin (GA)-dependent pathways. There are also multiple points of connection between the flowering pathways, for example, the low-temperature effect of vernalization is based on endogenous epigenetic effects, mediated by the degree of genomic DNA methylation.

In this section, we will focus on the effect of classical and more recently discovered phytohormones on the transition to flowering.

Gibberellins

The molecular mechanisms involved in GA signaling in flowering and other developmental processes have been recently and extensively reviewed. Physiological and genetic data have supported GAs as hormones that accelerate flowering in the model plant *Arabidopsis* and in other plants.

The application of physiologically active GAs to plants leads to early flowering in *Arabidopsis* and other plants such as *Lolium temulentum, Larix laricina* and *Pinus sylvestris.*

Moreover, the GA content increased in the shoots of plants induced to flower. Regulation by GAs may result not only from changes in synthesis, translocation and accumulation but also from sensitivity to the hormone.

In the absence of environmental factors that promote flowering, *Arabidopsis* maintains the transition to the reproductive phase via the GA pathway. This is supported by the lack of flowering of the GA-deficient mutant ga1 under photoperiodic conditions of day-length shorter than 10 h.

Moreover, over expression of GA biosynthesis genes or activation of GA signaling in the *spindly* (spy) mutant result in early flowering. The GA-dependent pathway to flowering requires the function of the products of genes such as GA1, *GAI, RGA, FPF1, SPY* and possibly *GAMYBs.*

The signaling pathway that drives GA-dependent transition to flowering may be regulated by the micro-RNA miR159, which seems to function by cleaving the mRNA encoding the GAMYB-related proteins and hence, by preventing the GA-induced activation of the floral meristem identity gene *LEAFY (LFY)* in *Arabidopsis.*

In contrast, the rice *GAMYB* gene does not seem to regulate the transition to flowering but the development of floral organs. A similar role in anther development has also been attributed to the *Arabidopsis GAmyb33* and *GAmyb65* genes, whose expression is restricted to anthers in part by the action of miR159.

Although GAs are essential for flowering of *Arabidopsis* growing under short-, but not long-day conditions, there is evidence to ascribe to GA a role in the promotion of photoperiod-induced flowering.

For instance, in *L. temulentum,* the application of certain GA molecules is as efficient as a single long-day pulse to induce flowering, GAs applied to intact leaves are transported to the apex and promote flowering, and long-day treatments induce a two fold increase in GA content in the apex.

Besides, a functional connection between GAs and the long-day pathway could occur via negative interaction between SPY and the GIGANTEA protein thought to act in the photoperiod pathway. However, the activation of flowering through the *Arabidopsis LFY* gene is regulated independently by GAs and the long-day pathway.

Brassinosteroids

It has been recently reported that *BAS1* and *SOB7* genes coding for cytochrome P450s in *Arabidopsis* modulate photomorphogenesis through brassinosteroid (BR) inactivation mechanisms. Both genes act redundantly in such a way that the double *bas1 sob7* mutant displays an early flowering phenotype.

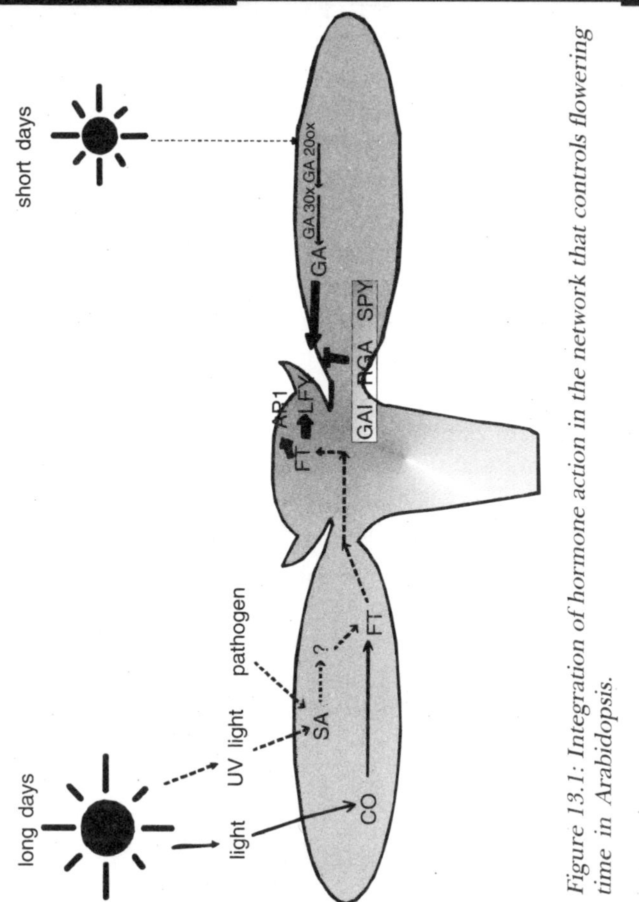

Figure 13.1: Integration of hormone action in the network that controls flowering time in Arabidopsis.

The positive regulation on flowering time exerted by BRs indicated by these data is in agreement with the late flowering phenotype reported for the *det2* mutant affected in BRs biosynthesis and the delayed bolting reported for the *bls*] (brassinosteroid, light and sugar *1*) mutant involved in regulating endogenous BR levels.

In contrast, other mutations in previously characterized BR-specific biosynthesis genes *DWFI, DWF4, CPD, BR6ox1* and *ROTS* do not seem to affect the timing of the transition from vegetative to reproductive stage, probably because of BR homoeostasis mechanisms based on feedback control of the expression of genes involved in its metabolism.

Auxins, Cytokinins and Ethylene

Auxins have been extensively characterized as hormones with essential regulatory functions in root and shoot development. They act by a strict control of transport and gradient accumulation patterns.

Many components of the xin signaling response have been identified and characterized including a number of Auxin/ indole-3 acetic acid (Aux/IAA) inhibitors and auxin response factor (ARF) transcription factors that seem to yield specificity in regulating different developmental processes through a combinatorial strategy.

Despite the relevant function of auxins in plant development, their regulatory role on the control of the transition to flowering in plants is some how secondary or indirect.

It has been reported that auxins in association with cytokinins, ethylene or abscisic acid (ABA) may modulate flowering time as suggested by the delayed flowering phenotype of some *Arabidopsis* mutants such as hyl1 (hyponastic leaves *1)* or alh1 (ACC-related long hypocotyl 1), which are affected in sensitivity to auxin, cytokinin, ABA or ethylene, respectively.

Also a regulatory connection between auxins and GAs has been proposed in the control of morphogenesis in pea plants. The late flowering phenotype of the na1 pea mutant seems to be explained by auxin regulation of GA biosynthesis.

Also recently, it has been reported that mutations in the *ARF2* gene confer delayed flowering to different mutant *arf2* alleles in *Arabidopsis*. Cytokinins regulate many vegetative developmental processes.

Despite physiological evidence reported about cytokinin implication in the control of flowering time, there is no genetic evidence supporting a role for this hormone in controlling the transition from vegetative to reproductive development.

Abscisic Acid

ABA regulates many growth and developmental processes and is especially relevant in regulating water- and osmotic-related stress. Most of the ABA-response mutants described display only subtle phenotypic defects in the absence of stress.

In contrast, the *ABA insensitive 8 (abi8)* mutant displays severe developmental defects including delayed flowering. Moreover, the *ABA hypersensitive 1 (abh1)* recessive mutation suppresses the late flowering phenotype conferred by certain FRI*GIDA (FRI)* and *FLC* alleles in *Arabidopsis* due to the inability of FRI to increase F*LC* mRNA levels.

Although an interpretation of these observations is that the effect of ABA on flowering may be indirect, the identification of the classical flowering time regulator FCA as an ABA receptor provides a direct link between this hormone and the onset of reproductive development, possibly as a response to stress conditions.

However, ABA may regulate flowering also through FCA-independent mechanisms since the double mutants ab*il fcal* and *abi2 fca1* flowered earlier than fca1 plants.

Salicylic Acid and the Stress-activated Transition to Flowering

The onset of flowering is tightly regulated by interactions between different pathways controlling flowering time. As a result, plants flower at the appropriate time of year to ensure efficient reproduction. However, this tight control may be overridden in stressed plants and premature flowering may occur.

A variety of stress factors including pathogen infection, drought, extreme light irradiation and temperatures have been reported to induce accelerated flowering in different plants.

Some of these stress factors, such as biotrophic pathogen infection or irradiation with ultraviolet C (UV C) light, cause increases in the endogenous salicylic acid (SA) content. Although a flowering promoter activity was assigned to SA in reports published in the 1970s and 1980s, no information on the mechanisms by which SA modulates flowering time was available.

It has been recently reported that UV light irradiation,

which induces SA production, can accelerate flowering through a SA-dependent mechanism, whereas mutations that confer SA-deficiency lead to late flowering in *Arabidopsis.*

The SA-regulated transition to flowering seems to be the result of interactions with the photoperiod-dependent and autonomous pathways but is independent of the functions of flowering time CO and *FCA* genes.

In any case, evidence points to a regulatory role of SA upon the expression of *FT,* whose RNA is transported from the leaves to the apex in order to activate floral meristem identity genes.

FLOWER DEVELOPMENT

Although aberrant morphologies of flowers have been reported after the application of several hormones and biosynthesis inhibitors, only two hormones have been unequivocally associated with flower morphogenesis and are likely to have a regulatory role in the differentiation that occurs during flower formation.

GAs have been implicated in the control of floral homoeotic gene expression and anther development, while auxin gradients seem to regulate ovary development and organ initiation, as we will summarize below.

A very clear hint of the involvement of GA in flower development is the male sterility observed in *Arabidopsis* GA-deficient *gal* mutants, in which microsporogenesis occurs, but pollen grains are not viable.

An equivalent defect is observed in the GA-deficient *d5* mutant of maize and in petunia plants treated with the GA biosynthesis inhibitor paclobutrazol, which formed anthers loaded with pollen grains, but the connective tissue and the tapetum were degenerated.

Moreover, the tomato GA-deficient *gib-2* mutant is arrested in an earlier developmental stage, prior to microsporogenesis, and is also sterile, similarly to the *myb33 myb65* double mutant in *Arabidopsis,* in which microsporogenesis is dramatically affected and the tapetum enlarged and eventually collapses.

However, GAs not only regulate late differentiation stages of anther and pollen development, but a deficiency of GAs in *Arabidopsis* causes retarded growth of petals, stamens and pistils, which can be rescued by knocking out negative elements of the GA signaling pathway expressed during flower development, such as *RGA* and *RGL2*.

However, fertility of the ga1 mutant is not fully recovered even after simultaneous elimination of RGA, RGL1 and RGL2, which is in agreement with a possible role for also RGL3 in pollen development.

In this context, GAs seem to be necessary to promote the expression of the floral homoeotic genes *APETALA3, PISTILLATA* and *AGAMOUS,* because ga1 mutants show lower expression levels of these genes, and a glucocorticoid-inducible form of RGA can repress their expression after dexamethasone treatments of nascent flowers.

The physiological relevance of this regulation is further supported by the observation that overexpression of *AGAMOUS* partially suppresses the floral defects of the ga1 mutant.

Finally, there is an additional role for GAs in later stages of flower differentiation. It has been shown that GAs produced in anthers are transported to the corolla and induce growth and pigmentation.

This latter effect can be attributed to the promotion of anthocyanin synthesis in petunia petals by GAs, which requires the coordinated upregulation of at least 15 genes that encode enzymes involved in flavonoid biosynthesis, including chalcone synthase. An essential role for auxin in the generation of new floral organs is based on multiple observations.

First, genetic evidence implicates auxin flux in the determination of floral organ number and patterning. Mutations in PIN-FORME*D 1 (PIN]),* a gene that encodes an auxin efflux carrier, result in only few flowers being formed and multiple structural abnormalities, including a decreased number (and reduced size) of sepals, petals and stamens, and a marked loss of valve tissue in the ovary.

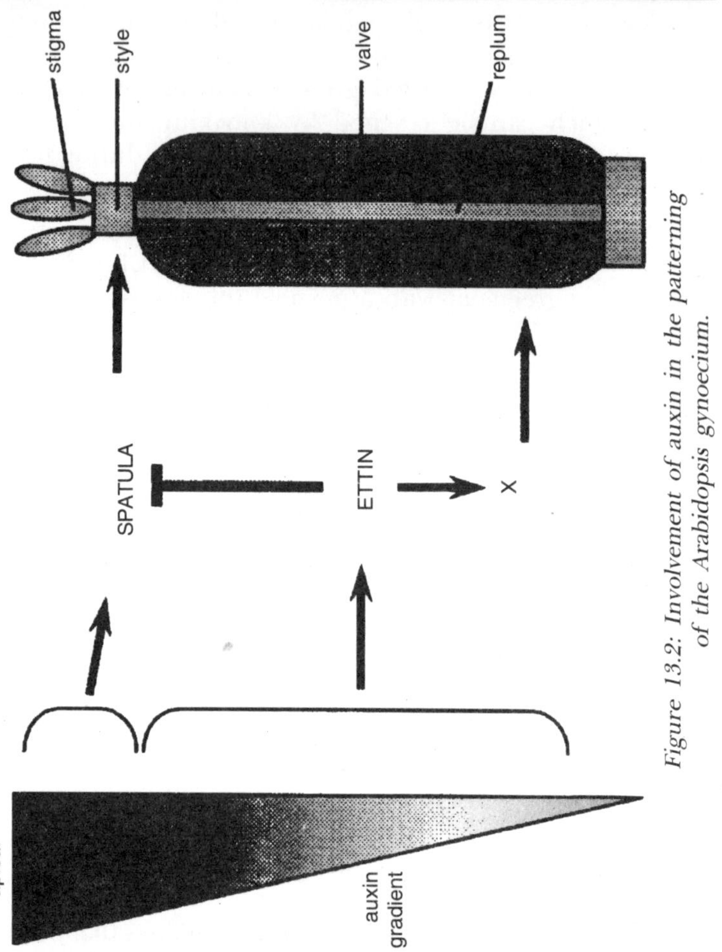

Figure 13.2: Involvement of auxin in the patterning of the Arabidopsis gynoecium.

This effect is phenocopied by applications of the auxin polar transport inhibitor N-1-naphthylphthalamic acid (NPA). Part of this effect may be attributed to the role of auxin in general organ outgrowth, as suggested by the observation that petunia *floozy* mutants, defective in a flavin mono-oxygenase required for auxin biosynthesis, do not show alterations in floral organ identity but the initiation of organ primordia is impaired at an early stage.

However, the defects in the specification of valve tissue in the gynoecium point to a more specific role for auxin gradients in the specifying patte ovary. This is particularly evident when interpreting the equivalent valve defect caused by mutations in *MONOPTEROS* and *ETTIN* , the genes encoding ARF5 and ARF3, respectively, two transcription factors that participate in auxin signaling.

In the current model, ETT would establish two boundaries in the ovary to mark the apical and basal ends of the valves, by responding to intermediate concentrations in an apical–basal gradient of auxin, and directing valve tissue differentiation.

Much of the role of ETT in valve differentiation would actually be to prevent downregulation of the style specific gene *SPATULA* in valve tissue, for which it might require the activity of additional proteins such as SEUSS.

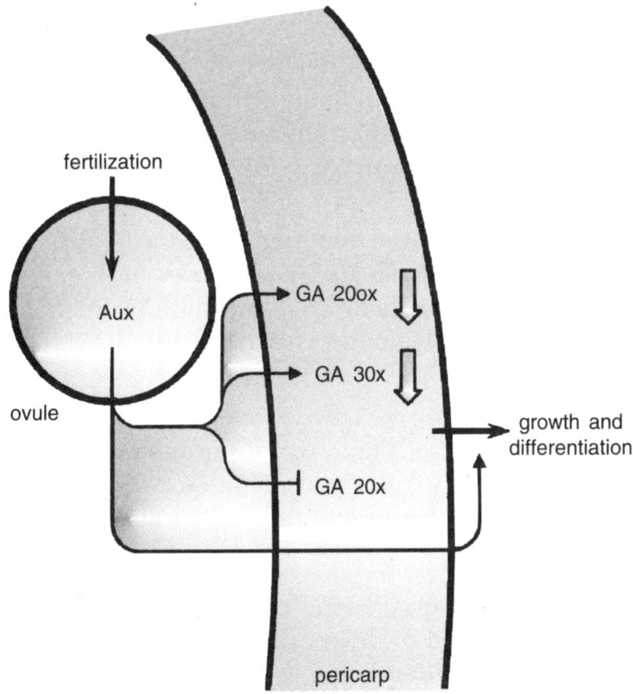

Figure 13.3: Possible mechanism for the interaction between auxin and GAs during early fruit development.

EARLY FRUIT DEVELOPMENT

Hormones have been used for a long time to induce fruit set in an agronomical context in many diverse species. In many occasions, hormone applications tend to increase fruit yield, but they are also used to induce the formation of seedless fruits.

Both effects may for instance be observed in certain citrus species and cultivars, and are also important in tomato, in which certain unfavourable environmental conditions reduce pollen production and thus fruit set.

From a basic research perspective, these observations have led to the hypothesis that in these treatments, the effect of the applied hormones reflects a role for the endogenous hormones in the early events during the formation of fruits.

However, there have been two alternative views of this phenomenon: one in which hormones trigger early fruit development upon pollination by activating the differentiation programme, and another one in which hormones are required only to direct nutrient resources to the differentiating fruit.

Cytokinins have been reported to induce parthenocarpy when applied to unpollinated pea ovaries and *Arabidopsis*, but correlative and genetic evidence for the implication of auxin, GAs and polyamines in early fruit development is stronger.

Although it is not possible to propose an unifying model for the involvement of the different hormones in the diverse types of fruits (fleshy fruits, pods, siliques, etc.), certain trends are common for all the species studied, as will be shown below.

Gibberellins

The first systematic studies in which a biochemical approaches was used to dissect the mechanism by which GAs regulate early fruit development were in pea.

Unpollinated pea ovaries, as in many other species, are program-med to senesce unless the appropriate stimulus is provided-generally ovule fertilization, but also treatments with GAs.

This system has been very useful to evaluate rapid changes in hormone levels following fertilization, and the conclusion is that GA biosynthesis is increased as a consequence of successful pollination, through the upregulation in the pericarp of the expression of genes encoding enzymes involved in GA biosynthesis.

Work with *Arabidopsis* has provided the genetic evidence that supports previous physiological and molecular studies, since mutants impaired in GA biosynthesis or signaling have been found to show defects in fruit initiation and growth. The involvement of GAs in early fruit development is not restricted to pods and siliques.

Pollination in citrus causes a very clear increase in GA levels and, more interestingly, citrus varieties that naturally produce seedless fruits (such as *Satsuma* or *Clementina mandarins)* have increased GA levels that correlate with the differential ability of the species tested.

This latter correlation has also been observed in fleshy fruits of tomato. For instance, the ovaries of several tomato *pat* mutants (parthenocarpic) have a higher GA content, and parthenocarpy is abolished with paclobutrazol.

However, the *pat-1* mutants have defects in ovule and anther development so, at this point, it is still difficult to assess if this alteration of GA metabolism is in fact the primary cause of the observed parthenocarpy.

Auxin

Auxin treatments are very effective in inducing fruit set in certain species, particularly tomato, but also *Arabidopsis.* Parthenocarpy in tomato has been associated with the accumulation of auxins in the ovaries, and it is generally accepted that the contribution of auxin is more important than that of GAs for early fruit development in tomato.

However, it has been reported that auxin derived from the apical shoot seems to prevent fruit development in the absence of the appropriate stimuli (i.e. fertilization) thus complicating the interpretation of the overall role of auxin in fruit formation.

Ovules are indeed a major source for auxin, and localized upregulation of auxin biosynthesis in ovules might trigger early fruit development, as supported by the generation of parthenocarpy in transgenic tomatoes and eggplants that overproduce auxin in ovules.

A possible mechanism for the initiation of fruit developm-ent might thus involve production of auxin in the developing seeds, and then activation of GA biosynthesis by auxin, which would direct growth and differentiation of the fruit tissue.

This model is supported by observed upregulation of GA biosynthesis genes in pea pericarp by 4-chloro-IAA, resulting in increased GA concentration.

Polyamines

There is varied evidence supporting a role for polyamines during early fruit development. For example, the activity of arginine decarbo-xylase, the enzyme that initiates polyamine biosynthesis, decreases at the end of ovary development, but a transient increase is observed after fruit set induced by GA treatments in unpollinated ovaries, consistent with the idea that polyamines are required for growth in general.

This is supported by the observation that application of polyamines can partially promote fruit development in unpollinated tomato ovaries, and that the concentration of endogenous polyamines is rapidly altered in tomato fruits after pollination.

Notably, there is a correlation between high spermine level and ovary senescence, and between low spermine level and fruit development induced by pollination, auxin or GAs in pea and in tomato.

This might mean that spermine is part of the signals that induce senescence in unpollinated ovaries, and pollination would reduce spermine levels (via GA and possibly auxin).

Nevertheless, this model lacks the support of genetic

evidence, since the available mutants defective in spermine biosynthesis in *Arabidopsis* have not been evaluated for fruit set or ovary senescence.

FRUIT MATURATION

Fruit maturation is a complex biochemical and physiological process that involves numerous changes in fruit attributes including organoleptic qualities, nutritional content and susceptibility to opportunistic pathogens.

The process is regulated by endogenous and external factors that include developmental gene regulation, hormones, light and temperature through a coordinated network of signaling pathways.

Fruit ripening varies among different species but all kinds of fruits mature essentially either in a climacteric or non-climacteric way depending on whether increased respiration and ethylene synthesis is required or not to complete the process.

Most of the progress in studying fruit maturation comes from the combination of three experimental systems: *Arabidopsis* as a model plant with dry fruits, and two fleshy fruit plants, tomato, as a model for climacteric fruits, and strawberry, as a model for non-climacteric fruits.

Ethylene

There is no doubt that ethylene is the best-known factor regulating fruit ripening. A vast amount of information coming from physiological approaches in different experimental systems supports this regulatory role, and the biosynthesis and action of ethylene in tomato is likely the best-studied experimental system in climacteric fruit maturation.

However, from the molecular point of view, most of the advances come from molecular-genetic studies on the perception and biosynthesis machinery of ethylene in *Arabidopsis.*

Perception of ethylene in *Arabidopsis* is mediated by the function of five receptors that act as redundant negative regulators of ethylene signaling.

In tomato, six ethylene receptors have been identified and characterized, and the genes encoding two of them, *NEVER-RIPE (NR)* and *LeETR4,* are strongly induced at the onset of ripening; however, their respective loss of function have opposite effects on tomato fruit ripening.

Downstream of the receptors, the putative MAP-kinase CTRI seems to act, by interacting with receptors, as a negative regulator of ethylene signaling in *Arabidopsis.*

Several *CTRI* homologous genes have been identified in tomato and other species and they show differential expression patterns, at least one of them being induced during ripening. Downstream of CTRI in *Arabidopsis,* the sequential function of *EIN2, EIN3* and *EIL* gene products connect to the function of the ERF1 transcription factor that regulate the ethylene signaling via binding to GCC-box promoter elements of target genes.

Homologues of *Arabidopsis EIN3, EIL* and *ERF* have also been identified in tomato as multigene families with at least a member of each family exhibiting ripening-induced expression. In non-climacteric citrus fruit, although ethylene production increases in young fruitlets, this hormone does not play an essential role in the ripening of mature fruits.

On the other hand, a cDNA microarray-based analysis of gene expression in ripening non-climacteric strawberry fruits allowed the identification of several ethylene signaling-related genes with patterns of expression associated with achene maturation.

Moreover, it has been recently reported that different ethylene receptors show increased expression during ripening of strawberry fruits coinciding with the production of a small amount of ethylene, which suggests that such a small increase may be sufficient to trigger ripening.

Auxin

Exogenous application of synthetic auxins to different plant species either hastens or delays ripening. Thus, it is controversial whether endogenous auxins act as positive or negative regulators of fruit ripening. Several Aux/IAA and

ARF transcription factors have been reported to be coordinately regulated by ethylene and auxins during tomato fruit maturation.

In fact, one of these genes, called *DR12,* belonging to the ARF family of transcription factors seems to play a role in tomato fruit ripening, as transgenic plants underexpressing the *DR12* gene displayed several defects including dark-green immature fruits and blotchy ripening. It has been reported that the decline in auxin levels supplied from the achenes to the receptacle during fruit maturation was associated with the onset of ripening in a non-climacteric fruit such as strawberry.

Microarray-based analysis of ripening strawberry fruits led to the identification of many auxin-repressed genes involved in different processes of fruit maturation such as pigmentation, cell wall metabolism and flavour/aroma synthesis.

BRs and ABA

The application of BRs to tomato pericarp discs led to accelerated ripening through a process that seems to be mediated by ethylene biosynthesis.

Moreover, the BR biosynthetic mutant *det2* displayed a reduced expression of an endo1,4-β-D-glucanase likely involved in the assembly of cellulose-hemicellulose network in the cell wall during ripening.

Also ABA seems to play a role in promoting banana fruit ripening through, at least in part, ethylene-mediated mechanisms. In ripening avocado fruits the rise in ethylene production precedes an increase in ABA biosynthesis from carotenoid cleavage.

The involvement of SA in the regulation of fruit ripening is somewhat controversial. It has been reported that treatment of banana fruits with SA delayed ripening.

However, the tomato calcium-dependent protein kinase *LeCRK1* is induced during fruit ripening as well as in SA- or ethylene-treated leaves, and its expression is undetectable in natural tomato ripening mutants such as *NR, Rin* and *Nor*. The function of SA during ripening may well be related to regulation of resistance to fungal pathogens in mature fruits. In fact, interaction between the *anthracnose fungus, Colletotrichum gloeosporioides,* with pepper fruits varies from *incompatibility* with ripe fruits to compatibility with unripe fruits.

Regarding this, a *PepThi* gene, which is pathogen inducible, is also activated by SA in unripe fruits. Another likely function of SA during ripening of climacteric fruits could be the regulation of ethylene production through modulation of the expression of ethylene biosynthetic genes. A wound- and ripening-induced 1-*aminocyclopropane*-1*carboxylate (ACC) synthase gene* from tomato is inhibited by SA.

CONCLUSIONS

As seen above, hormones impinge on multiple pathways that regulate reproductive development. The challenge for the next few years is the elucidation of the molecular mechanisms by which this regulation occurs, so that direct and indirect effects for particular growth regulators can be distinguished.

Acquiring this detailed level of knowledge seems particularly relevant if a long-term goal is to be able to fine tune-specific aspects of reproductive development without affecting the general architecture of the plants or other growth patterns.

Index

A

B

C

D

E

F

G

J

K

L

M

N

O

P

Q

R

S

T